Imaging the Divine

Jesus and Christ-Figures in Film

Imaging the Divine

Jesus and Christ-Figures in Film

Lloyd Baugh

Sheed & Ward
Kansas City

The illustrations in this book are used with the kind permission of the Film Stills Archive of the Museum of Modern Art (MOMA) in New York City (distinguished in the text as "MOMA"), and of the Photofest film stills archive also in New York (distinguished as "Photofest").

Sheed & Ward™ is a service of The National Catholic Reporter Publishing Company.

Library of Congress Cataloguing-in-Publication Data
Baugh, Lloyd, 1946-
    Imaging the divine : Jesus and Christ-figures in film / Lloyd Baugh.
       p.   cm.
    Includes bibliographical references (p. 237) and indexes.
    ISBN: 1-55612-863-0 (alk. paper)
    1. Jesus Christ in motion pictures. I. Title.
PN1995.9.J4B38   1997
791.43'632—dc21   97-2903
                                            CIP

Published by: Sheed & Ward
                115 E. Armour Blvd.
                P.O. Box 419492
                Kansas City, MO 64141-6492

To order, call: (800) 333-7373

www.natcath.com/sheedward

Cover design by James F. Brisson

Cover photo: *The Passion of Joan of Arc* (MOMA)

Contents

96526

I happily and gratefully dedicate this my first book to Alfredo and Natalia Cavaliere and their family. Over the years of my Roman experience, they have shared their lives, their faith, their hopes and dreams with me and have invited me to share mine with them. They are cherished friends who have taught me much about love, about spiritual freedom, about Christian committment, and about the meaning of Sirach 6:14-16. Cari amici, vi ringrazio.

Prologue

As popular myth would have it, professional scholars are people who necessarily live in isolation, self-condemned to the exclusive company of books
and scholarly journals, lurking the dark and dusty corridors of library stacks,
the terror of all in the reading room who might even whisper to one another
and proudly boasting of their latest electronic weapons on the battlefield of
data-basing and word-processing. Clearly they are poor souls and to be pitied.

My experience of professional scholarship – I admit to be a relatively
recent arrival in that camp and it is up to the reader to determine my standing
therein – obliges me at this point to do a bit of demythologizing. To begin
with the last point, my grasp of the esoteric intricacies of *WordPerfect 6.1*
and *Windows 3.1* (I have not yet been initiated into the *sanctum sanctorum* of
Windows 95.) is limited to the most basic of rituals and at least once a day I
have to rush to our computer center for a session of crisis management.
Though I admit to being somewhat sensitive to whispers in the reading room
and to the car alarms in the street outside, I am allergic to dust and so do
little lurking in the stacks. I live (and I daresay "thrive") in an international
and intercultural community of one hundred and twenty Jesuits, in which the
daily contacts and conversations are a rich humanizing experience. I am fortu-
nate that, since my field of work – both writing and teaching – is film studies
and theology, I am able to justify spending at least some of my research time
(and funds) for evenings at the cinema. And finally, I have been abundantly
blessed with many good colleagues and friends in whose company the liberating work of the Spirit goes on in me. It is this humanizing-divinizing community of colleagues, confrères and friends that I would like now to
acknowledge with gratitude.

This book finds its most immediate origins in a theology course I teach
at the Pontifical Gregorian University: "Images of Jesus in Film." And so, a
first expression of gratitude goes to Giuseppe Pittau, Rector of the University,
to Robert White, my Department Chair and to Jared Wicks, Dean of the Fac-
ulty of Theology, for their support of this interdisciplinary course, for their
ongoing advice and encouragement, and more immediately, for having allowed me a lighter teaching load this past year, thus affording me the time
and energy to complete this book.

An expression of profound gratitude goes also to the students who have
participated in this course, and in other parallel courses and seminars of mine,

and with whom I have tested many of the ideas expressed in this book. I am especially thankful to a number of my students who over the years have become colleagues and dear and trusted friends: Theo Hipp, Massimo Maffioletti, Maria Franca Tricarico, Dino D'Aloia, Benedetto Labate, Marta Giorgi, Dario Tokic, Denis Joassart. *Vi ringrazio della fiducia, vi ringrazio dell'amicizia.*

I would like also to thank the Rectors of three of the Roman Colleges – the Seminario Romano Maggiore, the Almo Collegio Capranica and the Collegio del Gesù – who in generously inviting me to direct cineforums in their colleges, have given me the possibility of further testing my ideas and of meeting my students on their own turf, always a good experience. Sincere thanks go also to Biancarosa Magliano of the Centro Studi USMI in Rome who two years ago recruited me for her editorial team and who has since then encouraged me and afforded me the possibility of publishing in article form some of the ideas developed in this book.

In reseaching the material for the book, I have spent several happy and fruitful months working in the libraries of the Institut des Hautes Etudes du Cinéma in Paris and of the British Film Institute in London. To the friendly and helpful research staffs of both institutions, many thanks. I am particularly grateful to David Sharp of the B.F.I. for his warm welcome and to the several members of the B.F.I. research team who patiently offered me the extraordinary possibility of last minute verification of data by telephone.

The final few months of a book project like this one can be hectic and stressful. I am thankful to my Jesuit community at the Gregorian which has been most supportive. I want also to acknowledge my profound gratitude and high esteem for my confrère, Jos B. Gavin, for his generous and expert service of proofreading the manuscript of this book, for making valuable suggestions for the organization of my material, and especially for his fraternal care and encouragement in several difficult moments. Also to another Jesuit confrère I owe a longer term debt of gratitude, Marc Gervais of Concordia University in Montreal who years ago and with much patience taught me how to "read" and appreciate a film and shared with me his love for cinema. He was then, and has often been since then, a light in the darkness and I suspect he will recognize his presence, both intradiegetically and extradiegetically, in this book.

I want also to acknowledge a number of people whom I have come to know here in Italy, who have become good friends and have enriched my life and my faith. They are treasured companions whose care and support have made possible the kind of intense committment necessary to bring to completion this book project and others. *Tante grazie a* Pier Luigi Fumagalli, Marco Foschini, Dimitri Tondo, Skirmantas Jankauskas, Cristián Sotomayor, Jack Hunthausen, Michael Pastizzo, Sebastiano Grasso *e alle famiglie* Cottone, Manicotto e Ciampi.

Lloyd Baugh
Rome, Italy
19 July 1996

General Introduction

From early in the Christian era, artists and simple believers have sought to create representations of Jesus the Christ. Among the earliest of these representations were the graffiti on the walls and tombs in the catacombs, and carved on sarcophagi: the "icthus" and later the fish design, the chi-rho sign for "Christos," the anchor sign, the peacock. Roman (pagan) mosaics were "converted" to Christian use, with the face of Jesus being superimposed over that of the sun god Helios. The cross sign and the representation of Jesus crucified came into use relatively late, as the crucifixion of Jesus was at first considered to be a shame and a scandal.

The representation of Jesus the Christ in early icons created by monks became so popular, and the spiritual and liturgical veneration of these images of a severe otherworldly Jesus so widespread, that it led, in the seventh century, to a serious conflict in the Church. One side, represented by the iconoclasts or image-breakers, insisted that the veneration of icons was in fact adoration and thus idolatry, the opposite side, best represented by John of Damascus, insisted that the Incarnation, that is Jesus, fully divine and fully human as determined dogmatically by the Council of Chalcedon (451), allows the representation of Jesus the Christ in art. The controversy was settled by the Council of Nicea (787), in favor of the representation of Jesus, a decision which clearly encouraged the continued development of the art of the icon and other forms of art which came to represent Jesus and the Christian mysteries.

Working in the east and then in the great cathedrals of Monréale, Cefalù and Ravenna, the mosaic artists of Byzantium represented Christ as the Pantocrator, a severe, transcendent figure, in a style developed first by the eastern iconographers. In western Europe, the stonemason-sculptors and the makers of stained glass sought to represent a Jesus Christ more divine than human, often making him larger than the figures around him, enthroned, transfigured or in judgment. The early medieval painters, on wood or in frescoes, also stressed the transcendent dimension, the divine nature of Christ. In the Middle Ages, dramatic artists began creating theatrical representations of the Christ and his passion, in the passion plays of Bavaria and elsewhere, and the mysteries of his life, in, for example, the great mystery cycles in Britain.

These representations in the beginning were primitive, in folk-art style, but they developed into highly sophisticated, formal dramas, some of which continue to be produced today, for example at Oberammergau where, interestingly enough, they are supported by a thriving popular-art industry of wood sculptures of Jesus. For centuries writers of poetry and later prose have represented Jesus the Christ – one thinks of John Donne, Gerard Manley Hopkins, Nikos Kazantzakis – as have composers of music and song, both classical, ecclesial and popular, the theatrical-musical representations of *Jesus Christ Superstar* and *Godspell* in the 1960s being well-known recent examples.

Beginning in the Renaissance, there was a radical and dramatic shift in the way the visual arts represented Jesus Christ. The two-dimensional, larger-than-life figure of Jesus seen against an abstract background, a figure more transcendental than immanent, gave way to a more this-worldly, incarnated figure, a "softer" Jesus, most often pictured three-dimensionally and in a historically- and culturally-specific setting, though not always first-century Palestine. In this later Jesus, often shown surrounded by people, the artists wanted to emphasize the human nature he shared with all men and women. If Renaissance art made Jesus human, the art of the Baroque period, while maintaining his humanity, made him strong and passionate, while later the art of the Romantic period made him sentimental.[1] This last development paved the way for a widespread growth of popular devotional images of Jesus, still dominant today, whose most evident quality is their exaggerated sentimentality and in large part, bad taste.[2] In reaction against this development towards the sentimental, many modern and contemporary artists have experimented with a rich variety of styles for the portraits of the Christ. Dali, for example, made him surreal and cosmic, Roualt liberated him by making him a clown and Chagall, both on canvas and in stained-glass, expressed Jesus as rooted in the messianic figures of the Old Testament.

If the representation of Jesus Christ was a constant theme in the six traditional arts, one might well expect it to be a theme of the seventh art, the cinema, an art form that is only a hundred years old. Clearly it is so. Already in the first five years of its existence, the new art form produced at least six films, all brief, as were all films in those early days, whose subject was the life and passion of Jesus the Christ. In its first hundred years, the cinema produced more than one hundred fifteen films that treated, in one way or another, some with greater and some with lesser success, the story of Jesus. They are films in a variety of styles, with a wide variety of approaches to the portrait of Jesus, and consequently with an astonishing variety of christologies. Some are quite orthodox, some further to the left; some are fascinating challenges to theology and the faith, others so banal as to be completely uninteresting, and some are unacceptable, erroneous, or downright heretical.

The history of cinema also demonstrates another approach to the person of Jesus the Christ, that is the figurative or metaphorical approach, a most valid way, that has always had a privileged place in the Judaeo-Christian tradition. The Old Testament used metaphors – the gentle breeze, the mother hen, the suffering servant – to represent aspects of God's self-revelation. In his ministry as represented in the gospels, Jesus repeatedly used metaphors and parables to speak of God and of himself as the revelation of God. From the very beginning the art of the Christian community created and developed visual metaphors to represent Jesus the Christ, for example, the fish, the pelican, the phoenix. From early in the development of cinema, film-makers have told stories in which the central figures are foils of Jesus and in which the plot is parallel to the story of the life, death and, sometimes, the Resurrection of Jesus, stories in which the "presence" of Jesus is sensed and discerned in the person and struggle of the protagonist.

There are two films, one early in the history of the seventh art and one much more recent, which serve as very apt introductions to this two-level approach to Jesus Christ in cinema, because in each film, both the direct and the metaphorical approaches to Jesus Christ are represented. In D. W. Griffith's epic film *Intolerance* (1916), a film with four parallel narratives running concurrently, the episodes recounting the story of the passion of Jesus are "framed" by episodes of three other stories of intolerance, narratives in which the innocent victims of human cruelty are clearly foils, in some sense metaphors, of Jesus. In Denys Arcand's film *Jesus of Montreal* (1989), a young actor playing the role of Jesus in a theatrical production, and thus "surrounded" by direct representations of Jesus, becomes, in his own life, a foil to Jesus to the point of experiencing, like him, a passion, a death and a resurrection. The terminology commonly used to qualify these cinematographic foils of Jesus is "Christ-figure," if the total dynamic of the film embodies the total dynamic of the Christ-event, or "Jesus-figure," if the character referred to embodies only some aspects of the life and death of Jesus, without any particular reference to his total salvific mission and to his Resurrection.

This book, then, is about representations of Jesus and Christ-figures in cinema. Part one is dedicated to the Jesus-film tradition, from its beginnings to the present day. It considers a wide variety of these films, doing a more detailed analysis of some of the major productions. In chapter one, we shall consider the beginnings of the Jesus-film tradition, from the first silent representations of the passion play till the early Bible epics. The second chapter focusses on two Jesus-epics made in Hollywood, Stevens' *The Greatest Story Ever Told* (1965) and Ray's *King of Kings* (1961). In chapter three, we shall look at the particular *genre* of the Jesus-film as musical, doing an analysis of *Jesus Christ Superstar* (1973) and *Godspell* (1973). The so-called scandal films about Jesus will occupy our attention in chapter four with a brief consideration of *Monty Python's The Life of Brian* (1979) and a major essay on Scorsese's *The Last Temptation of Christ* (1988). In chapter five, we shall discuss two films which represent well the later Jesus-film tradition: Zeffirelli's *Jesus of Nazareth* (1977) and Rossellini's *The Messiah* (1975). And in the final chapter of part one, we shall focus on the finest and most valid of the Jesus-films, Pasolini's *The Gospel According to Saint Matthew* (1966).

Part two of the book is dedicated to the filmic Christ-figure. In the Introduction, some consideration will be given to the notion of the Christ-figure, its advantages and its limits. In chapter one, we shall analyze Arcand's

Jesus of Montreal, a transitional film which fits remarkably well into the thematic structure of this book because it creates both a variety of portraits of
Jesus and a splendid, multi-faceted Christ-figure. The woman as Christ-figure
is the theme of the second chapter. In it, we will consider how five films,
Fellini's two classics, *Nights of Cabiria* (1957) and *La strada* (1954), and
three more recent creations, *Out of Rosenheim* (*Bagdad Cafe*) (1987), *Babette's Feast* (1987) and *Dead Man Walking* (1995) have as protagonists
women who are metaphorical representations of the evangelical-soteriological
mission of Jesus Christ. The third chapter shifts register considerably and
analyzes the classical western, *Shane* (1953), demonstrating how its director
George Stevens has strategically changed elements of the novel on which the
film is based, in order to embody in the person and actions of the protagonist-
hero of his film, the basic elements of the Christ-event.

In chapter four, we shall analyze how, in two versions of the same film
– *A Short Film about Love* (1988) and *Decalogue Six* (1988-89) – the Polish
film director Kieślowski creates two fascinating variations on the theme of
the Christ-event. The subject of the fifth chapter is Bresson's great masterpiece, *Au hasard Balthazar* (1966). In this daring frontier film, the French
artist embodies in the story of a small donkey, not only a profound study of
good and evil in the human experience, but also a complex and fascinating
parable of the Christ-event. In chapter six, we shall look at a wide variety of
films, first considering how the essential dimensions of the Christ-event are
represented in them, and then how certain typical guises characterize the
Christ-figure in film. Finally, in the seventh chapter, we shall consider several
films by two undisputed masters of cinema and of the Christ-film *genre*,
Tarkovsky and Bresson.

Part One

The Jesus-Film

Introduction

The Jesus-film is a much more complex reality than one might at first suspect, and this complexity is directly due to the subject. The film-maker who chooses to explore the Jesus-theme is obliged to face a series of decisions, choices and difficulties that are quite unprecedented in the history of cinema. It might seem a truism to say that the Jesus-film is based on the New Testament or the gospels. But even this fact, this "choice" made by the film-maker, is complex and fraught with ambiguity. The film-artist who wishes to tell the story of Jesus in the Bible must decide among the four quite distinct portraits of Jesus in the gospels of Mark, Matthew, Luke and John, the Jesus presented, if indirectly, in Acts of the Apostles and in the epistles, and the Jesus announced and even described in some of the books of the Old Testament. The artist may choose to represent only one of these Jesus-portraits, or a kind of synthetic, composite Jesus, including elements from all the biblical sources.

Having made this first and basic decision regarding a biblical Jesus, the film-maker faces a further series of problems. The New Testament, the gospels, were neither biographical nor historical documents, at least as we in the twentieth century conceive of "scientific" history and biography, but rather they were faith proclamations, and the number of straight biographical details in them is limited. Clearly the Gospel provides no physical description of Jesus. Further, the individual gospels are not always in agreement among themselves. At times, in fact, they seem to contradict one another. The style of the gospels is characterized by ellipses: details connecting separate episodes are lacking, time is telescoped, the stress is often on the spoken words of Jesus and often the concrete circumstances of his preaching and his miracles are not described. Only Luke has the infancy narrative, an account which is extremely elliptical, and the gospels reveal little or nothing about the first thirty years of Jesus' life. Finally, something obvious in regard to the gospels but of no little import in a Jesus-film, the "story," and especially its conclusion, is well-known. In the film, on the level of content therefore, there can be no surprises, no tension, no suspense, and this a clearly a disadvantage for a medium like cinema that requires a dramatic structure.

Another element in this delicate balance that is the Jesus-film, is the point of view of the film-maker towards the biblical material regarding Jesus. Is the artist a Christian believer or not? If yes, then what is the quality of that belief? Is it the faith of the fundamentalist who holds in the literal truth of every word of the gospels, or is it a more enlightened belief which recognizes the complexity of literary *genres* and forms within the gospels? Is it a vision of Jesus Christ that takes into consideration the wide-ranging results of centuries of scripture research and theological investigation into the figure of Jesus? If on the other hand, the basic point of view towards the biblical Jesus is that of unbelief, then is it the closed dogmatic unbelief of the militant atheist, or the rather open, searching unbelief of the agnostic? This question of the Christian belief or unbelief of the film-maker is already important when he or she is handling day-to-day elements of the public life of the historical Jesus; it becomes absolutely crucial when it is a question of representing transcendent elements of the manifestation of Jesus as the Christ, the Incarnation of God, questions such as the epiphany of God at the baptism of Jesus, the miracles, the Transfiguration and, of course, the Resurrection.

A further consideration in relation to the Jesus-film is that the nature and function of the *genre* "sacred scripture" is radically different from the nature of the *genre* "cinema." The former is that of the written word, born and transmitted in an oral tradition, believed to be divinely inspired and guaranteed, and now heard in liturgical settings or read in the context of prayer or academic research. The nature of the *genre* cinema is that of the audio-visual "word," mediated by an ever more complex technology and ever more powerful economic structures, and experienced largely in settings that are social-cultural and entertainment; and the cinema "word" is, in the most absolute way, not divinely-inspired or guaranteed, no matter how approved a film might be by church authorities. These are two worlds that have little in common, a fact that leaps to the attention when, in one of the many silent films about Jesus, the dynamic dramatic visual frames of action and expression are regularly interrupted by the static frames of the printed word, quoting the Bible. The dissonance is immediately evident. The question of the high technological dimension of cinema is critical to the Jesus-film when, for example, one realizes that digital electronics and techniques of virtual reality can create on-screen, in the most concrete, material, realistic terms, elements of Jesus' experience – the healing miracles or better, the Transfiguration, the Resurrection and the Ascension – that in the Gospel are described in metaphorical or poetic terms, or as in the case of the Resurrection not directly described at all, simply because they are manifestations of the transcendent divinity of Christ, of Holy Mystery, which by definition defy concrete, material representation.

The issue of the authenticity of the cinematographic representation of Jesus Christ becomes more complex when one considers that in many of the Jesus-films, the source material for the portrait of Jesus is not the canonical gospels but rather the non-canonical, apocryphal gospels or popular-devotional biographies of Jesus, documents which often reflect more biblical fiction than biblical fact. Sometimes the source material is novels whose fictional representations of Jesus are more projections of the personalities and problems of the authors than reflections of the historical Jesus or of the biblical Jesus Christ. In these cases, and even though the spectators may be convinced of seeing an authentic image of Jesus the Christ, they are in fact twice removed from the Jesus or the Christ of the gospels.

A further difficulty for the Jesus-film has to do with the undeniable fact that any film about Jesus Christ is preceded by the dense heritage of nineteen centuries of visual art on the Jesus-theme. This complex tradition is an issue or a stumbling block for the film artist who inevitably has to take a position in its regard. Some reject the tradition, some imitate it slavishly, some limit their contact to inspiration. At the same time, the maker of the Jesus-film has to bear in mind that the Jesus tradition in the visual arts is also a stumbling block for the audience. Most spectators[1] come to any film about Jesus with a whole series of preconceived notions and feelings about him, based on their religious and intellectual upbringing: how Jesus looks and sounds, how he moves and acts, how he relates to people and situations. This consideration is even more critical in the case of the spectator who is a believing and practicing Christian and whose world-view and life-choices are radically tied up with a personal spiritual existential experience of Jesus the Christ: it is highly unlikely that any filmic image of Jesus will be in full harmony with such a radically personal experience.

Then to this equation must be added a number of rather concrete practical considerations which have to do with the fact that film-making is a very public and very costly art form, that it exists and thrives in the context of a highly-structured socio-economic system of production and distribution. A Jesus-film, but for that matter, any film, costs a great deal: investors have to be found willing to finance it and producers have to ensure that the finished product will give the investors a return on their investment. These precise economic realities clearly have an effect on every aspect of the Jesus-film, including the nature and the quality of the Jesus created and portrayed in the film. Will the film be shot in the Middle East thus permitting the publicity campaign to claim it was filmed in the "authentic locations"? Will it fulfill the needs of the Spielberg-dependent filmgoers with spectacular, computer-generated effects, such as a virtual-reality Resurrection or at least a credible Sacred Heart? Will it recreate the authentic cultural-political ambience of first-century Palestine, the Pesach hymns at the Last Supper in Dolby quadraphonic sound? To get to the heart of the matter, which actor will be assigned the role of Jesus? Putting a well-known, popular star in the robes of Jesus may ensure profits at the box-office, but it creates major problems for the image of the Jesus thus created: an actor with well-known precedents in the intense psychological dramas of Ingmar Bergman inevitably embodies a Jesus full of existential *angst*; a good-looking blond teenage heart-throb becomes a California-surfer Jesus, the New York-bred, -trained and -accented method actor creates a confused, neurotic Jesus. But are any of the portraits of Jesus created by these high profile actors capable of embodying, in any adequate way, the Jesus Christ of the Gospel and of the Christian tradition? Or does their high-profile idiosyncratic "performance" not in fact get in the way of such an authentic embodiment?

The century-old history of the Jesus-film demonstrates a wide variety of attempted solutions to these problems. There is, for example, the use of non-professional or unknown actors, the creation of subplots to fill in the elliptical gaps in the Gospel accounts, the imitation of popular sacred drama, or the representation of Jesus by metonomy. In this latter case, the camera "sees" Jesus only from behind, or only his hand as it heals, or the hem of his garment, or his shadow: it is a particularly unfair and unsatisfactory solution. In the long term, none of these solutions have more than a limited success. As we shall now see, often these solutions are self-conscious and even clumsy and they can end up interfering with the authentic image of Jesus they are intended to enhance.

1

The Early Years

How are we to deal with the problems created by the appropriation of *sacred* texts by a medium of *illusion* like cinema, or by the adaptation of a story that is presumed *true* into a vehicle of *fiction?*[1]

This rhetorical question, intended to point out a major difficulty faced by the makers of the earliest films on the life and passion of Jesus, may be used as a critical tool to appreciate all the films of the ninety-nine year history of the Jesus-film. If the question poses serious problems for some of the more recent Jesus-films, for example, the very high-key *The Last Temptation of Christ* of Scorsese or the very low-key *The Messiah* of Rossellini, it seems to find a simple answer in the early passion films, which in both content and style seem to reflect the Gospel texts. As we have already suggested in our introduction, the New Testament texts are linear in style, highly elliptical, often syncopated, with little organic narrative and relatively little attention paid to psychological motivation of character and action. Further, our normal experience of the Jesus of the Gospel is composite, reflecting elements of the four versions: "We mix up all the versions in our heads and produce for ourselves a rough-and-ready harmony."[2] One scholar attributes the undisputed popularity of the early passion films at least in part to this correspondence between the biblical text and the film text: "The Passion is a story made to measure for the early cinema. A known story, already written down, elliptical in development, with texts that are syncopated and paroxysmal."[3]

The early Jesus-films are highly episodic in structure and content, composed of "series of tableaux, autonomous units."[4] Simple cuts and title cards join episodes and serve as rough transitions between them. The films evince "no shaping of . . . events into an integral narrative whole."[5] The real connections between episodes, the transitions, are spontaneously made by the "reconstructive capacities of the viewer familiar with the Gospels,"[6] that is, one who has already done that work of shaping and integrating the Gospel story as he or she has read or heard it. Rather than a narrative recounting of the story of Jesus or a fictionalized reworking of the Jesus-material, both of which become popular approaches later on in the Jesus-film tradition, these early films are more like "reminders, iconographically cued remembrances"[7] from the source-text that is the Bible.

This explanation clearly accounts for the curious fact that in the catalogues of a number of production companies, the early passion and life of Jesus films were available to buyers in various versions, with more or fewer episodes. From the Pathé catalogue, for example, "one could order a Passion Play in three different versions: in 32, 20 or 12 scenes."[8] In some cases, different versions were offered to Protestant and Catholic audiences: episodes (evangelical and extra-evangelical) involving Mary, the mother of Jesus were more often included in versions destined to Catholic audiences. Again, regarding the Pathé catalogue, offered as extra, optional sequences to buyers already owning a copy of the life-of-Jesus films, were the autonomous episodes of the miracles of Jesus. Clearly, the "goal of the Passion Play [film] was to illustrate and recall a well-known story rather than create a self-contained diegesis with narrative flow."[9]

The two earliest Jesus-films appeared in 1897, barely two years after the debut of the seventh art. *The Passion of Christ*, commonly known as the *Léar Passion*, was produced in France for a publishing house, La Bonne Presse, by the Société Léar. Based on a script written by Herman Basile, it was filmed "in a vacant lot in Paris, substituting actors for children at the last minute,"[10] and the finished film lasted only five minutes. All copies of this film have been lost. The second passion film, a record of the Passion Play performed at Horitz in Bohemia, was an American production,[11] financed by the theater producers Klaw and Erlanger, directed by Walter Freeman and filmed by Charles Webster and his crew in the Bohemian town. Entitled *The Horitz Passion Play*, it was composed of a maximum of forty-five scenes,[12] and included documentary footage of the town, the theater and the preparation of the actors in addition to scenes from the Old Testament and from the New Testament extending from the visit of the Magi to the Resurrection. Thanks to a carefully-planned and executed public relations campaign, including a preview showing to the Cardinal-Archbishop of Baltimore, James Gibbons, and a very successful tournée of Philadelphia, Baltimore, Boston, Rochester, Pittsburgh, Montreal and San Francisco, the film had a successful run in New York.

The Mystery of the Passion Play of Oberammergau, also known as *The Original Oberammergau Passion Play*,[13] a nineteen-minute film produced in the United States in 1898[14] with professional actors, had a rather more complicated genesis and history. Based on the seventeen-year-old scenario, written by Salmi Morse for a stage production of the passion of Jesus, which opened briefly in San Francisco but not in New York, it was filmed on the roof-terrace of the Grand Central Palace Hotel in Manhattan. The filming was done in late autumn, which resulted in some rather unevangelical snow in the Garden of Olives.[15] Starring Frank Russell as Jesus,[16] the film was directed by Henry Vincent, the famous theater director who, because he could not adapt to the new medium, was in effect replaced by William Paley and the actor, Russell. Including twenty-three scenes of the life of Christ from the shepherds of Bethlehem to the Ascension, it was publicized, as the title suggests, as an authentic film version of the Passion Play produced every ten years in the Bavarian village of Oberammergau. The revelation in the New York press that the film was a fake had virtually no negative effect either on the enthusiastic public which flocked to see it twice a day in New York, or on its distribution all over the Northeastern United States. The showing of the film was accompanied by a learned commentary of a certain Professor Powell (later replaced by a minister) and by the singing of a boys' choir, and it was enthusiastically approved by churchmen, both Catholic and Protestant. A copy of the film was bought by an itinerant Protestant preacher, who showed it all over the country at revival meetings, "the first time a rather suspect 'shadow world' was used as a power for religion."[17] The result was a success far greater that the producer had hoped for.[18] *The Mystery of the Passion Play of Oberammergau* is considered important in film-history and in the history of the religious film because it was one of the first examples of a recreated or fictionalized version of a historical event in film. Its producers, Richard Hollaman and Albert Eaves had "by faking and dramatizing scenes, unwittingly taken one of the first steps towards artistic expression in motion pictures."[19]

In 1899, the French film production company, Gaumont, produced the six-minute *Life of Christ*, which is important for two reasons. Its director was a woman, Alice Guy – "a distinct rarity in the Jesus-film genre"[20] – and in its various scenes, it imitated paintings by Old Masters, an oft-repeated technique in films about Jesus. The next year, again in France, Georges Méliès produced a short film, *Christ Walking on the Waters*[21] which, in spite of its extreme brevity – only thirty-five seconds – is significant in the history of the Jesus-film. In it, for the first time, a special filmic effect, a simple double exposure, was used to depict, as the title suggests, the miracle of Jesus walking on the Sea of Galilee.

The French film company, Pathé, produced three of the earliest Jesus-films. The first, released in 1902, *The Life and Passion of Jesus Christ*, was a respectable nineteen minutes long, and depicted thirty-one scenes from the New Testament, covering the life of Christ from the Annunciation to the Parousia. The second was the five-minute long *Life of Christ*, released in 1907. Pathé's third effort, *The Life and Passion of Jesus Christ*, which came out in 1908, was rather undistinguished, with "unimaginative set design and curiously gauche performers . . . and a few crude attempts at special effects."[22] It deserves, however, a place in the history of the Jesus-film, at least as a curiosity, because it was re-released *twice*: in 1914, with some new scenes edited in, and with color tinting applied by hand, titled *The Life of Our Saviour*, and again seven years later, with the title *Behold the Man!*, a version in which the earlier colored footage was framed by a modern narrative filmed in black and white.

In the United States, the Kalem production company, five years after its 1907 production of *Ben-Hur*, which brought a lawsuit for copyright violation from the author of the novel, General Lew Wallace (a lawsuit lost by the company), produced a life of Christ, *From the Manger to the Cross*. Directed by Sidney Olcott (who also did *Ben-Hur*) it was sixty minutes in length, the longest of the early Jesus-films and one of the first American feature-length films.[23] It was based on the so-called "Tissot Bible,"[24] and many of its shots reflected both the content and the compositions of the illustrations in this devotional book. In fact, Olcott's compositions often "improved upon Tissot."[25] It omitted the Resurrection of Christ, but included a dramatic suicide of Judas, and as optional scenes, "with an eye to exclusively Catholic audiences,"[26] two extra-evangelical scenes: on his way to Calvary, Jesus meets first his mother and then Veronica. The film had well-known professional actors – the British actor Robert Henderson-Bland played the role of Jesus – and it was shot, in large part, on locations in Egypt and Palestine. There is no doubt that the "authentic" location shots, for example, of Joseph, Mary and the Child Jesus resting on their flight into Egypt, with the Sphinx and the great pyramids behind them, were one of the reasons for this film's popularity at the box office and they set a standard of sorts for future Jesus-films.

Several other aspects of this production seem to anticipate elements common to later Jesus-film productions: the script (in a silent movie, limited to title cards) is faithful to the text of the gospels, anticipating Pasolini's *The Gospel According to Saint Matthew*; the lead actor wrote two books about his experience of playing Jesus, something that the director Franco Zeffirelli as director did seventy years later; and like Zeffirelli's film, *From the Manger to the Cross* remained very popular for years. Clearly, the film's length, which was three times that of its longest predecessors, anticipated the epic length of the later megaproductions. Early in the era of sound films, it was re-released with "a synchronized music and sound effects track, together with newly-filmed close-ups."[27]

The high point of the early Jesus-film was without a doubt, the Jesus-episode in D.W. Griffith's three-and-a-half-hour epic *Intolerance*, released in the United States in 1916. The film's four parallel episodes, woven together by alternate editing into "the single flowing form of a fugue,"[28] illustrate how the struggle of good and innocent people against hatred, cruelty and intolerance is a repeated theme in human history. In addition to the modern episode in which an innocent man is condemned to death during a violent labor-management conflict, and to the episodes of the cruel conquest of Babylon by Belshazzar and of the killing of French Protestants by Catherine de Medici, known as "The St. Bartholomew's Night Massacre," Griffith presented, in the briefest and "least developed"[29] episode, the story of the passion of Jesus. He introduced the passion with the episode of the woman taken in adultery and that of the wedding feast at Cana, the latter of which provided an opportunity extradiegetically[30] for some special effects – a dark cross appeared superimposed over Jesus as he solemnly performed the miraculous transformation of water into wine – and which became intradiegetically the occasion of the beginning of the plot of the Pharisees against Jesus which culminated in his crucifixion.

The Judaean episode of *Intolerance* is significant in the history of the Jesus-film for several reasons. First, its crucifixion scene, with its epic compositions and huge cast of extras, is nothing short of spectacular. Secondly, Howard Gaye's low-key portrayal of Jesus, clearly dated by today's esthetic norms, is considered "one of the most successful dramatizations of Christ on film,"[31] and set the standard for film portraits of Jesus for years to come. And finally, the film touches for the first time the delicate issue of how to represent the responsibility for the death of Jesus, an issue which must be faced even with the most recent Jesus-films. In his original version, and notwithstanding the presence on the set of a rabbi and an Episcopalian priest as advisors,[32] Griffith had shown the leaders of the Jewish community not only persecuting Jesus but also crucifying him; the director gave in to justified pressure from Jewish groups and "burned the negative already shot, refilming the [crucifixion] scenes with Roman soldiers substituted."[33]

To conclude this treatment of the earliest of the Jesus-films, we might consider one of the oddities of the *genre*, the 1918 film, *Restitution*. Its director and principal actor (as Jesus) was Howard Gaye, the Jesus of *Intolerance*. Perhaps the first "spin-off" film, that is, a film generated by a character or an episode in a previous film, it recounted in four episodes and in one-hundred minutes, the eternal struggle of humanity against Satan. In the triumphant climax of the film, Satan, having formed "an unholy alliance"[34] with the German Kaiser, met with Jesus, evidently well-resurrected from his crucifixion in *Intolerance* (in which the Resurrection was not represented). Perhaps wishfully anticipating the proximate end of World War I,[35] Gaye had Jesus defeat both Satan and the Kaiser. The film was no doubt popular, because ten years later, it was re-released in a shortened version and with the more dramatic title of *The Conquering Christ*.

A theme similar to that of *Restitution* formed one of the first of the Jesus-epics, the 1919 Danish work, *Leaves from Satan's Book*, an early film of Carl Theodor Dreyer. Based on a popular novel by Maria Corelli, and lasting over one hundred minutes, it imitated the structure of *Restitution*. The film has four episodes and documents Satan's largely successful attempts, by assuming a human identity, to corrupt people in different periods and different places: the Spanish Inquisition in fifteenth-century Seville, the French Revolution and the execution of Marie Antoinette and the Civil War in Finland in the period following the Russian Revolution. In the first episode, lasting twenty-two minutes, Satan, in the guise of a Pharisee, successfully tempts Judas to betray Jesus. The character of Jesus is clearly of secondary importance: in the foreground are Satan, the protagonist of the entire film, and Judas who struggles dramatically both before and after his sin. Dreyer portrays three moments in the final days of Jesus' life: a visit to the home of Simon the Leper where during a silent musical interlude Dreyer inserts, using a primitive dissolve-technique, a shot of Jesus as the good shepherd, then the Last Supper and the agony in the garden and the betrayal. It is clear in a number of shots that Dreyer is imitating Renaissance paintings. He wants to suggest Jesus's transcendence, his divine and human natures; but the formal, theatrical looks and gestures, the slow deliberate movements, reminiscent of the Jesus of *Intolerance*, create a Jesus who is strangely severe, impassive and set apart from the rest of the characters.

In 1923, four years after his classical expressionist film, *The Cabinet of Dr. Caligari*, the German director, Robert Wiene, made his passion film, enti-

tled *I.N.R.I.* Not based on the Bible but adapted from a novel by Peter Roseg-
ger, it was seventy minutes long and starred the husband-and-wife team of the
Danish Asta Nielsen and the Russian Gregori Chmara, in the roles of Jesus
and Mary Magdalene. Wiene shot some of the film on location in Palestine
and followed the already established tradition of basing his compositions on
masterpieces of Renaissance art. The silent *I.N.R.I.* was re-released in 1934 as
a "talkie," with music and voice-over narration, under the title *Crown of
Thorns*.

The uncontested high point of the era of the silent film about Jesus,
Cecil B. DeMille's *The King of Kings* was the first of a long line of monumental Jesus-films, the colossals. Following the first DeMille biblical spectacular, *The Ten Commandments*, in 1923, and preceding his epic story of the
persecution of the early Christians, *The Sign of the Cross*, in 1932, *The King
of Kings*, released in 1927, was nearly two hours in length. Based on a
screenplay by Jeannie MacPherson, and filmed in black and white, but surprisingly breaking into color for the Resurrection scene, the film tried valiantly, but not entirely successfully, to break out of the episodic, elliptical
structure of the earlier Jesus-films, into the more organic, narrative style that
characterizes its descendants.

The King of Kings is of interest in the history of the Jesus-film for a
number of reasons, most of which have to do more with its producer-director
than with the film itself. DeMille created around his lead actor, Henry B.
Warner, with his "carved Jewish profile,"[36] a kind of mystical star aura. The
actor, at forty-nine years of age undoubtedly the oldest film-Jesus ever, was
forbidden by contract to appear in public during the filming, and once in
makeup and costume, he was "transported in a closed car and wore a black
veil when leaving it for the set . . . and had to eat alone in a tent while on
location."[37] Another aspect of DeMille's legendary showmanship was his
elaborate strategy to offset anticipated negative reactions to his film from
Church authorities. He shrewdly retained as advisor the Jesuit priest, Daniel
A. Lord, one of those responsible for the U.S. Motion Picture Production
Code, and in addition held daily prayers during production led by repre-
sentatives of various religious groups, including Islam and Buddhism.[38] He
also had Mass celebrated on the set each morning, insisting it was "like a
constant benediction on our work."[39] Clearly the daily Catholic liturgy was
also "a good insurance policy against future attacks on the film."[40]

Despite this odor of sanctity, or at least of orthodoxy, around the set
and the production, DeMille inexplicably began his Jesus-epic with the thoroughly extra-evangelical episode at the lavish pleasure palace of a high-living
and scantily-clad Mary Magdalene, played by Jacqueline Logan. When the
Magdalene discovers that her lover Judas has forsaken her to follow a certain
preacher from Nazareth, she leaves the party-in-progress, hops on her chariot
and, as if imitating Ben-Hur, rides off to get him back. Upon meeting Jesus
she is converted and the scene of the ghostly seven deadly sins reluctantly
quitting her body, by the use of simple double exposures, is a dramatic high

point early in the film. It was as if DeMille, fearful of the insufficiency of the over-exposed biblical material, "felt that only the quick introduction of sex would grip and hold the audience."[41] After this unusual and dramatic opening, the film settled down to a "conventional and almost reverential treatment of incidents from the rest of Jesus' life."[42] The crucifixion, for example, was filmed in long shot, with crowds of extras, as if imitating a Breughel painting: the death of the God-man was too awesome and mysterious an event to be seen in the all-revealing close-up shots that are a staple of more recent Jesus-films.

Though even today some few critics approve of H. B. Warner's portrait of Jesus, saying that his "acting throughout is impeccable" and that he was a "a virile, charismatic figure, both convincingly human and convincingly divine,"[43] the overall effect of Warner's performance was to create a formal "static, otherworldly . . . a trifle effete"[44] and ghostly character, a "Hallmark-card Jesus, pious and untroubling."[45] Warner was neither the first nor the last such figure in the history of the Jesus-film. In spite of this weakness, DeMille's strategy worked and his *The King of Kings* was very successful. Distributed internationally, except in Poland, where it was banned,[46] it was "so widely seen, and occasionally shown on television well into the 1970s, that another major film version of Christ's life was not produced until the similarly titled *King of Kings* in 1961."[47]

After DeMille's "Magdalene to Resurrection" epic, the 1935 French film, *Golgotha* by Julien Duvivier broke some interesting new ground in the tradition by, in a certain sense, returning to its origins. The first sound film on the life of Jesus, it limited itself to the events from Palm Sunday to the Ascension, and as suggested by its alternate title, *Ecce Homo*, it placed much emphasis on the Jesus-Pontius Pilate encounter, giving the role of the latter to the famous actor, Jean Gabin, and that of Jesus to Robert Le Vignan. At one hundred minutes in length and complete with massive sets and crowds of people, it examined in a particular way the complex political realities against which the events of Christ's passion were played. Duvivier's film, although in many respects superior to its predecessors, manifested some of the weaknesses endemic to many of the later Jesus-films. The elaborate sets and huge crowds of extras, for example, did not promote a very profound treatment of the spiritual reality of the passion, of the mystery of Jesus' suffering. Another problem was the imbalance between the two principal actors: a powerful, dominant Gabin as Pilate who overpowers Le Vignan, a "sad, anguished, languid" Christ whose "distracted look and soft voice [make him] appear almost effeminate."[48] For some strange reason, the extant version of *Golgotha* is three-hundred meters shorter than the original version and almost all the close-up shots of Jesus are missing.[49] Perhaps this is another case of a certain reticence to portray too directly the more transcendent, mysterious dimensions of the Christ-event, a phenomenon which carries through to the second generation of Gospel spectaculars.

    Interesting at least as a curiosity in the development of the Jesus-film is a long series of films in which Jesus plays a very secondary, and at times ridiculous role, the so-called religious "peplum" films.[50] These action and adventure films often include characters named in the Bible or in ancient history, but they inevitably take great liberties with both historical and biblical facts. Most often they are based not on sacred scripture but on devotional novels, some of which provided repeated, if limited, inspiration to filmmakers: Edward Bulwer-Lytton's novel, *The Last Days of Pompeii,* inspired sixteen film adaptations, Henryk Sienkiewicz's *Quo Vadis?,* ten, Cardinal Wiseman's novel, *Fabiola,* three, and Lew Wallace's *Ben-Hur,* three.[51]

    These films imitated the production values and themes of many earlier and of most of the later Jesus-epics and featured massive sets, huge crowds of extras, ever more elaborate special effects, vibrant colors and elaborate musical scores. They were films full of action, mostly violent, with gladiators, chariot races and the liberation struggles of Christians and slaves. Inevitably too, they depicted the development of sentimental relationships: typically, an unlikely pagan-Christian love experience which resulted in the final conversion of the pagan. In these religious "peplum" films, the distinctions between good and evil were clear: the persecuted Christians were always good, the persecuting emperors were evil, often sadistic, sometimes insane.

    Then into this smorgasbord of action, melodrama and very vague religious sentiments, and as if hoping to give their product depth, credibility and respectability, the directors of these films introduced appearances of Jesus. Usually he was seen very briefly, sometimes as part of the action, sometimes in flashbacks or memory sequences. In a number of films, his face was mysteriously hidden from the camera, which pictured him from the back or registered only his hands or feet or, particularly mysterious, his shadow. One of the first of these films was the 1935 American production of *The Last Days of Pompeii,* directed by Ernest Schoedsack, the unlikely story of a gladiator-turned-horse-thief and occasional accomplice-in-crime of Pontius Pilate, and whose injured son is healed by Jesus. Late in the film, the gladiator, one Marcus, witnesses the crucifixion, and the director would have us believe that these two contacts with Jesus are responsible for his conversion and heroic martyrdom in Rome at the end of the film.

    Schoedsack's film is memorable for a number of things: Basil Rathbone's performance as a curly-haired and guilt-troubled Pontius Pilate; its impressive recreation of the eruption of Vesuvius, prepared by the same special-effects team as worked on *King Kong,* a film made two years earlier by the same director. This film Vesuvius produces "an amazing illusion of carnage and mass destruction."[52] *The Last Days of Pompeii* is also memorable for the total lack of correspondence to the Bulwer-Lytton novel and for the disrespect for historical accuracy with which Schoedsack shamelessly telescoped the time between the death of Christ in 30-33 AD, and the eruption of Vesuvius in 79 AD, to about twelve years. On the other hand, perhaps the least memorable aspect of Schoedsack's spectacular is its portrayal of Jesus, so inconsequential that the name of the actor who played Jesus was not included in the film's credits. Jesus was glimpsed very briefly only three times in the film: when he heals the son of Marcus, then seen from afar during the crucifixion, and finally in a double exposure "vision" to encourage Marcus as the ex-gladiator is about to die a martyr.

In 1951, Metro-Goldwyn-Mayer, perhaps the most important studio in Hollywood, made *Quo Vadis?*. The studio and the film's director Mervyn LeRoy were poised to take advantage of the post-War "return to religion"[53] in America, and they chose a sure bet: the novel, *Quo Vadis?*, had won a Nobel prize; that, and the no-fewer-than-nine previous versions of the film (all silent) seemed to guarantee its success. From the novel which tells the story of a worldly Roman officer who falls in love with a Christian slave, and who in the end converts to Christianity and saves his loved one from the lions, LeRoy created a film spectacular. With massive and elaborate sets, he represented the splendor of Nero's Rome and of the imperial court at Anzio. He gathered a roster of stars such as Robert Taylor, Deborah Kerr, Peter Ustinov and some eight thousand extras, including Elizabeth Taylor and Sophia Loren,[54] and he repeatedly staged scenes of triumphal marches and arena-executions of Christians, and, of course, the burning of Rome. Perhaps the dramatic high point of the film is the high-camp performance of Ustinov as an insane Nero. MGM's hunch paid off: the film cost seven million dollars but it earned almost four times that much. As in *The Last Days of Pompeii*, the even-vaguely biblical content of *Quo Vadis?* is minimal, limited to brief appearances by the apostles Peter and Paul. The role of Jesus is even more limited: a shot of him carrying the cross in the opening of the film, and then, during a climactic sermon of Peter, a flashback tableau of the Last Supper, a meticulously precise recreation of Leonardo da Vinci's fresco.

In 1953, Twentieth Century-Fox produced *The Robe,* directed by Henry Koster, and based on the novel by Lloyd C. Douglas. The first film produced in the new wide-screen Cinemascope, it introduced Richard Burton in the central role of the Roman centurion responsible for carrying out the crucifixion of Jesus. As Marcellus, Burton wins Jesus' robe in the toss of dice at the foot of the cross, and the possession of the garment then moves his life in new directions. After a period of questioning and crisis, and effected by the conversion of the woman he loves, he too becomes a Christian. In the conclusion they both die as Christian martyrs at the hands of the crazed Emperor Caligula. The film, which cost eight million dollars, was a resounding international success at the box office. The critics, on the other hand, were not so enthusiastic, noting something that could be said about most of these films of "Jesus in the bit part," namely, that the spectacular production values, the wide-screen photography, the monumental sets, the huge cast, the elaborate choreography, the constantly swelling musical score, militate against any hope of real, credible personal or spiritual development in the characters. In *The Robe*, Jesus is seen only in the opening scenes of the film, as he enters

Jerusalem on Palm Sunday, and then later at the crucifixion. He is shown
only from the back or from the knees down, and his voice is heard.

Even the Disney organization got into the business of making these
pseudo-religious spectaculars, with the 1959 film *The Big Fisherman*, based
on another Lloyd C. Douglas novel and directed by Frank Borzage.[55] A three-
hour long, wide-screen production made in California, it combines a rather
uninspiring version of the vocation of the apostle Peter with the melodramatic
(and unlikely) love story of a prince and princess. Jesus is glimpsed several
times but in an annoyingly indirect way: the camera shows only the hem of
his garment, or his hand extending awkwardly into the frame.

In 1959, the MGM studios produced *Ben-Hur*, directed by William
Wyler, the third film based on the novel by Lew Wallace.[56] This megaproduc-
tion had over three hundred and fifty speaking parts and more than fifty thousand extras. Memorable especially for the great sea battle and the twenty
minute chariot race that took more than three months to film, the film won a
record number of eleven Academy Awards. *Ben-Hur* narrates the epic story of
the adventures and vicissitudes of a Jewish prince condemned into slavery
and later adopted by a Roman noble. He returns to Palestine, defeats his great
enemy in a chariot race, discovers that his mother and sister, believed to be
dead, are in fact lepers. Reunited, they return to Jerusalem, searching for the
healer Jesus, only to meet him as he carries his cross to Calvary. After the
crucifixion, the mother and sister are miraculously healed.

Jesus is glimpsed indirectly in the static, Hallmark-card nativity scene
early in the film, and later at a well in Nazareth, when the adult Jesus, seen
from the back but emanating a mysterious supernatural light, offers water to
the slave, Ben-Hur. In another occasion, Jesus is seen briefly from behind, as
he preaches to the crowds. Towards the end of the film, as Jesus climbs to
Calvary, seen mostly from a distance or with his face strategically, and annoyingly, hidden by the cross, Ben-Hur returns the earlier favor and offers
him water. The crucifixion is filmed mostly in long shots, with a couple of
dramatic close-ups of Jesus' nailed hands, and of his blood dripping into
pools of water, thus preparing for the final healing of the two women who are
cleansed of their leprosy by the rain.

In *Ben-Hur*, as in many of these films in what one irreverent but perceptive critic calls "Hollywood's toga sweepstakes,"[57] not only does Jesus not
have a strong physical presence, but he is also quite purposely voided of any
serious moral or spiritual impact. "Divinity was out; humanity was in."[58] It is
interesting to note, for example, that in spite of Ben-Hur's meetings with
Jesus, that seem pregnant with significance, superstar Charlton Heston's hero
does not undergo a clearly Christian conversion: "No conversion of the hero
to Christianity was implied [but rather] a sense of spiritual movement toward
the idea of the brotherhood of man."[59] A vague conversion experience, so
ecumenical as to displease no filmgoer, perhaps as much as one can expect
from a Jesus who remains veiled and vague.

One of the last of what one critic refers to as the "endless list of extra-vaganzas . . . churned out"[60] by Hollywood, was the 1962 Columbia Pictures remake of *Barabbas*.[61] Based on the novel by Pär Lagerkvist and directed by Richard Fleischer, the film features a cast of stars, with Anthony Quinn in the lead, and has monumental sets, a dramatic music score and spectacular scenes, including explosions in a sulphur mine. The film narrates the rigorous adventures of Barabbas, as a gladiator and then as a slave, after the crucifixion of Jesus. Barabbas tries to blot out the memory of his contact with Jesus the day of his death but luckily for him, unsuccessfully. When in the conclusion of the film, Barabbas too is crucified, he dies repeating Jesus words, "Into your hands, I commend my spirit," and thus is redeemed. As if to set the note of apparently endless suffering that dominates this film, Jesus is seen being scourged at the pillar in the opening credits of the film. Later in the prison cell they share, he speaks with Barabbas. Finally, Barabbas witnesses Jesus condemned and crucified and he hears his dying words to God, "Into your hands. . . ."

In conclusion, and lest it be thought that only Hollywood produced these pseudo-religious "klinkers," in which Jesus plays a basically superficial and insignificant role, it is worthwhile to mention the largely unknown 1961 Italian-French production *Pontius Pilate*.[62] Directed by the Frenchman Irving Rapper, it purports to narrate the events of Christ's passion from the point of view of Pilate who, years later, reports the events to Caligula, the successor of Tiberius. Jesus is photographed much of the time from behind or is limited to the far right or the far left of the screen, and neither he nor Pilate nor anyone else are portrayed with any depth or sensitivity. In the history of the Jesus-film, Rapper's *Pontius Pilate* holds a unique record: the actor John Drew Barrymore, "in probably the most bizarre piece of gimmick casting ever seen, plays both Jesus and Judas, both of them badly."[63]

2

The Gospel According to Hollywood:
King of Kings and
The Greatest Story Ever Told

Another undoubted shortcoming of the Gospel according to Hollywood is
the habit of watering down the Bible in our pluralistic society so that it
gives the least possible offense to the religious sensibilities of all shades
of believers and unbelievers in the audience.[1]

In the early 1960s, after decades of representing Jesus as a secondary
character, Hollywood produced two major biblical films in which Jesus was
once again the principal character, *King of Kings* and *The Greatest Story Ever
Told*. Both films were made in grand Hollywood epic-spectacular style and
boasted important stars supported by hundreds of secondary actors, massive
sets, elaborate costumes, and no apparent limits on costs. Both films took full
advantage of all that the new film technology could offer: wide-screen images, ever more vivid colors, elaborate music scores and sound tracks and
special effects. It was precisely because of these high production values that
both films – "disedifying and even antireligious"[2] – were failures both in
transmitting faithfully the content and meaning of the Gospel narrative and in
representing adequately the person and significance of Jesus the Christ.

Nicholas Ray's *King of Kings*

The first of these "Jesus as Superstar" films is the 1961 MGM-Sam Bronston
production, *King of Kings,* directed by Nicholas Ray, who, six years earlier
had directed the award-winning *Rebel without a Cause*, for which the Jesus of
the new film is sometimes referred to facetiously as "a rebel with a cause."[3]
Over three hours in length, and costing eight million dollars, *King of Kings* –
a title that blatantly "exploited the title of Cecil B. DeMille's silent film, *The
King of Kings*"[4] – starred Jeffrey Hunter as Jesus and many other well-known
Hollywood actors. It featured the voice-over narration of Orson Welles – a
performance which went uncredited[5] – and included an omnipresent and dramatic music score, almost four hundred elaborate sets, hundreds of minor actors and two huge battle scenes. Once the production team[6] had decided to
make the film in this epic-spectacular style, then in order to attract the largest
possible viewing public, they had to effect two major transformations on their
basic source-text, the gospels. On the one hand, they had to transform the
spare, elliptical, linear, non-dramatic text of the gospels into a full, organic

narrative, characterized by dramatic action and movement, character interest and suspense, in order to grab and hold onto the attention of the audience. On the other hand, they had to transform the tough radical, uncompromising, prophetic content and tone of the Gospel text into a form that continued to edify, of course, but in a softer, safer manner, without offending or alienating any member of the viewing public. The challenge was to seduce gently the audience by amplifying the Gospel narrative and by domesticating its message. It was precisely in effecting this double transformation that the production team of *King of Kings* inevitably ended up making a film about the life and mission of Jesus that was historically, biblically and theologically inaccurate,[7] and that created a distorted and unacceptable image of Jesus the Christ.

Among the significant historical distortions in the film are the two battle scenes, in the opening moments and during the Palm Sunday sequence. Created to illustrate the conflict between the Romans and the Jewish zealots, and to give substance to the character of Barabbas, they are complete fabrications, introduced into the film "out of a desire not for fidelity to the Gospels but to the codes of 1950s and 1960s epics."[8] The distortions of the Gospel text are numerous. For example, Pilate and Herod Antipas, the latter described as an Arab, are continually pictured together during the film, in the end giving the impression that they and only they are responsible for the death of Jesus. Then the Roman centurion present on Calvary, a certain Lucius, is also present from the beginning of the film in crucial moments of Jesus life: at the slaughter of the innocents, later when Jesus is growing up in Nazareth and, along with Pilate's wife, at the Sermon on the Mount; at Jesus' trial in front of Pilate, where Lucius acts as his "defense attorney."[9] Finally, all of Jesus' preaching is concentrated in the grand-scale episode of the Sermon on the Mount. Several times, the biblical event represented in *King of Kings* is a complete falsification. For example, Mary – played by Siobhan McKenna, an "Irish touch for the Jewish mother"[10] – is gifted with an almost divine omniscience about her son's mission; she seems to know more about it than he does, and she annoyingly keeps dropping hints to this effect. Further, Jesus visits John the Baptist in his cell to encourage him before his death. Again, the film makes Barabbas and Judas friends and basically sympathetic characters and Judas' betrayal of Jesus is, in effect, a well-motivated and "not-ignoble calculation."[11]

Equally important, *King of Kings* deliberately omits some basic and important elements of the Gospel. For example, and evidently to avoid the accusation of anti-Semitism, totally and conspicuously absent from the film is the role of Jewish authorities in the persecution of Jesus throughout his ministry and in the conspiracy to arrest him and put him to death. "The Jewish priesthood is shown as under the control of the Romans, something which diminishes imputed Jewish guilt, and Jewish leaders hostile to Jesus are carefully balanced with others sympathetic to him."[12] The implication of this careful and entirely fictional machination is that "Christ died by default, and that not a single Scribe, Pharisee, Sadducee, priest or high priest had anything to do with it."[13] As well, a wide variety of absolutely crucial events in Christ's life, which have to do with the radical quality of his mission and with his divinity, are omitted: the Transfiguration, the raising of Lazarus, Jesus' predictions of his own death and Resurrection, his cleansing of the temple, his ongoing conflict with the religious authorities. The critic Bosley Crowther summarizes well both the facts and the effects of Ray's manipulation of the Gospel, saying that he has "obfuscated the healings, avoided the miracles and skipped altogether the judgment of Jesus as a blasphemer and seditionist by the Jews . . . the essential drama of the messianic issue has been missed."[14]

Beyond its specific historical errors and as a consequence of its biblical errors, *Kings of Kings* contains a whole series of serious theological inaccuracies, presumably not evident in the script when the film received the "formal approval of Pope John XXIII."[15] Regarding Jesus' miracles of healing, for example, in Ray's version, they are never deliberate moments of personal encounter which announce the Kingdom of God. Sometimes the miracles are reported after the fact and not by eyewitnesses, clearly a strategy of "asserting the . . . miracles, but in a modified form not involving their dramatization, and in a way taking refuge in the skepticism which on the surface is condemned."[16] Other times Jesus does perform the miracle but in a bizarre, impersonal way, without touching or speaking with the person healed. "One miracle is shown as a blind man shuffling along the street and accidentally colliding with the shadow of Jesus, the cure following without any act of faith whatever in the blind man, a sort of radioactivity kind of miracle."[17] This is faithful neither to the Gospel nor to the most elementary theology of miracle.

Further evidence of biblical and theological inaccuracy is the fact that Ray does not have Jesus create a community with his disciples, nor does he allow a community of believers to be formed around them. Then, the crucial issues of Jesus' divinity and of his consciousness of being the Son of God are not touched. "Not once in this film is Christ shown claiming divinity, and some scenes are so constructed that he seems to be disclaiming it."[18] Finally, Jesus' death just seems to happen: it is not freely embraced as a consequence of his mission and it has no soteriological significance.

If the integrity of *King of Kings* is vitiated by its specific treatment of the Gospel content, there are also serious problems with the film as a whole, that is with formal, extradiegetical choices of the production team. To begin with, the formal choice to beef up the Gospel text with series of subplots, interconnected by parallel editing and rapid cutting, confers an artificial soap-opera quality to the film. There is the story of the centurion Lucius and his gradual conversion; the story of Barabbas and Judas and the zealots, and their radical political option; the story of the strange partnership of Pilate and Herod; and finally, the peculiar and annoying story of Mary, the mother of Jesus as a much-sought-after spiritual counselor. The logical result is that Jesus gets lost in the process,[19] and the film remains "limp, spiritually empty,"[20] a "series of *tableaux* inspired by Christian paintings"[21] rendered statically with "the nature of an illustrated lecture."[22]

In the same vein, the choice to give an epic-spectacular quality to the film is implemented in a very uneven and inconsistent fashion: it seems to be limited to the Sermon on the Mount episode and to the two elaborate and unhistorical battle scenes. The battle scenes – one critic, making a pun, suggests that Ray had his attention more on "mounted cavalry than on Mt. Calvary"[23] – are purely gratuitous and have nothing to do with the Jesus-story. The Sermon on the Mount is clearly the *pièce de résistance* of Ray's film. In a scene which was to have been almost a half-hour in length,[24] and which took more than a month to shoot, Ray pulled out all the stops:

> All the characters of the story are assembled – Pilate's wife and Lucius, Barabbas and Judas, Nicodemus and Caiaphas, the disciples and Jesus' mother, the adulteress and Mary Magdalene. Starting with the Beatitudes at sunrise, Jesus talks to camel drivers, the rich young ruler, elderly people, cynics, merchants, members of the Sanhedrin, students and children.[25]

Martin Scorsese, who later omits the Sermon on the Mount from his Jesus film, was much impressed by Ray's version, speaking of the "extraordinary camera work, full of surprising angles," and he added enthusiastically, "Ray films it like a modern press conference."[26] In what is reputed to be "the longest traveling shot in the history of cinema,"[27] Ray staged the Sermon "as a question-and-answer session, in which he [Jesus] wanders freely among the multitudes."[28] Further, a variety of crucial and dramatic moments in the life of Jesus, represented directly in the gospels, are here described by Lucius to Pilate in perfect newscast style: "it was reported that. . . ." Finally, the passion and crucifixion, clearly a dramatic high point of the Gospel, are curiously and inexplicably represented in minor key.

Though Ray portrays the passion of Jesus and the crucifixion in a very subdued, controlled way, he adds to them two details, quite unjustified and if anything, in high key. The table for the Last Supper is Y-shaped, something absolutely unique in the Jesus-film tradition. In an interview, Ray attempted to defend his revolutionary choice with some elaborate and exaggerated reasoning.[29] Referring to the famous Last Supper fresco, he insisted that he did not want to imitate Leonardo da Vinci;[30] the "da Vinci" form of table would not permit the washing of the feet;[31] the Y-shaped table would allow Jesus to give the broken bread directly to everyone at table; and finally, in Ray's own words, the Y-shaped table represented "the cross not yet formed."[32] The other unconventional detail is that Ray shoots the raising of the cross with a camera situated above the head of Jesus. The dynamic result is quite disconcerting, shocking – possibly why Scorsese imitates it twenty-seven years later – and totally inconsistent with the very static quality of most of the film.[33]

There are also two major problems with the soundtrack of *King of Kings*. The melodramatic music score, that swells in all the right moments to modulate the right emotional response of the viewer, is a distraction, as is the choir behind the music which hums transcendentally throughout the film, and chants "Amen" at the end of the "Our Father" and a chorus of "Hallelujah" after the Resurrection. As well, the conspicuous and ubiquitous voice-over narration of Orson Welles, whose authoritative, booming voice connects episodes and redundantly explains things that are often self-evident, frequently seems superfluous, evidence perhaps that the producers did not trust the power of their images to carry the meaning of the events.

All of these problems and limits of the film as a whole, are reflected in the film's specific portrait of Jesus. First of all, the choice of "teen heart-throb"[34] Jeffrey Hunter to play the role of Jesus was clearly a strategic error. Though tall, well-built, blond, good-looking, he was an actor with little experience and "barely enough histrionic ability to play a Hollywood marine."[35] This well-tanned "teenage Jesus"[36] would have been more appropriate playing a California-surfer than the Palestinian prophet/Incarnate God. He portrays a strangely empty, "amorphous and passive,"[37] expressionless and almost inarticulate Jesus: "Christ is there as a physical presence, but His spirit is absent."[38]

Perhaps intuiting the limits of Hunter, Ray and company, tried to create an aura of mystery around him. Imitating the "old methods of the star-system"[39] as they had been applied to H.B. Warner, the first "King of Kings" thirty-four years earlier, the studio forbade Hunter to appear in public during the elaboration of the film, an enforced mystical isolation which extended also to interviews with the press.[40] Then Ray and the studio made a great deal out of Hunter's "fan-mag baby-blue eyes."[41] The object of repeated and intense close-ups in the film, these "aquamarine-blue, otherworldly, unsemitic eyes,"[42] – gigantic when projected from the seventy-millimeter film onto the wide screen – were meant to project Jesus' power, "transmitted through the mesmerizing gaze of Jeffrey Hunter."[43] Supported by "his clothes of white or pastel," the blue eyes represent the "natural moral purity of Jesus,"[44] and in the words of Sam Bronston, the film's producer, they "convey the visionary warmth of expression that gave Christ His instant appeal to people from all stations of life."[45] An even less credible justification of the repeated closeup of Hunter's eyes, from a film critic this time, is that "the blue represents the relief from suffering and guarantee of imminent redemption."[46] If the attention paid to Hunter's blue eyes seems exaggerated, even more bizarre is the attention given to his body hair. Apparently Jesus, clearly intended by Ray and company to fit into the "secular, idealized-heroic traditions of Hollywood masculinity,"[47] could not be permitted body hair, and so Hunter sports shaved armpits and torso. This strange detail – today almost perverse – is clearly evident during the scourging and crucifixion of Jesus and makes Hunter's Jesus a strong contrast to the two very hirsute criminals crucified with him.

Parallel to the limits imposed on the Jesus-character by the actor Hunter, the director and screenwriter seem determined to emphasize Jesus' humanity in an exaggerated way. The character of Jesus appears to suffer from a basic lack of human insight, a basic lack of self-understanding as a result of which he seems to stumble forward into the various events of his mission without having made any clear decisions in freedom. The most glaring example of this strange passivity, with which, for example, neither Barabbas nor Judas seem to be afflicted, is the moment of the crucial messianic decision to leave Galilee and go to Jerusalem. Jesus has been taking a break at home in Nazareth with his mother. When the apostles return to Mary's house from their missions and announce that it is time to go to Jerusalem, Jesus puts aside the chair on which he has been working and says, "I'll finish this work when I return." He evidently has little understanding of what awaits him in the Holy City. Astonishingly though, Mary understands, as she says a little too knowingly, almost smugly, directly into the camera, "The work will never be finished." Jesus hears her remark and seems confused.

The film does everything to limit the scope and range of Jesus' messianic identity and role. His preaching is limited to the scene of the Sermon on the Mount, and this gives it a detached, out-of-touch quality, anything but the case with the Jesus of the gospels. Then what Ray's Jesus does say is strangely without any incisive or challenging quality, almost an academic exercise. When an onlooker asks him rather forcefully, "Are you the Messiah?", Jesus calmly launches into the "I am the good shepherd" discourse, as if he had not heard the question. There are none of the parables, and there is no critical or prophetic edge to anything Jesus says in the entire film. Certainly too, there is nothing of the Gospel critique of the Jewish religious institutions of the time, no chasing of the money-changers from the temple, no discussion of what is licit on the Sabbath. Nor is there any reference to the issue of personal or social sinfulness: there is no summons to moral responsibility and conversion, no encounter with the rich young man, no conversation with the Samaritan woman at the well, no sense of eschatological urgency. Ray's Jesus seems oddly unaware of the Old Testament and his own sharing in that prophetic tradition. In fact, the film is almost void of references to Jesus' Jewishness, a most crucial aspect of his being Messiah, and of which the gospels give repeated testimony. In the end, when this Jesus dies on the cross, a thoroughly sanitized, domesticated version of that atrocious death, the event seems to be oddly disconnected with his life and mission.

If *King of Kings* generally skirts the issue of Jesus' prophetic messiahship, it decisively avoids the issue of Jesus' divinity. Ray's Jesus has absolutely no growing self-awareness of an exceptional degree of intimacy with God, to the point of addressing God as "Abba" or "Daddy." His only references to the Father are the "Our Father" prayer, and a couple of desperate "Father" gasps in the Gethsemane scene. All the passages of the Gospel that might suggest this relationship are avoided: Jesus as a boy speaking with the Scribes in the temple, already about his "Father's business" or the parables that address the identity of Jesus or the discussions along those lines with the disciples and the Pharisees.

The film makes a glaringly obvious "effort to rationalize or obfuscate"[48] Jesus' miracles. Only two minor miracles and one exorcism are represented.

The former are effected in silence and by the shadow of Jesus: no human contact, no kindness, no invitation to salvation. The latter happens by chance, the demoniac stumbling into Jesus arms while voices from off-screen shout, "He's crazy, he's crazy." Clearly these miracles "are ones that could have a psychological explanation,"[49] or "natural causes."[50] Some other miracles are reported but immediately dismissed and the major miracles are avoided – for example, the raising from the dead of Lazarus and of the son of the widow of Nain, the cleansing of lepers, the feeding of the five thousand.

Regarding the Resurrection, the confirmation by God of Jesus' salvific divine mission and identity, Ray and company fudge the issue once again. First of all, Jesus' own Gospel references to the Resurrection are neither depicted nor reported. Then the event itself is represented in a most unconvincing way: first by an all-too-human meeting of Jesus with Mary Magdalene near the tomb, and then by an eerie scene by the Sea of Galilee in which Jesus himself does not appear but his voice is heard amplified by a very artificial echo effect. Then using a "somewhat stagey, formalised device,"[51] Ray has a gigantic shadow appear, clearly that of Jesus, which then stretches across the beach, to form a perfect cross with the nets of the Apostles, accompanied all the while by heavenly chants of "Hallelujah."[52] Apart from the utter tackiness of these scenes, their "cumulative effect . . . is to emphasize the humanity of Jesus, while leaving the divinity in doubt."[53]

The Jesus of *Kings of Kings* is represented as a good and noble person, a person of virtue, but at best it is exceptional human virtue. In an effort to avoid offending anyone and thus risk the boycotting of the box-office, Ray and his team watered down the Gospel and consequently the figure of Jesus the Christ. The result is a strange, disembodied representation of Jesus, "neutralized . . . as the object of faith,"[54] a "Messiah of the secularized gentiles,"[55] a "non-denominational Jesus of pluralistic America,"[56] with which, one critic suggests, it was hoped to seduce the audience:

> The picture bends all its efforts . . . to keep Christ as neutral and undynamic as possible while at the same time lulling the audience into a pleasurable state of pietistic euphoria by parading the familiar words and images of the New Testament before them in pageant style.[57]

Judging *King of Kings* as a whole, this critic concludes: "A life of Christ should be an irresistible challenge to man's conscience. Instead, this one is a tranquilizing drug . . . and bad art."[58]

George Stevens' *The Greatest Story Ever Told*

In 1965, George Stevens made *The Greatest Story Ever Told* for the United Artists studio, based not on the Bible but on the 1949 best-selling book, *The Greatest Story Ever Told* by Fulton Oursler,[59] a fictionalized and "romanticized life of Jesus, which also took into account a series of ancient legends."[60] Filmed in seventy millimeter, wide-screen Ultra-Panavision, Stevens' *magnum opus* went wildly over budget "from an estimated $10 million to an actual $25 million,"[61] three times that of the previous record holder, *Kings of Kings*. By far the most costly Jesus-film ever made, *The Greatest Story Ever Told* was both "the apogee of the Passion Play [and] one of the box-office duds of all time."[62] If Stevens' film was, like its immediate predecessor, *King of Kings*, a colossal failure, it was clearly not because Stevens made the same errors as Nicholas Ray: in many ways, the two films are quite different.

Perhaps the major difference between them is that Stevens' Jesus is clearly meant to be divine, the incarnate Word, from the very beginning of the film. His identity as Son of God is clear to him and it is clear to us. Stevens has him speak repeatedly of God as "My Father," and when he is proclaimed by Peter and others as the Messiah, the Son of God, he affirms this identity. Further, this film, in contrast to Ray's is essentially faithful to the gospels, with a tendency to favor John's version. Almost all the Jesus-material is directly from the Gospel texts. The material having specifically to do with the conspiracy against Jesus, though not always precisely evangelical, reflects the spirit of those passages in the Gospel.

Stevens studiously avoids the elaborate and distracting subplots of Ray's film: "he steers away from fictional events, providing only as many as are necessary to hold the story together."[63] The Barabbas-zealot-revolt story, with its battle scenes, is gone; the Judas-Barabbas connection, in which Jesus becomes a pawn, has disappeared; Mary, the Mother of Jesus, is no longer the omniscient spiritual counselor; the roles of the centurion and the wife of Pilate are drastically redimensioned. By avoiding the distracting subplots, Stevens also avoids the constant parallel editing and rapid cross-cutting that gives *King of Kings* that devastating soap-opera effect. Because his material is basically and clearly evangelical, Stevens has no need of the voice-over narration that annoyingly dominates Ray's film.

Further, unlike Ray, Stevens does not totally avoid the delicate issue of the complex responsibility for Jesus' crucifixion. Accountable, along with Herod and Pilate, are Caiaphas and the Sanhedrin. Yet cleverly, and not really in contradiction of the Gospel accounts, "Stevens split[s] the Sanhedrin,"[64] opposing Caiaphas and company with Nicodemus and Joseph of Arimathea who sympathize with Jesus and argue against his condemnation. He divides the crowds of onlookers during Jesus's trial: along with the shouts of "Crucify him!" are heard cries of "Release him!"

All these differences between the two films notwithstanding, the basic concept and quality of Stevens' finished film is that of the biblical colossal,[65] and it shares with *King of Kings* some of the inevitable elements of that *genre*: massive sets, overpowering music score, elaborately choreographed crowd scenes and exaggerated length, with the basic version being more than three hours long. But these spectacular elements are not in themselves responsible for the failure of the film. The fatal flaw of *The Greatest Story Ever Told* lies elsewhere, namely in the total control that Stevens had over the project. George Stevens was not only the director of the film: he was also its

producer and the co-writer of the screenplay, which, in effect, gave him unlimited authority over the entire production.[66] In this situation, where there
were no limits on decisions, no questioning of basic concepts and their imple-
mentation, a kind of hubris set in, and, as in the case of more recent flawed
megaproductions by all-powerful directors, like Francis Ford Coppola's
Apocalypse Now (1979), Michael Cimino's *Heaven's Gate* (1981) and Kevin
Costner's *Waterworld* (1995), the result was a disaster, both critically and at
the box office. One critic, perhaps somewhat uncharitably, addressed precisely this problem when he described *The Greatest Story Ever Told* as a
"dinosaur," which he then qualified by adding: "Just as the dinosaur's huge
bulk concealed the tiniest of brains . . . this film enshrines a minimum of
spiritual and intellectual content."[67] In general, Stevens as a director-producer
had "one basic flaw that hampered many of his films: an obsession with perfection."[68] This flaw was in large part responsible for the incredible cost
overruns already mentioned, and for the evident problems experienced with
the editing of the picture. When the film was first released, *The Greatest
Story Ever Told* was four hours and twenty minutes long. Shocked by the
very negative reactions of audiences, Stevens put the film through a series of
at least seven further "editions," one of which was less than half the length of
the original version.[69]

At the same time this basic flaw also manifested itself in a series of
production decisions both about the film as a whole and about the character
of Jesus that have much to do with the failure of the film. Stevens' fundamental production concept for the film is already suggested in the fact that he
maintained the title of Oursler's book. In Stevens' mind, the awesome salvific
event of Jesus the Christ, the narrative of universal human redemption
through the extraordinary intervention of the incarnate Son of God, clearly
the greatest story ever told and a story in which he, as a devout Christian,
sincerely believed, required a vast, cosmic, universal, timeless framework.
Stevens' basic position was clearly announced in the opening and closing
scenes of *The Greatest Story Ever Told*, in effect, the frame within which the
action of the film takes place. There are the fresco images of a Christ Pantocrator, in the heavens and in the apsidal arch of a great cathedral and the
words of the Prologue of the Gospel of John and the music and sung words of
the "Hallelujah Chorus" from Handel's *Messiah*. But already in these opening
images is evident one of the problems which plagues the film: the image is
not that of a Byzantine Christ, but rather of the actor Max von Sydow, a
"strange . . . uncompelling figure,"[70] in his role of Jesus, "with a hang-dog
expression emphasized by his straight, lifeless black hair and beard."[71] The
photographic familiarity of the actor's face destroys the illusion of a genuine
image of the Christ.

In a further production decision of dubious merit, Stevens decided not
to make his film in Palestine, insisting that the Holy Land had lost all of its
biblical quality.[72] He chose to set his film in Utah and Colorado, "where
mountains and canyons are epic in scale,"[73] with the snow-capped Rocky

Mountains, the vast Grand Canyon, the churning Colorado river, dramatic gulches, buttes; the whole amplified by magnificent sunrises and sunsets and by exceptionally blue skies with fluffy white clouds, all photographed in wide-screen Technicolor. The critics immediately noted the inappropriateness of Stevens' choice: one spoke rather sarcastically of "sets by Hallmark, panorama by Grand Canyon Postcards, Inc."[74] Another explained that "the setting is impressive, too impressive . . . The Lord's Prayer gets lost in the scenery."[75]

The visually powerful, dramatic natural settings create a problem in a film about Jesus because they inevitably call to mind the settings of so many classical "big-sky Westerns of the Hollywood cinema,"[76] including Stevens' previous film, *Shane*, filmed in the same Utah and Colorado settings.[77] Jesus the Christ anachronistically and counterculturally inserted into the myth of the American West simply does not work. Further, Stevens did not realize that the spectacular beauty of the natural landscapes of the film was in extreme contrast to its massive and elaborate outdoor sets, the palace of Pilate, the courtyard of the Temple, to mention two of them. It was also in contrast to the obviously artificial sets created in studio, for scenes such as the Last Supper, clearly in imitation of Leonardo da Vinci's fresco, and to the highly artificial lighting, in perfect devotional holy-card style, in the scene of the crucifixion. Stevens had hoped that the extraordinary beauty of his landscapes would be experienced as "a visual equivalent for the ideas,"[78] that they would inspire the viewers to reflect on the beauty and power of the ideas of Jesus that his film was representing. He was wrong. In the end, the spectacular natural settings amplified, "magnified and sanctified in Cinerama and Ultra Panavision 70,"[79] simply distract the viewer from the much more profound and more subtle spiritual significance of the Christ-event.

Perhaps the most glaring production error that Stevens made was his "unfortunate decision to ensure box-office success by loading the picture with 'guest stars' . . . the effect is unintentionally devastating, almost totally crippling the film's believability."[80] Well-known actors in the role of Jesus and other Gospel figures "bring with them secular subtexts from their other films,"[81] which act as filters[82] that color or distort their representation of these figures and affect the way the viewers perceive, understand and react to them. In *The Greatest Story Ever Told*, these guest appearances or cameo parts – a "galaxy of talent"[83] – coming in to work for a day, are a terrible distraction. The cast included Roddy McDowall, Ed Wynn, Angela Lansbury, Shelley Winters, Sidney Poitier, Dorothy McGuire, John Wayne, Claude Rains, José Ferrer, Sal Mineo, Carroll Baker, Charlton Heston, Telly Savalas, Pat Boone, Martin Landau, Van Heflin, Donald Pleasence and Jamie Farr. Apart from turning the serious and sacred story of Jesus "into a prolonged version of Hollywood Squares,"[84] these far-too-familiar faces provide a "jarring note . . . since Jesus and the disciples were being played by relatively unknown actors."[85]

Further, Stevens aggravated the problem of the presence of these familiar faces by directing badly – with "elephantine pomposity"[86] – their performances. John Wayne, the Roman centurion appearing out of the blue on
Calvary, and proclaiming in his best Western drawl, "Truly this was the Son
of God" (pronounced "Gaad"), carries outrageous "overtones of stagecoaches
in Monument Valley."[87] Telly Savalas as Pilate is in his pre-Kojak days, but
he makes the kind of ironic comments and sly smiles that become Inspector
Kojak's trademark. Only the cigar is missing. Not only is the casting of Sidney Poitier as Simon of Cyrene, characterized as "a liberal gesture [and] gratuitous,"[88] by one critic and as having "evident antiracist intent"[89] by another,
awkward, but Stevens' choice to deny him even one word of dialogue is incomprehensible. Shelley Winters, having touched the cloak of Jesus, screams
in a high-pitched voice, "I am cured, I am cured," but Stevens does not indicate clearly what was wrong with her.[90] Charlton Heston as "a beefcake"[91]
John the Baptist, in "only mildly unkempt hair and Tarzan gear,"[92] overpowers every scene he is in, not because of the spiritual greatness of John the
Baptist, but because he is the superstar Charlton Heston. Fresh from the colossal hits *The Ten Commandments* (1956) and *Ben-Hur* (1959), he is too big,
too strong,[93] too well-known to be contained, even by George Stevens.

Stevens' "flawed direction"[94] extended beyond the awkwardness of the
guest stars. His style, described as "obtrusively, sometimes risibly 'dramatic,'"[95] often resulted in entirely inappropriate effects. For example, the
illogical echoing of the voice of Charlton Heston (John the Baptist) honed to
perfection on the Ed Sullivan (television) Show, as Jesus goes into and returns from the desert, keep the attention on the Baptist and not on Jesus. Or
again, when Jesus is preaching in the temple courtyard, Stevens has him include as his own the words of Saint Paul in the First Letter to the Corinthians
"Faith, hope and love abide, these three, but the greatest is love" (1 Cor 13):
"the effect jars."[96] Then in a piece of highly artificial and disturbing "editing-
à-la-Griffith," as Jesus dies on Calvary, Stevens has Judas commit suicide,
not by hanging but by throwing himself into the fiery pit in the courtyard of
the Temple, the only use of this peculiar structure in the whole film. One
critic tried valiantly to justify Stevens' choice here: "The Buddhist style of
[Judas'] death suggests the depth of his alienation from Jesus' message."[97]
The more convincing explanation, however, is that Stevens simply got carried
away.

Stevens' misguided direction is clearly evident in the long scene of Jesus as he preaches by night in the courtyard of the Temple. Jesus' marching
dramatically back and forth on the "stage" of the fiery pit, speaking violently
perhaps for the first time in the film, and eerily lighted by the burning torches
of the crowd, clearly, and disastrously, conjures up thoughts of an assembly
of Nazis[98] or a Klu Klux Klan rally.[99] Another failed scene is the strange,
almost hallucinogenic episode at Bethany, the home of Martha, Mary and
Lazarus, preceding Palm Sunday. For the most part the scene is in eerie silence, strange after the constant mood music in other scenes. In a dreamlike

atmosphere, Lazarus is led away from a grated window by his sisters. Jesus, his face hidden, is sitting on a throne-like chair by himself. The disciples, sitting in the background, begin reciting *sottovoce*, verses from Psalm 118 – "Oh, give thanks unto the Lord . . . for His mercy endureth forever" – which trance-inducing chant continues through the whole scene. Slowly, mysteriously, a woman, whom we presume is Mary Magdalene, comes forward and silently begins anointing Jesus' feet. The scene comes alive for a moment when Judas interrupts the anointing, fairly shouting his usual objection at the cost of the ointment. Jesus answers with the typical calmness of the King James Version of the Bible and the scene reverts to its previous lethargic key. The two sisters slowly come forward with white sheets and wrap them around Jesus' shoulders, as if they are a burial shroud: a very bizarre sequence.

The Last Supper is perhaps the best example of Stevens' misguided direction. Clearly imitating Leonardo da Vinci's fresco, the director fills the episode with perfectly balanced compositions, with Jesus in the center, apex of the pyramid formed by the disciples around him. The few movements, looks and gestures of the apostles are perfectly choreographed, perfectly symmetrical, perfectly timed. The very few movements of the camera are slow, deliberate, smooth to the point of tedium, causing one critic to speak of "the lugubrious solemnity"[100] of the approach. Likewise, the words of Jesus are slow, deliberate, ponderous in tone and rhythm, with long pauses between phrases, presumably to suggest spiritual density.[101] His looks are intense, sad, solemn; his gestures are deliberate, studied, contemplative, exaggeratedly so. Finally, when Stevens has Jesus extend his right hand over the bread and the chalice of wine, in the liturgical gesture of epiclesis, he seems anachronistically to be presiding at a Catholic Eucharistic service instead of a Hebrew Passover meal.

A further aspect of Stevens' faulty direction of *The Greatest Story Ever Told* is the overly-studied pictorial quality of many of his compositions, which amounts to "an exercise in *mise-en-scène* – and bluff."[102] Evidently he expected that this pictorial quality, often reproducing holy-cards in *style sulpicien*, such as the shots of Jesus during the Last Supper, or of the tender (and very static) Nativity scene, would inspire devotional thoughts and feelings in the spectators. He was very wrong. One critic summarizes the effect:

> Stevens' groupings are often wholly artificial: people standing on hillsides in painterly attitudes, listening to sermons or watching miracles, in a manner which proclaims (surely unintentionally), "This film has nothing whatsoever to do with everyday life as you, the audience, know and understand it."[103]

The highly pictorial *mise-en-scène* of the Sermon on the Mount episode is a good example of this static artificiality. Jesus is standing on the pinnacle of a cliff at the edge of the Grand Canyon, the apostles are seated on the ground, arranged equidistantly from each other in a precise semicircle around him. All are dressed in white. Beyond the apostles, Stevens arranges a wider circle of hundreds of listeners, all seated, silent and motionless, evidently rapt into ecstasy by the words of Jesus. More than half the frame of the composition is taken up by the extreme long and wide shot of the Grand Canyon in the background.

To add to these problems, the basic script of *The Greatest Story Ever Told* has some serious limitations. For example, Stevens has Jesus speak almost exclusively in phrases from the King James version of the gospels, including all the Thees and Thous, or at least the tone of the Scriptures. This places Jesus in a category apart from all the other characters, from the apostles down, who use colloquial vocabulary and speak in everyday tones and cadences. The contrast is particularly obvious, for example, when the "King James" Jesus (vonSydow) is speaking with the "New York cop" Pilate (Savalas). The inconsistency is very distracting. Further, for all the care he ostensibly took to maintain a high level of originality, Stevens' script contains "some of the most superbly banal lines in a fiercely contested field."[104] For example, when the overweight Victor Bono, playing the totally fictional Sorak, announces to Caiaphas the arrival of Judas, who is about to betray Jesus, he says, "We have a visitor," in a melodramatic, almost vampirish, tone that inadvertently reveals his background as a "heavy" in too many Hollywood "B" movies. Even Jesus has some insipid lines. When during his trial, he speaks to Pilate about "the God who loves you no less than he loves others," the Governor asks somewhat ironically, "Why have I not known him?," Jesus in all sincerity responds, "You have not looked for him." When the rich young man refusing to follow Jesus says to him, "Is wealth a crime?," Jesus answers, "No, but it can be a burden." The response is not only unevangelical but clearly it manifests disastrous extreme caution on Stevens' part: Jesus' weak response "takes the sting out of the eye-of-a-needle remark and clears Stevens' Jesus from any accusation of un-American tendencies that might be made by staunch Christian opponents of moral decay."[105] One critic, speaking of the banality of many of Jesus' lines, touches on a crucial issue: "We see Jesus utter a few pieces of good advice, but nothing that would explain why the Gospel set the world on fire."[106] It would appear that Stevens, in many of his production decisions, is motivated above all by "the desire to offend nobody – Jesus has no brothers and sisters (because that would offend the Catholics), the miracles are kept to a minimum (so as not to put a strain on the agnostics), the crowd is very half-hearted about crucifying Jesus (because that might look like anti-Semitism)."[107]

Clearly, all the above-discussed weaknesses in Stevens' film have a negative effect, at least indirectly, on the image of Jesus portrayed in the film. A Jesus, small against the awesome background of the Grand Canyon, is lost; a Jesus teaching the "Our Father" with the churning Colorado river behind him diminishes in power as a teacher; a Jesus facing the muscular superstar Charlton Heston as John the Baptist is displaced. But even more devastating to the image of the Savior in *The Greatest Story Ever Told* are two choices made by producer-director Stevens in direct regard to his Jesus: his basic concept of Jesus as "the Christ of faith rather than the Jesus of history,"[108] and his choice of "the rather dour"[109] Max von Sydow to play Jesus, and his subsequent weak direction of the Swedish actor.

There is no doubt that "of all the Jesus films of the sound era, *Greatest Story* was least interested in 'humanizing' the character of Christ."[110] Stevens downplays Jesus' concrete historicity. Little attention is given, for example, to Jesus' Jewishness. He visits the Capernaum synagogue but does not read the scriptures, as a up-and-coming young Jewish preacher would do. The Last Supper is clearly not a Jewish ritual meal. The episodes of the circumcision, of Jesus boyhood conversation with the scribes in the Temple of Jerusalem, of the wedding feast at Cana, of Jesus' controversies with the Jewish religious authorities concerning the Sabbath, are all missing from the film. "Even his family is played as a symbol."[111] The effect of these shifts and omissions is to reduce the concrete humanity and historicity of Jesus of Nazareth and "to represent a universal Christ."[112]

Repeatedly Stevens proclaims that Jesus is "the Divine One,"[113] from the words of the Prologue of the Gospel of John in the opening, to the "Hallelujah Chorus" at the raising of Lazarus and in the conclusion of the film, a rather clichéd proclamation of divinity: a music critics comments that "using Handel to ring down the curtain for the intermission was banal, but using it *again* — as the finale accompanying the Resurrection and Ascension – is inexcusable."[114] Stevens wants to suggest Jesus' divinity in the authority he wields over the disciples when he calls them, a vocation narrative described by James Wall as "taking one look at total strangers and immediately having them drop everything and follow him down the road."[115] The director's preference for the Christ of faith is also evident in the images of Christ as Pantocrator which act as a frame for the entire film, a choice which obliges Stevens to begin and end the film in a church, making it "resemble at times a church service."[116] What Stevens does not seem to understand is that in a medium as concrete, material and specific as cinema, universalizing Jesus in order to make him the Christ of faith reduces his humanity. In not "dealing with the historical moment"[117] and the cultural reality of Jesus, Stevens loses his human, incarnational dimension, his human nature, so absolutely essential to the Word of God who became flesh in a precise time and place and within a concrete religious culture. The Christ of faith thus becomes a Jesus of myth.

The second level of this serious problem of Jesus and the Christ of faith is Stevens' infelicitous choice of an "icy"[118] Max von Sydow, in 1965 a relatively unknown actor, to play Jesus. "In von Sydow's portrayal, he [Jesus] is so emotionally removed,"[119] far too "uncharismatic,"[120] "enigmatic and intellectual,"[121] "too distant, too foreign."[122] This emotional distance is obviously wanted by Stevens, but it has a negative effect in many episodes of the film. For example, totally absent in von Sydow's Jesus are the crucial human experiences of "humor and joy."[123] As well, between Jesus and the woman healed, there is no personal contact. The Jesus on the cross, filmed predominantly in emotion-cooling, extra long shots, as he continues to speak in the flawless English of the King James Version, seems hardly to suffer at all.

Further, one wonders why this Jesus is plotted against by the authorities and finally condemned and crucified. Clearly von Sydow's Jesus "is not perceived as a real threat to anyone,"[124] especially when compared to the strong, very physical and gutsy John the Baptist of Charlton Heston. One critic, somewhat exasperated, exclaims: "Surely, Christ was not the cold, humorless fish von Sydow makes Him . . . in his godly, solid, almost stolid portrayal."[125]

There is an excessive slowness and formality in von Sydow's movements, especially his annoying tendency to raise solemnly his clear blue eyes to heaven at the slightest provocation, a problem compounded by some very odd gestures. At climactic moments such as the raising of Lazarus and the teaching of the "Our Father," "he strikes poses reminiscent of an Egyptian dancer."[126] There are serious problems in the way von Sydow delivers his lines: his overly deliberate pronunciation of words; the distracting traces of his European accent, oddly out of place in a film in which everyone else speaks standard American English, and the "mystical" pregnant pauses in practically every sentence.[127] These traditional theatrical techniques may be appropriate on a passion play stage, where the audience is distant from the actor, but Stevens should have known better than to allow them in his von Sydow Jesus, perfectly visible, often in close-up, on the giant screen.

All the problems manifested in four hours of the film come to a head in the final sequence, that of the Resurrection, clearly a crucial episode in any Jesus-film for it must represent the awesome mystery of the victory of God-in-Jesus over death and sin. The scene calls for creativity, great delicacy and subtlety, virtues which at least in this film Stevens does not evince. In his climactic scene, Stevens seems to want to use, one last time, all his favorite tricks. A series of self-conscious dissolves move us and von Sydow from the apse of the church, in which the film began, to the sky and the clouds, shifting the still image of von Sydow-Jesus-Pantocrator from small to large size, from local to universal impact, from a mere fresco to the great transcendent reaches. A rather ordinary "special" effect created by the totally unmotivated use of an orange filter make the sky more dramatic and definitely more kitschy. All the while, at full tilt, the strains of Handel's "Hallelujah Chorus" artificially support the whole, while von Sydow's strangely disembodied voice, amplified by a cosmic sound system, promises to be with the apostles until the end of time. In the end, the silly technical effects, the vague, abstract quality of the scene and Stevens' style which at this point "disintegrates into utter vulgarity,"[128] deny the reality of the Resurrection, for they suggest that "what the disciples saw was an inspirational vision rather than the real man."[129]

3

The Jesus Musicals:
Jesus Christ Superstar
and *Godspell*

If today the film colossals of the 1960s seem rather odd, a rather outdated and ultimately counterproductive way of representing the story and the image of Jesus the Christ, the Jesus-musicals of the 1970s appear only slightly less odd, and certainly their way of representing Jesus Christ raises no fewer problems than the colossals. The two major examples of this "Jesus-musical" film *genre* were first theatrical musical dramas, produced and popular in the 1960s. In 1973, both were made into films: *Jesus Christ Superstar*, billed as a rock opera, and *Godspell*, billed as a folk-rock musical.[1]

The dramatic musical is a very particular *genre,* on the theater stage and especially in its adaptation to the film medium. Very different from the serious stage drama, the crucial elements of a stage musical are its songs, and the music and the dance numbers that accompany them. The development of the narrative is secondary: the story told is mainly a vehicle for the songs. The actions done, the words spoken are in function of the songs and music. Strong character development and precise motivation of characters becomes very secondary. The most tenuous motivation for singing a song is sufficient. In the musical drama, narrative space must be created for major production numbers, in which principal elements of the cast and chorus can sing and dance for several minutes. Regarding stage design in the musical, realism is not the crucial element. The setting must above all support the spirit of the music and song and the tone of a given scene or major number. In the musical drama, the spectator's suspension of disbelief is quite different from that required for a drama, say by Shakespeare or Arthur Miller. In a good musical, the spectator readily, enthusiastically accepts the unrealistic breaking into song and dance, the presence of chorus and dancers, the corresponding shifts in tone and register and then, after the production number, the return to relative normalcy until the next production number.

As a result of all of this, the identification and vicarious participation of the spectator in the experience of the protagonist – struggle, tension, tragedy, triumph, joy – is different, certainly more limited than in the case of the straight drama. The protagonist is perceived first and foremost as a singer-dancer, and only secondarily as a real person with a serious human experience. Concretely, this can be noted for example at the end of a performance when the spectators comment on a musical. They speak especially of the great music, the beautiful singing, the exhilarating dancing, the marvelous special

33

effects while they are less likely to talk about the human struggle of the protagonist or about the moral implications of the decisions made by various
characters.

When therefore, a musical drama is adapted to the *genre* of the cinema,
the reality becomes even more complex. Some of the rules and effects of
stage musicals pertain, but there are some important differences. In the film
version, through skilled camera work, the viewer comes into more intimate
contact with the characters. The point of view is no longer that of someone
sitting in the orchestra of a theater. The settings of the action can be real or
realistic, rather like what happens to Shakespeare's *Hamlet* when it is filmed
on location in a medieval castle. Of course, as in any film, the passage from
one time to another, from one place to another, is instantaneous. If in the film
musical, there seems to a greater intimacy, a higher level of realism than in
the stage musical, and therefore, theoretically, a greater possibility for involvement in the experiences of the protagonist, then this illusion of intimacy
is contradicted by the flimsy plot and superficial character development in the
film musical. The illusion of reality is particularly contradicted by the illogic
of the protagonist, seen in closeup, who repeatedly breaks into song. This is
especially so when the protagonist-singer is supported by a dense music accompaniment, whose source is not seen on-screen – a strange confusion of
intradiegetical and extradiegetical elements – and then joined by a chorus of
singers and dancers who conveniently appear out of nowhere and together
with the protagonist, create a major production number.

If the film musical is first and foremost a light entertainment piece like
The Wizard of Oz (1939) or *My Fair Lady* (1964) or *Hello Dolly* (1969)
whose subject remains on the level of fable or light fiction, the viewers understand. They accommodate themselves and shift their parameters to be able
to enjoy the entertainment without asking much more of the film. When,
however, the subject of the film musical is serious or tragic or involves a
profound and complex human experience or a well-known historical figure,
the problem is more complicated. Then the stakes are raised even higher
when the story told in the musical film is that of Jesus the Christ. Here the
subject is not only a historical person, but a human being believed by Christians to be the incarnate God, a human-divine being who is the object of a
profound existential faith committment on the part of many people, and
whose memory is preserved in a sacred, divinely-inspired book, the Bible.
Clearly in this case, the accommodation of the viewers to the musical dramatic medium is more difficult to effect. Their suspension of disbelief in
front of a singing, dancing Jesus, surrounded by singing, dancing disciples, is
less willing. Even if the suspension of disbelief be effected, a whole series of
questions must be considered regarding the reception of a Jesus hero of a
musical. What happens to the Christ of faith when he is represented singing
contemporary lyrics, surrounded by singers and dancers, and amplified by
Dolby stereo sound and spectacular filmic effects? What is the connection
between the Jesus met in the Bible or the Jesus Christ encountered in the

personal experience of prayer, and the Jesus Christ, singing superstar? What happens to the Good News, the message of salvation in the life, death and Resurrection of Jesus Christ, when it is mediated through the musical film?

Jesus Christ Superstar

Based on the hit Broadway musical of the same name by Andrew Lloyd Webber and Tim Rice, *Jesus Christ Superstar* was produced by Universal Pictures and directed by Norman Jewison. Filmed on location in the Negev Desert of Israel and slightly over an hour and a half in length, *Superstar* was the "largest grossing film about Jesus made in the sound era."[2] To suggest the mixed-media quality of the *Jesus Christ Superstar* phenomenon, "it all began with a single rock song, entitled 'Jesus Christ Superstar' . . . which immediately had an extraordinary success,"[3] and which led to an "album of twenty-eight musical scenes in two LPs."[4] Though the film's earnings of over $20,000,000[5] indicate its popularity, the record album of the musical was far more successful, earning almost twice that much.[6]

The plot of *Jesus Christ Superstar* hearkens back to the very early passion films. Insofar as the very loose dramatic narrative of the film can be considered a plot, it represents only the events of Jesus' passion, beginning with his anointing by Mary Magdalene and ending with his crucifixion. Though the film strangely includes one scene that belongs before the passion (Jesus called upon to heal the sick and crippled), the film omits the parables, the miracles, the teaching of Jesus, even his discourse around the Last Supper, which could ostensibly have been included. Even the events of the passion are telescoped and the personalities involved, except for a few, are only vaguely, lightly and superficially characterized: "the history of Jesus is reduced to the presence of a few figures who function less as individuals and more as personifications representing fundamental attitudes [towards Jesus]."[7] The narrative of the film stresses certain elements of the passion story, or adds and stresses elements that could be considered part of the passion in order to augment the dimension of conflictuality of the whole piece. Given much space in the film are the intense and high-key conflict between Jesus and Judas, the more low-key tension between Jesus and Mary Magdalene, the ongoing conflict between the High Priests and Jesus and the conflict between Jesus and both civil authorities, Pilate and Herod.

The structure of *Jesus Christ Superstar* reflects that of the early passion play films, as it creates a fictional frame around the main narrative of the film through "the device of introducing a group of young actors and actresses who are giving a definitive performance of *Jesus Christ Superstar*."[8] In the opening of the film, the small theatrical troupe, which at moments in the film, with great poetic license, becomes a huge cast, arrives by bus at a Roman ruin in the desert and at the end of the film, they get back on the bus and drive away. Clearly this device signals that the film is "an explicitly twentieth century re-enactment of the Gospels – a play within a play, so to speak,"[9] and thus justifies to some extent "the liberties taken with the Gospel text, and the modern tone"[10] of both the passion play and the film.

The timeframe of the play-within-the-film is extremely fluid, shifting continuously from present to past and back to present. The contemporary quality of the rock music and the lyrics of the songs create this fluidity, which is then supported by concrete material elements in the play. For example, the Roman soldiers wear khaki military pants, lavender tank tops and construction helmets; a vacationing King Herod dons Bermuda shorts and amber sun glasses; in an effective visual pun, the High Priests climb "high" on twentieth-century metal scaffolding; the merchants in the temple courtyard-bazaar sell postcards, drugs, military weapons, contemporary foreign currency and prostitutes, and to suggest the remorse felt by Judas, the film has him pursued across the desert by three huge tanks. This temporal fluidity is at times a distraction, thus reducing the impact of the story of the passion which is after all a narrative with a precise historical and cultural setting. One critic sees it as "an transparent projection of contemporary questions and problems."[11] Another, more outspoken, says that "seeking the effect of timelessness, the director mixes ancient amphitheaters, modern tanks, biblical costuming, a tourist bazaar and a traditional crucifixion in a melange that isn't so much timeless as mindless."[12]

In a certain sense, the fluidity of the time frame of *Jesus Christ Superstar*, as a film about Jesus the Christ, is the least of its problems. The film has many other limitations in this regard, elements that get in the way of its creating an effective image of Jesus Christ, faithful to the Gospel and to the Christian faith. First and foremost among these is the almost total lack of correspondence between the film and the Gospel: "the film can hardly be called biblical in any strict sense."[13] The director Jewison rather casually characterizes his film as "a pastiche, that's all it is! Try to make it more important than it is and you get into trouble."[14] Clearly a choice made by the authors of the original rock opera,[15] and then by the director of the film, neither in its portrayal of the events of Jesus' passion, nor in the characterization of its personalities, nor in the words they sing – "paraphrase replaces the language of the Gospel writers"[16] – nor even in the spirit of what is said and done, is there anything authentically of the Gospel in *Jesus Christ Superstar*. In this sense, "the film is all fiction."[17]

This basic non-correspondence with the gospels is most evident in the film's portrayal of Jesus, which will be discussed below. But it is also evident and problematical in many other dimensions of the film. Webber, Rice and Jewison, in reinterpreting and retelling the Gospel story without the authenticating spirit of the actual gospels, end up creating some strange and confusing effects, among them a disquieting lack of consistency and coherence, in style and content experienced repeatedly throughout the film. Do they perhaps want to create the first postmodern gospel? The film careens from Judas on a desert mountaintop to Roman soldiers in lavender tank-tops, from references to the Nazi Holocaust (Caiaphas speaking of a "permanent solution" to the problem of Jesus) to images of the Arab-Israeli Yom Kippur War (Judas pursued by tanks); from a temple courtyard-bazaar of "secular vices . . . human weaknesses"[18] to the Last Supper as a picnic under the olive trees in Gethsemane reinforced with an unmistakeable visual reference to Leonardo da Vinci's fresco; from an agony in the garden scene, supplemented by a hallucinogenic rapid montage of details of Old Masters of the crucifixion (twenty three shots in twenty-four seconds) – the Flemish School reduced to the "purest kitsch"[19] – to King Herod "catching some rays" on his barge and insisting with spoiled-child petulance that Jesus, already in chains, "turn my water into wine" and "walk across my swimming pool."[20]

There are also problems inherent in a passion account which takes the form of a "total" musical. In *Jesus Christ Superstar* not one word is spoken and every word of the dialogue is sung. The text of the film prescinds completely "from the theater musical and bases itself on the original album . . . Jewison suppresses the dialogue and relies only on the music and the images."[21] The strong, often violent, overpowering quality of the rock music is distracting, and in fact reaches bizarre extremes, for instance, in the singing-screaming match between Judas and Jesus in Gethsemane. The contemporary lyrics, the diametric opposite of the King James Version English of Jesus in *The Greatest Story Ever Told,* reduce the psychological distance between the characters and the audience: "no small part of the audience's ability to identify with *Superstar* is to be found in the colloquial familiarity of the rock lyrics, which create closeness rather than distance."[22] Yet a Jesus who screams at his disciples, "there is not a man among you who cares if I come and go," or who says of Mary Magdalene, "She's always tried to give me what I need right here and now," is perhaps just a little too familiar.

Further, the casting of *Jesus Christ Superstar* created some problems. Jewison cast Ted Neeley, a white, as Jesus, Yvonne Elliman, a native Hawaiian, as Mary Magdalene, and two black men as Judas (Carl Anderson) and Simon the Zealot (Larry T. Marshall). Given the already-discussed dramatic frame, and the contemporary quality of the passion play-within-the-film, this multiracial cast might even be acceptable. But the casting of a black to play Judas brought accusations of racism, accusations that in fact do not stand up to the evidence of the film. Different from the weak and evil figure of the gospels, Jewison makes Judas a forceful and dynamic man, clearly stronger and more attractive than Jesus. One critic comments that "Judas is a better part, and Anderson steals the movie with his athletic dynamism, snarling rage and quick, intelligent movements.[23] From the opening moments of the film, Judas is genuinely concerned and caring for Jesus and Judas' (Anderson) rendition of "I don't know how to love him, I don't know why he moves me" after his betrayal of Jesus is one of the most profoundly touching moments of the film.

If *Jesus Christ Superstar* can be defended against the charges of racism, it is much more difficult to dismiss the repeated charges of anti-Semitism leveled at the film. Clearly, the film places the blame for the death of Jesus on the Jews. Shifting the account of the Gospel, neither Webber and Rice nor Jewison attempt to attenuate the responsibility of the Sanhedrin for the death of Jesus. They make Pilate a weak and fearful man and Herod a spoiled child and a comic figure. Their responsibility for Jesus' death is diminished by these characterizations. On the other hand, the Sanhedrin, first appearing in black cloaks on the scaffolding above the ruin, "like giant vultures roosting on the branches of a tree,"[24] are portrayed as strong, determined, politically astute and sadistically evil.

It is obvious that many of the above-discussed difficulties with the film interfere indirectly with its portrayal of Jesus, but undoubtedly the most serious deficiency in *Jesus Christ Superstar* is its direct representation of Jesus. The problems of this Jesus begin with a straightforward extradiegetical element, that is the choice of the actor Ted Neeley for the role. Neeley is of slight build, with straggly, stringy blonde hair and blonde mustache and beard. Neither his presence nor his movements and gestures nor his high-pitched voice are capable of embodying a character of moral strength: "Neeley is curiously weak as Jesus . . . he looks faintly ridiculous bursting spontaneously into falsetto song."[25] Neeley's weakness is then amplified in comparison with the forceful presence of his two supporting actors, Carl Anderson as Judas and Yvonne Elliman as Mary Magdalene. Both in body and in face, they are stronger personalities, and their rich, powerful singing voices, especially that of Anderson, clearly dominate that of Neeley. The critic Tony Rayns speaks rightly of "Carl Anderson's powerhouse Judas against Ted Neeley's ten stone weakling Jesus."[26] As well, moving with these two actors to the intradiegetical level, clearly the characters they play are intended to be stronger than that of Jesus. With Mary Magdalene, Jesus remains passive, while she struggles with crucial issues in her relationship with him. Judas dominates Jesus because, on the one hand, in a radically new perspective for the Jesus-film, Jesus is seen from Judas' point of view,[27] and on the other hand, Judas is painted as a more robust, more vigorous, more coherent and more attractive personality than Jesus.

If the Jesus of *Jesus Christ Superstar* comes out second best when compared to the figures of Judas and Mary Magdalene, then when he is compared to the Jesus of the Gospel, he is completely outclassed. *Jesus Christ Superstar* takes "great liberties with its protagonist."[28] As a result, most of the actions, words and attitudes of the Jesus of the film are thoroughly unbiblical, both in fact and in spirit. In the gospels, Jesus is a powerful miracle worker, who out of love and mercy heals and liberates people from infirmities, physical, mental and moral, thus announcing the dynamic presence of the Kingdom of God. In one of the most bizarre episodes of *Jesus Christ Superstar*, an episode chronologically out of place in a passion play, Jesus is given the opportunity to act as a healer. The scene recalls the cult-horror film, *The Night of the Living Dead* (1968). Alone and depressed, Jesus walks into a ravine where without warning dozens of nightmarish creatures dressed in black rags seems to emerge from the cracks and crevices, and crawl, "Blob"-like, toward him, demanding to be made whole. At first confused, Jesus then tries to get away, screaming:

> There's too many of you
> Don't push me
> There's too little of me
> Don't crowd me
> Leave me alone.

Clearly this Jesus has neither the ability nor the desire to combat evil, to do any healing, and Jewison ends the scene ends with a shot from above, showing Jesus totally overwhelmed, swallowed up by these people.

The Jesus of the Gospel, a Jew, drives the money-changers out of the temple as a religious act, dramatically demanding a renewal of faith and religion. A prophetic, messianic act, it gets him in trouble with the Jewish religious authorities. In *Jesus Christ Superstar*, the raging of Jesus through the bazaar (though he screams "My temple," its connection with the Temple of the Gospel is quite unclear) is more an act of justified anger at a variety of secular vices. The gesture makes "Jesus a more humanistic leader than the religious leader of the Gospels."[29] In the Gospel, in that final period of his ministry, Jesus has an understanding of his growing conflict with the Jewish authorities and of the inevitability of a tragic conclusion; yet he moves forward with courage and conviction. In *Jesus Christ Superstar*, Jesus seems to be quite oblivious of the conflict until he is arrested, and even so, he seems to have lost all conviction as he moans, "I'm not as sure as when we started. / Then I was inspired. Now I'm sad and tired."

The Jesus of the gospels multiplies his teaching in that final period of his mission. The eschatological discourse in the Gospel of John is six chapters long and clearly asserts Jesus' care for his disciples and for the future of his teaching through them. It unequivocally and repeatedly asserts Jesus' awareness of the presence of the Father, his sense of profound intimacy and identification with the Father, his faith-filled submission to the Father's loving divine will, his understanding of the redemptive, salvific significance for humankind of his impending death. In *Jesus Christ Superstar*, there is no teaching, except perhaps for one pseudo-beatitude, rather out of place in the Palm Sunday procession: "You are blessed. There is not one of you who cannot win the kingdom!" Rather than expressing care for his disciples and their future and the future of the community, he selfishly, neurotically and ignobly complains:

> I must be mad thinking I'll be remembered.
> Yes I must be out of my head.
> Look at your blank faces.
> My name will mean nothing . . . ten minutes after I'm dead.

Further, *Superstar*'s Jesus makes no specific references to the Father,[30] not even in Gethsemane when he prays to God as "God," not as "Father," and there is certainly no sense in this Jesus of a relationship of intimacy and identity with God, and no sense at all of the soteriological significance of his impending death. If anything, his God is a sadistic killer who offers no explanations, and Jesus is an nervous masochist, complaining, "Can't you show me now I would not be killed in vain /. . ./ Show me there's a reason for your wanting me to die /. . ./ Kill me, take me now, before I change my mind."

In the gospels, the Last Supper is a Jewish ritual meal, the feast of the Passover, presided by Jesus at the height of his human and spiritual power and freedom, and who, out of love for his disciples and those who would follow them, creates in this meal a new memorial, the Eucharist, to ensure his ongoing presence in their midst as a sign of hope. In *Jesus Christ Superstar*, the Last Supper is a picnic, the institution of the Eucharist is rather improvised and tenuous: "For all you care, this wine could be my blood /. . ./ For all you care, this bread could be my body."[31] Jesus is sad and bitter, disillusioned by his disciples, telling them to "stick to fishing from now on," and he concludes the "ritual picnic" in a violent shouting match with Judas, screaming in a high pitched voice: "You liar! You Judas!"

If there is no clear correspondence between the Jesus of *Jesus Christ Superstar* and the authentic Jesus of the Gospel, it should come as no surprise that there is no correspondence between Jewison's Jesus and the Jesus of the Christian faith and of authentic Christian theology. To put it bluntly, *Jesus Christ Superstar* is "a theological disaster."[32] This Jesus has no real prophetic or messianic identity or role. There is no sense of his Jewishness and so no sense of his continuity and discontinuity with the prophets of the Old Testament. There is no question of the establishment of the Kingdom of God, neither future nor present and active here and now.[33] There is certainly not the slightest indication of Jesus' being divine, the Christ,[34] the incarnate Son of God, and neither Jesus' death on the cross, nor the Last Supper have any redemptive or soteriological significance, either for him or for humankind.

In a total inversion of the tradition biblical epic, and clearly anticipating Martin Scorsese's anti-heroic Jesus of *The Last Temptation of Christ*,[35] *Jesus Christ Superstar* gives us a Jesus who is "not a heroic figure who struggles with the Devil . . . not the great speaker who casts a spell on people . . . nor the great healer and miracle worker."[36] Not only is Jesus' human nature underscored, completely downplaying his divine nature, but in his mere humanity he reveals himself to be weak, confused, uncertain of himself and of his friends and selfishly, neurotically preoccupied with whether he will be remembered.[37] Involved in two relationships which are, to say the least, ambiguous,[38] suggested by the languid soulful looks and lingering touches with both Magdalene and Judas,[39] this Jesus is a man troubled, even dominated by anxiety and doubts, and who it seems clear never overcomes any of these limits. Given this representation of Jesus, the title of the film takes on clear ironic significance: this Jesus is neither the Christ, nor is he anything but the most venal and hollow Superstar.

Two scenes at the end of the film which seem to want to counter the image of Jesus as anti-hero, in effect do little to ennoble him or to change his status. First there is the spectacular "Jesus Christ Superstar" scene immediately preceding the crucifixion.[40] Jesus, in a fresh white robe and his hair and beard neatly-combed, faces Judas in an arena. Judas, apparently "resurrected"[41] from his suicide, descends "miraculously" from above. Dressed in a "high camp, Las Vegas style, white Sly Stone jumpsuit,"[42] decorated with tassels and sequins, surrounded by showgirls, and supported by a spectacular light show of crosses in white and gold on the background, Judas sings to Jesus as if in the present day:

> If you'd come today, could've reached a whole nation
> Israel in 4 BC had no mass communication.
> Was dying like that a mistake?
> Or did you know . . . that you would be a record breaker?

The scene, preceded by a shot of the scourged and bloodied Jesus who inclines his head to one side and closes his eyes, is meant to suggest – again anticipating Scorsese – "the last temptation of Jesus Christ Superstar." It is "a vision of Jesus, who puts the meaning of death on the cross into question."[43] That this scene represents a temptation is also suggested by the fact that it "is not the final word, but is superseded by the parallel edited-in-scene of the way of the cross"[44] and by the crucifixion which follows. The problem, however, is that if this is a temptation, then Jewison does not show Jesus resisting and overcoming it. At least Scorsese does that. Jewison shows him carrying the cross, crucified and dying. A strange sense of inevitability seems to inform the scene and there is certainly no evidence of a divine choice, no evidence of even a human choice.

Without a doubt the most crucial aspect on any film about Jesus is its representation of the Resurrection, because this final "act" is at the heart of the identity of Jesus as the Son of God. It is the divine vindication of his christological claims. In *Jesus Christ Superstar*, "the Resurrection is at best ambiguous."[45] The passion play-within-the-film ends with the death of Jesus on the cross at which point, Jewison shows the actors of the play boarding the bus on which they arrived at the beginning of the film, and driving away. Judas (Anderson) lingers in the doorway of the bus as if looking or waiting for someone. Jesus (Neeley) is not shown boarding the bus. The final shot of the film, a slow zoom away from an empty cross on the hillside, with a splendid setting sun behind it, barely allows barely a glimpse of a shepherd leading a flock of sheep under the hillside, clearly a reference to the epic *Ben Hur*.[46] Jewison has already twice shown a shepherd leading his sheep in the film, so the conclusion that this shepherd is the resurrected Jesus is quite unwarranted. Clearly, this rather strange representation keeps the crucial issue of the Resurrection open and unresolved and both the film and its protagonist remain ambiguous till the very end.

Godspell

The second of the Jesus-musicals released in 1973 was *Godspell*, produced by Columbia Pictures and directed by David Greene. Lasting about one hundred minutes, the film, which has as subtitle, "A Musical Based on the Gospel According to St. Matthew," is based on the stage play by the same name, originally written as a non-musical as "part of a master's thesis by John-Michael Tebelak."[47] First performed as a workshop production by a group of actor-graduates of Carnegie Mellon University, at the "off-off-Broadway's La Mama,"[48] it was produced and directed by John-Michael Tebelak. "Only later did it become a musical with the addition of songs by Stephen Schwartz,"[49] and as a musical, it opened off Broadway, "on May 17, 1971, at the Cherry Lane Theater,"[50] after which it went on the road playing in a number of cities, nationally and internationally.

The title already suggests the theme of the film: *Godspell,* "Gospel," an Old-English word which means "good news." The film is not a reconstruction of the life of Jesus of Nazareth according to historical principles, but rather an "actualizing,"[51] in a contemporary setting, in contemporary language and cultural modes, and in contemporary spirit, of the Christ-event. "God-spell," the "spelling" of God, a new spelling or telling of the "good news," is "a kind of miracle play,"[52] a modern parable, a "re-enactment, this time in New York locations,"[53] of the total salvific event that is the life, teaching, death and Resurrection of Jesus the Christ.

Greene's film, though a musical, and though often compared to *Jesus Christ Superstar* (most of the time negatively) is in fact radically different from that film, in style, in content, in impact and in the image it proposes of Jesus Christ. If the stylistic convention or key of *Jesus Christ Superstar* is the rock opera which relates it in some sense to the biblical spectaculars, the principal stylistic key of *Godspell* is that of the "musical comedy."[54] Mixing "vaudeville and theater with circus and pantomime,"[55] it also reflects the conventions of the carnival, burlesque and old movies and the atmosphere of clowns and clowning.[56] Clearly *Godspell*'s medium is not the high-key, often violent, all dominating rock music and song of *Superstar.* It features low-key folk music and some ragtime, in effective counterpoint with the spoken word which, reflecting the origins of the play, has precedence. The film has no major, attention-getting production numbers, in fact, the director Greene says that "There isn't much in *Godspell* . . . which calls attention to itself."[57] The singing and dancing proceed organically, naturally from the dialogue and actions of the narrative, as do the multimedial references to film, mime, puppetry and slapstick comedy. Greene's idea was to focus attention on the performers rather than on his own virtuosity as a director, "to make it seem as if the kids were doing it all."[58] Not one of the actors is a well-known or a star. Greene insists: "I felt very strongly that if one got star performers they would tend to change the concept into a starring vehicle,"[59] and one of his assistants adds, "*Godspell* is a very naive concept in the first place, and we all felt it should be presented simply, without tricks."[60]

Regarding costumes, in *Godspell*, the forced, high camp, at times surrealistic models of *Jesus Christ Superstar*, are replaced by simple, playful, do-it-yourself costumes, reflecting in a low-key, impressionistic manner, the personality and role of the person wearing them.[61] In its settings, *Godspell* does not imitate the suggestive, exotic, at times surrealistic settings of *Superstar*, nor does it seek the actual locations of any of the Jesus-stories. Again Greene explains his intentions for this modest production: "My instructions to my designer . . . were to make it look as if the picture hadn't been designed."[62] The film begins in New York City, big, boisterous, tough, impersonal, alienating, ordinary: New York here representing any great metropolis, or urban civilization, or humankind, in need of salvation. It ends with the same noisy, chaotic metropolis, but now about to be "invaded" or blessed by the saving grace of the Christ-event just renewed. Within this frame, the setting of the main narrative of the film remains New York, Central Park, fountains, city streets, the harbor, houses and skyscrapers, but a very different New York, ideally quiet, peaceful, with empty streets and unpopulated buildings, reflecting not so much an objective reality as the intense subjective, liminal reality being lived by the personalities of the film, as they leave all they have to live the "God-spell." Stylistically then, *Godspell,* a low-cost production at $1,300,000,[63] is straightforward and unassuming. It refuses "to pretend to be anything more than it is . . . a series of stories and songs, like the Bible . . . told with the directness that simple stories need: with no tricks, no intellectual gadgets, and a lot of openness."[64]

Godspell is radically different from *Jesus Christ Superstar* also in its content. Whereas *Superstar* is above all a passion play, limiting itself to the final period of Jesus' life, Greene's film in effect covers most of the Gospel. Its narrative is continuous. There is no parallel cutting among episodes of Jesus and Judas and Mary Magdalene and Pilate and Herod. Jesus is present in, and is a principal focus of each scene; each scene leads to the next easily and naturally. Perhaps the major intradiegetical difference between the two Jesus musicals is that *Godspell* is infinitely more faithful to the gospels. Adapting material from Matthew and to a lesser extent from Luke, it reflects the overall structure and dynamic of the association of Jesus and his disciples. In many details of dialogue and action, and in its overall theme, the Good News of salvation comes into the world, and in its spirit, of joy, mercy and forgiveness, gratitude and love, *Godspell* represents in a surprisingly consistent way, the story of Jesus the Christ. Concretely, *Godspell* opens with a kind of Genesis creation-narrative. The Creator God, heard in voice-over, solemnly proclaims that he is God and King and that he has created all that exists and thrives in the world. Having set this clear biblical context, Greene introduces the figure of John the Baptist[65] who summons disciples together, from various occupations, largely dissatisfactory, in the city, brings them to the Bethesda fountain[66] in Central Park and baptizes them. Jesus appears by the fountain and is baptized by John,[67] at which point he becomes the leader of the disciples (Jn 1).

There follows in the course of the film a series of moral teachings of Jesus, all of them taken directly word for word from the Gospel of Matthew: the beatitudes, the teaching concerning love of neighbor, the law and the prophets, anger, turning the other cheek and the disciple as salt of the earth (Mt 5), the teaching regarding the serving two masters, doing almsgiving in secret and the lilies of the field (Mt 6), the teaching about the judgment of others, the golden rule and the response of God to prayer (Mt 7), and finally, Jesus' words about the judgment of the nations (Mt 25). If in *Godspell*, the moral teachings of Jesus are spoken by him, the film represents six of his parables in the form of sketches and burlesques, acted out, dramatized by the disciples. These include: the good Samaritan (Lk 10), the prodigal son (Lk 15), the rich man and Lazarus (Lk 16), the Pharisee and the tax collector (Lk 18), the sower of the seed (Mt 13) and the unforgiving servant (Mt 18). By placing the "teaching" of Jesus' parables in the hands of the disciples, *Godspell* is suggesting two important biblical-theological concepts: the closeness of the disciples to the Master, and the oral tradition of the teaching of Jesus to the Christian community.

The controversies of Jesus with the Pharisees are concentrated in one disturbing episode towards the end of the film, in which Jesus comes face to face with a giant monster-puppet, animated from within by the disciples, and which suggest the presence of evil even in those closest to Jesus. All the major points of this fatal conflict are included: the question of the authority of Jesus (Mt 21), the question of paying taxes (Mt 22), the greatest commandment (Mt 22), the denunciation of the Scribes and Pharisees (Mt 23), and Jesus' lamentation over Jerusalem (Mt 23). The narrative of the film then continues with the Last Supper, Jesus' betrayal by Judas, the crucifixion and death of Jesus, and, as we shall see below, his Resurrection.

In *Godspell*, the nature of the narrative is that of an "impressionistic view of Jesus"[68] and of the Gospel story. More an "interpretative reading of the Gospel"[69] than a precise historical rendering, the film clearly omits a number of concrete details of the gospels normally included in a Jesus-film: the infancy narrative, precise spatial and temporal coordinates, the healings, exorcisms and miracles, the confession of Peter,[70] Jesus' prophetic cleansing of the Temple[71] and then all the details of his arrest and trial. The settings of many of the Gospel actions are impressionistic transpositions, more appropriate to the New York City ambience: the baptisms take place in a fountain, the Last Supper in a junkyard on Ward's Island that has been cleaned up by the disciples, the crucifixion on the storm fence that encloses the junkyard.

In its actualizing of the Gospel, *Godspell* also effects a number of significant shifts in the text of the Scriptures: among Jesus' disciples, there are women and men; in the episode of the judgment of the nations, both the chosen sheep (just people) and the rejected goats (sinners) are invited to enter the kingdom, a representation of what theology refers to as the universal salvific will of God. Perhaps the most important shift has to do with the clearly privileged relationship of Jesus with the John the Baptist-Judas character.[72] *Godspell* makes the Baptist-Judas character the strongest, the most attractive of the disciples and it gives him several privileged learning moments with Jesus. In the end, Jesus forgives Judas for the betrayal; it is Jesus who kisses him twice. Judas is "crucified" with Jesus and the other disciples on the storm fence and he is one of those who carry Jesus back into the city in the conclusion of the film.

Given the impressionistic quality of the narrative of *Godspell*, and given the fact that considerable accent is placed on the teaching of Jesus, there is nevertheless no doubt that the Jesus of this film is a clearly defined, delineated and complex figure, and as has already been suggested, a very different figure than the protagonist of *Jesus Christ Superstar*. First of all, *Godspell*'s Jesus is divine, the Son of God. The intimacy of his relationship to God is repeatedly underlined, and when he prays in the Gethsemane scene, his personal address to his Father, in contrast to the cold, formal tones of *Jesus Christ Superstar,* is heartfelt and convincing. The Gospel's echoes and tones, repeatedly heard in Jesus' teaching, in his references to the Kingdom, in the fact that he is considered as Lord and as Master by his disciples, and in the sacramental nature of his celebration of the Last Supper, all affirm Jesus' divinity.

The Jesus of *Godspell* is one who speaks, and perhaps more importantly, who acts with authority. He has no moments of self-doubt or confusion. He fulfills his mission with coherence and moral strength and is sensitive to the reality around him and ahead of him. The moments of sadness and pain he experiences towards the end of the film, he lives with the noble conviction of their soteriological significance. But the spiritual authority and power of this Jesus does not separate him from those around him, as does the cold authority of Max von Sydow's Jesus in *The Greatest Story Ever Told*. In *Godspell*, Jesus participates in the activities of his community. He adds conclusions or explanations to the parables his disciples recount, and he sings and dances with them.

Radically different from the neurotic, egoistic protagonist of *Jesus Christ Superstar*, this Jesus is a patient and gentle teacher, who evidently takes pleasure in the progress of his disciples. At times he is firm, as when he corrects Judas, but it is clearly in favor of the truth and for the well-being of Judas. *Godspell*'s Jesus is a liberator. His teaching is meant to free his disciples from what limits them and to allow them to free one another. At the Last Supper, in a gesture which represents the didactic washing of the feet (Jn 13), Jesus begins by wiping dabs of theatrical make-up from the faces of the disciples. By the end of the sequence, they are "washing" one another. Jesus is also an infinitely merciful Lord, suggested in two particularly powerful and significant moments, neither of them strictly speaking evangelical. First, in the judgment of the nations sequence, when having in justice condemned the sinners (goats) to eternal damnation, Jesus is moved by mercy and he calls them into the kingdom with the justified (sheep); second, when at the moment of Judas' betrayal, Jesus realizes his friend's awkwardness and perhaps reluctance. He kisses Judas twice and folds him into his arms in a powerful embrace, a grace-filled embrace which seems to have effect later in Judas' salvation.

The Jesus of *Godspell* lives for his disciples and dies for them. In death, he is with them and strengthens them. He sends them back into the world from which he called them, to spread the Gospel, the Good News: "Long live God." Which bring us, once again, to the crucial point of any film representation of Jesus: the Resurrection. In *Godspell*, though there is no direct representation of the Resurrection of Jesus, "the film ends on a clear note of hope,"[73] and the Resurrection is suggested. The morning after the crucifixion, in which all the disciples, including Judas, have participated, they gently remove Jesus' body from the cross (fence), and dancing, clapping their hands, and singing "Love live God" and "Prepare Ye the Way of the Lord," they carry him out of the park and back into the city. Anything but discouraged or afraid, not in hiding, but animated and strengthened by the spirit of joy and hope that only Jesus alive could give them, they bring the Gospel, the Godspell, their salvific experience of God-in-Jesus back into the everyday hustle and bustle life of the metropolis. Clearly, in the closing of *Godspell*, the film's director, Greene is suggesting that Jesus lives, for the disciples, for the city and for us.

Certainly the most original aspect of the figure of Jesus in *Godspell*, and perhaps the most important for his identity as the Divine Messiah, the incarnate Son of God, is that he is represented as a clown. "Of all the Jesus images in film, this one diverges the most from the dominant tradition of the blond bearded young man."[74] Dressed in red clown shoes, brightly colored pants with orange suspenders, and a t-shirt emblazoned the stylized Superman "S" emblem (evidently an ironic reference), this "gentle hippy with a Jimi-Hendrix-Afro-look, painted clown's eyes and a red heart painted on his forehead"[75] is without a doubt the polar opposite of the superstar-Jesus or the biblical epic-Jesus.

The depiction of Jesus Christ as a clown in art is not new. Dostoevsky represents Jesus as the fool in *The Brothers Karamazov*, Rouault paints him as a clown, and the Quaker hymn proclaims its faith in Jesus as "the Lord of the Dance." Neither is this cinematographic approach to Jesus as clown unique to *Godspell*. "The clown-figures in Bergman's *Sawdust and Tinsel* (or *The Naked Night*) (1953) and Fellini's *La strada* (1954) both drawing their inspiration from Chaplin's *The Circus* (1928) (his own Christ film),"[76] precede *Godspell*'s divine clown. As we shall see later in this book, several other films represent Jesus as a clown, and with good results. Building on this "tradition of Christ as fool, and of Christianity itself as a form of folly,"[77] *Godspell*'s Jesus, a kind and sensitive clown, a Lord of the Dance and the Song, creates a community with his disciples and, being free, gives them freedom to enjoy the experience with him. Jesus-the-clown calls his disciples out of the everyday world of routine, obligation and stress into a mysterious wonderful world, a world in which everything is possible, in world in which the play-reality is more authentic and significant than the objective, scientific realities of everyday living. All this is not all that different from what Jesus does with his disciples in the Gospel.

In this liminal space, Jesus-the-clown plays with his disciples and teaches them to play, to clown. In a "totally irreverent but thoroughly enjoyable . . . game of parable telling,"[78] Jesus instructs them in words and song and they learn to teach each other. He loves them, lives and dies for them, and saves them. They in turn become instruments of song and dance and play and in this liminal space, bring salvation to others. In the Judaeo-Christian tradition (but not only) liminality has been understood one of the dimensions of mystical experience, the profound experience of God.[79] The mystic or visionary moves out of the normal dimensions of time and space into the mysterious, timeless realm of the Divine. This dimension of liminality in the film suggests a further significance of the film's title: *Godspell* as the spell of God, the fascination, the ecstasy of God, the mystical experience of God.[80]

The intense experience the disciples of *Godspell* have of God-in-Jesus is liminal. It takes place within a space and time that is, at the same time, beyond space and time. It is lived in situations that are specific and physical and, at the same time, beyond the specific and meta-physical. It is an experience that is both real and mysterious. Of crucial importance for the disciples in *Godspell*, this is not an experience in which they stop and linger, for their own self-indulgence, a kind of mysterious "high" experienced selfishly for its own sake; their experience of the "spell-of-God" moves them courageously to give it to others. In the hymn "The Lord of the Dance," the Lord called disciples, James and John, and because they danced with him, "the dance went on." In *Godspell*, the most eloquent sign of the divine Lordship of the protagonist is that after his death, in the disciples who danced with him, the dance and the song go on.

4

The Scandal Films:
Monty Python's Life of Brian and
The Last Temptation of Christ

Monty Python's Life of Brian,[1] a 1979 British production directed by Terry Jones, has the dubious privilege of being the only Jesus-film in the key of satirical comedy. A cinema spin-off from the hugely successful British television series, *Monty Python's Flying Circus*, *Life of Brian* is clearly within the "firm tradition of British humor . . . which depends on the juxtaposition of the unexpected with the ordinary,"[2] a brand of humor which does not easily translate into other languages and cultures, wherein lies one of the major reasons for the film's limited success.

Life of Brian, the group's "most sustained [cinema] effort to date,"[3] was radically different from the television series. This difference was judged positively by some critics, who for example note that, compared to the fragmented, gag-after-gag, style of their television show and previous films, "*Life of Brian* adopted a refreshingly coherent plot structure."[4] It is precisely this coherent plot structure that was criticized by others: "The *Life of Brian* is far less funny than a Monty Python television show . . . the plot line forces a linear and even logical approach on performers whose genius always lay in the lack of such a next-step approach."[5]

Given what was popularly rumored to be the theme of the film, a Monty Python version of the life of Christ, it is not surprising that things did not go smoothly with the financing and production of the film. Early on, the producers, EMI, got nervous with the protests regarding the film, and with the excuse of the costs becoming excessive, canceled their participation. To the rescue came a friend of several of the Monty Python crew, the ex-Beatle George Harrison who, together with a banker friend, put the necessary funding together, and the work got underway. Because of its structural weaknesses, the finished film had only minor critical success and because of the limited appeal of the Monty Python style of humor, it had only limited international distribution. For example, it was never released in Italy.[6]

The producers need hardly have worried, for *Life of Brian* is "patently . . . not an attack on Christianity,"[7] and in fact it is not even a film about Jesus. In ninety minutes of running time, the only visual references to Jesus are a brief shot of a crib at Bethlehem at the beginning of the film, in the most tacky Christmas postcard style, complete with glowing babe and singing choirs of angels, and a couple of distant shots of him during the Sermon on Mount, with a crowd of thousands gathered adoringly on the hillside in the most classic Hollywood style.

The film deals exclusively and most irreverently with the "parallel tale"[8] of the impossibly zany adventures of one "Brian Cohen," natural son of a Roman centurion and a Jewish woman – as always in Monty Python, she is played outrageously by a man. Born at the same time as Jesus, Brian later joins a Jewish liberation movement, mainly to get away from his oppressive "Jewish mother." As a member of this political activist group, Brian must write anti-Roman graffiti on the walls of Jerusalem and participate in an ill-fated plan to kidnap the wife of an elegant but lisping Pontius Pilate. Pilate in any case prefers his dubiously macho pal come from Rome, "Biggus Dickus," who, though splendid in his military leathers, speaks with a lisp like Pilate. Because of his dangerous activities, Brian is relentlessly pursued by the Roman authorities. He escapes briefly by being accidentally picked up by extraterrestrials in a low-flying space ship which later is shot down in a Star Wars battle and crashes into the Jerusalem bazaar. In his very spontaneous public-speaking debut, Brian unwillingly acquires a following of very unbalanced and very charismatic types who insist on mistaking him for the Messiah. His sandal and his gourd, both dropped by Brian as he tries to escape the enthusiastic crowd, become the focus of their devotion. Though "a reluctant messiah whose impact proved somewhat less pervasive than that of his contemporary Jesus Christ,"[9] Brian is nevertheless arrested and condemned to crucifixion, an experience which he shares rather optimistically with the other hundred odd victims that day, as on their crosses, they sing and sway in perfect harmony, "Always look on the bright side of life."

"A sustained, explosively funny lampoon of Biblical-Roman Empire epics,"[10] *Life of Brian* "successfully sends up the kind of reverent, choir-laden, star-studded gospel dramatizations habitually perpetrated by the cinema industry on behalf of God and Mammon."[11] This satirical criticism of Hollywood treatment of the Bible story is announced in the opening of the film: a fancy credits sequence at the beginning, with visuals imitating those of the "toga-and-sandal epics,"[12] and music reminiscent of the James Bond movies, followed by a special effects Bethlehem star crossing the sky and a flicked-on spectacular sunrise behind the outlines of the Magi. The film goes on to poke fun at the pseudo-biblical classics of the past, *"Ben Hur* at the head of the line"[13] – with an afternoon of sport at the Jerusalem Colosseum, "around tea-time" – and it sends up other "movies like *The Greatest Story Ever Told* and *King of Kings*,"[14] with the pseudo-spectacular scene of the Sermon on the Mount which echoes the parallel scene in both of those films.

A good part of *"Brian's* humour resorts to memories of the classroom."[15] In one of the funniest sequences, a law-and-order rabbi, master of ceremonies at the daily late afternoon stoning, "sends one of the participants to the back of the crowd for chucking their rock too soon."[16] The rabbi ends up being stoned by the over-enthusiastic crowd. In another scene, a night-patrolling centurion in severe British schoolmaster style, "corrects the Latin grammar in Brian's graffiti,"[17] "*Romanes eunt domus*," and then, instead of arresting him for sedition, orders him to write it one hundred times on the walls of Jerusalem. In a third hilarious sequence, a group of fashionably leftist Jewish Liberation terrorists, trying to justify philosophically a coup, discover to their chagrin how well off they really are under the despised Romans.

Regarding God, Jesus Christ and the Bible, *Life of Brian* is anything but sacrilegious. One critic puts it quite succinctly: "As for the brouhaha about blasphemy, that's a load of poppycock. God is not mocked."[18] In fact, the film is "almost deferential to its source. In many ways, particularly visually, the film is a lot less vulgar than most Hollywood forays into the Holy Land."[19] While often considered very irreverent, particularly by people who have not seen it, *Life of Brian*'s "satire is directed more at biblical films than [at] the original story."[20] Almost none of its humor, whether in single lines, some "wickedly acute,"[21] or in more extended scenes like the daily stoning, has to do with Christ.

In its satire the film does level considerable criticism at abuses of religion and perversions of religious sentiments, thus satirizing "the hypocrites, the false prophets, the gullible, the fighters for freedom who feud among themselves."[22] As such, "it's a brilliant metaphor for how the world has used Christ's message."[23] Particularly effective in this regard is the episode of the Sermon on the Mount, a set-piece, *de rigueur* in every Jesus-film. In the Monty Python version, the attention is on the crowd rather than the speaker. The people in the back cannot hear, and so each offers his own interpretation of what Jesus is saying: "Blessed are the Greek," "Blessed are the cheese-makers." To the general admiration of all the professionals in the crowd, the latter beatitude is interpreted by one of the evidently bourgeois bystanders as "Blessed are the manufacturers of general dairy products." Before long, disagreements and name-calling ensue and a free-for-all breaks out. It takes a crowd-control squad of burly Roman soldiers to subdue the disturbance, and all the while, out of earshot in the background, Jesus continues his sermon.

If any one group is singled out for particular criticism in *Life of Brian*, it is the "fundamentalists of *any* faith,"[24] individuals and groups who give themselves to "political and religious intolerance,"[25] either as leaders or as followers. In the film, the freedom-fighting guerillas "destroy themselves by backbiting each other to death [and] the worshipers are thrown off the true path of love by the urgent need to persecute and destroy all those who do not believe as they do."[26] The overly enthusiastic disciples of Brian who camp outside his mother's house and refuse to leave in spite of her repeated exhortation to "piss off!" delivered in a marvelous cockney accent, soon break into factions. There is the group of the "gourd," led by a radical-chique-feminist-ideologue terrorist, whose political passion under the unlikely fatal attraction of Brian is converted one night to passion of another kind, and the group of the "sandal," in fetishistic devotion to the sandal accidentally left behind by Brian as he runs from them. There is also the radical hermit, living nude in a

shallow desert pit, whose eighteen-year silence is broken when Brian falls
into his pit. The hermit's only source of sustenance, a mulberry bush, is plun-
dered by the hungry crowd when Brian will not perform a loaves-and-fishes-
type miracle.

The Last Temptation of Christ

Martin Scorsese's Jesus-film, *The Last Temptation of Christ,* produced in the
United States by Universal-Cineplex Odeon films and released in 1988, is
interesting for several reasons, all of them interrelated. Its production had a
long and much-travailed history. On its release the film raised a storm of
protest from a wide variety of Church people and organizations, while its
portrait of Jesus is, without a doubt, the most original and the most controversial of all the filmic images of Jesus. As is evident from its title, Scorsese
bases his film on the 1955 novel, *The Last Temptation,*[27] written by Nikos
Kazantzakis, and in a sense the film's troubles begin there.

Kazantzakis' novel presents a non-biblical Jesus beset by doubts and
fears about his identity and mission, constantly, oppressively tempted by evil.
A human being much more than the incarnate Word of God, this Jesus is
strongly tempted also sexually, and only by a superhuman effort of the will is
he able to achieve a final victory. Kazantzakis, though repeatedly nominated
for the Nobel prize, was excommunicated as a heretic by the Greek Orthodox
Church and his novel was placed in the index of forbidden books by the
Catholic Church.

The first producers, in the early 1980s, of the Scorsese film project
were Paramount Pictures, who attempted to deal with the early protests from
fundamentalist Protestant groups by insisting that the film project, only in
pre-production, be given "a new working title – 'The Passion.'"[28] When the
letters of protest continued to pour in, Paramount nervously called together a
group of "eminent theologians"[29] to advise them concerning Scorsese's project. The seminar concluded that "while there were obvious risks, *The Last
Temptation of Christ* deserved to be made."[30] Paramount did not want to take
those risks and in 1983, the project was terminated.

Scorsese then looked for financing in France, where Jack Lang, the
Minister of Culture "had a policy of offering support to non-French film-
makers of international standing."[31] Lang, an admirer of Scorsese, was very
interested in his film but when, in the wake of public protest over the Godard
film, *Je vous salue, Marie* (1985),[32] the Archbishop of Paris, Cardinal
Lustiger, wrote a letter of "solemn warning to President Mitterand about the
misuse of public funds for a project founded on subverting scripture,"[33] the
French backed off. Only in 1987 was Scorsese's project accepted by Universal Pictures: he had to slash the film's budget from $15 million to "a lean
$6.5 million for Universal,"[34] but the picture he had so longed to make was
underway.

When *The Last Temptation of Christ* was released in 1988, it unleashed "a firestorm of controversy."[35] In fact, the public protest against the film was "far more widespread and volatile than any previous criticism directed against a Hollywood religious film."[36] In America, the objections came from Catholic archbishops and Protestant TV-evangelists.[37] In Italy, Franco Zeffirelli, whose 1977 film, *Jesus of Nazareth* is one of the Jesus-classics, reacted very strongly: without having seen the film, he condemned it at the Venice Film Festival as "truly horrible and totally deranged,"[38] and on national television, he fired a second salvo, saying that *The Last Temptation of Christ* was a product of "that Jewish cultural scum of Los Angeles, which is always spoiling for an attack on the Christian world."[39] Though some of the criticism of *The Last Temptation* was reasoned and precise – one American Bishop rightly wrote that the film is "equally defective on the theological level and on the esthetic level"[40] – the general tenor of the protest "can be gauged by a placard seen in Chicago: 'God doesn't like this movie,'"[41] and by public prayers to the Deity to nuclear bomb the cinema in Manhattan where *The Last Temptation* was being shown. Finally, "the U.S. Catholic Conference called for a nationwide boycott of the film, the first such boycott the conference had ever recommended."[42]

At the risk of oversimplifying the wide range of objections to Scorsese's film, many of which will be dealt with later in this chapter, it seems clear that the major objection of the protesters to *The Last Temptation of Christ* had to do with the long final sequence of the film, in which Scorsese has Jesus come down from the cross and walk into an earthly paradise, where in rather rapid succession, filmically at least, he marries first Mary Magdalene and then, as a widower, Mary, the sister of Lazarus. By her and her sister Martha, he has a number of children. The problem is that people who had not seen the film, or who had seen it but not very perceptibly, had no idea that these "offending events occur in a *fantasy* sequence,"[43] a daydream-like temptation to the domestic life carefully formulated by Satan to dissuade the crucified Jesus from living fully his mission of salvation. Further it is a temptation sequence represented by Scorsese as a fantasy, something evident in the film language of the sequence, and as a temptation-fantasy that Scorsese has Jesus overcome: he returns to the cross and dies victorious. The real weaknesses of *The Last Temptation of Christ* lie elsewhere as we shall see.

At the time he took on *The Last Temptation* project, Martin Scorsese was a well-established and internationally respected film-maker, an *auteur* in the full sense. That, and the seriousness and tenacious dedication he devoted to the project oblige us to treat the film seriously. Already as a child, growing up a Catholic in New York, Scorsese dreamed of this project: "At age ten he had drawn the story boards for a movie he wanted to make on the life of Christ."[44] As a film student at New York University, Scorsese studied "previous biblical films based on the gospels."[45] He himself reveals his early hopes to do a Jesus-film: "This desire is evident in *Jerusalem, Jerusalem!*, a script I wrote in the mid-sixties, where the Passion of Christ is played out against a background of the Lower East Side of Manhattan."[46] Scorsese's interest in Kazantzakis' novel spanned more than thirty years of his life: "In 1961 a Greek friend, John Mabros, told me about *The Last Temptation* . . . but it really started when Barbara Hershey gave me the book in 1972."[47]

The long and difficult negotiations with Paramount and Universal, the conversations with the widow of Kazantzakis to ensure the rights to the novel, the drastic budget cuts, his personal participation in the writing and re-writing of the script, all attest to the seriousness of Scorsese, as does his impassioned and by and large intelligent defense of the film and his vivid personal interest in every phase of its production: "Around 1983, I subscribed to the *Biblical Archeology Review*, and a lot of our art direction came from that magazine."[48] Interestingly and ironically, it is precisely this seriousness of Scorsese, this audacious personal commitment to the *Last Temptation* film, that contains the seeds of the film's weakness and consequently, the drastic limits of the film's image of Jesus.

First of all, it is significant that Scorsese chooses to base his Jesus-film on Kazantzakis' controversial novel and not on the gospels themselves, as is the case with Pasolini's film, about which Scorsese said: "I was moved and crushed at the same time by the Pasolini film because in a sense it was what I wanted to do."[49] Secondly, and though Paul Schrader has the on-screen credit as scriptwriter of *The Last Temptation of Christ*, Scorsese, along with the New York film critic Jay Cocks, is responsible for most of its dialogue and much of its action. Which means that, in the inevitable process of editing or streamlining the five-hundred page novel into a two-and-a-half hour film, it is Scorsese who decided what to omit, what to add, what to change, all of which effect shifts in the figure of Jesus and his significance. Here we shall mention only two of the many examples of shifted meaning in the film. If Kazantzakis devotes much time to the relationships of Jesus with most of his disciples, thus creating a complex and vibrant community in which Jesus lives and matures in his vocation, Scorsese in effect reduces this community to one disciple, Judas, and gives Jesus an almost exclusive, and fundamentally unbalanced, relationship with his betrayer. Then, Scorsese adds the bizarre, gory "Sacred Heart" scene, not even vaguely suggested in Kazantzakis, which not only betrays Scorsese's own subversive[50] misunderstanding of this traditional Catholic icon,[51] but also makes of his Jesus an unbalanced and masochistic refugee from a Cronenberg horror movie.

Another dimension of the evident seriousness with which Scorsese undertakes the *Last Temptation* project is his wide knowledge of cinema. Scorsese is one of the new generation of American film-makers, which includes also Coppola, Spielberg, Lucas, De Palma, whose basic formation is academic. Scorsese graduated in Film Studies from New York University in 1964, and later taught film there.[52] His wide academic acquaintance with cinema and films makes Scorsese susceptible to the tendency of academism, a tendency clearly perceptible in *The Last Temptation of Christ*, that is, of making his film self-consciously in reference to, or in reaction against, other Jesus-films. For example, he much admired Pasolini's *The Gospel According to Saint Matthew* and Rossellini's *The Messiah*. From the latter, his *Last Temptation* inherited "the primitive setting to Christ's mission;"[53] from the former, an aggressive style of editing. In Scorsese's own words, "I love the way Pasolini did the miracles . . . when Jesus cures the leper . . . Just a simple cut, and it's so shocking and beautiful."[54] Scorsese in effect admits the critical dimension of his "academic" approach when he says about *The Last Temptation*, "I wanted to use Kazantzakis's concepts to tear away at all those old Hollywood films . . . and create a Jesus you could maybe talk to, question, get to know."[55] Clearly he wanted to avoid the "very emphatic and vulgar . . . full-blown Hollywood"[56] style of *King of Kings*, and of *The Greatest Story Ever Told*, the "antiseptic quality, hermetically sealed holiness that didn't teach us anything new about Jesus."[57] With these other films quite consciously in the background, Scorsese's film at times takes on aspects of a postmodern pastiche of contents and styles, and his Jesus, formulated in virtue of the strengths and weaknesses of these other images of Jesus, often manifests a rhetorical character inconsistent with other elements of the film.

To some extent, Scorsese's desire to avoid the limits and exaggerations of the Jesus-film tradition bears good fruit. One theologian comments on the freshness and originality of *The Last Temptation of Christ*:

> One notices how free it is of the ponderous solemnity that so typifies the genre. Gone are the endless choirs of angels singing in the soundtrack. Gone are the awestruck audiences surrounding Christ. Gone is the starchiness that tends to mummify the actor playing the lead role.[58]

In a largely justified and successful effort to de-Westernize[59] the ambience and the texture of the Jesus story, Scorsese shot his film in Morocco.[60] The location, the costumes and the rich variety of Middle-Eastern music in Peter Gabriel's sound-track, give *The Last Temptation* an undeniable "exotic orientalism,"[61] which in itself may be good. On closer examination however, this exotic orientalism turns out to be far more Arabic than Hebrew. In the Cana episode, for example, the wedding ritual, the costumes, the music and dance are all Arabic and Muslim, as are the criers at the tomb of Lazarus and the dance and the extradiegetical music and song during the Last Supper.

Somewhat paradoxically, in the script of *The Last Temptation* and in the spoken dialogue, Scorsese seems to want to re-Westernize his film. Certainly in an attempt to render his characters more dynamic or immediate, and perhaps "to substitute for Kazantzakis' use of the 'demotic' language of the Greek peasantry rather than the 'puristic' language of Athenian intellectuals,"[62] Scorsese has his characters use plain language, "contemporary phrasing and speech patterns"[63] and "rough, unsophisticated American accents."[64] He obviously does not realize that this decision, resulting, for example, in a Judas (Harvey Keitel) who sounds like a streetwise New York tough, is in logical contradiction of the exotic de-Westernized ambience of the rest of his film. A New York critic recognized Scorsese's self-contradiction, calling it as "one of the film's great incongruities . . . the language . . . is often as intentionally flat as the imagery is starkly glorious."[65]

Reacting against the limited and stereotypical role of women in the previous Jesus-films, Scorsese wanted to update the Jesus-story by a significant and strong presence of women throughout his film. Mary Magdalene is portrayed as one of Jesus' disciples, and she and Martha and Mary participate in the Last Supper. *The Last Temptation of Christ* is the only serious Jesus-film to allow this. Scorsese justified his daring move with characteristic ingenuousness and somewhat limited eucharistic theology: "Jesus was so great, I just couldn't see him telling the women at the Last Supper, 'Wait in the kitchen.' . . . He would have them take part in the first Mass."[66] A closer study of these strong characters, however, reveals that in them there is little new. Scorsese keeps them very much within the limits of "traditional conceptions of women."[67] In *The Last Temptation*, and even in the mind of its Jesus, woman is still "the earthly other to spiritual man"[68] and her role is limited to that of embodying "sexuality and domesticity."[69] Scorsese seems not to appreciate that the Jesus of the Gospel has an infinitely more enlightened view of woman and gives her nothing short of a revolutionary role to play in the establishment of the Kingdom of God.

In consciously rejecting the grand epic style of at least the American tradition of Jesus-films, their stiff formality, and the consequent unnatural and unevangelical static quality of their Jesus-figures, meant to suggest his transcendence, his divine nature, Scorsese wanted develops a simpler and more dynamic style, a more personal, reachable Jesus, more in touch with issues that trouble contemporary humanity. Unfortunately he missed the mark. With Kazantzakis' aggressive psychological-epic style hovering in the background of his consciousness, and because his own interests and struggles lie more with the psychological than the spiritual, the iconoclast Scorsese seems to lose control of his creation. Thus, the indisputable and complex interiority of *The Last Temptation*, in both style and content, ends up being more psychological than spiritual while its Jesus becomes more a study in pathology than a prophet and spiritual leader.

At the time that he made *The Last Temptation of Christ*, Scorsese, with ten feature films to his credit,[70] was already internationally recognized as an *auteur*, an artist whose *corpus* of films, limited in large part to the contemporary urban American experience, clearly manifested discernible and repeated themes and stylistic elements. The protagonist of the Scorsese film tends to be an anti-hero, an outsider, a misfit, living a struggle against the world and within himself, and whose struggle more often than not ends in failure. He is usually male and almost always seconded by a friend who does little to help him resolve his problems. The victim of sexual confusion, repression and obsession, the Scorsese anti-hero is introspective often to the point of neurosis, a condition often signaled by complex interior monologues. This situation leads inexorably to outbursts of violence, physical, verbal and psychological, usually marked by blood, which seems to be one of Scorsese favorite symbols. The style of the Scorsese film is equally idiosyncratic. Characterized by rapid camera movements and unconventional angles, purposely unbalanced and shocking compositions, dialogue often violent in tone and content, forceful, aggressive editing and a rich, complex and often relentless sound mix, the Scorsese style tends to overpower the viewer.

Even a superficial viewing reveals that *The Last Temptation of Christ* manifests "striking parallels to Scorsese's early Italian-American work."[71] Stylistically, it has all of the typical elements mentioned above. Certainly one of *The Last Temptation*'s dominant stylistic traits is its extremely dense "multicultural New Age sound"[72] music of which one critic justly says, "the source of its hypnotic, trance-like rhythms is Peter Gabriel's musical score [which] accounts for much of the doleful sorrow, a good bit of the cacophonous shock, and a large part of the raw sensuality."[73] Equally dominant are Scorsese's nervous and aggressive camera movements and very peculiar camera angles. Jesus is repeatedly seen from above: "The startling overhead shots of his [Scorsese's] earlier films are revealed here as God's POV [point-of-view]."[74] Also unusual is Scorsese's particular use of the editing technique of the rapid lap dissolve which violently telescopes time, used for example during the call of the disciples scene and the Last Supper.

The Last Temptation clearly reveals thematic interests common to many of Scorsese's films: "faith and sacrifice, guilt and redemption, sin and atonement."[75] In its two principal characters, Jesus and Judas, it contains one of the classic elements of the Scorsese canon, as Richard Corliss explains:

> He [Scorsese] knew that Kazantzakis's story could be the ultimate buddy movie. For 15 years Scorsese has been directing secular drafts of it. Two men, closer than brothers, with complementary abilities and obsessions, who must connive in each other's destiny.[76]

If a Jesus-film in tough, aggressive *Mean Streets* or *Raging Bull* style is already uncomfortable, then a Jesus neurotically dependent on Judas – "two men from the 'neighborhood'. . . each needing the other to fulfill the role he has chosen to play"[77] – is a serious problem. Further a Jesus Christ aptly described as "Scorsese's most privately anguished being,"[78] and the "central character of his canon, a smalltime weasel on the fringe who is heretofore usually Italian and definitely lunatic,"[79] is totally unacceptable and has nothing in common with the Jesus of the Gospel. In his *Last Temptation,* Nikos Kazantzakis creates a Jesus of fiction who goes well beyond the Jesus of the Gospel to the point of heresy. Scorsese, in his *Last Temptation,* creates a Jesus in his own image and likeness, a first-century preacher who "suffers from twentieth-century angst,"[80] a "paradigm of his gallery of heroes,"[81] who often only vaguely resembles Kazantzakis' creation, and who is little more than a strange burlesque of the Jesus of the Gospel.

Clearly then, one of the reasons for this limitation of *The Last Temptation of Christ* is that Scorsese, facing the unique challenge of representing

Jesus on screen, was unable to shift registers, to take some distance from his usual thematic and stylistic modes of expression and to develop an approach more appropriate to the exceptional subject. It is very true that given his previous work, "one can clearly see the attraction Christ as *dramatis persona* holds for Scorsese."[82] It is equally true that in remaining bound to his previous work, Scorsese's film and his Jesus Christ are fatally flawed.

Regarding the creation of *The Last Temptation of Christ* and its limitations, a third element comes into the picture: the question of the personal faith vision of Martin Scorsese. Clearly, for a person about to create an image of Jesus Christ, even though based on the vision of Kazantzakis, his personal beliefs regarding the Christ, his own understanding of Jesus and his mission, and his salvific action, are of prime importance. Scorsese is clear about his own religious identity: "I am a Catholic,"[83] and he continues, "I'm a devout Catholic even if I'm not a 'good' Catholic . . . I believe and I pray."[84] Concerning who Jesus Christ is for him, he is equally clear: "I believe that Jesus is divine."[85] "He's God."[86] Regarding the Resurrection, his position is quite orthodox, if not too sophisticated: "I do believe in the Resurrection. I can't exactly say what it means, beyond a kind of transcendence."[87]

But behind these basic statements of Scorsese's belief, significant in themselves because they indicate a valid point of departure, a more complex puzzle begins to reveal itself. Scorsese grew up a Catholic in Little Italy, New York City, in the 1950s and this implies a variety of religious experiences whose influence continues to be felt in his films even today.[88] For example, two of Scorsese's earliest memories are of the religious icons with which he grew up: "My grandmother . . . had the portrait of the Sacred Heart. And also the niche with the statue of the Virgin Mary grinding the snake under her foot."[89] It is significant that both are, in Scorsese's sensibility, violent images, and that the Sacred Heart image – "a painting that hangs in millions of Italian and Italo-American living rooms"[90] – had such a particular and profound effect on him: as early as *Mean Streets* "Scorsese had wanted to include his dreams of the sacred heart in his movies."[91] Scorsese also admits an interest in another religious icon of particular importance for *The Last Temptation*: "At that time (first communion) I was fascinated by images of the crucifixion and drew endless pictures of it,"[92] the first moments, perhaps, of a lifelong preoccupation with religions that have blood sacrifices, and which preoccupation certainly makes itself felt rather heavily in the film.

As a child, Scorsese attended Catholic parochial school, "at St. Patrick's Old Cathedral [with] Irish nuns, the Sisters of Mercy."[93] Having decided "at the age of ten"[94] to become a priest, as an adolescent he entered the seminary: "At the age of fourteen, I went to Cathedral College, a junior seminary on the Upper West Side."[95] This is an important detail because Scorsese himself and many film critics repeatedly refer to his "seminary training," purportedly in preparation for the priesthood, as if it had gone on for years. One biographer speaks of the young Scorsese's "ministry and witness . . . to outcasts and despairing"[96] and of his departure from the seminary as leaving behind "the

Roman collar."[97] Implied in these references to Scorsese's seminary training is the conclusion that it had provided Scorsese with an extensive and profound theological background, clearly (they suggest) qualifying him, perhaps as no other film-maker, to create a valid filmic image of Christ. The fact is that in the junior seminary, more a high school for aspirant seminarians than anything else – it was a day school only: "we went home every night"[98] – the boy Scorsese would have studied no theology in any serious sense and in any case, his stay was rather short lived: "I was expelled after a year, because I really didn't have my mind on my work: I had met a young lady with whom I fell in love."[99] However fuzzy the specific details of Scorsese's religious formation may be, its legacy is clear. He himself says "'unequivocally' that his inheritance was 'a major helping of guilt, like a lot of garlic.'"[100] Guilt, for sure, but also a struggle with sinfulness, especially of the sexual variety, the kind that is always mortal, probably augmented by scrupulousness; a fascinated preoccupation with violent suffering and bloody sacrifice, as the inevitable result of human sinfulness; and a kind of naive, literal understanding of the basic Catholic symbols.

The themes and limitations of Scorsese's religious education are abundantly evident in *The Last Temptation of Christ*. Just as "Scorsese the seminarian was beset by voices, overcome by urges, and bedeviled by desires [with] dreams of bliss in a woman's arms,"[101] his Jesus suffers neurotically through much the same experience, and in a sense, Christ's victory in the conclusion of the film is the victory that Scorsese (still?) hopes for. The masochistic and obsessive fascination with the cross is there too, as is the liberal pouring out of sacrificial blood, both human and animal. Let us consider two typical, though seldom noted, exaggerations. In the opening minutes of the film, Scorsese has Jesus, who builds crosses for Roman executions, actually help nail a victim to a cross. In a tight close-up of Jesus' face, Scorsese shows blood from the victim's foot splatter on Jesus' face.[102] Not only is the image shocking; it also represents a physiological contradiction: since blood in the foot flows very lethargically, such a violent splatter is impossible, except for Scorsese's special-effects technician. Later in the film, Scorsese has the episode of the wedding at Cana open with the slaughter and disembowelment, shown in dripping close-up, of the lamb for the meal.[103]

Repeatedly, *The Last Temptation* reveals a naive and rather superficial use of traditional Christian symbols. The bizarre "Sacred Heart" scene – the density of the gesture of Jesus removing his heart "in the manner of a Filipino faith-healer"[104] augmented by strange red lighting in the expressionist manner and by the blood dripping into a pool of water, causing it to boil – is non-evangelical and non-Kazantzakis. Further, in its awkward materialism, it evinces a total misunderstanding of this mystical devotion popular in the Church since the seventeenth century. More significantly, it creates a seriously-distorted image of Jesus and of his divine love.

The sanguinary "grotesqueries"[105] continue in the Last Supper scene, in which the sacramental wine turns into the actual material blood of Jesus, complete with convenient clots for the close-up camera.[106] If this Last Supper scene "verges on the cannibalistic,"[107] consider how it might have gone. Scorsese describes how in his script for *The Last Temptation*, Paul Schrader had a "literal version of the Last Supper in terms of swallowing the flesh and blood of Jesus."[108] Mercifully for the viewer but inconsistently, Scorsese's maintains only half of Schrader's idea – the wine becomes blood, the bread remains bread – inviting the theologically astute viewer to conclude that in the case of *The Last Temptation*'s Jesus, the miracle of transubstantiation is only half successful.

Scorsese attempts to justify in *The Last Temptation of Christ*, this exaggerated emphasis on blood which has become one of the primary trademarks of his films.[109] He argues for example that "blood is very important in the church. Blood is the life force, the essence, the sacrifice. And in a movie you have to see it."[110] The logical process of his reflection is a little less clear when he explains further: "I tried to show [in *The Last Temptation*] that the sacrifices of animals lead to the sacrifice of the Cross . . . Sacrifices took place in the Temple, under the supervision of the priests. It must have looked like a slaughterhouse."[111] Scorsese begins with a valid point, then he does an exaggeratedly literal reading of a sacramental symbol and ends by justifying turning what in the Gospel and in Kazantzakis is the Passover ritual meal into a "Eucharistic river of blood."[112]

In *The Last Temptation of Christ*, the grotesqueries are not exclusively sanguinary. Scorsese makes of the baptism scene at the Jordan, a psychedelic Hari-Krishna meeting with weird hypnotic overtones. John the Baptist becomes a "seducer and rapist of spirits"[113] and the penitent faithful, his "groupies, literally shaking with the rhythms of 'transcendental meditation.'"[114] In Kazantzakis, the healing miracles are spread throughout the ministerial activity of Jesus. Scorsese concentrates them in one unforgettable, apocalyptical scene. He has Jesus descend alone into a dusty valley, where he is quite literally attacked by a mob of strange creatures, presumably in need of healing, who pour out of a tower and rise out of the ground. Like refugees from *The Night of the Living Dead*, or from the parallel healing scene in *Jesus Christ Superstar*, they grab and tear at Jesus – this *grand guignol* ballet is filmed in slow motion – and only the arrival of the disciples, in the nick of time, assures Jesus' survival.

In at least one scene of the film, the music on the soundtrack becomes one of these grotesqueries. Chosen by Peter Gabriel, but ultimately the responsibility of Scorsese, the music during the Last Supper scene is all wrong. First of all, it is Arabic and not Hebrew music, and it is heard during the most solemn part of the Last Supper scene, a Jewish ritual Seder, as Jesus institutes the sacrament of the Eucharist: "This is my body . . . This is the cup of my blood." This quite incredible juxtaposition,[115] a classic postmodern pastiche, one of many in the film, is totally inappropriate, if not downright offensive and blasphemous, both to Christians and Muslims. The section of the soundtrack in question is identified by Peter Gabriel as follows: "Baaba

Maal, a Senegalese singer, did the traditional Moslem call to prayer which is used in the Last Supper scene."[116] It is not, in fact, the classical Moslem "Call to Prayer," but rather a song in Arabic based on the Islamic profession of faith or creed, which says textually: "I believe that there is no God [Allah] but God [Allah] and that Mohammed is the One Sent by God [Allah]." In the song this phrase is repeated, as are other words in praise of Mohammed as the Prophet and the Beloved of God.[117]

There are several other problems and contradictions with the inclusion of the Moslem credal hymn in this scene. Islam denies categorically the notion of the incarnation of God, thus denying the divine identity of Jesus Christ as incarnate Word of God. It also denies the possibility that God-in-Jesus "incarnates himself" in the bread and wine of the Last Supper and the Eucharist. So, for Islam, the use of the profession of faith for a scene which proposes this incarnation of God in an "infidel" religion is unacceptable. Clearly for Islam, Mohammed and not Jesus, is the ultimate and greatest Messenger of God, and with him, the Revelation of God concludes. Finally, there is the fact that Jesus in this scene, having been portrayed as weak, ineffectual, neurotic, paranoid, throughout the film, is shown once again to seem quite unsure of what he is doing. While the Islamic creed is heard, Jesus glances nervously from side to side as if seeking confirmation from his disciples, and Scorsese photographs him from a slightly high angle which has a diminishing effect on his person. Were it not completely anachronistic and illogical, one might wonder if Jesus is nervous in this occasion because he hears the Muslim creed and it adds to his doubts about his identity and mission. After all, if Allah is the only God, then clearly, Jesus cannot be divine.

Behind these strange and disconcerting scenes, there are some fundamental theological misunderstandings and errors on Scorsese's part, most of them having to do with Jesus. For example, Scorsese admits Jesus' double nature, but then he goes on to conclude, erroneously: "Because of his dual nature, human and divine, every moment in His life is a conflict and a victory."[118] Evidently, Scorsese does not want to imagine that Jesus might have achieved an equilibrium, a serenity, in his human-divine existence, something that is very clear in the Jesus of the gospels. Further, Scorsese seems to have problems even with Jesus' human nature: "Jesus is wracked by doubt and fear . . . But he's not weak at all. He just has the doubts we all have. He struggles all the time because it's part of his human nature."[119] No doubt growing up in Little Italy, New York, especially for a sickly child as Scorsese had been, life was a constant struggle, but to project that experience on Jesus of Nazareth and on human nature in general is simply unacceptable.

Regarding Jesus' healing miracles, and flying in the face of the overwhelming evidence of the gospels, and even in Kazantzakis, Scorsese suggests strong resistance and struggle on Jesus' part. His explanation is very strange: "Every miracle, everything that gets him closer to his destination, also brings him closer to his death, closer to the Crucifixion, and that is something he doesn't want."[120] Scorsese is far from a theology of miracle which sees the thaumaturgical gesture as Jesus' authoritative offering of healing and reintegration, out of sheer love for the poor and afflicted, and as a sign of the establishment of the Kingdom of God.

The problem is not that Scorsese does not know the gospels, or that he is totally incapable of reasoning theologically. In answer to a question about whether Jesus of Nazareth knew from the beginning that he was God, he answers correctly: "Maybe, maybe not. There are hints both ways [in the gospels],"[121] and he goes on to speak intelligently of details in Matthew and Luke. Clearly he has done his homework. But Scorsese's eagerness to create a Jesus closer to his own experience, in his own image and likeness so to speak, gets in the way. He therefore ends up arriving at outrageous conclusions like the following, where he misinterprets both Kazantzakis' Jesus, at least a little, and the Gospel Jesus, badly: "this neurotic – even psychotic – Jesus [of Kazantzakis] was not very different from the shifts of mood and psychology that you find glimpses of in the Gospels."[122]

> Scorsese's interpretation of Christ coalesces images that haunt all his earlier films – disorienting, disturbing, and evocative archetypes of fear, guilt, and desperation; overpowering, unsettling, and visceral visions of blood, sexuality, pain, suffering, and ecstasy.[123]

In his basic understanding and portrayal of Jesus, Scorsese's initial intuition is good. Responding to Kazantzakis' earthly Jesus, reacting against the monumental Hollywood Jesus, he wants to restore Jesus' humanity, to portray him as a real human being, "a Christ who laughs and cries and dances,"[124] who experiences fully a wide variety of very authentic human thoughts and feelings who, like all human beings, develops in his self-awareness and in his understanding of what he is about in the world. But somehow, in the concrete expression of this intuition, something goes wrong. Every time he gives Jesus a moment of authenticity, Scorsese then seems to lose control of his creation. For example, with a touch of genius, Scorsese gives the early scene of the first parable a marvelous freshness: Jesus, finding himself with a group of people, simply begins to talk. Speaking awkwardly, uncertainly at first, the parable seems to take shape as he speaks it. The natural spontaneity of Jesus' discourse and of his gestures is entirely credible. The problem however, is that this is the way Scorsese has Jesus speak throughout the entire film, even at the end, always awkward and uncertain, as if he never develops any self-confidence or skill, as if he never speaks with authority. In the classical episode of the wedding at Cana, Scorsese shows Jesus dancing, an original, credible and useful first-century Palestinian touch, but its subtle effect is lost when he has Jesus follow up the miracle of the water-into-wine with a late-twentieth-century and very American grin and ironic toast to the surprised servants. Scorsese gives his Jesus moments of confusion and doubt, certainly consonant with an authentic human existence. But he does not allow his Jesus to resolve his confusion in any kind of definitive way; he permits him no normal human development, maturation, so that at the end of the film Jesus is still struggling with the same issues and problems as at the beginning.

One explanation of this fundamental imbalance in the Jesus of *The Last Temptation of Christ* has to do with Scorsese's understanding of the situation in first-century Palestine. His research revealed the intense divisions that characterized that period, the complex models of Messiah that were awaited, military, priestly, mystical, and he discovered "in this divided society the model for his conflicted Jesus."[125] This concept of a conflicted and troublesome Jesus was well served by Scorsese's choice of an actor for the role. Having considered Robert De Niro, Chris Walken, Aidan Quinn, and Eric Roberts,[126] Scorsese cast Willem Dafoe, "blondish and blue-eyed in the Anglo-Saxon physical tradition of Jesus,"[127] an explanation which would seem to contradict Scorsese's desire to give a Middle-Eastern texture to the film.[128] Given Scorsese's basic concept, Dafoe, an actor trained in alternative theater circles in New York, "whose off-beat looks have cast him [in previous films] as an ideal villain,"[129] and whose Jesus "embodies incoherence overlaid with all the nervous intensity associated with Method acting,"[130] is undoubtedly the best choice for an unbalanced Christ.

Scorsese-Dafoe's Jesus "is indeed very human, full of weakness, self-doubt and ambivalence."[131] His fear is unequivocally manifest at the beginning of his mission, when Scorsese has him say *sottovoce* to Judas, as he begins to speak to the small crowd, "What if I say the wrong thing? What if I say the *right* thing?" It is again shockingly clear in the close-up of his terrified face when Lazarus, whom he has just raised from the dead, embraces him, or in the slightly high-angle shot of him at the Last Supper, when, having said over the bread "This is my body," his expression clearly suggests he is not at all sure of what he has done. Scorsese's Jesus, like that of Kazantzakis, is "a man caught in an identity crisis,"[132] out of which trap he never emerges:

> Merging his research with his rereading of Kazantzakis, Scorsese envisioned a human Christ, unsure of whether he was merely an ordinary mortal or a divinity incarnated, and equally uncertain whether his mission was to engender a family, save a nation, reform a religion, or forge a new path to salvation.[133]

If the various Jesus-figures of cinema that precede Scorsese-Dafoe's are conceived and portrayed as heros, either in high key in the Hollywood version, or in low key, in Pasolini and Rossellini, the protagonist of *The Last Temptation of Christ* is decisively an anti-hero. On the intradiegetical level, in his words and actions, this Jesus is anything but strong, decisive, authoritative, morally integrated, a model for others. His anti-heroic identity is further underlined by a whole series of extradiegetical, or stylistic, elements. For example, the very first image of Jesus is a vertical shot from above, picturing him huddled in the dust as if trying to protect himself: hardly the Master of the Universe. As he saves the life of Mary Magdalene from the angry and homicidal crowd, Scorsese pictures Jesus in a long shot, with both arms raised, a strong stance, but he subverts the authoritative quality of this image by making it a high-angle shot with an inevitable diminishing effect: hardly the Savior of the world. Again at the Last Supper and in the "Sacred Heart" scene, Jesus is photographed from above, dominated not dominating, and the expressionistic lighting and the corresponding shadows on Jesus' face, make him more a confused and reluctant vampire, and certainly not the Incarnate, Loving Word of God.

The humanity of the Jesus of *The Last Temptation of Christ* goes beyond being merely weak and indecisive. His anti-heroic existence manifests very clear signs of classic neurosis. A man oppressed by a sense of tragic destiny which permits him no freedom of movement or choice, he is also almost pathologically incapable of making decisions in moments of crisis. Further, Scorsese's Jesus, like Scorsese's Johnny Boy, Travis Bickle and Jake LaMotta before him,[134] "exhibits classic masochistic symptoms: seeking submission, pursuing pleasure through suffering, and finally, with the aid of his closest friend, setting up his own death."[135] Though ostensibly the leader of the community of apostles, he remains a loner relating only to Judas and then in a dependent-submissive and at times even sexually ambiguous manner: "the boldest . . . image of their affinity . . . comes when the camera looks down on Jesus asleep in the protective embrace of his friend 'my brother.'"[136] Scorsese suggests the terrible solitude, social and psychological, of Jesus in the two-shot sequence of Jesus carrying his cross. After a brief vertical shot from above, he represents the *via dolorosa* in a very long (sixty second) shot, in deliberate, painful slow motion, which manifestly imitates the sixteenth-century painting of Hieronymous Bosch, "Christ Carrying the Cross."[137] Already Bosch's image is violent – "Christ almost suffocated in the middle of the frame by the faces of the mob and . . . overwhelmingly sadistic, the facial expressions of those characters"[138] – but its violence is somewhat attenuated by the inclusion of two more positive figures, the good thief and the Veronica, sympathetic to Jesus. Characteristically, Scorsese omits these two, thus creating a "more extreme"[139] image.

Again like most of Scorsese's anti-heros, Jesus' neuroses extend to his sexuality, which often seems to be the dominant, if not only, dimension of his humanity.[140] He lives his relationships with women in a troubled, immature, unintegrated manner, wracked by fear and guilt. His public rejection of his mother is exaggeratedly violent in word and tone,[141] and many of his contacts with Magdalene fairly steam with confused and repressed desire. For this, Scorsese, much more than Kazantzakis, carries the responsibility. For example, in Kazantzakis, on the occasion of the first meeting between Jesus and Mary Magdalene, Jesus waits in the open-air courtyard of Magdalene's compound, observing the lighthearted conversation of the other men, while the woman meets her clients behind closed doors. Scorsese, evidently wishing to raise the temperature, moves the scene into a narrow corridor of a room, in which Magdalene, nude on a bed behind a gauze curtain, and pictured repeatedly in voyeuristic close-ups, entertains each man in full view of all the oth-

ers, including Jesus, who watch in oppressive and sweaty silence. One critic
captures well the atmosphere of the scene when he justly compares the room
to a "porn cinema or a 'peep show' on 42nd Street."[142]

Neurotic is not enough for a Scorsese anti-hero. His Jesus is diagnosed
by critics as "contradictory, almost schizoid,"[143] as "fragmented, almost
schizophrenic,"[144] as "suffering from a conflict of dual personalities."[145]
Scorsese himself describes him as "often psychotic: he sees visions, hears
voices, has persecutory hallucinations and fainting fits."[146] This profound imbalance in Jesus manifests itself perhaps most clearly and shockingly in his
relationship with God. From the very first sequence of the film, Scorsese has
Jesus experience his heavenly Father as "a predatory God,"[147] an eagle-like
creature who sinks his claws into Jesus' brain, and from whom Jesus, rather
understandably, seeks repeatedly but unsuccessfully to escape.

The radical imbalance is evident also in Jesus' unpredictable and drastic
mood shifts, from passive fear to shocking violence in words and actions and
back to total paralysis. A dramatic example occurs after Jesus, fashionably
complete with Rambo bandana on his head, violently chases the money
changers from the temple courtyard for the second time.[148] Accompanied by
Judas, he is about to storm into the temple with a furious crowd, when all of
a sudden, caught between the high-priests and the Roman soldiers, he freezes,
and has to be led away, whimpering, by his disciples. *The Last Temptation of
Christ*, like most of Scorsese's films, in fact, is very violent: intradiegetically,
extradiegetically, it pounds the viewer into submission.[149] In a film about a
psychotic, homicidal taxi driver or about a heavyweight boxing champion, the
violence may be acceptable. In a film about Jesus Christ, even based on the
novel of Kazantzakis in which the violence is minimal, it is both esthetically
and theologically inappropriate.

A Scorsesean anti-hero par excellence, a man fearful, troubled, divided
within himself, isolated from the human community, subject to hallucinations,
fainting fits, sudden mood shifts and violence, the Jesus of *The Last Temptation of Christ* fits well into Scorsese's canon and is no doubt "Scorsese's
extreme idea of a human saviour."[150] But as a reflection of the Jesus of the
Gospel, which he *is*, in spite of the protests and disclaimers of Scorsese
pleading that he is "only interpreting Nikos Kazantzakis's vision of the Messiah in one controversial novel,"[151] the Jesus of *The Last Temptation of
Christ*, even more than that of Kazantzakis, is a terrible distortion:

> His humanity and frailty are emphasized to the exclusion of any pres-
> ence, dignity, or inner strength that would lend him credibility. This Je-
> sus is simply too neurotic, tormented, and unsure of himself to be not
> only mortal but also divine."[152]

Before going on to consider the significance of what is considered by
many to be the most scandalous aspect of the film, the long episode of "the
last temptation," let us consider briefly and in a "theological way" several
further dimensions of the Jesus of Scorsese in the first part of the film and

reflect on how they correspond both to Kazantzakis' Jesus and to the Jesus of the Gospel and so of the Christian faith.

Scorsese creates a Jesus who misunderstands and resists his messianic identity, who "tries to evade God's call by taking up the most odious profession possible for a Jew,"[153] that of making crosses for Roman executions, an ambivalent figure, perturbed by confusion and indecision about his mission and destiny. In this, he is quite faithful to Kazantzakis. Today, almost all theologians justly admit some degree of gradualness in Jesus' coming to understand his identity and mission: it would be theologically untenable, for example, to pretend that Jesus as an infant had full knowledge and understanding that he was the incarnation of the Eternal Word of God. If we take seriously the incarnation of God in Jesus of Nazareth, we must also accept that like every other human being, Jesus matured in his understanding of who he was and of what he was to do, that he grew, as the Gospel says, in "wisdom and grace and age before the eyes of God and man" (Lk 2:52). The problem is that Scorsese is not content with a simple growth of awareness in his Jesus. Evidently that is not dramatic or extreme enough for the Scorsesean anti-hero. So he has his Jesus oppose his own divine identity and vocation, a rather typically post-Freudian, late twentieth-century position, unlikely in first-century Palestine, and certainly unacceptable to any serious theologian or believing Christian. Regarding Jesus' messianic mission, no respectable theologian would "go so far as to say that Christ actively worked against it."[154]

Formulating this problem another way, Christian theology has since its beginning maintained that Jesus Christ is, at one and the same time, fully God and fully human. The Council of Chalcedon, of which Scorsese knows and speaks intelligently,[155] solemnly defined that belief as true and as an article of faith. On the one hand Scorsese does not deny the divinity of Jesus, that is, his being God. In fact, as we have seen, he affirms it. On the other hand though, Scorsese shows Jesus violently resisting God, trying to escape from God and God's influence. Trying, that is, to escape from himself. This, for the believing Christian, and logically for Scorsese, is erroneous. As one theologian puts it, "theologically it is untenable that Christ should be portrayed as . . . running away from God when he himself is intimately united to that very Godhead."[156]

A further serious theological problem with the Jesus of *The Last Temptation of Christ* has to do with his rapport with the disciples. In this matter, Kazantzakis is much closer to the biblical evidence and Scorsese diverges widely from both Kazantzakis and the gospels. The Jesus of the Gospel calls each of his disciples individually and by name, a crucial point, and together they establish a community of love, in which he teaches them, observes and comments on their behavior, and entrusts to them his mission. The Gospel Jesus, in a certain sense, needs the disciples, and his relationship with them is rich, varied and mutually beneficial. In Scorsese, Jesus does not call the disciples by name. In a strange scene on the shore of a lake, Jesus, flanked by Judas who, in a reversal of the biblical protocol, has already chosen him, stares very intensely at the sons of Zebedee as they clean their nets. They, of course, immediately leave all and follow him. Group apostolic vocation by hypnosis, is both humanly and theologically unacceptable. Then as Jesus and the first disciples walk across the countryside, Scorsese edits in a series of lap dissolves "to multiply Jesus's disciples as he gains followers."[157] This is evangelization by magic and facile cinematic effects; here there is no question of personal call and response, no question of human liberty, and certainly no question of grace. While Kazantzakis devotes much attention to the community of the disciples, and to their individual contacts with Jesus, Scorsese's disciples – "small-minded, spineless men . . . insubstantial . . . particular and insular"[158] – remain an almost indistinct mass, with apparently little contact among themselves and no significant contact with Jesus. Which seems to be quite alright with this Jesus, for the interior conflict that Scorsese gives him is "a solitary struggle that never goes beyond self-scrutiny, not a communal experience to be shared."[159]

It is not entirely true, however, to say that Jesus' struggle is solitary. Scorsese gives him Judas. "Almost invariably at Jesus's side, Jesus's symbiotic second self,"[160] Scorsese's Judas, different from that of Kazantzakis, usurps Peter's role[161] as leader, and John's as "beloved disciple."[162] As in most of the films in the Scorsese canon, including the most recent *Casino,* in which the male bonding is the most profoundly dynamic, also in *The Last Temptation of Christ*, "passion principally exists between men, whether expressed through love or brutality; here it is basically the love that passes between Jesus and Judas,"[163] and so it ought to be no surprise that the betrayer's kiss in Gethsemane is "a desperate kiss of love."[164] Theirs is a "combative relationship,"[165] often violent both verbally, physically and especially psychologically: "Judas and Jesus together, moreover, constitute a psychodrama [that is] bloody and self-destructive."[166] From the outset, Scorsese provides extradiegetical evidence of Judas' domination: Harvey Keitel physique, thick muscular body, red Afro-style hair and beard, easily overpowers a rather wimpy-looking Dafoe, as does his strong voice and tough guy New York accent. Repeatedly Scorsese places Judas (Keitel) in the dominant position in compositions, as in the episode of the call of the sons of Zebedee, with Jesus (Defoe) below or to the side. Often Scorsese has Judas precede Jesus and walk with more determined strides than he. Evidently, the outcome of the Jesus-Judas psychodrama is the further diminishment, the moral and spiritual destruction, of the character of Jesus.

The Bible speaks of Jesus as the Way, the Truth and the Life, Son of the Living God, Wonder Counselor, Light of the World, Prince of Peace. Christian theology speaks of him as the Eschatological Prophet, Eternal Word of God, Alpha and Omega, the Beginning and the Consummation of the Universe. Non-Christian religions and even secular thought, while rejecting his divinity, consider Jesus a great prophet, a peacemaker, a revolutionary thinker, a champion of the poor and oppressed, a liberator, a great moral and spiritual leader. Scorsese, while insisting Jesus is divine and the Christ, creates a film image of him that has little of the divine and the Christ. Scorsese's all-too-human portrait of Jesus misses the mark,

> . . . by not supplying a convincing portrait of his spiritual leadership . . .
> It is difficult to believe this man did enough to distinguish himself from the would-be prophets and saviors running around at the same time, much less that he would save the world.[167]

If in the beginning of this chapter, we downplayed the importance of the controversial "last temptation" sequence, to seek the weakness of the Scorsese's film elsewhere, let us now return to that much-discussed passage, first to clarify some serious misunderstandings about it, and secondly to demonstrate how it does, in fact, have a further negative effect on the film and on the image of Jesus therein.

Among the misunderstandings about this passage is the conception of its length, relative to the rest of the film. The commonly-held notion is that the "last temptation" sequence is very long, that it "occupies about one third of the three hour film,"[168] thus creating a serious imbalance in style and content. In fact the film is about one hundred and sixty minutes long,[169] and the final episode is approximately thirty minutes long, and so occupies one fifth, twenty percent, of the film. This is twice the length of the "last temptation" episode in Kazantzakis' novel. Scorsese streamlines the content of the episode, for example he mercifully removes all references to the apostle-evangelist Matthew, already busy writing his "gospel" about whose falsified "revisionist" content Jesus complains bitterly.[170] But at the same time, Scorsese slows down considerably the rhythm of the "last temptation" episode.

A second and more significant objection often voiced is that the "last temptation" episode is not clearly distinguished from the rest of the film as a fantasy- or dream-sequence.[171] This objection is simply erroneous and evinces either bad will or extremely underdeveloped film appreciation skills. Scorsese makes it quite clear both at the beginning and at the end of that sequence, that he is shifting registers, away from objective reality – Jesus on the cross – and then later back to that reality. At the outset, as the temptation is about to begin, Scorsese bleeds out the very dense sounds of the music and the shouts of the crowd, while continuing to show their violent gestures; very eerie, this first total silence of the film. The visuals of Jesus coming down from the cross and entering the earthly paradise have a languorous unearthly dream tone, an effect underlined by the highly elliptic quality of the editing: Jesus "ages" perhaps forty-five years in twenty minutes. The "reality" thus portrayed is clearly subjective and unhistorical, an illusion. Scorsese's return to reality at the end of the "last temptation" sequence is more violent and thus even more clear. The shouting of the crowds and the dense and violent music kicks in very suddenly, and equally suddenly Jesus is back on the cross: the fantasy-temptation is over.

The third and most common objection to this passage is that it shows a Jesus not only interested in sex but rather more than usually active therein, as he effects two marriages, one adultery, and has a flock of children. The "last temptation" then, would be sexual. The critics are unanimously in agreement that this is not Scorsese's intention: a woman film critic says: "Whatever else this Jesus may be after, it's not sex,"[172] and a male Catholic theologian slightly more cautiously says that "the temptation is not primarily sexual."[173] In the temptation scene then, Scorsese represents:

> Jesus [who] imagines what might have been. The temptation is to ordinariness, the domestic ordinariness and family happiness of spouse, children and quietly growing old – the avoidance of the heroic call to be for others, to self-sacrifice.[174]

The text of the film clearly insists that the fantasy is not spontaneous in Jesus but rather conjured up by Satan, in the form of the young girl, a guardian angel" who appears at the foot of the cross and then accompanies Jesus,

> . . . who seeks to trick him into forsaking his Messianic mission . . . to convince the suffering and celibate Christ at the moment of his ultimate sacrifice that his destiny was not to be the savior of mankind, but rather an ordinary married Jew with a family.[175]

However, even if we accept the "last temptation" episode as a fantasy-day-dream about domesticity, it is still shocking to see Jesus with three different women, quite calmly being unfaithful and committing adultery, living and fathering children in a relaxed *ménage à trois*. It is interesting that in this last detail, Scorsese, perhaps without realizing it, is picturing a custom common in Muslim culture, in which up to four wives are licit, but strictly forbidden in first-century Israel.

A final comment regarding Jesus and sex: though Scorsese represents his protagonist as being tempted to live out his sexuality, the gospels offer no evidence in the matter. It is just the opposite. The Gospel makes it clear that Jesus lived his sexuality within the option of celibacy, in a personally-integrated, socially-liberating manner. Clearly such an option does not make for popular cinema. Is it just possible, that in their sexually-active fantasy-Jesus, Scorsese and Kazantzakis could be projecting their own, and a typically twentieth-century, preoccupation? Is it possible, as one critic suggests, that *"Temptation* is a working out of Scorsese's demons, not Christ's?"[176] Perhaps a more telling objection to the "last temptation" episode, if we are to believe its basic logic, would be to the quality of the existence that Jesus leads in his own fantasy world. Scorsese creates a strange, lethargic Jesus, a lackluster, inert figure,[177] whose actions and attitudes are a vague echo of those of the zombie-like Lazarus after he is raised from the dead. He shows little real human passion or love in any of his three relationships and he grasps onto his children, as if he needs them more than they need him.

In the conclusion of the film, Scorsese's Jesus returns to the cross and achieves his final victory, which in Christian theological terms is also the salvation of the world, the victory of the whole creation, but only because he is once again shamed into action by Judas. This confirms what is perhaps the most serious doctrinal lapse of the film, namely that "only through the efforts of Judas . . . is the establishment of Christianity made possible."[178] The expression on Jesus' bloodied face in the concluding shot of the film as he says, "It is consummated," has nothing of the sense of the cosmic moral-spiritual victory that it should be announcing. A disturbing, masochistic grin, it would be more appropriate on the face of a heavyweight boxing champion after winning a title fight. Perhaps the film should have as its title "Raging Messiah."[179]

The greatest specific challenge to any director making a Jesus-film is how to represent Christ's Resurrection. The Bible does not describe it, but rather records its effects, its aftermath. Christian tradition makes it a crucial article of faith: the Resurrection is the confirmation of the cosmic victory of God-in-Jesus over death and sin and thus, a confirmation of the divinity of Jesus. It is not a historical event in the strict sense that it was witnessed by someone and so there are no precedents for its portrayal. Theology speaks of Christ's Resurrection as a meta-historical event, a reality beyond the traditional material, physiological, psychological categories, and so, by definition an event impossible to represent materially.

Scorsese's solution to the problem is most original. First of all, he admits all the above difficulties and courageously refuses the facile and unsatisfactory "solutions" of most other Jesus-films. Then he offers a kind of abstract-symbolic interpretation of the Resurrection, presenting a rapid montage, "a burst,"[180] of flashing colored lights, of blue, green, red, orange, with yellow and white dominating.[181] Lasting eighteen seconds, with vigorous drum music and the ringing of joyous, jubilant church bells in the background, it comes very close to effectively suggesting the Resurrection.[182] But two elements, one of which Scorsese could have easily avoided, subvert the power of this Resurrection montage. In the sequence, there are several glances of pieces of sprocketed film: a material element in this abstract poetry of Resurrection, they confuse and distract. Then, in the background of the music and church bells, Scorsese maintains the shrill wailing of female voices begun in the final shot of the crucifixion scene. Had this sound of death faded out after several seconds, Scorsese's Resurrection might have worked.

Perhaps, the most surprising and innovative dimension of Scorsese's *The Last Temptation of Christ,* and something noted by very few of the critics, is that it represents Jesus subjectively: "Only the Scorsese film offers a subjective Jesus."[183] Repeatedly, Scorsese represents the reality of events as Jesus himself perceives them. Repeatedly, the viewer sees and hears things with the eyes and ears of Jesus. Privy to his innermost thoughts and feelings, Scorsese has the viewer assume his point of view.

A thematic and stylistic pattern well established in the *auteur*-Scorsese's work, most evident perhaps in *Taxi Driver* and *Raging Bull,* and the basic organizational pattern of his recent *Casino,*[184] this subjective point-of-view dominates *The Last Temptation* from the outset: "the entire film is a kind of extended interior monologue of the man coming to terms with himself."[185] The very first words of Jesus, as he grovels in the dust under the attack of the predatory God, are in fact his most intimate thoughts, heard in voice-over, which reveal him as "pained, awkward and self-analytical in these early moments."[186] In the temptations in the desert scenes, we are "in" Jesus' mind and feelings. In his early scene with Mary Magdalene, we are almost embarrassingly privy to his experience of "guilt, sorrow and even longing,"[187] and before the gaping black hole of Lazarus' tomb, we share the almost unbearable tension of Jesus' silent but monumental struggle with death.

Scorsese creates this high subjectivity of Jesus in large part through the interior monologue, but also by having his physical presence dominate the screen, a very different approach from that of Kazantzakis who devotes extensive scenes to the disciples and others. In the film, Jesus is present in all but five scenes: "This almost total occupation of the screen is the precondition of the film's intensely subjective feel."[188] This dominant presence of Jesus is supported by "a battery of devices suggesting interiorisation, full and semi-subjective point-of-view shots . . . travelling point-of-view shots taken from unstable hand-held cameras, registering highly emotive situations,"[189] all of which dramatise his subjectivity. With consummate skill, Scorsese even creates instances of aural subjectivity, for example "the sounds of everything but the water bleeding away when Jesus meets the Baptist,"[190] the horrifying buzzing of flies at the open tomb of Lazarus, the sudden silence to indicate the beginning of Jesus' last temptation and the shocking return of the violent ambient noise, when Jesus conquers the temptation and returns to die on the cross.

The Jesus-film tradition, even in its finest creations, limits itself almost exclusively to objective portrayals of Jesus, to seeing and hearing him as others see him, as fascinating and challenging as that can be. A tradition that wants to portray only the divinity of Jesus, even if in a reductionistic way, that is, by interpreting this divine dimension as material power and majesty, aloofness and distance, human perfection, it avoids dealing seriously with the Incarnation of God, with Jesus' humanity in all the limitations of that humanity. Scorsese takes up a considerable challenge: "To subjectivize Christ is to release questions . . . disrupting traditional representations, in which the primary question is how others relate to Christ not how he related to himself."[191] In daring to do so, Scorsese is creating a kind of cinematographic parallel of the fascinating branch of christology that investigates the question of the self-consciousness of Jesus, the thematic of his gradually maturing understanding of his identity, of his relationship with the Father, and of the mission of salvation he was to accomplish.

If the creation of *The Last Temptation of Christ* was a challenge for Scorsese, then the experience of it is certainly a challenge for the serious viewer. We are accustomed to hearing Jesus' words and seeing his actions, first in the Bible and then in film. We are not at all accustomed to being privy to his interior life, his thoughts, his joys, his fears, his temptations. That the Jesus of Scorsese dances and laughs is surprising. That he experiences fear in Gethsemane, we are used to. But that he struggles regularly with temptations, and that uncertainty and anxiety are part of his everyday life, is not easy for the Christian to accept. Further, that this interior monologue, troubled, filled with anxiety and pain, be dominant in the film, that this "interiorised voice of Jesus" regularly interrupt events "in a typically unstable interrogatory form,"[193] gives the film a moral and stylistic density that is very difficult to deal with.

After all is said and done, it seems clear that the fatal weakness of *The Last Temptation*'s subjective Jesus is in the film-maker's anthropology. Scorsese's Jesus is weak, uncertain and riddled by guilt. He is fascinated, even pleased, by his own suffering, at times seeking it out, clearly indicating dimensions of neurotic masochism. He moves with high energy though phases of frenetic activity, aggressive preaching, and violent criticism of the authorities, and then he falls into periods of passivity, impotence, depression, clearly symptoms of a manic-depressive psychosis. His human relationships are without freedom and strangely imbalanced. He dominates all the apostles except Judas, by whom he lets himself be dominated. His relationships with women are marked by confused feelings of guilt and desire that in the end are never resolved even minimally. Scorsese's Jesus shifts repeatedly in his understanding and acceptance of his divine identity, as if there were a profound and unbridgeable gap between his humanity and his being the Son of God. This creates a theological problem. While it is theologically acceptable to say that Jesus of Nazareth at some point struggled with his identity, it is theologically unacceptable to represent him as having never arrived at a point of serene self-understanding and integration. Scorsese's Jesus, who imagines God as a violent, rapacious bird of prey who pursues and attacks him, obliging him to do and to be something he does not want, manifests serious symptoms of paranoid schizophrenia.

In spite of Scorsese's written disclaimer before even the title and the opening credits of the film[194] – "This film is not based on the Gospels. It is only a fantasy research on the eternal conflicts of the spirit" – this is a film about Jesus the Christ. And Jesus the Christ is the figure on whose life, death and Resurrection Western civilization is based. For the Christian, and thus for Scorsese, who insists on his Catholic faith, Jesus is not just another historical figure, however great, but now dead and gone. For the Christian, Jesus is risen: he lives here and now, dynamic and efficacious, in every human being and in every dimension of human culture and civilization. In *The Last Temptation of Christ*, Scorsese represents this Jesus the Christ not only with a low christology, but with a very low anthropology, so low that he almost ceases to be normally human. The kind of operation made by Scorsese "applied to a figure who, for the Christian world, represents the Son of God, the apex of religious impulse, is absolutely unacceptable."[195]

5

Two Recent Classics: *Jesus of Nazareth* and *The Messiah*

Jesus of Nazareth

Franco Zeffirelli's 1977 *Jesus of Nazareth* is different from most of the Jesus-films treated in this book. It was conceived as a film primarily for television, and as a result, it exists in three versions, two for television – a shorter version of six and a half hours, usually shown in two parts and a longer version of eight hours, divided into four parts – and the third, further abridged version, for the cinema.[1] A British-Italian co-production[2] for NBC Television, it was produced by Sir Lew Grade at a cost of $18,000,000.00.[3] With a major music score by Maurice Jarre, a script by Anthony Burgess, and a "star-packed"[4] international cast, it met with immediate success,[5] a long-lasting success when one realizes that in many countries, *Jesus of Nazareth* has been broadcast twice yearly, at Christmas and Easter, since 1977, and has drawn most respectable segments of the viewing audience on those occasions. Given this exceptional success with the world-wide public, and given its distinctive style, it does not surprise then that from some critics, *Jesus of Nazareth* has received a very good press: "directed with such restraint, beauty, and obvious sincerity that it stood as something of a revelation in comparison to the many previous versions of the Savior's life,"[6] Zeffirelli's film is considered by many "the finest adaptation of Jesus's life ever made."[7]

Jesus of Nazareth, probably because of its ongoing popularity with the television public, is also the most widely-marketed Jesus-film ever made. Consider the evolution of the film and of the industry of spin-off products that it has inspired. The film itself was made in three basic versions, the television version of which is regularly re-marketed every Christmas and Easter. The film was also issued in regular video cassettes and then in a didactic video version, subdivided into sections of twenty-five minutes or so, for use in Catholic catechetical work: this latter version spawned a devotional-catechetical study guide for the cassettes.[8] A glossy and expensive "coffee table book" based on the film was published, with a minimum of text and replete with dramatic photographs, and further, the Burgess-Zeffirelli script of the film "was *novelized* by William Barclay."[9] Finally, a book of personal memoirs was published by Zeffirelli, *Il mio Gesù*, (*My Jesus*), his reflections on various aspects of the preparation, filming and post-production work on his Jesus-film.[10] Issued recently in a "Super Best Seller" series and full of superlatives – those in the book, meant to promote the film, and those on the cover, meant to promote the book – it is clearly intended as a marketing tool.

Referring to itself, perhaps only a bit presumptuously, as an "extraordinary book," "a true story, rich with humanity and religious feeling, testimony of one man's relationship with the divine," it promises to cover "every spiritual problem" met during the elaboration of the film.

This discussion of the marketing strategy developed around *Jesus of Nazareth* may seem irrelevant to a treatment of the Jesus-figure in Zeffirelli's film, but in fact as we shall see, it has much to do with kind of Jesus represented in and by the film. From the beginning *Jesus of Nazareth* was intended to be a didactic film for a mass television audience. Zeffirelli himself insists on how he finally accepted to do the film out of "moral responsibility"[11] and because he was convinced that with seven or more hours of television at his disposal, he could accomplish "a grand piece of work which would be useful to everyone, to believers and unbelievers alike."[12] And, paraphrasing his producer Vincenzo Labella, Zeffirelli goes on to explain how he believed that in a moment of general moral crisis in the West, "a crisis of all the traditional values and all the ideals, his film might make people realize how much they are losing, either stupidly or maliciously."[13] Once the work on the film got underway, Zeffirelli began to see himself not only as a moral reformer but even as a religious prophet: he said that in the film . . .

> I was interested in the possibility of telling the story fully and clearing
> up unknown areas in our faith, plus the political stories behind them. I
> felt that I was putting an end to centuries old misunderstandings about
> the Jews and Jesus, that I was destroying medieval attitudes.[14]

In keeping with the didactic intention of the film, and the corresponding desire to reach a television mass audience, Zeffirelli formulated a very middle-of-the-road approach to the biblical material at his disposal. He certainly saw the Hollywood Jesus-films, for he reacted against them. He also knew Pasolini's *The Gospel According to St. Matthew* and quite openly rejected its approach.[15] Discussing his own concept of Jesus, Zeffirelli notes the error of the Marxists in appropriating Jesus to the socialist cause,[16] a not-so-veiled reference to Pasolini's presumed Marxism and to his hard-talking, tough-acting, fast-moving, no-nonsense, no-compromise Jesus. Zeffirelli's Jesus, therefore, would require a more moderate theological approach. He must not be too human, nor too divine; he must not be a fire-and-brimstone religious reformer, nor a Messiah of the poor and suffering, nor confrontational prophet of faith that does justice. Better a "soft" Jesus, a moderate conciliatory Messiah, along classic hagiographical lines: "a consoling Jesus, who does not disturb consciences nor cause them any crisis."[17] Zeffirelli did not want a challenging Gospel of radical truth or an innovative Gospel of spiritual liberation or uncompromising love but rather a Gospel "relived in the spirit of a pre-conciliar [Vatican II] apologetic."[18]

> He does everything he can to avoid confronting himself or his audience
> with the difficult, demanding nature of his subject. For Zeffirelli the Gos-
> pel story is straightforward to the point of banality. There are no alarm-

ing implications. The resurrection is no more disturbing or important than
the waking of the sleeping princess in Walt Disney's *Sleeping Beauty*."[19]

Zeffirelli's Jesus is soft, banal because the Gospel story he represents in
Jesus of Nazareth has been thoroughly banalized, a complex operation which
in the film proceeds at multiple levels. Let us consider first the procedure of
banalization as it is manifest in the content of the film. It is certainly true that
Zeffirelli includes many of the traditional episodes of the gospels, beginning
with the betrothal of Joseph and Mary, the Annunciation, the birth of Jesus at
Bethlehem, Jesus with the elders in the Temple. He represents the baptism of
Jesus at the Jordan, the calling of the disciples and a generous series of his
healing miracles: a demoniac, a paralytic, the servant of the Roman centurion,
the man born blind; the raising of the daughter of Jairus and the great miracle
of the raising of Lazarus. Zeffirelli also represents the miraculous catch of
fish, the miracle of the multiplication of the loaves and fishes, the meeting of
Jesus with Mary Magdalene and with the rich young man and much of the
preaching of Jesus, including a number of parables, the beatitudes, the Our
Father. He depicts Peter's confession of faith, the episode of the woman taken
in adultery and the scene of Jesus chasing the money changers from the Temple. Zeffirelli devotes careful attention to the events of the passion: the Last
Supper, Gethsemane, the trial of Jesus before Pilate, the crucifixion, the depo-
sition from the cross, and in conclusion, the Resurrection.

One might get the impression from the above that Zeffirelli's representation of the Gospel story is quite complete, and quite in conformity with
the Gospel texts. But it is not so. Considering first the Gospel episodes Zeffirelli omits from his treatment, an interesting pattern begins to emerge: missing are the temptations of Jesus in the desert, the wedding at Cana, the
Transfiguration, the storm on the lake and Jesus walking on the water, the
encounters with lepers, most of the traditional dynamic of the betrayal of
Jesus by Judas, and finally, much of the physical suffering of Jesus during the
passion. Some of these omissions suggest Zeffirelli's desire to avoid representing Jesus as too divine, too transcendental, what in theology is called a
too-high christology. Others suggest that he wanted to avoid unpleasant
scenes or episodes that show Jesus too human (a too-low christology) or on
the cutting edge, in an uncompromising position.

When questioned about the omission of the temptations in the desert,
Zeffirelli said rather lamely, "In that episode, in fact, one reaches the mystery, pure and simple, and mystery in itself cannot be represented, especially
in a weak and insufficient medium like cinema,"[20] and he continued, "The
torment of Jesus [in this dialogue with Satan], too interior to be rendered
exterior, risked leading the spectator into a dangerous confusion."[21] Zeffirelli's explanation is not very logical: cinema is not capable of representing
mystery and yet he devotes a long episode of his film to representing the
great mystery of the Incarnation, the Annunciation to Mary.[22] At the end of
his statement, however, he gave away the real reason for the omission of this

and other "difficult" passages of the gospels: his desire to avoid disturbing the spectator. One critic offers a similar explanation:

> Why is Zeffirelli so frightened . . . of the Temptations in the Wilderness, of the idea of Judas betraying Christ on purpose . . . Why does he tell a story if he feels constrained to wriggle out of its way whenever it becomes uncomfortably uncompromising? He's doing for the Bible what the Reader's Digest does for novels, and it's the very inoffensiveness of the thing that ultimately makes it so offensive.[23]

Zeffirelli's alteration – he would use a word like "development" – of the Gospel is manifested in a whole series of shifts and alterations and additions to the original narrative, whose purpose clearly is to render the evangelical material less radical, mysterious, challenging, to predigest it for the viewer. For example, calling the infancy narratives a "zone of the Gospel that has need of our contribution of poetry,"[24] Zeffirelli proceeds to give a domestic tone to a whole series of episodes of this early part of the Gospel. He has Anna the mother of Mary discuss the arrangements for the wedding with Joseph, who is a fine-looking, sturdily-built young man. He places the betrothal ceremony in the village square, with the group arranged not in a tight circle as would normally be the case, but in a precise horizontal composition, with Mary, Joseph and the rabbi in the center, as if they were posing for a photographer. A further homey detail: when Mary gives Joseph a necklace and everyone in the crowd appropriately mumbles, "It's beautiful," one of the participants looks directly into the camera and with a hand-gesture more Italian than Middle-Eastern, repeats, "Beautiful!" This kind of shot, rupturing the dramatic illusion of the scene in order to play to the public, is very popular in television comedy but in a film on the life of Christ, it is quite inappropriate.

In the Annunciation scene, Zeffirelli is not satisfied to create rather artificially a sense of mystery, with light and the sound of wind and almost baroque camera angles and movements, but then, lest this mystery be too much for the public to bear, he domesticates it by having Anna wake up and, like a good "Jewish (or Italian) mother," insist on knowing what's going on. Later, again to avoid the mystery of the event, he has the local rabbi, and not an angel as in Luke's Gospel, convince Joseph not to repudiate the pregnant Mary. Then in a totally extra-evangelical, and rather sentimental episode, Zeffirelli depicts the death of Joseph who, assisted by Mary, dies praying "Into your hands I commend my spirit," from Psalm 31.

With the calling of the disciples, Zeffirelli gives full play to his imagination. Wanting to suggest a St. John capable of writing the most theological of the gospels, Zeffirelli makes him "an intellectual . . . the only one."[25] He has Jesus interview John before issuing the call to discipleship, an interview by which we discover that John has been away studying. Zeffirelli makes the disciple Thomas a servant of Jairus, who on witnessing the great miracle, speaks with Jesus and follows him. In both cases, Zeffirelli's fantasy-changes temper the radical nature of the event. Regarding Mary Magdalene's meeting with Jesus, Zeffirelli, disregarding the fact that there is no evidence in the gospels that she is a prostitute, has her return home only to be teased and provoked by the vulgar neighborhood toughs. When she reacts in kind, one of her neighbors, sensing Magdalene's desire to reform, tells her about this Jesus who is all forgiving, and the woman determines to meet him. Later on Calvary, Zeffirelli makes Magdalene want to come to the foot of the cross with Mary. When the soldiers impede her, Mary, the mother of Jesus, insists she is a "member of the family" and gets her by. Evidently having Mary tell a lie, while certainly non-biblical, is not a problem for Zeffirelli. In other "developed" passages, John visits Mary, Jesus meets Barabbas and tries to convert him and Mary arrives in Jerusalem for the Passover with the Nazareth rabbi.

Perhaps the most original "development" in *Jesus of Nazareth*, certainly the one most noted by the critics, is the creation *ex novo* of the Temple priest, Zerah. This invention of Zeffirelli[26] seems to have the sole function of deflecting from the historical-biblical characters of the film the responsibility for Jesus' death, in short, the function of absolving the biblical Jews, that is Judas and the Jewish people of Jerusalem. Without going into all the details, it is clear that Zerah, who is shown to be "on good terms with virtually everyone in the Gospels,"[27] manipulates a "well-intentioned Judas"[28] into handing over Jesus and then he betrays Judas. In the end, Zeffirelli's Judas is a victim, not a villain.[29] Zerah is also the key figure at the meeting of the Sanhedrin (Jn 11:46-57), reconstructed fictitiously by Zeffirelli. During the debate, both Joseph of Arimathea and Nicodemus defend Jesus while Caiaphas presents theological arguments against him. Finally, in spite of the protests of Joseph and Nicodemus, it is Zerah who, with astute political argumentation, ends the debate against Jesus. The conclusion to be drawn is that Zerah is to blame and that many good Jews did not want Jesus' death. Zerah is present at the betrayal and arrest of Jesus, and at his trial before the religious tribunal, where once again, he counters the extra-evangelical defense of Jesus by Arimathea and Nicodemus, and sends him off to Pilate. Before Pilate, it is Zerah, of whom Pilate is fearful, who intervenes strongly against Jesus and thus reverses "Pilate's lack of interest in bringing about the crucifixion."[30] When in the "Ecce homo" scene, many in the crowd call for the liberation of Barabbas and the crucifixion of Jesus, a number of voices are heard calling for the release of Jesus, "a just man," clearly a non-evangelical detail, subtly inserted by Zeffirelli, again to attenuate the Gospel's blaming of the Jews.[31] "In Zeffirelli's Judea no one's to blame. Except Zerah. Without Zerah, Christ would never have reached the cross."[32]

A further problem with *Jesus of Nazareth,* one that ultimately has a negative effect on the film's Jesus, is the fact that it is structured according to the norms of television drama, and with a view to later compartmentalization into didactic video cassettes. This has a disastrous effect on the film in its version for the cinema. In general, the narrative is very carefully structured into brief, self-contained scenes, following upon one another in rapid succession, and each one carefully connected to the preceding and following ones by narrative and thematic bridges. One has the impression of a flawless organic development of the "story," very pleasing and reassuring in a fictional adventure film or love story, but unacceptable in a film that deals with the life and passion and death of Jesus the Christ. In *Jesus of Nazareth* every detail of the narrative is explained, prepared for, followed up and predigested for the viewer. There remain none of the crucial ellipses of the biblical text, none of its mystery, none of its radical questions to, and demands on the reader. Thus the film is rather like a typical television show.

With nothing in the film that shocks or challenges, either in content or in style, the viewing public of *Jesus of Nazareth* does not have to make an effort to understand or appreciate the film, as they do for the films of Rossellini and Pasolini, and, for different reasons, for the film of Scorsese. The large number of important characters in Zeffirelli's film, for example, is never a problem for the viewer. These are all more or less of the same importance dramatically in the economy of the tale. They are all given a minimum of characterization and human interest, often entirely original with Zeffirelli's version (John's intellectualism, Judas' naivete, Joseph's remarkably good character), and each character is smoothly woven into the plot in easy harmony with all the others. Zerah is the obvious example: he is so carefully inserted in the plot that most viewers do not even suspect his alien nature. Lulled into lethargic acquiescence, they simply presume he is one of the original biblical characters.

In *Jesus of Nazareth*, nowhere is there even the breath of excess or exaggeration, for everything is in good taste. All the apostles and other major characters are good-looking, if not downright beautiful, and pleasing physically. There are no lepers to be seen, Magdalene's unbiblical pre-conversion activities are only discretely suggested, a minimum of sacred blood is shed during the passion, and the *via crucis* and crucifixion are tastefully brief and relatively nonviolent.

Franco Zeffirelli began his career in show business as a successful scene designer and later director for the lyric opera. He learned his craft very well – the "wise virtue of the 'illustrator' or 'scene designer'"[33] – a fact evident in all his films, and certainly not lacking in *Jesus of Nazareth*, regarding which one critic speaks of the "exceptional esthetic refinement."[34] More specifically, the photography of Zeffirelli's film reveals this talent. First there are the powerful close-ups of famous faces: the great Laurence Olivier, in the full maturity of his powers as the just man Nicodemus; Anne Bancroft, as Magdalene, righteously angry when the disciples dismiss her account of the Resurrection; the handsome young Greek actor, Yorgo Voyagis, as a very Hebrew-Palestinian Joseph, with jet black hair and side curls; and especially, the quite spectacular first view of the young Virgin Mary, the perfectly-featured, definitely-Caucasian Olivia Hussey who, first half-hidden behind the threads of her weaving loom but then, accompanied by a cresting wave of music, rises dramatically[35] to reveal the breathtaking splendor of her refined beauty. Apart from the dramatic close-ups, Zeffirelli's photography is also characterized by the "very studied quality of the compositions,"[36] in which, one French critic gushes, "Zeffirelli reaches the level of the painterly masterpieces of the Renaissance tradition."[37] Particularly able with group compositions, Zeffirelli also deals well with more limited pictures, as evidenced by the spectacular chiaroscuro effects of the Annunciation scene, the perfect balance of the image of the betrothal ceremony, and the long shots of the Last Supper scene, clearly inspired by Rembrandt.

Regarding famous faces, we discussed in the previous chapter how Nicholas Ray overloaded his *The Greatest Story Ever Told* with well-known actors in major and even minor roles, thus creating a fatal imbalance. We also have noted in this chapter how Zeffirelli wanted at all costs to avoid the errors and excesses of the Hollywood Jesus-films. And yet he falls right into the trap. If anything, *Jesus of Nazareth* has even more big names than Ray's failed epic. They include: Anne Bancroft, James Mason, Ernest Borgnine, Laurence Olivier, James Farentino, Claudia Cardinale, James Earl Jones, Stacy Keach, Donald Pleasence, Michael York, Christopher Plummer, Fernando Rey, Anthony Quinn, Ralph Richardson, Rod Steiger, Peter Ustinov, Cyril Cusack, Ian Holm, Ian McShane and Olivia Hussey.[38] Clearly Zeffirelli's "unfortunate decision to use 'name' actors"[39] is one of the major flaws of his film, and one of the major reasons for the perceived weakness of his Jesus. The character of Jesus ought to stand out morally and dramatically. Zeffirelli's Jesus gets lost "in the shuffle" of "guest stars."[40]

Beyond the photography and the stable of stars, the spectacular quality and box-office success of the film is guaranteed by Zeffirelli's truly impresario coordination of the impressive Moroccan landscapes and locations, the crowds of extras, the carefully-designed and coordinated costumes, and the rich musical score which swells appropriately and always tastefully to punctuate crucial moments. The "dreamlike landscapes, these movements of huge crowds, the decor, extraordinary and yet paradoxically so close to the real, give to the entire work an impact and a credibility never achieved in the many films of this genre."[41]

Impact and credibility, there certainly is, but their quality is that of fiction, not of biblical fact. A self-conscious quality of fiction, a tone of self-aware theatricality pervades the entire film, and in the end gives it a fatally unreal, densely baroque texture.[42] The self-consciousness clearly affects the performances of the gallery of stars appearing in the film:

> One could see from the first frame that everyone in this technicolour never-never land was fully aware of their massive cultural, historical and pictorial importance. People in biblical epics always seem to know there's a camera on them.[43]

A good example of the theatricality of *Jesus of Nazareth* are the very filmic zooms into close-ups on the faces of principal actors in crucial moments, a technique that dominates television soap operas. Another is the utter theatricality of Olivier's voice-over recitation of the suffering servant song from Isaiah during the crucifixion, as if Zeffirelli did not trust the dramatic intensity of the images to carry the meaning. There are also the illusion-rupturing words of actors-characters spoken to the camera, and so to the viewer: "major actors drawing attention to themselves in minor roles."[44] These elements, plus the perfect coordination of the costumes, the total appropriateness of every note of the Maurice Jarre music score, and the virtuoso composition and filming of many scenes, such as the Annunciation, all draw attention to themselves as fiction rather than to the very real mystery of the life, death and Resurrection of Jesus the Christ they are meant to represent.

The problem with the self-conscious, fictional quality of *Jesus of Nazareth*'s precise design, esthetic refinement, balanced beauty and careful coordination, quite appropriate in a La Scala or Metropolitan Opera production of *Aida* or *Don Giovanni*, is that in a film, and especially a film on Jesus of Nazareth, based on the lean, elliptical, challenging, tough text and style of the gospels, it translates into dramatic artificiality, meant, rather like a Hallmark Easter card, "to be decorative, to look pleasing and tasteful."[45] Perhaps in Grand Opera, Zeffirelli's training ground, more is better: more color, more music, more crowds, more beautiful faces and more dramatic dialogue. But the "more" of *Jesus of Nazareth*, though it is carefully-created and tastefully-coordinated, is definitely not better. Rather, it transforms the prophetic biblical content and themes into popular spectacle, that brings favorable reactions from what one critic calls "the mass of the believers-consumers,"[46] but that is void of authentic artistic and religious impact. In the end, as it was perhaps in the beginning, Zeffirelli's film is "a great spectacular work, graced with all the prerequisites imposed by the mass media, able to impose itself on the worldwide cinema and television markets."[47]

Some critics who liked *Jesus of Nazareth* defend it by insisting, as does Leandro Castellani, that it "provided an authentic spiritual experience to a huge number of television viewers in the whole world."[48] But in fact, to qualify a $28,000,000, eight-hour television spectacular, broadcast to hundreds of millions of people, as a "authentic spiritual experience," is at least exaggerated, if not simply unacceptable. Castellani seems to sense this problem, for he then tempers his first enthusiastic statement, saying that "the proposed religious experience [of *Jesus of Nazareth*] is perhaps in low-key compared to the lesson in religious culture that it offers.[49] A Catholic priest and critic, taking his cue from the argument for the indisputable right of the masses to authentic spiritual experience, says with evident irony:

> Is it not clear that the masses have need of the Sacred? And what could be better than a Jesus brought down to a level accessible to the masses? What better than a Jesus become spectacle? While always, of course, showing great respect for the [biblical] texts.[50]

Yet does *Jesus of Nazareth* indeed show such a great respect for the biblical texts? Zeffirelli's film is based mainly on the Gospel of John, but even a superficial study of the dialogue indicates that there is a wide variety of words spoken in the film. There are words taken from the gospels and there are words similar to those in the gospels, but "taken from their context, manipulated, summarized or changed."[51] Then there are words taken from "extra-evangelical [apocryphal] historical sources and elaborated with an even greater liberty than those from the Gospels"[52] and finally there are "many other words, the fruit of fantasy or invention."[53] Typical viewers inevitably get lost in the confusion of words, and in the end presume they are all biblical, and therefore that what they are seeing is a faithful version of the biblical accounts.[54] In this massive manipulation of the biblical texts, Zeffirelli clearly had in mind a didactic approach to the world-wide television audience for which his film was destined, a popular audience in which he cannot presume a biblical culture nor a particular desire to acquire such a culture.

It is with a didactic purpose that Zeffirelli, for example, has his text give information that the typical viewer might need but is not contained in the Gospel. Thus he leveled "the way towards a facile understanding of things that in themselves are not easy to grasp."[55] It is with the same didactic purpose that Zeffirelli edits the more difficult discourses of Jesus, lightens the longer and heavier scenes by dividing them up and adding "human interest" sequences such as the rabbi of Nazareth who congratulates Joseph on the occasion of Jesus' bar mitzvah, and introduces moments of humor. The problem with this operation of didactic "adjustment" or simplification is that the "resulting 'sense of reality' is really the product of many [filmic] tricks which work together to create a '*trompe l'oeil*' effect."[56]

Jesus of Nazareth explains itself. It presents to the viewers within its very text, made up of words, images, music and narrative structures, a predetermined meaning, a pre-digested interpretation[57] which renders the audience benevolent and passive, if not lethargic. At the same time, it "tends to exhaust the whole context [of the biblical scene], giving no space to other possible interpretations,"[58] and reduces the radical, challenging nature of the sacred text to the level of pseudo-naturalistic, popular mass media drama.[59]

The last thing one should impute to Franco Zeffirelli is bad will. Quite clearly he wanted to make a good film, one which genuinely communicated the person and the message of the Jesus Christ in whom he openly professes faith. Earlier in this chapter, we made reference to a book of memoirs written by Zeffirelli concerning the making of *Jesus of Nazareth*. This little book, which we shall now discuss briefly, is a valuable document for two reasons: on the one hand it is an eloquent testimony to Zeffirelli's deep faith and personal and professional sincerity, and on the other, it inadvertently provides the explanation for some of the radical limitations of the film.

The basic point we wish to make here is that the book, *Il mio Gesù*, provides evidence that Zeffirelli, whose professional commitment was to film a life of Christ in didactic style that would be "in some sense useful to all,"[60] in fact from the beginning had some rather strange and very subjective notions of the project and of himself in relation to the project, which reduced his objectivity, his ability to take artistic distance from the work, his perspective and his ability to judge and to be critical. Early on Zeffirelli began to see the film project as a kind of personal divinely-ordained mission to act as a prophet for the new generation, to reveal the truth and wonder of Jesus Christ in a new and convincing way, to perform "an act of love towards Christ."[61] In the book, he speaks of his experience of making this film as "my road to Damascus,"[62] thus comparing himself to St. Paul and his film to an experience of the Risen Christ. Entering further into subjective isolation, Zeffirelli rejects biblical and theological experts who might criticize his way of seeing things and suggests that he is among those who have their minds "open to the things of the Spirit."[63]

Not only this, but if we are to believe Zeffirelli's account, once the production work began on the film, it acquired the dimensions of a religious experience for him. He speaks almost mystically of "the star that certainly guided all of us,"[64] thus imagining himself as one of the Magi, and logically his film as the Christ Child, and again confirming his role as a prophet. Repeatedly in the book, Zeffirelli suggests the presence of divine providence behind the scenes of the film, manifesting itself quasi-miraculously in moments of difficulty and crisis, thus giving his *Jesus of Nazareth* a status second only to the gospels themselves in divine inspiration. This pseudo-inspired status seems to account for the aura of exaggerated sanctity with which he surrounds the characters of Mary and Joseph, all of it the fruit of his imagination. For example, it is not enough to maintain that Joseph was "a very pious man";[65] Zeffirelli has to insist that after "the visit of the Magi, all [Joseph's] doubt vanished."[66] His prophetic self-assurance seems to justify Zeffirelli's rather wide poetic licence with the infancy narratives and his elaborate didactic strategy for Mary and Joseph:

> I used the story of Joseph and Mary to represent the true nature of the Jewish people and at the same time to reveal our pitiful and shameful distance from a world of purity and values which inspired the thoughts and the actions of Jesus' contemporaries.[67]

Perhaps the greatest casualty of this sentimental-mystical confusion in Zeffirelli was the figure of Jesus as interpreted by Robert Powell. Originally intended for the role of Judas, Powell was given the role of Jesus after a screen test which became for Zeffirelli almost a sign from on high that the English actor was divinely ordained for a more important role. Perhaps Zeffirelli's lack of objectivity is no more evident that in the following statement about that "providential" screen test:

> We became aware that something was happening that made us think of a miracle, almost a "transport, a transformation of the material" as if spontaneously around this man [Powell] was forming itself an image of which he was the medium. Even more impressive was a kind of light "not his" which was moving into him.[68]

Zeffirelli seems to see in Powell the divine dimension of his protagonist, a mysterious quality which he senses especially in the eyes and voice of the English actor:

> Powell's eyes, which are the doors to the spirit like no other part of the
> human body, became two intense beacons of light . . . his voice took on
> mysterious and remote echos as if it were evoking and communicating
> messages of unknown dimensions.[69]

Yet at the same time, he speaks of the importance of Jesus' being very human: "Jesus is there [by the Jordan, with the disciples] but he is so human that he cannot be recognized among the others."[70] At times, Zeffirelli seems to exaggerate the demands he places on Powell and so, on his Jesus:

> Every thing, every word, every gesture of Jesus had to manifest this double [divine/human] aspect . . . because from his every sign, from his very word, emanated the power of a superior contact with God, a contact between God, him, and earthly things.[71]

Always humbly, Zeffirelli relies on his own talents as director to bring about the divine revelation: "I succeeded in raising and extracting from his personality that dimension in him that was ready to speak of things divine."[72]

Though some of the critics are almost totally negative toward *Jesus of Nazareth*, it would be exaggerated not to recognize several undeniable merits of Zeffirelli's film. First of all, there is no doubt that compared to the Hollywood spectacular-epic treatment of the Jesus story, *Jesus of Nazareth* shines out in its difference. Except for its cast of stars, and perhaps its rather dense music score by Maurice Jarre,[73] Zeffirelli's film has none of the heavy-handed excesses of its American cousins: no cast of thousands, no elaborately-recreated palace and temple sets, no "Grand Canyon" desert panoramas, no battle scenes justified by the zealot cause. Thanks to Zeffirelli's stage experience, most of the details of the more domestic scale of *Jesus of Nazareth* are tasteful, well-coordinated, well-shot and well-edited.

Of considerable interest, especially for those who wish to use the film as a didactic instrument, is the fact that in the long history of the Jesus-film, Zeffirelli is the first to place the story of Jesus in an "authentic, and historically justifiable, Jewish milieu."[74] After the California-surfer-Jesus of George Stevens, the Grand Canyon-Old West-Jesus of Nicholas Ray, and a variety of other culturally-anachronistic representations of Jesus, almost all of them reflecting American or at least Western European roots, the first-century Jewish-Palestinian setting of *Jesus of Nazareth* is notable. The authenticity of the Middle Eastern costumes, hair styles and domestic and social customs are particularly evident when *Jesus of Nazareth* is viewed back-to-back to Scorsese's North African and Muslim "imitation." A number of other elements give the film a certain tone of authenticity: the rabbi as a community leader and source of help and advice, the several scenes in the synagogue, the betrothal and marriage liturgies of Mary and Joseph, the bar mitzvah of Jesus and the Last Supper as a Seder liturgy. The repeated references to the Old Testament support and enhance this authenticity. Evidently much careful research went into this dimension of Zeffirelli's film and for this *Jesus of Nazareth* is to be recognized as a valuable didactic or catechetical aid, "a kind of propedeutical text . . . for those who have not read the Gospels,"[75] accompanied by orientations that modulate the sentimentally-fictional excesses of Zeffirelli which otherwise would acquire an undeserved seal of authenticity

Perhaps the greatest virtue of Zeffirelli's *Jesus of Nazareth* is its indisputable success, "the merit of having attracted the attention and the sympathy of a large number of viewers to the figure of Jesus."[76] No one disputes that it has been seen by more people world-wide than any other Jesus-film. In part this triumph is due to careful marketing, to the regular transmission of the film on television, and to the related fact that *Jesus of Nazareth*, having been made for television, works particularly well in that medium. Also responsible for its popularity is the simple fact that the film is well-made. Alluding to the criticisms of *Jesus of Nazareth* for its popular approach, one priest-film scholar asks rhetorically: "Would a simpler, more austere and less attractive approach have met with the same favorable reaction?"[77] If one is to judge by the more limited popularity of the more austere Jesus-films of Rossellini and Pasolini, the answer is clearly no.

Its merits notwithstanding, the basic problem of *Jesus of Nazareth* still remains that in opting for the popular approach aimed at a mass audience, Zeffirelli had to sacrifice subtlety, moral complexity and spiritual depth, both in the overall story, that is in the narrative of the Gospel, and in the figure of Jesus represented therein. In the elaborate didactic narrative, much of it Gospel-fiction rather than Gospel-fact, the authentic Jesus is largely absent. The Jesus who is present in the narrative remains a somewhat banal fictional hero, one element among many others. On the level of popular dramatic fiction, the character of Jesus is less interesting than many of the others, partly because the better-known actors draw attention to themselves and their characters, and partly because Zeffirelli was more free to be develop their personalities.

Zeffirelli's Jesus is a rather traditional, middle-of-the-road, somewhat conservative image of the Savior.[78] Visually, he has a strong face and expression with very intense eyes, which at times seems to have the quality of a Byzantine icon, but his real depth and intensity ends there. In his behavior, he is strong, self-assured, authoritative and charismatic, but never exaggeratedly so, for Zeffirelli also makes him kind, gentle, vulnerable. A paragon of balanced conformity, he is neither too human nor too divine; and he is certainly not demanding nor innovative nor radical in any sense. Intended for a mass television audience, Zeffirelli's Jesus does not disappoint that public: superficially characterized, rendered inoffensively, materially mysterious and sentimentally human, surrounded by attractive supporting personalities and a well-unified and smoothly-developing narrative, he is an ideal domestic Savior. In the end, however, and precisely because he is so domesticated, this Jesus has little to do with the mystery of Jesus Christ of the Gospel.

The Messiah

Roberto Rossellini's *The Messiah* is an Italian-French co-production,[79] with the substantial investment of two million dollars from the Family Theater organization of Father Patrick Peyton in the United States. Filmed in Tunisia where Rossellini had previously filmed the biblical *Acts of the Apostles*, *The Messiah* is a relatively long film at two and a half hours. Rossellini's last film, released in Italy in 1975, two years before his death, "never made it to the States,"[80] where it is still relatively unknown.[81]

To situate *The Messiah* within the canon of Rossellini's films, we must first recall that Rossellini is universally recognized as one of the most important and influential film artists of all time. An *auteur* in the full sense of the term, he is one of the creators of the film style known as neorealism. His films *Open City* (1945) and *Paisan* (1946), made in the immediate postwar period, are paragons and classics of that style, which in one way or another marked all of Rossellini's films, including *The Messiah*, made thirty years after *Open City*. Secondly, we should remember that even though Rossellini put his religious upbringing behind him, his Catholic education and the Catholicism of Italian culture had a profound influence on his films. Religious themes and elements imbue most of his work. Of his twenty-eight feature films, four have specifically religious subjects,[82] and a number of others have significant religious subtexts.[83] Thirdly, in the several years before *The Messiah*, Rossellini made a series of didactic films for television,[84] and clearly the shift towards a didactic approach, and the different exigencies of the television medium, had a conditioning influence on the style and content of *The Messiah*.

The major difference between *The Messiah* and all the Jesus-films considered so far in this book, has to do with the fact that it is part of "the didactic cycle"[85] of Rossellini, films which take a "pedagogical look at a great man in history, usually representative of an age in which some profound psychological shift in human consciousness took place."[86] Rossellini's basic idea in *The Messiah* was to represent the historical Jesus in as much as he is known from the gospels, in as objective and dispassionate a manner as possible, in order to inform the viewers, to teach who Jesus was and what he said, in order to edify them and show them the way to wisdom. This starting point, a radical break with the Jesus-film tradition, determines a number of aspects of *The Messiah*. For example, the basic tone of the film is tranquil, peaceful – "Rossellini is serene"[87] – very different from the stormy, tormented quality of Pasolini's *The Gospel According to Saint Matthew*, subject of our next chapter. Rossellini's fundamental attitude is "logical and didactic,"[88] and so before the figure of the Jesus of the Gospel, Rossellini maintains a certain distance. He observes, as it were "from above, the development of events,"[89] as opposed to Pasolini who, as we shall see, gets fully involved.

The serene tone of *The Messiah* is to a great extent determined by a further choice of Rossellini related to the didactic nature of the film, namely that of stressing more the message of Jesus than his figure, more the words of Jesus than his person. In order to bring about this shift in focus, Rossellini abandons the "traditional idea of a dramatic protagonist,"[90] and of the dramatic structure normally given to the Jesus-film. He chooses the more austere "cinema of prose,"[91] to express his ideas about Jesus, a shift away from the poetic, dramatic cinema of his earlier films (*Open City, Paisan*) and usually characteristic of the Jesus-film. In *The Messiah*, therefore, the dramatic spectacle, essential element of all the Jesus-films examined thus far, is "attenuated by the didactic intention, is purified of its negative characteristics and enriched with intellectual stimuli, thus involving the spectator not sentimentally but intellectually."[92] A further characteristic of the basic anti-dramatic, didactic austerity of *The Messiah* is Rossellini's decision to focus mainly on Jesus, on a this-worldly Jesus, eloquent preacher, wise teacher. This determines a radically different point of view for the viewer, accustomed to the divine Jesus, wonder-worker. "In wanting to guide the viewer in the search for meaning in the life of Jesus, he [Rossellini] wants the eyes to move, not towards the heights of the heavens . . . but along the surface of this dusty planet."[93]

Rossellini gives *The Messiah* a structure which promotes the priority of the word as "the absolute protagonist"[94] of the film, a structure which first of all is linear and not dramatic. There is no rising and then falling action, no suspense, no turning point or climax. There are no flashbacks, no introspective or fantasy sequences. The episodes depicted are "swift transcriptions, without any emotional emphasis or dramatic construction."[95] The temporal structure of *The Messiah* is chronological and very regular. Except for the brief prologue set in the Old Testament time of Samuel and Isaiah, the film follows the experiences of Jesus "day by day, as if it were a chronicle."[96] The linear plot structure of the film is also very elliptical, reflecting the essential nature of the Gospel texts. It does not attempt, as does the more organic, non-elliptical structure of *Jesus of Nazareth*, to fill in the gaps between episodes in the life of Jesus, to create logical and credible connections between them. The linear and elliptical structure of Rossellini's narrative makes it fast-moving, as is its figure of Jesus-the-teacher. The structure of the film thus underlines the urgency of Jesus' teaching mission.

Rossellini sees his *Messiah* as having a very straightforward, uncomplicated structure: in his own words, it is an "accurate historical reconstruction . . . of daily life, of the most normal data, into which environment is situated the event . . . everything becomes very simple."[97] However, looking at it from the outside, *The Messiah* is just a little more complex than this. The film is composed mainly of episodes from the gospels, not always connected, whose purpose is to illustrate not so much the life of Jesus but rather elements of his teaching, his doctrine. Clearly, Jesus is central, dominant, not so much as a physical or psychological presence, as he is in *The Greatest Story Ever Told* or in *The Last Temptation of Christ*, but rather more as a moral or intellectual presence, significant for what he says and does, for his being a Master.

This "saying and doing" of Jesus suggests what is a kind of double and parallel design in the didactic structure of *The Messiah*. There are the words of Jesus, spoken in a formal and slightly archaic tone, almost as if removed from the events, almost like the words of an oratorio, declaimed by actors seated on stools on an empty stage.[98] Then, parallel to these teaching words, Rossellini blends in Jesus' actions, no less didactic than his words, actions which are always performed in the concrete circumstances of the material world in which Jesus lives. His actions – and Jesus seems always to be doing something with his hands – have a double function. They anchor his otherwise perhaps too abstract words in a specific material context. At the same time, the activity of Jesus and of his followers has the effect of de-dramatizing his words, of rendering them less doctrinal and more morally efficacious. Contrasting Rossellini's film with Pasolini's on this point, the critic Luigi Bini says:

> Different from what happens in *The Gospel According to Saint Matthew* of Pasolini, in *The Messiah*, the Word does not assault. Rossellini defuses whatever dogmatic force it might have by putting it on the lips of Jesus while he is busy at carpentry work or talking to a small group.[99]

In its content, Rossellini's film "demonstrates a substantial fidelity to the Gospel text."[100] Containing little that is not taken from the gospels,[101] *The Messiah* privileges material taken from the Gospel of John,[102] but it also includes material from the other three evangelists: the visit of the Magi is taken from Matthew, the episode of Jesus teaching in the Temple at twelve years of age, is from Luke, the conflict of John the Baptist with Herod, and his subsequent imprisonment and execution is from Mark. Many of the parables are from Luke, and the beatitudes and Jesus' criticism of the Pharisees are from Matthew, as is the conclusion of the film at the empty tomb.

Among the parables included by Rossellini are: the sower of the seed, the leaven in the bread, the mustard seed, the stories of Lazarus and Dives, of the good Samaritan, and of the good shepherd. Rossellini also incorporates Jesus' teaching regarding the new law of love, then the beatitudes which are the basis of this new law, the teaching regarding prayer to God as Father and finally, before the Last Supper, the crucial action of Jesus' washing the feet of the Apostles as a lesson regarding charity and the "ministry of service,"[103] the cornerstone of the Christian community.

In contrast to the significance it gives to the teaching of Jesus, *The Messiah* clearly downplays his miracles. Rossellini represents only four miracles, three performed by Jesus: the miraculous catch of fish, the multiplication of the loaves, the healing of the man born blind, and then the Resurrection. This is itself a major shift from the classical tradition of the Jesus-film, for which the miracles with their dense dramatic power are a favorite set-piece. A further shift from the filmic miracle-tradition is that Jesus' wonders are represented not directly but elliptically, by metonomy. Rossellini shows not the miracle itself taking place but rather its effects: the blind man healed, not the healing, the abundant bread, the huge number of fish caught, the empty sepulcher. Other miracles are referred to as rumors. For example, regarding Lazarus, an episode conspicuously absent from *The Messiah*, we hear only of the report that a dead man was brought back to life.

Rossellini has three reasons for this very different approach to the miracles. Clearly he wants to stress the enlightened humanity of Jesus the teacher – of this we shall speak more later – and so he makes an "effort to remove every supernatural element from the narrative."[104] Further, the indirect approach reflects the way most people at the time of Jesus would have learned of his miracles,[105] and in a way it reflects the oral tradition already active during Jesus' lifetime. Finally, Rossellini's minimalist approach to the miracles has to do with his conscious stylistic preference in *The Messiah*, and it reflects his critical attitude "not so much towards the original [biblical] text, but towards the film medium which has the possibility of creating a spectacle."[106] He wants to avoid "the romantic touch, created by marvels,"[107] something cinema can do, and the Jesus-film has always done, "too easily with special effects."[108] Rossellini himself explains:

> If you show miracles in a film, you can do anything, even flying carpets. So what kind of credibility can you give the thing seen? I wanted to make a film that would be appreciated by people of our time . . . If I had underlined more the prodigious aspects [of the Gospel], I would have alienated the non-believers. But I think that even believers can find sufficient moments for their faith in the film.[109]

In addition to his dramatically understated treatment of the miracles, Rossellini effects a number of further shifts away from the Jesus-tradition in *The Messiah*. He augments the importance of John the Baptist, making him a strong and effective foil to Jesus, especially regarding his method of teaching. The Baptist, who is the narrative connection between the Old Testament prologue and the main body of the film, has an Old Law prophetic approach. His style is hard, anguished, urgent, world- and culture-denying. Rossellini's Jesus is well integrated in the world, full of the joy of living and of being with other people, and his teaching is edifying and affirming.

In this film in which Jesus preaches constantly, audaciously, with authority, and in which he teaches others to teach, a unique theme in the Jesus-film tradition, it is this preaching, whose doctrine is clearly in contrast to the doctrine of Judaism, that incurs the wrath of the Jewish religious authorities and their subsequent death-plot. Jesus is put to death because he is an eloquent and effective Master. Regarding the death-plot, Rossellini is very faithful to the Gospel tradition, if not to the Jesus-film tradition, in making no move to absolve the Jews.[110] He places the blame for Jesus' death on the Jewish leaders and on the crowd who, before Pilate, call for Jesus' crucifixion, a decision for which Rossellini was criticized in Italy, and which he defended by referring his critics to the text of the gospels.

A further dimension by which *The Messiah* stands out from the other Jesus-films is Rossellini's treatment of Jesus' parables and teaching, around which he creates a complex and convincing didactic atmosphere. In the way he represents Jesus' teaching, Rossellini suggests the development of both the oral tradition and of a didactic-catechetical methodology; he suggests that already in the oral tradition, which is the foundation of the Gospel texts, there was a didactic intentionality and approach. *The Messiah*, for example, represents Jesus teaching not only the small groups who gather to hear his wise words, but also the disciples, so that they can themselves become teachers. "The parables of Jesus pass from mouth to mouth: Jesus tells them to the disciples and they repeat them in villages where they are sent to preach."[111] The parables re-told by the itinerant disciples become an early witnessing to Jesus as the Messiah, "a primitive catechesis."[112] Several times in *The Messiah*, Rossellini shows the Gospel teaching and parables originating not with Jesus the Master, but, "in an original confirmation of the oral tradition of the communities from which the gospels originated, his followers: the parables of the Kingdom begun by Jesus and continued by Mary, Peter and so on."[113]

Perhaps the single element which stands out most in *The Messiah* is its strong representation of Mary, the mother of Jesus, a representation very different from that of the other Jesus-films, and one based more on Christian tradition than on the Gospel texts. Mary is present beside Jesus throughout the film – "the camera follows Mary who continually follows Jesus"[114] – and as part of "the inner circle of his disciples,"[115] she participates along with them in his teaching ministry.

> Discrete and concerned . . . she is lost in the crowd which is listening to the diatribe [of Jesus] against the "whitened sepulchers." She is in a corner of the court of Pilate and she leaves it running, stumbling, falling in anguish.[116]

Mary is present at the crucifixion; she receives Jesus' body and leads the disciples to the empty tomb. It is to her that Rossellini, in the final seconds of the film, gives the responsibility of signifying the Resurrection. As the first one to "believe in the risen Christ, Mary is the paragon of the faith."[117] Curiously enough, and unique in the Jesus-film tradition, Rossellini has Mary remain ever young, not changing throughout the film. Along with her crucial role in suggesting the oral tradition of Jesus' preaching, this detail seems meant to accentuate her "symbolic and metahistorical significance."[118]

In its content and in its style, Rossellini's approach in *The Messiah* is one of "constantly choosing the 'poor,' the anti-spectacular,"[119] as a way of focussing more clearly on the essentiality of the message. Consequently, the film has little of what is common in the Jesus-film tradition:

> In *The Messiah* . . . done away with were the classical pictorial and the popular iconography . . . the Hollywood spectacular; pathos; shadows; eclipses; storms; lightning and thunderclaps; earthquakes; showy miracles; intense visual expressions on well-lighted and well made-up faces; the hieratic gesture . . . violence, horrors; crowd scenes; the exhaustion of the man Christ; the suggestiveness of his words, his stories; the 'depth' of his stare; the abyss intuited in his eyes.[120]

In *The Messiah*, Rossellini adapted to the Gospel story a style of film-making to which he was, at this late point in his career, well-accustomed, a style that has its roots in neorealism, giving an austere, rigorous, almost documentary quality to the narrative, a style which reaches its fruition in the clean, sober, almost scientific quality of the film-essay. *The Messiah* is not a cinema of poetry nor a dramatic cinema, but rather a cinema of prose. In his film, "Rossellini subtracts, removes everything that appears superfluous, reduces the arguments to the bone, proposes a series of essential elements, creates an airy and light structure, a transparent network of images and sounds."[121] Based on reduction, with "not one superfluous accent, not one note above the line, not one emphatic sentence or image,"[122] it is an anti-spectacular approach, in contrast to the style of the Hollywood Jesus-film, constructed on the principle that "more and elaborate is better," an anti-naturalistic style in contrast to the pseudo-naturalistic approach of Zeffirelli's *Jesus of Nazareth*, built of sentiment and manneristic domesticity.

Every shot, every composition, every camera movement of *The Messiah* is austere and precise: "Rossellini . . . reached a level of essentialness almost unimaginable"[123] totally void of all "emphatic or rhetorical accentuation."[124] Nowhere does Rossellini indulge in the self-conscious creation of beautiful images or compositions typical of Zeffirelli's film: he avoids "all narcissism of style."[125] A fine example of this humble austerity can be seen when Rossellini makes visual references to popular iconic images. He does not turn them into breathtaking filmic-devotional *tours de force*, like Nicholas Ray's pseudo-Leonardesque Last Supper scene for example, but carefully "purifies them of every possible pious air or retrograde mannerism."[126] In one of the final sequences of the film, after Jesus is taken down from the cross, Rossellini has his body rest in the ever-young Mary's lap. The reference to Michelangelo's "Pietà" is clear and quite striking, and Rossellini keeps it from becoming sentimental by breaking the pious spell. He has Mary ask the Magdalene to bring her the balm for the anointing of Jesus' body. This is austere, essential iconography, at the service of "helping the spectator understand the facts."[127]

Rossellini avoids the galleries of stars employed by Zeffirelli and Ray, using unknown and non-professional actors. He never privileges one actor in the compositions, for which "the use of the close-up is almost unknown,"[128] and he directs them not to say "their lines and move like actors or protagonists. They speak and gesture with the natural quality, the simplicity of ordinary people."[129]

> The words – those of the Gospel – instead of being wrapped (as they usually are) in a kind of sacred aura, are pronounced almost inadvertently, between one everyday action and another: while walking, eating, resting.[130]

Rossellini clearly rejects the dramatic effect, for which the Gospel narrative provides plenty of opportunities. At the beginning of the film, for example, he represents the slaughter of the innocents in a discrete, almost undramatic way, a choice consciously made, says Rossellini, to counter a contemporary habit: "Of course, showing the slaughter of the innocents today can be a major dramatic scene, in the sadomasochistic style of film-making so in vogue today."[131] Rossellini justifies the uncharacteristically small group of Jews asking for Barabbas at the trial of Jesus by insisting on historical accuracy: "Of course, there were only those who were directly interested in the question. . . . Not all the Pharisees were the same."[132] For Rossellini, rejecting artificially dramatic effects, though they are clearly pleasing to the audience which wants thrills and chills even from the life of Jesus Christ, is the "rejection of seduction."[133] In the film-essay, there is no need for seduction: the truth speaks for itself.

In addition to rejecting crowd scenes, spectacular sets, complex choreography, all typical elements in the Jesus-film tradition, *The Messiah* eschews elaborate editing: no flashbacks, no parallel subplots, no introspective or fantasy sequences. Jesus and the other characters of the film move quickly and a great deal, and Rossellini's camera, "an attentive and very mobile observer,"[134] moves continuously to follow them. The extensive use of the *plan-séquence* shot,[135] combined with the judicious use of the zoom lens[136] – remarkable, for example, during the Last Supper scene – adds to the dynamism of the photography. The resulting rhythm of the narrative has a quality of urgency which is everywhere evident, for example, in the episode of the rich young man and in the representation of the passion "in a few incisive glances,"[137] and which is matched only in Pasolini's film.

The anti-spectacular and anti-naturalistic style of *The Messiah* is not only most appropriate for a film-essay on the life of Jesus Christ, the style becoming an "external characteristic of the physical and social ambience in which Christ lived and worked,"[138] but the sobriety of the film reflects and respects the style of the Gospel itself: "this simplicity is . . . also the essential quality of the Gospel whether from the literary or the theological point of view."[139] Convinced that the "encounter between the technical medium and the sacredness of a text can take place only on the basis of a substantial simplicity,"[140] and largely through the carefully disciplined style of his film,[141] Rossellini is able to "liberate the [Gospel] event from clichés, from from the accumulated incrustations of centuries."[142]

Rossellini succeeds admirably in creating a striking and effective film-essay on Jesus of Nazareth, and in doing so, he supersedes most of the Jesus-films that have gone before his.[143] Yet *The Messiah* has limits as a Jesus-film, limits due to a great extent to Rossellini's stylistic and formal choices which, of course, have an effect on the content of the film and ultimately on the figure of Jesus represented therein. Perhaps these limitations are nowhere clearer than in the two concluding episodes of the film, the passion and death of Jesus and the Resurrection. If in the Gospel, the passion and Resurrection narratives are the absolute high point, the culmination, both dramatically and theologically, of the life and mission of Jesus, in Rossellini's film they are radically redimensioned, becoming merely the final events of his life, almost a kind of epilogue. First, regarding the passion of Jesus, Rossellini, "proceeding with his lean and intentionally elliptical account, wanting to privilege the understanding more than the feeling,"[144] represents a Jesus, hardly aware of his impending death, contrary to the Gospel accounts, and then remarkably calm, almost unconcerned with the whole business. In the Gethsemane scene, he says only once, "Father, take this cup," and in the subsequent events, the horror, the physical and mental suffering of death by crucifixion are minimalized.

> Rossellini skips over the most cruel aspects of the Passion, he avoids the direct portrayal of the scourging and the insults to which the condemned man is subjected by the soldiers, leaves aside the *via crucis* so as not to fall into the usual cliches.[145]

Jesus arrives quickly on Calvary and almost as quickly dies. It seems oddly like the noble, stoical death of a hero, like that of Socrates, rather than what it was in reality and in the Gospel accounts: a horrible and shameful death as a criminal and the utter failure of his earthly mission. In simplifying Jesus' passion and the events leading up to it, Rossellini almost suggests that his death was a chance occurrence, as if things might have gone differently. There is little of the Gospel understanding of Jesus' growing awareness of the inevitability of his death and none of the sense of Jesus' freely choosing that death in obedience to the will of the Father, as a sacrifice for the salvation of Israel.

Regarding the Resurrection, Rossellini, clearly wanting to avoid the kitschy, highly emotional, highly-filmic spectacle-Resurrections of Stevens and Ray, represents the great miracle most indirectly, through the report of Mary Magdalene, the empty sepulcher, and the concluding shot of the film, of Mary, shedding joyful tears as she looks up into the blue sky. Biblically and theologically however, the Resurrection is attested not so much by the empty tomb – an ambiguous sign at best – as by the continuity of relationships between the risen Lord and his disciples, through the post-Resurrection appearances.[146] In Rossellini, there is no upper room (Jn 20:19-23), no meeting of the road to Emmaus (Lk 24:13-35), no reunion at the Sea of Galilee preannounced by Jesus (Jn 21). Rossellini's treatment of the Resurrection suggests that it is merely the final act of the life of Jesus of Nazareth, that it has no real implications for the life of the disciples or the community. "The triumph of the resurrection to which the final images allude . . . seems more like the inextinguishability of a word of truth and love than the glorification of the person Jesus."[147] Certainly too, Rossellini gives to the Resurrection no sense of a divine confirmation of the earthly mission of the Word of God, no sense of the cosmic victory of Jesus the Christ for the future of humanity.

The limits of Rossellini's vision, as suggested in these concluding sequences of the film, manifest themselves also throughout the text. In *The Messiah*, Rossellini does not represent the Annunciation, nor the angel of God who speaks twice to Joseph, nor the voice of God heard at the baptism of Jesus, nor the temptations of Jesus in the desert, nor the Transfiguration, nor the raising of Lazarus. In the gospels, these events point to the exceptional, divine nature of Jesus as the Messiah. Rossellini's Jesus is "without a divine dimension, a normal person among normal people"[148] All of Jesus' actions have "an everyday, antiheroic quality,"[149] his miracles are "never denied, never affirmed,"[150] and insofar as they are, in a very limited, indirect way represented, they "are human actions."[151] Rossellini does not represent Jesus' conscious intention of working the miracles as efficacious signs of the advent of the Kingdom of God. Rossellini does not represent Jesus' final exhortation to the apostles – "All authority in heaven and on earth has been given to me. Go therefore and make disciples of all nations" (Mt 28:18-19) – nor does he indicate the Gospel distinctions between disciples and apostles, and between Peter and the others. Clearly his purpose is to downplay the institutional aspects of Christianity and the question of authority in that formal community. Yet in doing so, he removes a critical aspect of Jesus' messianic identity and mission.

Clearly, the fundamental idea of Rossellini's film, unequivocally announced in the title, is that of Jesus as Messiah. The problem for the Christian believer is Rossellini's model of Messiah, because in his film, "the nature itself of the Messiah is only partly represented."[152] The Jesus of the Gospel and of the faith of Christians announces the long-promised salvation of the people of God, and in his very existence, in his person, he constitutes that salvation. In his life, and his sacrificial death and Resurrection, he brings about that salvation. In Rossellini's film, the Messiah is "message and not salvation."[153] In his film, Rossellini justly wants to avoid the emotional, sentimental excesses connected with the passion, the pathetic effect, clearly a manipulation of the viewers. In doing so however, he creates a Jesus-Messiah who is a teacher, a man of superior wisdom, the Master, but "not the servant of Yahweh,"[154] the suffering servant announced in Isaiah.

Rossellini's wise Messiah, though clearly not the military-political leader expected by the people, as suggested by Rossellini's prologue, is one who identifies with the workers, the poor, the powerless. An innovator, who wants to change things, to renew the culture, his words often "indicate an attitude of break with the traditions of his society."[155] This Jesus is certainly a Messiah of liberation, "in his way revolutionary, uncompromising in his opposition to the legalism of the religious and social ideas of his time."[156] In short, Rossellini's Messiah is:

> the carrier of a word of dignity and of love: a word to contemplate as a sublime ideal of humanity. The Jesus of the Gospel is not only this: he is the Word who saves, call to conversion, communication of life and not only of wisdom."[157]

Rossellini's personal understanding and commitment regarding Jesus is of significance here, as will be Pasolini's in the following chapter. Rossellini says of himself, perhaps somewhat ironically, that he is an agnostic.[158] But his films, as we saw earlier in this chapter, indicate more than a passing interest in a variety of religious experiences. One film critic, Virgilio Fantuzzi, who knew Rossellini personally, advises caution to whomever would summarily reject Rossellini's vision of Jesus:

> Rossellini is not a believer, at least not in the strict sense of the word, because he admits to have moved away from the dogmatic formulas of the Catholic Church in which he was educated. But this does not mean he should be defined as a-religious.[159]

Fantuzzi goes on to suggest that perhaps some degree of non-belief in one who makes a film about Jesus might not be such a bad thing: "Paradoxically, it could be said that one should be a little secular, a little distant [from the Gospel] to appreciate the powerful impact generated by the shocking newness of the Gospel."[160] Rossellini himself said of Jesus: "I believe that the greatness of Jesus is unique, even for one who does not have the faith. All his preaching has to do with the raising up of human beings, of their dignity."[161]

Though Rossellini did not explicitly profess a personal belief in Jesus' divinity, his *Messiah* does leave open that possibility to the spectator. In what it says about Jesus, in what it does not say, and perhaps most importantly in its revolutionary style, which radically reduces much of the filmic interference usual in the Jesus-film, *The Messiah* offers important clues and points in the direction of his divinity. Fully recognizing the limits of the film, Fantuzzi insists that Rossellini's film is in substantial conformity to the Gospel:

> The film cannot be defined as a secular reading of the sacred texts. The religious message of the Gospels remains such in the film, insofar as the critical revision of the director does not lead to a substantial modification of the text, nor to the production of new meaning not already contained at least in the spirit of the [Gospel] text.[162]

6

The Masterpiece: *The Gospel According to Saint Matthew*

Pier Paolo Pasolini's film, *The Gospel According to Saint Matthew*,[1] in the minds of most serious critics is still the greatest, the most authentic and "the most religious film on Jesus ever made."[2] It was premiered at the International Film Festival of Venice on 4 September 1964. An Italo-French co-production,[3] it was given important awards at the Venice Festival but unfortunately, for a variety of reasons, it did not receive a wide distribution in the United States, and "got most of its showings on college campuses after its initial theatrical release."[4]

Pasolini's Jesus-film project began two years earlier during a visit to Assisi. While guest of the Catholic cultural organization, *Pro Civitate Christiana*,[5] in October 1962, and more or less confined to the house by the town's busy preparations for the visit of Pope John XXIII – to whose "dear happy memory" Pasolini later dedicated the film – the director found a copy of the New Testament on his bedside table. He turned to the gospels, and in his own words, "that day . . . I read them from beginning to end, like a novel."[6] The experience was like a bolt of lightning for Pasolini, who describes how he felt "an immediate need to 'do something' – a terrible, almost physical energy."[7]

In 1964, when *The Gospel According to Saint Matthew* came out, Pasolini was forty-two years of age. A prolific writer and man of culture, he had already published some twenty-eight books of poetry and essays, film scripts and novels, and in cinema he had worked on the scripts of some fifteen films, and had himself made five films.[8] Active also politically, Pasolini had been a member of the Italian Communist party, from which he was expelled in 1952 because of the scandal caused by his publicly-admitted homosexuality and some run-ins with the law in this regard. His short film of 1963, *La ricotta*, got him in trouble once again: the film was judged blasphemous and insulting to the Catholic faith, the religion of the state.[9] Pasolini was arrested, tried and given a four-month suspended sentence.

It is from this rich, varied and troubled background that Pasolini, a kind of national Italian *enfant terrible*, came to the project of making *The Gospel According to Saint Matthew*, and there is no doubt that this background left its mark on the film and on the portrait of Jesus which it presents. For example, Pasolini's past can be sensed in his preference for Matthew's Jesus: he was attracted by "the revolutionary quality of his [Jesus'] social diversity, of his non-violence, of the power of moral thought."[10] One senses it in Pasolini's objections to the other gospels: "Mark's seemed too crude, John's too mystical, and Luke's, sentimental and bourgeois."[11] Further, Pasolini insists that "Matthew is the most 'worldly' of the evangelists . . . and the most revolutionary."[12] And he continues enthusiastically:

> The Christ [of Matthew] who moves through Palestine is really a revolutionary whirlwind: anyone who comes up to two people and says, 'Throw away your nets, follow me, and I will make you fishers of men,' is totally revolutionary.[13]

Clearly, Pasolini was fascinated, inspired by the strong, aggressive Jesus of Matthew's Gospel. He himself confesses that the words of Jesus that struck him and drove him to make the film were: "Do not suppose that I have come to bring peace on the earth. I have not come to bring peace but a sword. For I have come to bring division, a man against his father, a daughter against her mother' (Mt 10:34).[14] Should there be any doubt as to his basic point of view, Pasolini adds: "I had in mind to represent Christ as an intellectual in a world of poor people ready for revolution."[15] Clearly, Pasolini had in mind something quite different from a biography of Jesus: "This film is simply the visualization of one particular Gospel, that of St. Matthew. It's not a life of Christ."[16] He explains further:

> I did not want to reconstruct the life of Christ as it really was. Instead, I wanted to tell the story of Christ plus two thousand years otf Christian tradition, because it took two thousand years of Christian history to mythologize that biography . . . My film is the life of Christ plus two thousand years of history told about the life of Christ.[17]

If Zeffirelli created a very free adaptation of all four gospels, in the end producing a work more of fiction than Gospel, and Rossellini, an austere amalgam of the four gospels, Pasolini, inspired by the raw power of Matthew's text, was determined to be utterly faithful to it: "My idea is this: to follow the Gospel according to Saint Matthew point by point, without making a script or adaptation out of it. To translate it faithfully into images, following its story without any omissions or additions."[18] Regarding the dialogue of his film, Pasolini insists that "the spoken words should be rigorously those of Saint Matthew, without even a sentence of explanation or bridging, because no image or word added can ever reach the high poetic level of the text."[19] Pasolini was faithful to his intention: in fact, "not one word in the film is Pasolini's invention."[20] The only exception is his insertion of several passages from the old Testament book of Isaiah, prophecies regarding the Messiah, additions which Pasolini rightly justifies by noting that "Matthew's text is full of citations from Isaiah, so I thought it would be licit to add a couple."[21]

Different from Zeffirelli's Jesus-film, which was intended to reach the popular public of the mass television audience, and from Rossellini's, whose purpose was to teach and edify, Pasolini, the poet, saw his film more as "a poetic work, which would express all his 'nostalgia for the sacred, the mythical, the epic.' "[22] Given his hopes for his film of the Gospel, clearly in explosive contrast with all the Jesus-films made to that time, Pasolini was aware of the delicacy of his situation; he well understood how the critics, both of the left and the right, would scrutinize his finished work. He explains his dilemma: "I walked on the razor's edge: trying to avoid, from my point of view, a uniquely historical and human vision, and from the point of view of the believer, a too mythical vision."[23]

Pasolini was not the only one nervous about this project. When he asked the *Pro Civitate Christiana* group for help, its director so,ught the advice of the powerful and conservative Giuseppe Cardinal Siri, archbishop of Genoa, who courageously encouraged him to promote Pasolini s project, writing: "To further the conquest of culture for God, something indeed has to be risked . . . in certain cases even prudence counsels daring."[24] As a result of Siri's letter, *Pro Civitate Christiana* gave financial assistance to the film.[25] Pasolini's film-in-progress was also followed by two Jesuits from the Centro San Fedele of Milan and by the somewhat skeptical theologian Romano Guardini, "who expressed a systematic lack of confidence in the possibility of representing Jesus through an actor."[26]

The controversy which had accompanied *The Gospel According to Saint Matthew* from its beginning made itself felt on the evening of its premiere at the Venice Festival. Anticipating a negative reaction from the far right, the police chief of Venice tripled the usual number of police and *carabinieri* around the *Palazzo del Cinema* at the Venice Lido. Yet the noisy Fascist demonstrators outside did not prevent the overall warm reception of the film and more importantly, did not prevent its being awarded the Special Prize of the Jury. If a Gospel film was a controversial choice for the secular Prize of the Jury, the same film by an avowed Marxist was equally controversial choice for the prize of the International Catholic Film office (O.C.I.C.), which justified its award to Pasolini in the following statement:

> The author . . . has faithfully translated, with simplicity and piety, and often movingly, the social message of the Gospel, in particular love for the poor and the oppressed, while sufficiently respecting the divine aspect of Christ . . . this work is far superior to earlier, commercial films on the life of Christ. It shows the real grandeur of his teaching stripped of any artificial and sentimental effect.[27]

Giovanni Cardinal Urbani, archbishop of Venice, present at the film's premiere at the Festival, was annoyed by it. A biblical scholar and professor, he complained: "Pasolini hasn't understood the Gospel. Jesus isn't like that."[28] Without realizing it, Urbani was voicing the objection that many Catholics, unfamiliar with the text of Matthew, would make to the film over the years. The Cardinal however, at the suggestion of one of his assistants, then read through the Gospel of Matthew in one sitting and changed his mind about the film: "I realized that, although he was a layman,[29] Pasolini had projected Matthew's very same Jesus on the screen, with great fidelity, word for word."[30]

There is some evidence that Pope Paul VI saw the film, and it was shown officially to the eight hundred Catholic bishops assembled in Rome for Vatican Council II. They evidently liked it, for there was a "burst of applause at the end of the film."[31] Three weeks after the Venice premiere, and in spite of some negative comments in a review of the film in the authoritative Vatican newspaper, *L'Osservatore Romano,*[32] O.C.I.C. conferred another honor on *The Gospel According to Saint Matthew,* the prize for the best religious film of the year, awarded appropriately enough at Assisi, where Pasolini's project had begun two years earlier. In a remarkably carefully-worded statement, the Catholic film organization without knowing it, anticipated the Vatican's "rehabilitation" of *The Gospel According to Saint Matthew* some thirty-two years later, when the film was included in a listing of great religious films.[33] In 1964, O.C.I.C. said of the Marxist-athiest Pasolini: "The author, who is said not to share our faith, had given proof, in his choice of texts and scenes, of respect and delicacy. He has made a fine film, a Christian film that produces a profound impression"[34]

If Zeffirelli wrote a book about the making of his film which has become a valuable hermeneutical instrument for the interpretation of his film, Pasolini went one better and gave us two films which can serve as hermeneutical instruments for *The Gospel According to Saint Matthew.* The first is *Sopralluoghi in Palestina,* a documentary film made just before *The Gospel According to Saint Matthew* and released in 1964; the second is *La ricotta,* made in 1963, when the Gospel project was already on Pasolini's mind, and released with three other short features in a film under the title *RoGoPag.*[35] The first film is a straightforward account of a trip through the Holy Land that Pasolini made with a priest-friend, Don Andrea Carraro. Its soundtrack registers the ongoing dialogue between the two men and, supported by the visuals, reveals why in the end Pasolini chose to make his film in Italy. Between the lines, so to speak, the film suggests a great deal about Pasolini's understanding and appreciation of the Gospel story, his political-social ideology, and his plans for the Jesus of his film. The second film, a biting satire on Italian culture and taste in art, tells the tragicomic story of Stracci (literally "Rags"), an "eternally hungry"[36] sub-proletarian bit actor in a film of Christ's passion, playing the part of one of the thieves crucified with Jesus. As Orson Welles, in the role of the obese and cynical Marxist director of the film-within-the-film, pontificates over the preparation of kitsch living-tableaux of the removal of Jesus from the cross, in garish colors and in imitation of minor Renaissance paintings,[37] poor Stracci actually dies, in black-and-white, in a "new sacrifice on the cross."[38] Though, as indicated earlier in this chapter, *La ricotta* got Pasolini in serious trouble with the law, it remains his most "explicit criticism of the makers of the historical-biblical epics,"[39] and, in both its style and its content, it prepared the way for a new approach in *The Gospel According to Saint Matthew,* a film which announced, for the first time, "that a biblical film can become a work of art."[40]

In keeping with his political ideology, and consistent with his esthetic preferences announced in *Sopralluoghi in Palestina* and in *La ricotta,* Pasolini made two other crucial decisions regarding his Gospel. Having decided that making the film in the Holy Land was out of the question, Pasolini determined to make it in Italy,[41] and in doing so, he opted for an analogical approach to the biblical realities. He searched in Italy for "landscapes and faces that would be analogous to the historical counterparts of the Gospel."[42] In Pasolini's own words, "for the people of that [Gospel] time . . . I substituted an analogous people (the subproletariat of southern Italy) and for the landscape, I substituted an analogous landscape (the Mediterranean Italy of the deep south)."[43]

Apart from a few sequences filmed near Rome, the scene, for example, of Jesus' baptism is in the Chia river valley near Viterbo, the Gethsemane scene, in an olive orchard "halfway up the hill between Hadrian's Villa and Tivoli,"[44] most of the film's settings are in the deep south. The mountain desert of the temptations is Mount Etna in Sicily, the town of Barile in Puglia, where until only a few years ago, there were people still living in caves, is Bethlehem. The seaside Cafarnaum is a village near Crotone; Nazareth and Jerusalem are Matera and especially the old town known as the "Sassi."[45] The palaces of the film are the fortresses left by the Normans on the coasts of Puglia and Lucania, and the desert through which Jesus walks with/the apostles is in Calabria.[46]

These authentic, timeless settings and the equally authentic and timeless peasant faces of most of Pasolini's actors, marked by centuries of abandonment, poverty and suffering, give an unmistakable political valence to his *Gospel.* By "setting the subproletariat Palestine, colonized by the Romans, the 'imperialists' of two thousand years ago, in the most economically-depressed areas of Italy today,"[47] by making the perpetrators of the slaughter of the innocents into Fascist bullies, and the Roman soldiers in Jerusalem into the "*Celere,*" Italy's violent, rapid intervention, anti-riot police, Pasolini was making an unmistakable ideological statement critical of the central government in Rome and of its Christian Democratic leadership. Consequently, the Jesus of Pasolini's film, in his strong critique, already present in Matthew's Gospel, of the religious and social institutions of his time, is by analogy making a parallel critique of contemporary Italian institutions.

Clearly connected to the esthetic-ideological decision to film his *Gospel* in poverty-stricken southern Italy was Pasolini's parallel decision to give it the look of the popular religious drama, such as the Passion Play of oberammergau and "those enacted by citizens of many European villages every year."[48] A brilliant intuition, Pasolini's choice "to give to the tragedy of Christ the character of the popular sacred pageant,"[49] makes his film absolutely unique in the history of the Jesus-film genre.[50] More the evocation of the meaning of the Gospel in and through the new reality, than the historical or sociological reconstruction of its narrative, Pasolini's *Gospel,* like the sacred pageant, is conceived as a "series of 'scenes' without internal connections, juxtaposed one to the other, according to the sense of the Gospel and beyond any historical logic."[51]

The authentic settings, the simple stylized costumes and the choice of actors all submit to this new logic, as does the style of acting. Given the words from the Gospel of Matthew, Pasolini's actors "repeat them as they are, without interpreting them . . . with the dialectal inflection of the simple people, with the usual, age-old gestures of the poor."[52] It is easy for these simple non-professionals to avoid the pitfalls of the method actor. Pasolini has them perform without imposing "their own personal interior logical and psychological modulation."[53] The final result in *The Gospel According to Saint Matthew* is quite unique in the Jesus-film tradition, a rigorous yet harmonious "blend of words and images into a unified whole."[54] Like the gospels themselves, the film does not have a dramatic structure nor climactic scenes. An the film, as in the gospels and the popular pageants, the various sequences seem uniform in tone, flat, equal among themselves, even interchangeable. It has something of the marvelous effect of "the Gospel read in the choir of an empty church, by the monks: the drama is stripped of all secular passion; it becomes spoken prayer, incised in the stones."[55]

When Pasolini, still a committed Marxist even after his expulsion from the Italian Communist party, chose to make a film based on Matthew's Gospel, evidently the question arose of his "problematical atheism,"[56] of just who Jesus was for him. In the very Catholic and very political Italy of the 1960s, the question became an issue of public debate and clearly affected the way people, and critics in particular, reacted to the film. Concerning his belief, Pasolini himself said, in a somewhat ambiguous way:

> To put it very simply and frankly, I don't believe that Christ is the son of God, because I am not a believer, at least not consciously. But I believe that Christ is divine: I believe that is him humanity is so lofty, strict and ideal as to exceed the common terms of humanity.[57]

In spite of this apparently atheistic stance, Pasolini was quite sincerely convinced that "at the deepest level, Marxism and Christianity had profound affinities,"[58] and in part his decision to make *The Gospel According to Saint Matthew* was motivated by the hope that it might serve to bring about a reconciliatory dialogue between Marxism and Christianity, a "radically unconventional alliance."[59] He elaborated this hope in a courageous interview published in *L'Unità*, the Communist newspaper in Rome: "Catholicism must be capable . . . of taking into account the problems of the society in which we live; and so too must Marxism face the religious moment of humanity."[60]

In spite of Pasolini's good will and hope, and in spite of the accolades to the film at the Venice Festival and in some Church circles, *The Gospel* alienated conservative Catholics who, using blatantly *ad hominem* argumentation, accused Pasolini of being a communist and thus concluded that his angry Jesus was nothing but a "revolutionary prophet, an anti-bourgeois guerrilla."[61] Evidently they had forgotten that Jesus, especially Matthew's Jesus, was "troublesome, a sign of contradiction,"[62] clearly a dimension that Pasolini was honest and courageous enough to underline. Though some progressive Catholics were happy with the film, members of the political left, especially in Italy, were "highly critical of the idea of a serious film on Christ

. . . [and attacked] the film on the basis that it did not deny Christ's divine nature."[63] Clearly the Catholic-Marxist dialogue had a long way to go.

Beyond the purely political dimension of Catholic-Marxist confrontation on the field of Pasolini's *Gospel,* there is of course a more fundamental and more crucial issue, that is the question of whether or not the Catholic, or Christian faith is the necessary background for the creation of an acceptable image of Jesus. John May puts the question succinctly: "The assumption is that intention or belief – or lack of it – inevitably governs artistic achievement."[64] If one subscribes to this assumption, in effect, judging a film not on its own merits but on the presumed belief or non-belief of its author, then one has to accept both Scorsese's and Zeffirelli's images of Jesus as valid, and one has to discard both Rossellini's and Pasolini's images. Further one would have to discard a whole series of films traditionally considered as religious, for example, *A Man for All Seasons* (1966) and *Thérèse* (1986), because their creators are not believers. one would also have to explain how Pasolini's *Gospel* can be included in the Vatican's listing of great religious films, and how a Catholic critic, voicing the opinion of many serious Catholic thinkers, can say about it: "The Jesus film of a committed Marxist is until this day the most successful example of a filmed Gospel; it fulfills equally well filmic, theological and religious criteria."[65]

Another problematical dimension of Pasolini's *The Gospel According to Saint Matthew* is its autobiographical content and themes, which at times interfere with what he himself wanted to be a faithful translation into images of the Gospel text and spirit. Pasolini's already-quoted definition of the kind of Christ he wanted to represent, "an intellectual in a world of poor people ripe for revolution,"[66] is also quite obviously a definition of himself, and of the role he wished to assume in Italian culture. on viewing the film several years after it came out, Pasolini admitted: "I don't believe I have ever created anything more my own, more perfectly measured to me, than the Gospel,"[67] and he went on to explain that the film is "dense with my own personal themes and motivations."[68]

Clearly the political subtexts identified above are personal themes of Pasolini's, as is the idiosyncratic fact that in his film he gave the roles of the members of the Establishment to artist and writer friends of his, many of them well-known to Italian audiences of the 1960s,[69] while the roles of most of the apostles and the bit-parts went to unknown non-professionals and simple peasants. Here Pasolini is being inconsistent with his own intention to give his film the quality of the popular religious pageant. More to the point, there is also a personal subtext in the film, that is, Pasolini quite consciously creates a parallel between himself, angry intellectual, cultural and moral prophet, rejected by his own people, and the angry prophetic Jesus he represents in his *Gospel.* Nowhere is this autobiographical element more poignant, and perhaps more distracting, than in the fact that Mary the mother of Jesus, played by Susanna Pasolini, the director's mother, is present at the crucifixion.[70] Here Pasolini is blatantly violating his own rule of absolute faithfulness to Matthew's text. In Matthew, Mary is not present on Calvary. Further, there is the unequivocal suggestion that Mary (Susanna Pasolini) collapsing in paroxysms of grief at the foot of the cross, is crying not only for the Jesus crucified but also for the son Pier Paolo "crucified" by the cultural, political and moral Pharisees of his generation.

Perhaps the most significant, and in a sense the most disturbing, of the "autobiographical elements which vein"[71] Pasolini's *Gospel,* insofar as it pretends to be faithful to Matthew's Gospel, is what Maurizio Viano, author of a recent major study of Pasolini's films, refers to as the "phallocentrism"[72] of the film, a powerful subtext created in part by Pasolini's homosexuality. Recalling two crucial women in the typical Jesus-film, Salome and Mary Magdalene, the first usually portrayed as a temptress playing an erotic power game with Herod, the second, usually suggested as a "locus of loose sexuality on its way to repentance, with more or less explicit hints at a relationship with Christ,"[73] Viano demonstrates how Pasolini shifts the conventional representations. In turning Salome into a "blank-eyed, virginal figure, who performs an asexual dance with grace and levity,"[74] Pasolini "desexualizes an episode which is likely to have had strong [hetero]sexual connotations."[75] Pasolini avoids the distraction of Mary Magdalene by removing her altogether and he turns Mary of Bethany into an awkward woman who is "neither young nor sensuous." Further, in this phallocentric subtext of the film, the desperation of Mary, the Mother of Jesus, on Calvary can be seen as a representation, on the part of Pasolini, of his own mother's "maternal anguish in front of the 'diversity' of her offspring."[77]

In Pasolini's Gospel, "beauty and visual dominance go to men, unquestioningly. Christ himself and some of the apostles are indeed beautiful young men.[78] So are many of the Roman soldiers, the rich young man and many of the peasants. over and over again the camera – Pasolini himself was often behind the camera – lingers just a little too long on their languid Latin good looks. Perhaps the most surprising, and ultimately revealing, element of the autobiographical and phallocentric subtexts of *The Gospel According to Saint Matthew,* and an element unnoticed by the critics, is the appearance in a cameo role of Ninetto Davoli, Pasolini's young and longtime companion in a relationship that created public controversy.[79] In a scene after the killing of John the Baptist, Jesus is walking along a hillside with disciples. They come upon Davoli playing innocently in the field with a little child. Jesus looks at him and smiles and he smiles back, the disciples smile, everyone smiles. one of the disciples ask "Who is the greatest in the Kingdom of Heaven?" and Jesus answers speaking the familiar lines of Matthew 18:3-7, including the words: "The one who knows how to make himself small like a child is the greatest in the Kingdom of Heaven, and whoever receives a child like this one, in my name, receives me."[80] With the presence of Ninetto Davoli, and the lingering eye-contact between him and Jesus, Pasolini gives these words from Matthew a second and very personal meaning: that of a provocative,

evangelical, if not divine, justification of his own much criticized relationship
with Davoli.

The protagonist, then, of Pasolini's *The Gospel According to Saint Matthew* is not the historical Jesus; neither is he a historical-cultural reconstruction, as is the Jesus of Zeffirelli's film. He is too single-minded to be the
introspective, neurotic Jesus of Scorsese,[81] and too impatient to be the gentle
and wise Master of Rossellini. A "Christ essentially tied to the biblical tradition,"[82] he is not a composite figure as are Zeffirelli's and Rossellini's, but
rather a crystal-clear and consistent image of the Savior in the Gospel of
Matthew. "Matthew's Christ is an angry Christ. And anger is precisely the
dimension which Pasolini's visual translation wishes to highlight."[83]

If anger is a highlight of Pasolini's Jesus, a dimension which, because it
is so unusual in a film-Jesus, tends to dominate the consciousness of the
viewer who sees the film only once, it is certainly not his only characteristic.
A vital and energetic figure, he "strides through the film with great vigour
and intensity."[84] He is an intense, "rugged Jesus,"[85] who seems neither to
have nor to need a home or resting place. His "relentlessly dynamic"[86] quality
is emphasized by his appearance, that of a "a slight Mediterranean type, thin
and dark, his hollow cheeks slashed by a beard, a 'rabbi' devoured by an
interior fire,"[87] a "severe Christ, with Byzantine features."[88] If Rossellini's
Jesus is always doing something with his hands, Pasolini's seems always to
be on the move, "striding determinedly forward to fulfill His destiny as the
Son of God,"[89] and almost always talking while he walks. often Pasolini's
camera pictures him from behind, from the point of view of the disciples as
they try to keep up with him. Jesus' words acquire greater power because
they are spoken as he moves, or as he stops and twists his body to look back
at them, and at us.

Pasolini's Jesus is sure of himself, with never a hint of the self-conscious hesitation, not to say confusion, of Scorsese's Jesus. Yet, Pasolini
makes it clear that his power and decisiveness finds its source not in himself,
a self-made, self-sufficient, prophet-preacher, in the manner of Nicholas
Ray's Savior, but in his mysterious contact-identification with the Father. In
one quite beautiful shot, understated in its simple austerity, Pasolini shows
Jesus in early morning prayer, kneeling with his arms uplifted in the *orante*
position, absolutely still, while his disciples do their early morning ablutions
in the background. At one point, Judas begins to walks towards Jesus, but
then stops in his tracks, not daring to interrupt the sacred space of Jesus'
communion with God. In the Gethsemane scene, Pasolini represents another
form of Jesus' oration: rejecting the traditional iconography of a Jesus kneeling in prayer almost passively awaiting his fate, he shows Jesus pacing back
and forth, almost like a caged animal, as if ready and almost impatient to live
the passion.

The Jesus of Pasolini's *Gospel* is prophetic, in the sense of seeings profoundly and critically into the present situation, and from that analysis "con
fronting authority and making serious demands on his followers."[90] In his

words and actions, he is rough, direct, at times undiplomatic, an "inspired peasant."[91] Jesus' words are often "spoken brusquely, as if blows with a stone:"[92] his "Get behind me, Satan!" correction of Peter, for example, is shocking in its vehemence, both for Peter who is clearly taken aback, and for the viewers of the film. Jesus' prophetic role is largely that of defender of the poor and the oppressed and correspondingly, that of criticizing the oppressors, the cultural and religious establishment of his time. He is a "Christ proud and pugnacious . . . who puts into play all his powers and his very life for the good of his oppressed people."[93]

Given this tough, prophetic quality of Pasolini's Jesus, then to qualify him as "emotionally remote,"[94] as a "cipher . . . an almost abstract figure,"[95] as only "sign, myth, symbol, allegory,"[96] or as an "intolerant Christ, who admits no alternatives, no 'either-ors,' " is simply to miss one whole dimension of this Jesus. Pasolini repeatedly shows him responding with mercy, gentleness and kindness to the disciples, to the people who come to him for healing and perhaps especially, to the children. One of the mistaken impressions many people have of Pasolini's Jesus is that he never, or hardly ever, smiles. one critic, for example, noting an encounter between Jesus and some children, says: "For the only time in the film, Jesus smiles, a smile that comes almost against his will."[98] This is simply not true. When this Jesus smiles, he smiles warmly, freely and fully: "surrounded by children in the temple, he laughs with joy which reveals . . . the heaven in which He has such confidence."[99] As well, Pasolini's Jesus, a man with an "intense love of life,"[100] smiles often: when he meets John the Baptist and when he calls James and John to follow him, when he speaks of the lilies of the field and when he is about to do the multiplication of the loaves and fishes. When Jesus heals the leper, there is a marvelous warm exchange of smiles between him and the man; and when Jesus cures the cripple, he smites at him and later he even speaks gently and reasonably to the Pharisees. During his triumphal entrance into Jerusalem, Jesus is anything but solemn. He is clearly enjoying himself and participating in this popular manifestation. Again, during the Last Supper, he smiles and speaks with kindness to the apostles. Pasolini's Jesus is also capable of sadness, as suggested in his reaction to the departure of the rich young man, and clearly manifested when he hears of the execution of John the Baptist. In a very human reaction, on that occasion he cries and almost seems discouraged .

The fact remains that the Jesus of Pasolini's *Gospel* still strikes the viewer as a severe and angry man. We have already suggested, many critics interpret this irascible and eloquent severity as a projection of Pasolini's own political ideology: Pasolini an angry Marxist, his Jesus, "a fiery young first-century revolutionary – sort of a young Fidel Castro."[101] Perhaps the problem is more that of projection on the part of the critic or viewer, who judges Pasolini's Jesus according to the norms of other, softer filmic portrayals of Jesus: "The point is, of course, not so much that we are in front of a Marxist

Christ, as that He is not the gentle, all-loving Jesus of conventional Catholic iconography."[102]

All of the above discussed characteristics of Pasolini's protagonist do make him radically different from all the other filmic representations of Jesus, but in no way do they put into question his being Son of God. There are however, aspects, dimensions of Pasolini's Jesus, and of his *Gospel,* that are problematical and that prevent his being a full and coherent reflection of the Matthean Jesus.

The Gospel of Matthew was written for a community off Jews who had converted to Christianity. In it, over and over again, Jesus is unequivocally identified as the Messiah or the Son of God. Yet, as we have seen, there is evidence that in his representation of the Matthean Jesus, Pasolini has down-played certain aspects of Jesus' divinity.[103] The absence of the major miracles and the Transfiguration, and of the corresponding confessions of faith in Jesus are evidence of this, as are the lack of references in Jesus' preaching to the Kingdom of God and the absence of most of the parables. A more serious problem with Pasolini's Jesus, however, has to do with a couple of fundamental weaknesses in Pasolini's representation of his humanity and involves elements that ultimately deny the full meaning of the Incarnation. The Incarnation of God-in-Jesus, the new Adam, as St. Paul refers to him (Rom 5:12-17), among other things means that Jesus of Nazareth was a fully integrated human being, within himself, in the world and with other people. In contrast, Pasolini's Jesus is a "world renouncer."[104] He is not only, to paraphrase the Gospel, not *of* the world, but also not *in* the world. In a sense, Pasolini's Jesus is so angry, so severe, so intolerant, that at times – for example, his cursing of the fig tree – he seems to reach the extreme point of denying the creation and thus negating the Incarnation, which after all is an ultimate vote of confidence of God in favor of the creation. A world-renouncing Jesus cannot be the Savior of the world.

If Pasolini's Jesus is not well integrated into his world, he is even less integrated into human society. Solitary, aloof, he is "a kind of Biblical intelectual who, despite an intense desire to be 'organically' linked to the people, cannot breach the immeasurable gap between them." Perhaps most evident in the Sermon on the Mount sequence, but also in many other moments of the film, Jesus seems separated from the people and even from his disciples. He does have encounters, conversations with people and even, as we have seen, moments of human tenderness, but these are usually very brief, evanescent. There is little evidence of "profound understanding or communion."[106] one critic admits "the distance between the crowd around Jesus and the figure of Jesus himself," but he argues that this distance "is quite orthodox and already in Matthew."[107] A close analysis of the film's images suggests, however, that the "distance" in Pasolini's *Gospel* is more extreme, more radical than in the text of Matthew, and that it is willed by Pasolini, who emphasizes it by the way he photographs his Jesus in relation to the people. The Jesus of the Sermon on the Mount, for example, shot in close-up, talking and talking, while not one listener is to be seen, is a powerful image of eloquent solitude. The repeated wide-angle compositions in which Jesus is to one side of the frame in close-up, with the crowd far in the background, emphasize his distance from the people, as does the oft-repeated image of Jesus from behind, while talking as if to himself.

Certainly, there are elements of the world-renouncer and the solitary man in the Jesus of Matthew. But this severity in the written text of Matthew is to some extent attenuated by the imagination of the reader who assimilates it. In Pasolini's *Gospel,* a dense visual and aural text, the severity of the Jesus of Matthew's written text is forcefully augmented. In stark black and white, a severe-looking Jesus, seen often in close-up, speaking violent words in violent tones with violent gestures, moving incessantly, almost always separated from the people around him, a separation augmented by the silence and passivity of Jesus' followers, an "indistinguishable mass,"[108] is almost too much. The clearest example of this extreme Jesus is in Pasolini's episode of the Sermon on the Mount, a figure about whom it is fair to say:

> Christians will be troubled . . . by this authoritarian master, commanding men and the elements, sublime Pantocrator, but without a private life, without feelings, with no humor and without that sovereign ease in his humanity where they [the disciples] learned to see the face of God.[109]

It is something of a truism to say that the final image or scene of a film has a particular valence or power, and that it can thus confirm the meaning proposed throughout the film or substantially shift that meaning. The Resurrection scene with which Pasolini concludes *The Gospel According to Saint Matthew* a good example of this. The episode is so powerful, so positive, so faithful to Matthew's Gospel, that as a film experience it effectively counters the problematical aspects of the person of Jesus noted above. The sequence is complicated and dense but the point can be made by noting a few of its elements. A "Gloria" heard quietly in the background from the time Jesus is taken down from the cross till the "explosive" opening of the tomb at the "Amen" of the hymn, clearly prepares for the glorious victory over death. The arrival of the women, the opening of the tomb, found empty, the angel of the Resurrection and its words of hope, all happening very fast, clearly suggest the power and urgency of this new life. The explosion of the unusual "Gloria," of the Congolese "Missa Luba,"[110] with its pounding drums and joyful voices, as the tomb opens and continuing till the end of the film, recalls the divine intervention of God in the Annunciation scene in the opening of the film, when we first hear this music, and it suggests a similar divine intervention in this conclusion. The closing shot of the film, shows the disciples and others running to greet the risen Lord on a hillside, as he commissions them to "Go therefore and make disciples Qvf all nations . . . and remember, I am with you always." (Mt 28:19, 20). The power and forward movement the whole scene is most persuasive, it resounds with the mystery of the Resurrection-victory of Jesus the Christ over death. But Pasolini is most convincing and unambiguous about his Jesus when he represents "the disciples running joyously towards the risen Christ in a burst of visual energy that sweeps the emotions of even the most skeptical spectator along with it."[111]

Part Two

The Christ-Figure

Introduction

> The Christ figure in allegory follows the main thread of the Christ story, while disguising it through a surface narrative and relying on the viewer to provide the necessary continuity. The figure is strong enough to exist by itself, but points to a meaning far beyond this existence for its ultimate truth.[1]

Beyond the explicitly biblical representations of Jesus in film, none of which, as we have seen in the first part of this book, is entirely satisfactory, all of which present the perceptive viewer with esthetic or theological problems, there is a whole series of films which represent the Jesus-story, the Christ-event, implicitly, in analogical form, films which may provide a more satisfactory approach to the person and event of Jesus Christ.[2] These Christ-figure films, which will be the object of our investigation in this second part of the book are from various periods, and belong to various *genres* and styles but they all have two elements in common. They submit to two levels or registers of interpretation, the direct and the analogical, the literal and the figurative; and on the figurative or metaphorical level, they accept a reading that is biblical and christological. They are not unlike the parables of Jesus which, when "read" on a literal level, remain brief narratives of human experience, but when interpreted metaphorically, fairly explode with theological or christological significance.

At least four dimensions of the Christian tradition itself justify the use of analogy or metaphor to image the divine. First of all, the Christian faith is one which finds its meaning in images. Genesis 1:27 reveals that God created the human being in God's image; the human person is an image of God. St. Paul insists that Christ is the image of God.[3] The New Testament recognizes in the Old Testament a variety of images or figures of Christ: the suffering servant of Isaiah, Isaac about to be sacrificed, Jonah who spent three days in the mouth of the whale, Moses who led his people out of bondage, the redeemer and lawgiver. Even Jesus used figures to speak of himself: the good shepherd, the light in the darkness, the way, the truth and the life, the living water. St. Paul insisted that though a sinner, he (and all committed Christians) was "conformed to the image" of Christ (Rom 8:29) and he called on Christians to imitate his imitation of Christ, that is, to become figures of Christ as he was a figure of Christ (1 Cor 11:1). Thus images of human beings and of Christ, images of human reality, and that includes film images, have a powerful theological valence. Further, the Christian faith is incarnational: it insists that God reveals God's-self in and through matter and in Christ – human matter – and not only once but in an ongoing way. Matter and material images are good, are in a certain sense, divinized and sacralized. Further still, Christianity is a storytelling religion, a religion of the Bible, which in large part, is narrative:[4] God telling God's story and the human story. It is a religion which finds its identity in the narratives of the creation, the fall, the promise, and in the "story" of salvation fulfilled in the Christ-event. Then, Christians know about this crucial Christ-event through the gospels, four narratives; and they know and meet God today through these narratives. Jesus in his ministry, revealed both God and himself through parables – "simple narratives that dramatize human conflicts . . . in the mode of fiction"[5] – through allegories, symbols and metaphors.

The critic Ronald Holloway points to four different levels or modalities for the analogical representation of Christ in film. The first level is when the Christ-figure functions merely as a sign: "The Christ figure is not a figure at all, but a mold to fit the Christ of tradition in simplified terms."[6] This is the typical use of the Christ-figure in overly-simplified films of Christian catechesis or propaganda. The second level is when the Christ-figure is represented as a myth: "Christ figure as myth leans on the cultural significance of Christ without turning to the questions of belief or historical truth."[7] As we shall see later, the typical example of this are the *Superman* films, or films which include only occasional or even single visual metaphors of Christ. On the third level, "the Christ figure as symbol concentrates on the primary significance of Christ for the Christian faith, his role as redeemer, adapted to the problems of this world."[8] Finally on the fourth level, the Christ-figure is the central figure of a narrative, which in all of its parts runs parallel to the Christ-story: the modality of extended metaphor or allegory. In most of the films we shall consider in this second part of the book, the Christ-figure functions at this level.

The cinematic Christ-figure is to be found in films of every *genre*: dramatic films, westerns, science-fiction films, comedies and satires, adventure films, films of social and psychological analysis and, as one might expect, religious films. As we have already noted, the Christ-figure has been an element in film from the beginning of the seventh art, in D. W. Griffith's *Intolerance,* till the present day, in Tim Robbins' *Dead Man Walking.* A critical dimension of the work of great film *auteurs* such as Tarkovsky, Bresson, Dreyer, Ford, Buñuel and Pasolini, and in single films of less significance artistically, the Christ-figure occurs in films by Christian artists, and in the work of film-makers who profess to be troubled believers, agnostics or atheists. The Christ-figure is embodied in a wide variety of forms: it is found in women and men and children; in saints, martyrs, nuns, priests and bishops; in clowns, fools, madmen and even in a donkey; in criminals, alcoholics, down-and-outers, lawmen and gunslingers.

At times, the Christ-figure is an overall dominant presence in the film and the christological action its governing theme; at other times, the Christ-figure is a *leitmotiv* parallel to the major theme. Sometimes, the Christ-figure is a metaphor repeated several times in the film, for example in a character whose identification with Christ emerges only for brief moments Finally, the reference to Christ can be a single image or shot, occurring only once in the film, at which point the term "Christ-figure" has a rather limited significance, in that it does not in any way refer to the dynamic of the protagonist in the entire film. For the Christ-figure to be fully authentic then, "the significant, substantial resemblance to Jesus is essential,"[9] both in the character in question, and in the central dynamic of this character's story.

A further distinction has to do with the difference between "faith-inspired representations of Christ and the more humanist, even atheistic, projections of the Jesus persona."[10] The fundamental point here is that the historical figure, Jesus of Nazareth, has a dual identity today: for the believing Christian, he is Jesus who is Risen, the Christ of faith, dynamic and active in our world; for the non-believer, he remains a historical figure, who lived and died and who now belongs to human culture, and as such is available to that culture as an secular icon, just as the Christ of the faith is for the Christian a sacred icon. Neil Hurley makes a distinction between "Christ figures and Jesus transfigurations in cinema,"[11] insisting that they are "differentiated on the basis of whether one affirms, at least implicitly, faith in Christ . . . or whether one draws on the universal cultural symbolic value of the Jesus persona."[12] Often, as we shall see, the Christ reference is a single and solitary visual or aural metaphor; Hurley would say this is a "Jesus transfigurations in the narrow sense (where the secular literary and historical traditions [of Jesus of Nazareth] serve as subtext for the film)."[13] When the metaphors are repeated, or extended to become the basis of narratives that reflect the fundamental dynamic of the Christ of the Christian faith, then, Hurley would say, we have classical "Christ figures (where the notions of messiahship, divinity or resurrection are demonstrably at work)."[14]

At this point, we must confront a delicate issue, one already raised in part one of this study, concerning the Christian faith or faithlessness of the film director. The basic question is: for a Christ-figure to be authentic, does the film-maker have to be a believing Christian? Can film-makers who claim to be atheist or agnostic create a valid metaphor of the Christ of the faith, or are they limited to creating Jesus-figures? In answer, three brief points can be made, which intend to justify the possibility of a non-believer's creating a filmic Christ-figure. First, it is crucial to interpret and judge the film first of all on its own merits, before asking the faith-qualifying question of the film-maker. Secondly, if a film-maker who professes to be an atheist can make a film about the life of Jesus (Pasolini's *Gospel According to Saint Matthew,* for instance) which receives the almost unanimous approval of Catholic critics, and the official recognition by the Catholic Church, then surely this film-maker or others can create a valid Christ-figure. Thirdly, the question of belief, non-belief, troubled belief, searching, agonized non-belief, is an extremely complex one. The lines of demarcation between belief and non-belief are sometimes very unclear and often include wide areas of grey. Perhaps, in fact, the sincere and coherent searching of the agnostic can be a valid position from which to search, to reflect artistically on the Christ-event by creating a Christ-figure.

The Christ-figure is neither Jesus nor the Christ, but rather a shadow, a faint glimmer or reflection of him. As a fully human being, the Christ-figure may be weak, uncertain, even a sinner, that is may have all the limits of any human being in the situation at hand. The Christ-figure is a foil to Jesus Christ, and between the two figures there is a reciprocal relationship. On the one hand, the reference to Christ clarifies the situation of the Christ-figure and adds depth to the significance to his actions; on the other hand, the person and situation of the Christ-figure can provide new understanding of who and how Christ is: "Jesus himself is revealed anew in the Christ-figure."[15]

Perhaps the first conscious attempt to use the dynamic of the Christ-figure in a film was in D. W. Griffith's monumental three-hour film, *Intolerance*. The film as we have already noted is composed of four stories, four episodes of human intolerance and cruelty, edited together in parallel: the conquest and destruction of Babylon by the Persians, the story of the passion of Jesus, the massacre of the Huguenots by Catherine de Medici (the St. Bartholomew's Night Massacre) and the contemporary fictional account of an innocent man, a worker arrested during a strike and condemned to death. In Griffith's film, the story of Jesus is the prime example of intolerance and as such, it provides a hermeneutic for the interpretation of the other three stories. The victims in the other episodes are understood and appreciated in reference to Jesus as the archetypal innocent victim. As Christ-figures, they then act as reciprocal hermeneutics for the event of the passion and death of Jesus: that archetypal event is widened, amplified because in a certain sense, Christ dies anew wherever an innocent woman or man dies because of human injustice and intolerance. This pattern of reciprocity is repeated whenever a filmmaker creates in the protagonist of a film, a figure of Christ. In the general introduction to this book, we coupled Griffith's early film with Denys Arcand's *Jesus of Montreal*. Let us now consider that film.

1

A Film of Transition:
Jesus of Montreal

Set in the city of Montreal in the present time, *Jesus of Montreal* tells the
story of Daniel Coulombe, a young unemployed actor, who is hired by the
priest-director of a Catholic shrine to update the text of a passion play presented each summer in the gardens of the shrine, and then to produce the new
version. The young man, bright, creative, charismatic, forms a collective with
a group of four actors whom he calls from various activities: Constance is an
unemployed actress working in a soup kitchen, Martin has been dubbing foreign porn movies, Mireille, young and very pretty, has been acting in television commercials that accentuate her body and René has been dubbing a
documentary about the origins of the universe. Daniel does library research
into the question of the historical Jesus, he speaks with a biblical scholar, he
consults his companions and together they produce the new script. The result
is a demythologizing text, radically different from the previous one. Among
other things it casts doubt on the divine origin of Jesus and therefore on his
divinity, by making him the illegitimate son of a Roman soldier, shifts around
events from the Gospel tradition and in the end seems to skirt the question of
the reality of Jesus' bodily Resurrection.

The opening night performance reveals a "very involving show,"[1] that is
original, full of action, movement and color, and elicits a very favorable reaction from the audience. Not so enthusiastic is *Père* Leclerc, director of the
shrine. Shocked by this all-to-human portrait of Jesus, and (especially) afraid
of the reaction of his religious superiors and the board of directors of the
shrine, he threatens Daniel. Thanks to coverage by the mass media, Daniel's
career seems ready to take off, but then almost immediately, he begins getting
in trouble. Reacting in holy wrath to the abuse of Mireille during auditions
for a beer commercial, he destroys some television equipment; at the end of
the second performance of the passion, he is arrested and put on trial, and
refusing the offer of help from a lawyer, he pleads guilty. The clever and
corrupt lawyer, Richard Cardinal, who specializes in managing media personalities, tries to persuade Daniel to become his client, promising him a "career
plan" and a brilliant future.

While awaiting the decision of the judge in his case, and against the
veto of *Père* Leclerc who wants the four disciples to produce the old version
of the passion play, but encouraged by his companions, Daniel decides to go
ahead with another performance. Before the end of the crucifixion scene, a
large contingent of police interrupts the performance and insists the people go
home. A free-for-all ensues, the cross is knocked down and Daniel's head is

crushed under the wood. Rushed to a hospital emergency room, too crowded to care for him, Daniel seems to recover and, accompanied by Mireille and Constance, he wanders through a subway station, preaching apocalyptically. In the end, he collapses and, rushed to a second hospital, he dies. The two women donate his organs for transplanting, and while two sick people recover, one with Daniel's heart, the other with his eyes, the lawyer Cardinal tries to enlist the cooperation of the disciples to form a theater in Daniel's memory. Only Mireille, the youngest, whom Daniel loved, resists the temptation and walks alone on the mountain of the crucifixion.

The context of *Jesus of Montreal*, both of the creation of the film and of its setting, is the postmodern post-traditional, "post-Catholic"[2] society of French Canada in the late 1980s. Until the 1960s Québec was a traditional Catholic society and culture. It put a premium on such values as a classical and Catholic education; large families characterized by fidelity, care, loyalty; a church-centered Catholic faith and *Weltanschauung*, with the institutional church considered as important as government; the virtues of hard work, honesty, respect for others, hospitality.

The "Quiet Revolution," "*la révolution tranquille*," of the 1960s and '70s changed all that rather drastically. The uncontested benefits of *la révolution tranquille* were many: a growth of pride in the French language and culture; the widespread democratization of political and social institutions, much good social legislation; the growth of the entrepreneurial class, with corresponding economic benefits for all; a greater openness to North American culture in general; a just shift in the monolithic political and economic power of the Roman Catholic Church. These changes were however accompanied by a wide range of negative changes in French Canada with rather devastating effects on that society and on individuals in it. Materialistic economic interests came to dominate many aspects of life which became vitiated by rampant consumerism, savage competition, and status- and success-seeking at all costs. Culture, now mass-mediated, commercialized and superficialized, became a commodity, an industry. Social relations, governed by economic rather than moral considerations, became manipulative, abusive and inhuman. The traditional family structure began to break down, the victim of economic stress, the "normalization" of short-term "no strings" relationships, divorce and the smorgasbord approach to sex. The Catholic religion, both as a personal faith and as a social, cultural structure, was replaced by new gods and new rituals, those of psychology, science, technology, astrology and sex.

Denys Arcand entered this fray as an *enfant terrible* of French-Canadian cinema and culture, a "Savonarola."[3] In his 1985 film, *The Decline of the American Empire,* he issued a stinging criticism of Québec society, which he accused of having sold out to the worst aspects of the dominant American culture, of having surrendered its distinctiveness and become a colony of the American empire. In *The Decline*, by focusing his attention on the dynamic of four couples, university professors, partners, lovers, who spend an evening and night at a cottage on a lake near Montreal, Arcand represents in their narcissistic attitudes and activities, in their casual infidelities and cruelties, and especially in the utterly mediocre quality of the pseudo-intellectual discussion, a microcosm of a tired, jaded, effete, navel-gazing society, materialistic, hedonistic and obsessed with sex. The critic Luigi Bini commenting on Arcand's film, speaks also of "the bitterness that broods beneath the varnished surface of this hedonism."[4] Behind the clever witticisms, the bright repartee, structured in an elegant, chamber-comedy style, Arcand reveals a society incapable of communicating beyond the most superficial banalities, and void of spiritual-moral values, a lost generation. The film concludes that "hedonism and lives based purely on the pursuit of pleasure are ultimately unfulfilling."[5] All the promise, the "sound and fury" of *la révolution tranquille*, ends up, suggests Arcand, in this moral and spiritual *cul de sac*, signifying nothing.

Four years later, Arcand, having lost none of his prophetic anger, continued his cinematic criticism of Quebec society, by turning his attention this time to the mass media, the culture industry, the world of advertising and the Church. But if, in *The Decline*, his criticism is bitter, cynical, without hope, in *Jesus of Montreal*, and notwithstanding the tough, hard-hitting quality of the film, Arcand does make a strong statement of hope, both in what he says, the content of the film, and in how he says it, its style. If *The Decline* pictures French Canadian society as a human and spiritual wasteland, desperately in need of salvation, then *Jesus of Montreal* announces the good news of that salvation, a hope embodied in the life and death of the young actor-director Daniel Coulombe, and in his identity and function as a Christ-figure.

In order to speak adequately about Daniel as a Christ-figure and about how and why Arcand constitutes him as such, we must backtrack briefly and address the reason for dealing with *Jesus of Montreal* film at the beginning of the second part of this book. As already suggested in the introduction to part two, *Jesus of Montreal* is a transitional film and this transitional quality is also an essential dimension of the salvific process carried forward by the protagonist of the film. Put most simply, if in the first part of this book we have explored the development and the variety of the explicit portrayals of Jesus Christ in cinema and if this second part of the book, we are to consider the implicit, metaphorical representations of Jesus in film via a wide variety of Christ-figures and Jesus-figures, then Arcand's film bridges the gap between these two approaches. The film has a Christ-figure,[6] the actor-director, Daniel Coulombe who, together with his companion actors, represents in their day-to-day lives and work, a variety of precise evangelical elements and situations.[7] At the same time, the film also presents a series of explicit portraits of Jesus Christ which become foils or a contrasting background to the Christ-figuring of Daniel. Arcand couches his social-moral-cultural criticism of Québec society precisely in the contrast, the dynamic confrontation between Daniel as Christ-figure and the Jesus-portraits among which he moves. Finally, Arcand very creatively and boldly embodies this confrontation in his protagonist Daniel by having him develop and then perform the role of Jesus in the passion play. In fact, Daniel becomes a Christ-figure precisely because he is the writer-director-actor of the passion play and because as such he has chosen to create the Jesus he does, both in the text of the play and in his performance. There is no doubt that the most powerful, most fascinating dimension of the film is precisely the ongoing tension of distinction-identification between Daniel-actor and Daniel-Jesus from the opening scene of the film when Daniel-actor is "proclaimed" as Daniel-Jesus by another actor and John the Baptist-figure, "the forerunner,"[8] till the end of the film when both Daniel-actor and Daniel-Jesus "die" on the cross.

Arcand undertakes the complex dynamic of the creation of a Christ-image in Daniel, via contrast with explicit images of Jesus early in the film when Daniel as writer of the updated passion play, beginning his personal research, comes face to face on a television screen with an excerpt from the previous version of the play. A few seconds of the videocassette is sufficient. The highly-theatrical performance in which the character of Jesus is lost behind the exaggerated gestures, the bombastic voices, the stylized costumes and choreography, is definitely not the model of Jesus that Daniel is looking for.[9] The second explicit image of Christ encountered in the film is the larger-than-life stone statue of Jesus condemned to death, the first station of the cross, in the garden of the shrine, which Daniel approaches and contemplates in silence as he begins his work on the new play, and then seen on several occasions both before and during the performances of the play. Imposing, monumental, static, impassive, it serves as a stage setting, a background, rather than as a model of Jesus, in the same way as the smaller liturgical stations of the cross seen later in the interior of the church as the final "passion" of Daniel is about to begin.

There is also the historical Jesus of the research undertaken by Daniel in order to update the script of *Père* Leclerc. A mysterious, elusive figure – Daniel says, "I'm beginning to realize that it's almost impossible to understand" (49) – "met" in the books of the national library and in the controversial and secret documents given him by a nervous theologian, a figure contoured by a few possible dates, some names, a few facts about crucifixion and iconography, this Jesus is for Daniel an access point to the Jesus Christ of the Gospel, who then becomes the concrete, dynamic, flesh-and-blood protagonist of the passion play. This latter "performed" Jesus really has little to do directly with Daniel's scientific quest for the historical Jesus. Arcand never shows Daniel with the Bible or consulting the gospels, but clearly they are the principal source of the material in the passion play: Arcand says, "I was also interested in creating a paraphrase of the passion . . . to model my own personal writing on that of the Gospel according to Saint Mark."[10] The concrete, vital, dynamic, living Jesus of the Gospel is the most important "Jesus" Daniel meets, the Jesus Christ he "becomes."

Arcand suggests another explicit image of Jesus later in the film. After Daniel is arrested, *Père* Leclerc convokes the cast of the passion play and

tries to convince them to substitute his traditional script. They respond negatively. Defending their own script and performance, they ridicule his and the
directorial instructions he tries to give them by parodying a scene from the
play in four distinct styles: *à la Comédie Française*, in method-acting style,
in *Québécois* dialect, and as a Japanese Kabuki actor would do it. In addition
to making fun of *Père* Leclerc, Arcand is here commenting on the phenomenon of the mass-mediated Jesus, the postmodern Jesus of the culture industry,
clever adaptations, audience-pleasing, but in the end, all style, no content.
Leclerc gets the point, the actors laugh and, approaching from behind Leclerc,
Daniel renders judgment on their theatrical models of Jesus by miming a gesture of *hari-kiri* and falling to the ground. Arcand gives to Daniel's gesture a
double significance: it is clearly a conscious rejection of the travesties of Jesus perpetrated by the culture industry, and ironically, it has a prophetic quality, as if Daniel senses the nearness of his own death.

Beyond these material images of Jesus, Arcand puts Daniel, and through
him, the viewers of the film, in contact with a series of less material images
of Jesus, those of the faith-understanding of a number of people he meets. In
these confrontations, also Daniel's faith in Jesus becomes clear. First, there is
the traditional faith-image of *Père* Leclerc, which seems to move from the
liberal pole at the beginning – he recognizes the limits of the thirty-five year
old version of the Jesus of the passion play, and its need of renewal – to the
orthodox pole when Daniel's version proves embarrassing and he wants to
return to the old version. Leclerc's faith is problematical: neither very clear
nor very solid. He insists at one point that "you can make the Gospels say
whatever you want. I know, from experience" (113), and in the end, having
confessed his hypocrisy, he seems to want to substitute the radical, dynamic
truth of Jesus Christ with a false Christ who offers easy comfort. In his final
appearance, after the death of Daniel when, preferring the comfort of his
clerical world, he closes his window to the thunderstorm and, symbolically, to
Jesus crucified, he seems to have lost his faith. Daniel models his Jesus differently.

Early in the film, in the library where Daniel has begun his search for
the historical Jesus, a strange librarian reassures him in a almost breathless
whisper, "It is He who will find you" (36). Seen again with an even-stranger
male companion after the premiere of the passion play, the woman's strange
esoteric, mystagogic, New-Age faith, is a mix of gospel, astrology, theoso-
phy, paranoia and sentimentalism:[11] "Jesus is so sweet, so positive" (92).
Daniel's Jesus has nothing to do with this one. In his brief conversation with
the theologian who nervously warning him of danger, furtively hands him
some pertinent archaeological-theological documents, Daniel meets an image
of Jesus which seems to be more a systematic intellectual construction, subject to change when the next issue of the favorite archaeological journal
comes out: no feelings, no courage, no commitment, no passion. This is certainly not Daniel's image of Jesus.

Among the members of the audience of the passion play, Daniel encounters the simple charismatic faith of a Haitian domestic who, twice during
the opening performance, overcome by emotion, identifies Daniel-Jesus with
the Jesus of her faith and rushes up to him begging for help. There is also the
rather rough, practical faith of the security guard, who during the passion play
directs the audience from one scene to another. An agent of comic relief, at
one point while explaining the ending of the play, he insists: "He dies on the
cross and afterwards he rises from the dead. Come on, lady, there's no mystery in that" (164). The man obviously does not appreciate the irony of what
he says.[12] For Daniel, there *is* mystery.

Finally, Daniel encounters the strange, post-Christian, neo-pagan "faith-
ignorance" of people who have seem to have no familiarity with the story of
Jesus. There is the woman who objects to the suspension of the final performance of the passion play during the crucifixion, insisting "We want to know
how it ends" (164). There is also the friendly young policeman who, apologetically arresting Daniel-Jesus on the cross at the end of the second performance, says: "I would've liked to see the ending" (135). Daniel's calm,
understanding response to this man who is arresting him, "You'll come
back," is a beautifully Christ-like moment.

Among these neo-pagans, the sophisticated but sleazy lawyer ranks
high. He certainly knows the Jesus story, but his offhand remark to Daniel
during the "temptation" scene – "Jesus Christ is an extremely fashionable
personality these days" (143) – reveals a faith in Jesus more as a media-
opportunity and money-making proposition than as personal Savior. Daniel
does not meet the lawyer another time. Arcand makes the court psychologist
less blatant than the lawyer, but no less pagan. In very objective scientific
tones, she asks Daniel, "Don't you find playing in the Way of the Cross on
the mountain rather ridiculous?" Daniel significantly responds, "Playing Jesus
. . . is anything but shabby" (139). This is a crucial moment in the film, for
whatever Daniel's position was in the beginning, Arcand is here suggesting
that his faith in Jesus, his commitment to Jesus is consciously taking root.

The Jesus of the passion play created and played by Daniel is clearly
the most vivid, dynamic and vital explicit portrayal of Jesus of Nazareth in
the film. In one sense, he is the "Jesus of Montreal" of the title, though nowhere in the film does Arcand give a title to the passion play.[13] Arcand situates this Jesus in a colorful, fast-moving dramatic presentation, with a cast of
four supporting actors and a number of original and dramatic effects. Moving
through an abridgement and rearrangement of the Gospel accounts, with, as
we have already noted, a precedence given to Mark, this Jesus works wonders: he walks on water, restores sight to a blind woman, raises the daughter
of Jairus. He preaches strongly and convincingly to the people, at times violating the limits of dramatic illusion and talking directly to the audience, offering them bread. He forms a company of disciples who recognize him as the
Messiah. He is condemned, scourged, crucified and dies. In a very original
scene which recalls the post-Resurrection appearance to Thomas, the disciples

at Emmaus and Pentecost, Daniel-Jesus rises from the dead. The faith of the disciples is renewed and they offer life and hope to all.

The play, and especially its Jesus, are taken seriously by the audience, who pay close attention and whom Arcand makes become "followers" of Jesus, since they follow him from station to station. The play is taken seriously by the media people and the critics, who insist it is "the show of the summer" (117), and by the clever lawyer Cardinal, one of "the sharks of show-business,"[14] who sees a good opportunity to make some money. It is taken very seriously by *Père* Leclerc, who is scandalized by its portrayal of Jesus as the illegitimate son of a Roman soldier, and hence Mary as an "unwed mother" (113). But perhaps most important of all, the passion play is taken seriously by the actors, who want it to go on at all costs, even when it is canceled by Leclerc, and by Daniel, who has created this Jesus and thus believes in him, "lives" in him: "it is no surprise that . . . as the performances of the play continue . . . Daniel, the Christ-figure, identifies with Christ."[15] If Daniel rejects the Jesus of the previous version of the passion play, the mediated Jesus-caricatures of his friends, and the Jesus of theology and of the faith of the esoteric librarian, he definitely stands by the Jesus of the passion play who is his creation in the writing and in the performing. All the evidence, therefore, seems to lead to the conclusion that also for Arcand, this Jesus of the passion play is the one, the "Jesus of Montreal" of the title of his film.

Yet it is very definitely not so. Having, through Daniel, created the passion play, Arcand then as creator-director of the film and as creator of the Christ-figure recognized in Daniel, subverts the passion play, weakens its impact, by a variety of techniques which we shall now discuss. In weakening the impact of the Jesus of the play, he strengthens the position and impact of Daniel as the Christ-figure of the film. This process of the subversion of the passion play takes a number of forms. On a first level, Arcand subverts the play by turning some of its personages into caricatures: the effete, philosophical Pilate, with his exaggerated make-up, studied gestures and vaguely tongue-in-cheek lines; the sadism of the High Priest who hovers in the background threatening Pilate; the bombastic Simon Magus and another magician, non-evangelical characters who seem to enjoy flying over the audience, propelled by fireworks and a crane.

On a second level, Arcand gives some sections of the passion play the quality of postmodern pastiches, "collections of pre-existing images, bits of culture, put together in a clever/clever fun/fun way."[16] The scene in which Jesus walks on water is transparently inspired by the scene a few minutes earlier of the actress Mireille "walking on water" in a perfume commercial. The reference in the post-Resurrection dialogue to the need for hope in this "enigmatic universe" (82) is inspired by the science documentary at the beginning of the film. Perhaps most obvious of all is the double reference to the "To be or not to be" soliloquy from *Hamlet*: the actor who wants it included in the passion play, eliciting laughter from Daniel, and then the recitation of the soliloquy during the Resurrection scene, creating the added irony that no one in the audience of the play, not even the sophisticated culture hounds, recognize its source. We do though, and that makes the difference. It creates distance between us and the passion play, it relativizes its significance, with the intended effect of enhancing more the significance of the "real" story of Daniel and his role as Christ-figure.

On a third level, we meet Arcand's subversion of the passion play in the variety of interruptions that seems to plague it and that keeps reminding us, the film audience, that we are watching a show within the show. First of all, Arcand never allows us to see the entire play uninterrupted; we see it three times, and each time, only in excerpts.[17] Then Arcand creates a series of humorous interruptions of which Marc Gervais comments: "The power of these sections [of the play] is temporarily broken again and again by gags."[18] There is the Haitian domestic who twice interrupts the performance with her declarations of faith; the security guard who subdues this woman and loudly reminds her that "this show, it's the actors who are putting it on, not you" (79), and who, in a distinctly working-class accent, herds the crowd from station to station. The effect of each of these "unexpected" interruptions is to break the fictional frame that we film viewers build around the performance, to break the psychological process of the "willing suspension of disbelief" by which we "enter into" the action of the *via crucis* and accept it as real. When Arcand's interruption jolts us out of that "willing suspension of disbelief," we automatically disbelieve the passion play which has been revealed to be an illusion and we fall back on the previous illusion-become-reality in whose favor we have, at the beginning of the film, willingly suspended our disbelief: the story of Daniel, a reality and a suspension of disbelief not once interrupted.

Another technique Arcand uses, more subtle this time, is, on several occasions during a performance, to allow the precise limits or contours of the structure of the passion play to become extremely fluid or to disappear altogether, moments in which "life starts imitating art."[19] For example, Daniel-Jesus, speaking on the difficulty for the rich man to enter the Kingdom of God, says the words directly to a superstar television actor, flanked by stunningly beautiful identical starlets. Or again in the second performance, when Daniel-Jesus warns the people against trusting hypocritical priests, he fairly spits out the words at *Père* Leclerc and his two superiors. Further, during the three performances of the play, Arcand often films the action in such a way that, in the frame are included members of the audience, looking on, following the actors, arriving at the crucifixion. The effect of this technique is again to relativize the passion play, to keep reminding the film audience that they are witnessing a theatrical production and that this Jesus is in fact not Jesus but an actor.

No doubt the most significant technique, and perhaps the most subtle, Arcand employs to subvert the passion play, is that he inserts it within another story, that of Daniel and his companions, a story which exists before and after the passion play, and which continually intrudes on it.[20] The film audience already knows the story of Jesus' passion: "The Christ story is taken for granted."[21] What interests in the passion play is the technique, the style, the interpretation given by the director and the actors. Clearly of greater interest is the story of Daniel, the real protagonist of the film. Marc Gervais explains this two level dynamic precisely, and adding a third level, anticipates the further development of Daniel as a Christ-figure: "We are distanced [from the play], yes, but also pulled into that other story, the story of Daniel – and paradoxically, through that other story, into the experience of Christ himself."[22]

A further level on which Arcand relativizes the moral seriousness of the passion play, of the "serious" portrait of Jesus based on scientific research,[23] is that he makes it very popular with the audience, which breaks into enthusiastic applause and bravos at the conclusion of the first performance and defends the final performance from the interruption by the police. Daniel as actor and director, justifies the play to a livid *Père* Leclerc, insisting on this positive audience reaction: "But it [the play] works! They follow!" (113). Popular with the audience, it is very popular, too popular with the mass media people on whom Arcand centers his attention at the end of the premiere: a radio show hostess, with tears in her eyes, cries out, "My God!" (84) but the irony of her expression is lost to her. A television talk-show hostess gushes, "It's beautiful, it's rich. It's strong. It's so strong" (84), while an ever-so-slightly gay but very serious theater critic, grasping Daniel's hand, says with high self-importance and a very pregnant pause, "I like it . . . a lot. It's a show not to be missed!" (84). Arcand undermines the import of these comments by revealing that these three media personalities have made precisely the same comments, the same gestures, to the attractive young lead actor at the end of the Dostoevsky piece in the prologue of the film.

Then Arcand makes the personal reactions of the media personalities to the passion play take the form – the very next day (a minute or so later in the film) – of a full-blown media event.[24] In a devastating satire in which he represents "the theater critics and their eccentricities . . . in a scathing manner,"[25] Arcand edits in parallel the radio show and the television show of two of these personalities, and then has them contradict each other regarding Daniel: "He graduated with highest honors from drama school," "a young self-taught actor, who never went to theater school," and the gushing comments of the evening before continue: "the hit show of the summer," "[Daniel] is *the* new show-biz personality," "a show which *really* involves you," "a *must*" (118-119). Clearly here, Arcand is further subverting the passion play by allowing it to be co-opted by the mass media and, shortly after, by the culture industry in the person of the smooth and sleazy lawyer, who tries to seduce Daniel into his stable of show-biz clients, or, as he insists on calling them, "friends" (142).

To sum up, Arcand subverts the passion play, creates distance between it and the audience, for one and only one reason, his desire to focus attention on Daniel-the actor-the man. Thus, Daniel and his story, lived out against the background of the passion play, assume both in their main contours and in their details, incontrovertible dimensions of the Gospel events, clearly creating in Daniel a Christ-figure.

Let us first consider some of the main contours of Daniel as a Christ-figure. Many aspects of Daniel's origins, his family, his past life, remain a mystery, though there is the suspicion of his having been on a "spiritual quest" (184), which in a general way reflects the divine mystery of Jesus' origins and of his hidden life as he prepares for his mission. When Daniel begins his activity of preparing the passion play, the first thing he does is to search for disciples. He accepts them as they are and calls them out of the activities they are in by offering them something more valid. That is precisely what Jesus did. Then Daniel is without a home; he creates community with his disciples by breaking bread (pizza) with them, and in him, the disciples experience new meaning and significance, spiritual freedom, in their lives.[26] In the text he writes and in the events "around" the play, Daniel reveals himself to be a perceptive and courageous critic of both secular and religious institutions. First, he attacks the mass media-advertising industry to which he reacts violently as Daniel and the inconsistency, cowardice, hypocrisy of *Père* Leclerc; then, as Daniel-Jesus, he attacks the arrogant and avaricious priests with their titles, privileges and power. This pattern also reflects the experience of Jesus. Then, "rendered a Christ-like figure by these events, he [Daniel] pursues the parallels to their tragic conclusion."[27] His criticism and actions having become intolerable to the Establishment, a threat to their power, he is persecuted and dies on a cross.[28] Then, again like Jesus, Daniel experiences a "resurrection," both in his body whose organs give life to others, and in the memorial theater established in his name, rather like the Church which is the "Mystical Body of Christ."[29]

Arcand has Daniel reflect aspects of the Christ-event also in a dense network of intricate details which are never gratuitous or unjustified references to the Gospel, but always have precise meaning on both levels of the allegory. For example, Arcand points to the christological identity of Daniel when he has him identified as being a greater one by his friend, a John the Baptist-figure, to whom Daniel has come "to be inspired" (21) for his role as Jesus. Daniel-actor always wears white as he does in the role of Jesus.[30] Like Jesus, he is thirty years old when he begins his work; he is open, tolerant of individuals no matter what their weaknesses, but he can get into a holy rage when he faces hypocrisy, injustice, institutional abuse of people.[31]

Like Jesus, Daniel has a privileged relationship with women: they are among his first followers and they and not the male disciples accompany him in his passion and death[32] and they visit his "grave," where the two young women in the conclusion of the film sing the "Stabat Mater" at the point where he died.[33] Daniel submits to being washed by Mireille, whom he has saved from "prostitution" in the advertising industry, clearly a reference to Mary Magdalene who washes Jesus' feet. Arcand has Daniel live in the apartment of Constance along with Mireille, suggesting the relationship of Jesus with Martha and Mary, and insofar as it is these two women who sign the documents for the organ transplants at the end of the film, they might be said to be present at his "resurrection."

Beyond allegorical parallels, it is especially in the quality of Daniel's relationship with the two women that Arcand has him reflect Jesus. Arcand makes Daniel celibate,[34] a celibacy which he lives in a mature and fully-integrated manner, a way of being with others which, like that of Jesus, is open, welcoming and freeing. Both Mireille and Constance seem to have had negative experiences with men: Constance is not married but has a daughter; Mireille, "Arcand's central image for matter yearning for more,"[35] has been living with a "playboy director"[36] of sexist television commercials, a caricature of Roman Polanski, who insists that as an actress her "greatest talent is her ass" (48). Arcand has Daniel, who in this represents the possibility of "pure love,"[37] redeem them from these abuses, and given the leering perverted sexuality of the lawyer in the film, and of the characters in his previous film, Arcand makes Daniel-Jesus into the protagonist of and "apocalyptic battle" between a balanced and "tender sexuality" and a "diseased sexual imagination."[38]

Furthering Daniel's association with Jesus, Arcand has him chase the money-changers, that is the media people making a sexy and sexist beer commercial, out of the temple (the theater), which should be dedicated by higher rituals. When he is arrested for this drastic action, he appears before the judge without a lawyer. Like Jesus, Daniel speaks with moral authority, for example when he is defending the innocent in the theater, when he speaks the truth about himself with the court psychologist and when he is criticizing the abuse of power, the perversion of the truth in his own church in the passionate discussion he has with *Père* Leclerc before the final, tragic performance of the play.

When Daniel goes to lunch with the lawyer, Richard Cardinal,[39] they meet on the top floor of a skyscraper. The lawyer explains to Daniel all the fame, riches and power that can be his, with him (Cardinal) as his agent and career planner. Then in a remarkable zoom-to-close-up shot of the two men face-to-face in a window, the city below them, Arcand has the lawyer say to Daniel in a conspiratorial whisper, "This city is yours, if you want it" (145). This temptation in the desert-wasteland of the modern metropolis has a wider focus than the analogous scene in Scorsese's *Last Temptation* film, in which "the emphasis is mostly on sex, and the devil speaks with Barbara Hershey's vocal chords."[40] More faithful to the biblical account of the temptations of Jesus in Matthew 4, Arcand "restores the focus to broader temptations to deceit and power . . . indicting the fashion for greed and celebrity that have made lawyers like 'Cardinal' the power brokers of our age."[41] Around this same time, Arcand has the John the Baptist-figure "beheaded," victim of an advertising executive (Salome): his head appears in a publicity campaign for a new perfume. Thus the young actor becomes also a Judas-figure, who has betrayed his art (theater) and his messiah, Daniel.

Moving into the sequences of the film parallel to the passion of Jesus, in an atmosphere heavy with foreboding, Daniel together with his disciples has a final meal, of wine and bread (pizza). During the meal he has a moment of doubt, which Reinhold Zwick sees as a reference to the agony in the garden.[42] The meal, picnic-style, takes place in a park-garden on the mountain. Though aware of the dangers involved, Daniel decides to do one more performance of the passion play as a confirmation of his salvific relationship with his disciples (134), by which Arcand gives to his subsequent death a sacrificial-salvific dimension. As already noted, Daniel dies on the cross, his death marked by a thunderstorm, as was the death of Jesus. The strange scene between the "death" of Daniel on the cross and his final collapse, in which he descends into the depths of the earth, a subway station, and wanders about delivering apocalyptic warnings and predictions, is clearly a reference to Jesus' apocalyptic discourse in Mark's Gospel.[43] It is a delirium totally justified within the diegesis of the film: in Arcand's own words, "Coulombe has just spent three months putting together the show. . . . An actor who undergoes such a shock [brain injury] could not help but be delirious . . . about the show, about what he has read, about what is living in him."[44]

Finally, there is the question of the Resurrection. Since we shall deal with the "resurrection" of Daniel again below, suffice it to say here that Arcand suggests several parallels between the popular understanding of the Resurrection of Jesus and the events "around" Daniel after his death. The transplant of his organs, that is the sacrifice of his body and blood on the cross-shaped operating table, which gives life, sight, hope to others, is a positive, grace-filled analogy of the death and Resurrection of Jesus. It is not by chance that the doctor, commenting on Daniel's type "O" blood, says "That's a godsend" (181). One critic sees several levels of christological significance in this: "This (eucharistic) blood, sent through the Holy Spirit, is rare and saving."[45] Regarding the organ-transplants, in making one recipient English and the other Italian, Arcand gives a universal quality to this salvific resurrection gesture.

Arcand also points to the "resurrection"-living-on of Daniel in the proposed theater company to carry his name. The parallel is, as we have already noted, to the founding of the Church, the "Mystical Body of Christ," in which the resurrected Christ lives in his members. This second parallel is less grace-filled than the first: the theater project is formulated by the lawyer Cardinal, the tempter of Jesus, and will have the weak Martin Durocher (literally, "of the rock," and so, Peter) as its first president, and with profit as one of its *raisons d'êtres*. Behind it all, the theater company becomes an image of a corrupt, hierarchical Church, with profit as its moving force and Satan as its inspiration. We shall speak more of this reference later. Arcand, perhaps at his most sarcastic here, has Mireille, the youngest of the disciples, walk out on the meeting in Cardinal's office. She returns to the mountain of the crucifixion, to mourn the death of her savior and perhaps to experience his resurrection.

Arcand makes it quite clear throughout the film that the correspondence between Daniel as the Christ-figure and Jesus is by analogy, that is it respects the distinction between Daniel-man-director-actor and Jesus the Christ of the Gospel, of the Christian faith. In other words, Daniel Coulombe, in the uniqueness and specificity of his life, has experiences which can be seen to be parallel in meaning to events in the life of Jesus Christ as transmitted in the gospels. There are however, several points in the film at which the parallel lives of Daniel as Christ-figure and Jesus Christ cease to be parallel, but converge and meet. They are moments in which the christological dimension of Daniel-Christ-figure is so strong, comes so close to the Christ he is representing, that the distinction fades and, however briefly, the Christ-figure and the Christ figured seem to be the same person. It would appear that we are here before a situation that is quite unique in religious cinema, in the cinema of the Christ-figure.

The most evident of these situations is that of Daniel's dying on the cross. Though at first glance, Daniel's death on the cross may seem to be accidental, while Jesus' surely was not, a closer analysis reveals that the violent confrontation between the police and the crowd resulting in Daniel's death is the logical conclusion of the conflict, ever increasing, ever more confrontational, between Daniel and *Père* Leclerc and the shrine authorities. Daniel seems to have an ominous sense of how this conflict might end when, after the conversation with Leclerc the night of the premiere, he seems depressed and says to his disciples, "I only hope it lasts" (116), a remark that seems to echo the earlier comment of one of the disciples who speaks of the danger of producing a tragedy on stage: "When you act in a tragedy, misfortunes often happen" (55). Also in the gospels, Jesus has a sense of impending tragedy.

Twice during the performance of the passion play, Arcand brings the text of Jesus' words so close to the reality that Daniel-the-actor is living in that moment, that Jesus' words seem to be Daniel's own. Once when Daniel-Jesus is speaking of the difficulty for the rich man to enter the Kingdom of Heaven (71), Daniel-the-actor walks over to a man in the audience and speaks the words directly to him. Soon after this man is identified as a famous, and, one presumes, rich film and television star. Who then speaks the words? Daniel-Jesus or Daniel-the-actor and Christ-figure? Or again, more dramatically this time, during the second performance of the passion play, when Daniel-Jesus is warning the people to beware of corrupt priests, he walks over to *Père* Leclerc and his two superiors, stares at them and says: "Do not ever insist on being called 'Rabbi' or 'Reverend Father' or 'Monsignor' or 'Your Eminence'" (132). Clearly this is a moment in which the conflict of Jesus with his church and that of Daniel with his, overlap, are one.[46] There is also the fascinating and disturbing scene, already referred to, near the end of the film, in the subway station, in which the dying Daniel-actor, no longer in the role of Jesus, staggers from person to person, crying out apocalyptic warnings. These are words taken from the Gospel of Mark and a scene not

"played" in the passion play. It is Daniel-the-actor speaking, but his identification with Jesus as the eschatological prophet is very deep.

This brings us to the fascinating question of Daniel-the-actor's consciousness of being a Christ-figure. An important theme in the theological
investigation of the historical Jesus, is the very complex issue of the developing consciousness in Jesus, as human being, of being a prophet, the Messiah,
the Incarnation of God. The crucial and analogous issue about *Jesus of Montreal* is whether Arcand suggests in Daniel any consciousness of being a
Christ-figure, that is of going beyond the mere role of Jesus in a play. Does
Arcand give Daniel any awareness that, in his own personal experience as a
man, as an actor, producing this passion play and living these conflicts, he is
reproducing the pattern of the life of Jesus the Christ? The question put simply is: does Daniel come to identify himself with Jesus Christ? Or to put it
another, and perhaps more provocative way, is there evidence in the film to
suggest that Daniel-the-actor, perhaps remembering the prediction of the esoteric librarian – "Are you looking for Jesus? . . . It is he who will find you."
(35-36) – has any sense of meeting in his concrete human experience the
Jesus of the Christian faith, of experiencing a "brush with the mystery of
Jesus"?[47]

Concerning this issue, Zwick says that Daniel's "destiny becomes ever
more like that of Jesus" and he asks rhetorically if it is possible that Daniel
"can play Jesus with such intensity . . . without a conscious self-identification
with the role?"[48] Arcand himself seems to suggest an answer to Zwick's question when he speaks more generally about *Jesus of Montreal* being a film
about actors: "I wanted to examine the paradox of the actor: he never knows
where the role [he is playing] begins or where his own personality ends."[49]
Beyond Arcand's own reflection, there is also considerable evidence in the
film to suggest that Arcand does intend some degree of such self-consciousness in Daniel. When, for example, the mysterious librarian walks away from
Daniel, Arcand has him look at her with interest, with no evident gesture of
rejection or ridicule. At the time, this reaction is of little obvious import but
later, in retrospect, it becomes important. Further, in the first of the two interruptions of the passion play by the Haitian woman who recognizes Jesus in
Daniel, he, though a fine actor and presumably capable of dealing with interruptions, remains curiously shaken, immobile, silent, troubled. Is it only because of the interruption to the play or is it because the woman has struck
some chord in him, has reminded him of something he has already considered? The already-discussed violent words spoken, perhaps ad-libbed, to the
three priests might also suggest some awareness of self-identification with
Jesus as does the apocalyptic monologue in the subway station. No doubt the
most significant detail for suggesting a self-identification with Jesus occurs at
the end of the second performance of the passion play. Daniel-the-actor is
hanging on the cross, eyes closed, playing the dead Jesus. The crowd has left
and at the foot of the cross remain only the two policemen, there to arrest
him. Arcand has Daniel remain eyes closed, silent, "as if in a bodily medita-

tion-contemplation of the death of Jesus and the policemen have to explicitly 'wake him' out of it."[50]

Though Arcand's film won a variety of international awards, including the O.C.I.C. ecumenical prize at the Cannes Film Festival in 1989, and though it has been well-received by church groups all over the world, it is often criticized and often the rationale of the criticism touches the question of Daniel as a Christ-figure. The first two typical objections can be dealt with expeditiously. One point often made is that the Christ-figure in Daniel is severely weakened, ineffectual, because the image of the Church in the film is exaggeratedly negative, a caricature, and that renders the christological quality of Daniel's death not credible. Not so! The image of the Catholic Church in the film is embodied in *Père* Leclerc, and in him Arcand creates anything but a caricature. Leclerc is a carefully-drawn, well-developed, complex tragic figure.

Another typical objection to Daniel as Christ-figure has to do with the community he creates with his four disciples. It is "too democratic," vaguely communistic, as is the "collective script" (44) Daniel proposes to write with them: they are all equal and Daniel is no spiritual leader. It is clear that Daniel forms a community with his disciples, a community in which they are healed and grow in spiritual freedom. It is also true that one suggestion of a disciple – the "To be or not to be" soliloquy – becomes part of the script, perhaps in the same way as the Gospel Jesus entrusted aspects of his mission to his disciples. But it is also overwhelmingly clear that, like Jesus, Daniel is the moral, creative and organizational leader of the company, and it is he, not the others, who suffers and dies.

The principal objection of Catholics to the film, and so to Daniel as the Christ-figure, is its portrayal of the Resurrection, both as Daniel-writer-director presents it in the passion play and as it is represented metaphorically and analogically in the events following Daniel's death. The former is not our concern here, and in any case, Zwick's excellent analysis demonstrates well how Arcand-Daniel's version is a complex, subtle and valid representation of the Resurrection.[51] Regarding the portrait of Daniel as Christ-figure, clearly its full effectiveness depends on the representation of the Resurrection-event. Just as Jesus of Nazareth would not be The Christ without the Resurrection-event, in the same way no Christ-figure is fully-satisfactory unless, on some level, the Resurrection is suggested and justified in his experience.

In Daniel as Christ-figure, Arcand represents the Resurrection of Jesus the Christ in three aspects of the events following his death. On a first level, he suggests the "resurrection," or at least the living-on of Daniel in the establishment of a theater company in his memory, which, as we have already noted, is a transparent reference to the establishment of the Church. But many object to the "blasphemous" nature of this "resurrection": this "church" in which Daniel-Christ-figure will live on and his work continue, is being founded by the sleazy lawyer, the great tempter. Clearly, as we already have said, this is a tough criticism of what Arcand sees as the exaggerated hierar-

chical and economic dimensions of the Church, the sinfulness of the Church.
To those who cry "Blasphemy" the response is simple: the Catholic (or Christian) Church, *casta meretrix*,[52] in its two thousand years of existence has always struggled with the element of its own sinfulness. Witness to this are the
recent public "apologies" of Pope John Paul II for the injustices the Church,
as institution, and so as the Mystical Body of Christ, has committed against
the Jews, against women, against the Protestants. Yet the Church has never
ceased to be a living mystical embodiment of the resurrected Christ. Thus
Arcand's analogy is acceptable and fruitful especially regarding Daniel as
Christ-figure. He is not sinful but his "embodiment" in his disciples can be;
as we have already noted, one of the disciples maintains her integrity and
thus, the integrity and purity of the legacy of Daniel in her.

On a second level, Arcand represents analogically the Resurrection of
Christ in the experience of Daniel in the new life and hope given to the re-
cipients of Daniel's transplanted organs. Three details included by Arcand,
beyond the already-noted universal aspect of this new hope, are particularly
significant. First, the first words spoken by the man who receives Daniel's
heart is "God!" (185) as if a prayer, a song of praise, or perhaps a cry of
recognition. Second, at the head of the hospital bed of the woman who receives Daniel's eyes, Arcand places an image of the Sacred Heart of Jesus,
visible for only a few seconds, but long enough to suggest the presence of
Daniel-Christ in this reality. The third detail is earlier, during the transplant
surgery on Daniel. Arcand has him outstretched on the cross-shaped operating
table: a surgeon preparing him for the surgery paints the centre of his chest
with a red disinfectant. It becomes a transparent image of the Sacred Heart,
Jesus giving his heart, himself, out of love, far more significant and credibly
imbedded in the analogy, than the *grand-guignol* and thoroughly unevangelical "Sacred Heart" scene in Scorsese's *The Last Temptation of Christ*. An
accusation often levelled at this analogy of the Resurrection in Arcand is that
it is too heavy, too material, and therefore, not spiritual: a "technological
micro-resurrection,"[53] an accusation that does not stand up to the evidence.
First, Arcand is creating an analogy of the Resurrection of Jesus Christ, in the
concrete, specific experience of a physical, material human being. So it is
quite permissible for the "carrier" of the analogical meaning to be material.
Second, Arcand determines that the reactions of both "witnesses" to the "resurrection" of Daniel to be spiritual: one praises God and the other expresses
gratitude. Finally, Arcand makes of the transplant surgery only one of three
"carriers" of the "resurrection" of Daniel. It is supported, in different ways,
by the founding-of-the-Church analogue and by a much more original analogue, dense with Resurrection meaning, in the conclusion of the film, which
we shall now consider.

Normally, during the closing sequence of a film, when the credits appear on the screen, the audience begins to leave the cinema. Those who follow this example at the end of *Jesus of Montreal* will miss one of the most
significant moments of the film, namely an extradiegetical statement by Ar-

cand proclaiming the resurrection of Daniel, his protagonist Christ-figure. The shot, some two hundred and seventy seconds long and noted rather deceptively in the script as "End Credits" (188), is apparently one uninterrupted *plan-séquence* shot,[54] and begins in the subway station. At the very spot where Daniel has collapsed and died, analogically the tomb of Jesus, two young women are singing, in a "slow and highly dramatic"[55] way, the conclusion of Pergolesi's "Stabat Mater." They are the same two women who, in the prologue of the film, were singing in the choir of the shrine where they saw Daniel for the first time, and who later auditioned for the beer commercial, where they witnessed Daniel-Christ-figure at his most prophetic. In this scene Arcand is suggesting that they too have become his disciples: they visit his "grave," they have chosen a life of "evangelical" poverty, relying on handouts from passersby, they continue singing and this time the words, which continue on the soundtrack long after we no longer see the singers, are a Resurrection prayer:

> When my body dies,
> Grant that my soul not be denied,
> The glory of Paradise.
> Amen.[56]

After a slow zoom away from the singers, Arcand shifts his camera to observe them from far above (perhaps the point of view of the "risen" Daniel). At this point he begins the *plan-séquence* with a slow, very steady movement of the camera to the left. The two singers disappear and the camera moves into what seem to be an abstract image of the interior of the earth and the cosmos. It moves horizontally for seventy-five seconds, all the while the singing voices reminding us of Resurrection hope until almost imperceptibly, the horizontal movement become vertical, of an order that is "not logical but purely symbolic."[57] The credits of the film begin to appear, in white letters against the background of the horizontal and then the vertical movement through the earth. At first these credits are still, fading in and fading out, but after forty-five seconds, they too begin to move vertically. At this point, and for two full minutes, Arcand boldly creates a *double vertical movement,*[58] continuing the Resurrection hymn, through the earth, then into a building, the shrine's church, past a stained-glass window, composed of three vertically-reaching Gothic *flèches,* with a blazing white morning sun breaking through it, a traditional symbol of Easter. The movement continues upwards out of the church to the skyline of the city at dawn, and finally, to the mountain top, where in the final seconds, the camera rests on the empty cross. In this remarkable concluding shot, Arcand is saying directly to us, the viewers of his film – we are the only witnesses to this extradiegetical "resurrection" – that in the death of Daniel, Christ-figure, "a new morning dawns."[59]

2

The Woman as Christ-Figure:
La strada, Nights of Cabiria, Babette's Feast, Out of Rosenheim (*Bagdad Cafe*) and *Dead Man Walking*

The logical place to begin any discussion of the woman as a filmic Christ-figure is in the good number of films dedicated to women saints: the extensive Joan of Arc cycle, with its two masterpieces by Dreyer and Bresson, Alain Cavalier's recent film on Thérèse of Lisieux, *Thérèse* (1986) and perhaps Augusto Genina's award-winning, but little distributed, *Cielo sulla palude* (1949), the story of Maria Goretti, saint and martyr. The point we are making here is that the woman saint is a Christ-figure because she lives fully her Christian vocation to be *imitatio Christi*, because she quite consciously conforms her life and her death to the pattern of the life and death of Christ. In this sense, as the stories of these women saints develop, we begin to see behind or within them, images or reflections of the ideal of humanity-achieving-Divinity represented by Jesus Christ.

These women saints we have just mentioned, and of whom we shall speak further in the "Saint as Christ-figure" section of chapter six, are easily recognized as Christ-figures against a background of highly-principled spiritual and moral struggle, involving global forces of good and evil, martyrdom, sainthood, with significant public, ecclesial and historical consequences. It is a struggle between, on the one hand, the highest spiritual ideals lived out with intelligence and integrity, with nobility and heroism, and, on the other hand, monumental powers of evil, in some sense almost equally matched with those of good. The filmic images of these Christ-figures, universally-recognized spiritual giants, struggling against sophisticated forces of evil, have the effect of edifying the viewers, challenging them to move towards this level of spiritual integrity.

But not all women Christ-figures are saints. In this chapter, we shall consider how the women protagonists of five films, not one of them a saint, represent in their persons and in their lives and struggles, various patterns of the life, death and Resurrection of Christ. The two films of Fellini we shall now discuss move us into a very different world from that of the saint, an environment which, at first glance, might seem to have little or nothing to do with considerations of spiritual integrity and heroism, with two protagonists who seem to be light years away from anything near sanctity or *imitatio Christi*.

To imagine how the protagonists of *La strada* and *Nights of Cabiria* can be considered Christ-figures, we have to adjust downward our spiritual sights. It might help to recall that, in addition to the biblical image of Christ in the Resurrection or the Transfiguration, or as the miracle-worker-healer-teacher, there is also the image of Christ in the suffering servant of Yahweh spoken of by Isaiah in the Old Testament, and the image of a Jesus powerless on the cross. There is also the Jesus who touched and healed untouchables, outcasts, who took seriously his association with sinners and prostitutes, an element of the New Testament accounts that we perhaps tend to sanitize today. If we take seriously this Jesus who fully incarnates himself into every dimension of human experience, and who may have thus appeared to be a failure, an anti-hero, it is a little easier to imagine how Gelsomina of *La strada* and Cabiria of *Nights of Cabiria*, in addition to having much in common with each other,[1] can also be seen to have enough in common with Jesus Christ to justify considering them Christ-figures.

Fellini's *La strada*

Set in northern Italy in the early 1950s, Fellini's *La strada*, a film considered by many scholars and critics as one of the absolute masterpieces of world cinema, and a "profoundly Christian work,"[2] tells the strange and tragic story of Zampanò, an itinerant performing strongman, and Gelsomina, a simple girl sold to Zampanò by her mother and forced by him to be his assistant and, when he has no one else, his bed-partner. Gelsomina submits to this degrading slavery blindly, helplessly. In the course of their wandering – the road in Fellini being almost always a metaphor of the journey of life – Gelsomina comes to self-awareness and understanding of her mission in life through her conversation with two people. The first is a circus tightrope-walker called "The Clown,"[3] the second is a nun who offer Gelsomina and Zampanò overnight shelter in the barn of her convent. In her relationship with "The Clown," described by one critic as a "spiritual flirting,"[4] simple little Gelsomina is enlightened and strengthened in her resolve. In their brief conversation concerning a pebble, become one of the best-known scenes in world cinema, "The Clown" explains to Gelsomina, caught in a moment of discouragement, that like the pebble, even her life has meaning, and that she is meant to continue helping Zampanò, otherwise he would have no one to take care of him. The nun encourages Gelsomina, sympathizing with her misgivings and speaking to her of spiritual freedom in her relationship with Zampanò, words which then inform all that Gelsomina does.[5]

Thus Gelsomina resumes her mission with renewed vigor. When, however, Zampanò, in a fit of jealous rage, brutally kills "The Clown," Gelsomina goes into a decline and, abandoned by her man, she dies, a death which takes place off-screen. Some time later, Zampanò finds out about her death and, in the conclusion of the film, one night after a violent, drunken spree, he ends up kneeling on the beach, facing the ocean, and in a graced moment of self-awareness, he breaks down and cries.

Fellini has Gelsomina live in a squalid world of poverty, brutality, and violence, and in that world, he gives her a shiftless, nomadic existence, moving from town to town, in and out of circuses, her only home the small trailer attached to Zampanò's motorcycle. Handicapped socially if not mentally, "Gelsomina is an outcast from society . . . throughout her life, her insignificance has been revealed to her again and again,"[6] and with Zampanò, she is little more than a slave.[7] In her clown's make-up and costume, Fellini seems to underscore the ridiculousness of her person, and in her death, not represented on-screen, he seems to suggest the absurdity of her existence and the "tragic interdependence"[8] of her relationship with Zampanò. According to this interpretation, the film becomes the melodramatic and hopeless tragedy of a common woman and its conclusion, "infinitely sad."[9]

Two elements in the film, however, oblige the serious viewer to go beyond this first level of interpretation. Firstly, there is the irrepressible innocence and vitality of Gelsomina and her growing self-consciousness – "a spiritual odyssey along the road"[10] – best represented in the close-up shots in which Fellini creates, especially in her eyes, a veritable icon of goodness. Secondly, the no-less-than-miraculous conversion of Zampanò at the end of the film defies understanding,[11] unless it is somehow connected to Gelsomina's goodness and to the death she suffers because of that goodness. It is precisely his particular attention to these two points that prompt André Bazin, the great film critic and theorist, to see *La strada* as "a phenomenology of the soul and perhaps even of the Communion of Saints, at least of the interdependence of salvation."[12]

Re-examining various moments of the film from this new perspective, an interesting pattern regarding Gelsomina begins to emerge which demonstrates definite christological elements, and allows us to interpret the film as "a purely spiritual odyssey, once which can be summarized in three stages: misery, sacrifice, redemption."[13] There is Gelsomina's situation of total subjugation, helplessness and passivity, in which one can perceive elements of a self-emptying incarnation. The fact that the sea is a recurrent image in the film, clearly associated with Gelsomina, visited twice by her and then by Zampanò, is not by chance: in the opening of the film, "Gelsomina kneels before the sea as if in a last moment of confidence, perhaps in a final giving up of herself . . . she seems to receive a sort of consecration from it."[14] In the conclusion, the drunk and desperate Zampanò is at the same sea, an image of "apotheosis, of beginning, of sacramental birth, as Zampanò bathes himself in Gelsomina's element, the sea."[15] Fellini himself would seem to confirm this spiritual significance of the sea when he says: "The great sea and the distant sky which I like to show in my films are not enough: beyond sea and sky, through terrible suffering perhaps, or the relief of tears, God can be glimpsed – his love and his grace."[16] Gelsomina's meeting and subsequent friendship with "The Clown," in which she first sees him wearing angel's wings and balancing on a tightrope high above the town square headed towards the church, is a "vehicle of grace for Gelsomina."[17] Their subsequent conversation "around" the pebble – "the parable of the pebble"[18] – in which he confirms her meaning in life, her vocation to save Zampanò, clearly suggests an experience of divine mission.[19]

Gelsomina's encounter with the gentle nun provides the occasion of the final of three temptations,[20] like those of Christ, to forsake her mission, a temptation which, like the other two, she resists. After this, Gelsomina renews her commitment to help Zampanò in, among other things, his strongman act in which he breaks chains tied around his chest (his heart). The chains take on important symbolic significance, becoming moral-spiritual bindings or limits, as much as iron ones. Fellini makes this motif of Zampanò's chain-breaking evident from the beginning of the film in such a way that it functions as an extended metaphor of the change-conversion in Zampanò, which does not happen all of a sudden at the end of the film but begins much earlier.[21]

If Gelsomina is a "pure spirit of love"[22] and a Christ-redeemer-figure, Fellini makes Zampanò into a metaphor of human nature in need of redemption: "Zampanò is Everyman – after the Fall: he is selfish, brutal, boastful, irreverent, and insensitive to everyone and everything except his own needs and survival . . . For Fellini, Zampanò is both Adam and the prodigal son."[23] Then the director represents in Gelsomina's commitment to her man nothing less than the saving mission of the incarnate Word of God in Jesus Christ, a mission which reached its climax on the cross. Zampanò's slaying of "The Clown" out of jealousy and anger signals the beginning of Gelsomina's passion, an experience anticipated earlier in the film as Fellini repeatedly associates her "with images of crucifixion and martyrdom."[24]

It becomes a Calvary along which Gelsomina shoulders a double cross. Assuming both Zampanò and "The Clown" she "carries the crime of one and the death of the other."[25] Her indistinct crying "which transcends mere words" is not unlike the silent prayer of another woman-Christ-figure: "the silent movement of the lips of the Joan of Arc of Dreyer, at the heights of inconceivable suffering."[26] At this point Zampanò's total brutality seems to be victorious, especially when it is revealed that after he has abandoned her, Gelsomina dies. Her death is by all appearances a failure, a total nonsense, something underscored by Fellini when he has Gelsomina die off-screen. It is an image of the paradox of the death of Jesus, a sign of contradiction, considered a shocking failure by the apostles judging by their behavior. But Fellini then suggests that Gelsomina's death is a "saintly folly,"[27] that in her passion, Gelsomina is an image of the "suffering servant of Isaiah, by whose stripes Zampanò is reached."[28]

In the final scene of the film, "Gelsomina, in spirit, brings Zampanò back to the sea,"[29] and there he is touched by grace incarnated in her and by her "redemptive love,"[30] a spiritual force represented by the notes of her music which in this scene "builds in crescendo"[31] and the Christian overtones of the beckoning ocean waves which Fellini has associated with the little woman from the opening scene of the film. Gelsomina who undertook her saving mission by the sea, completes it there, as her "'sacrifice' (as Fellini puts it) . . . become the means of Zampanò's 'redemption.'"[32] In the awesome experience of self-awareness and sorrow, a veritable "dark night of the soul,"[33] he breaks the moral-spiritual bonds that have limited his life and in Fellini's own words, "he slowly raises his gaze up towards the sky."[34] Zampanò is redeemed.

Fellini makes Gelsomina a simpleton, a clown, a ridiculous little person of no apparent significance, living in a squalid, unspiritual world in which she seems to have no chance of impact. Yet, because of her sacrificial life and death which brings about the spiritual liberation, the salvation of the man she loves, we can recognize in her a magnificent Christ-figure.

Fellini's *Nights of Cabiria*

"A profoundly religious film . . . a story of genuine death and resurrection, redemption, 'salvation,'"[35] Fellini's *Nights of Cabiria* represents the life of a woman, Cabiria, who because of her wide-eyed," Chaplinesque"[36] naivete and basic innocence, makes for an unlikely hooker. Already in the opening of the film, set in a squalid *borgo* on the outskirts of Rome in the mid-1950s, Cabiria is a victim of robbery and attempted murder at the hands of a lover-client. However, not easily discouraged, she returns to work in the noisy, violent suburban piazza, full of hope for the future. When business there becomes too complicated, she shifts her activity to the downtown *via Veneto,* where she is picked up by a movie star who is drunk and has just fought with his *fidanzata.* At his luxurious villa, Cabiria is almost immediately discarded by him when the *fidanzata* shows up, and Cabiria spends the night in his bathroom. Soon after, she makes a pilgrimage to the nearby Sanctuary of *Divin' Amore* where she prays for the grace to reform her life, a grace that does not appear to be conceded. One night in a burlesque theater, Cabiria submits to hypnosis on stage and, to the delight of the raucous all-male audience, she expresses her love to an ideal lover. Afterwards, a man from the audience repeatedly declares his love for her and finally proposes marriage. Cabiria seeing this as the answer to her prayers, closes with her previous life, sells her little house and comes to the wedding rendezvous with her life savings. The man, obviously a fraud, takes her money and abandons her. Cabiria, "in a state of darkness and despair"[37] and wanting to die, drags herself out of the woods. On the road, "Fellini's perennial symbol of life,"[38] she meets a group of young people dancing and singing. As she walks on the road back to town (and, metaphorically, to life),"[39] at first afraid, diffident, she then lets them encircle her and responds to their festivity with a "wondrous affirmative smile"[40] that speaks of hope and joy.

Cabiria's identity and function as a Christ-figure does not exactly declare itself explicitly in the plot of the film. Nor does it jump to the attention in her two ill-fated attempts to have an experience of grace: one, while "at work" one night when she begins to follow a small Corpus Christi procession but is distracted by the arrival of a favorite truck driver; the other, her ill-fated pilgrimage to the *Divin' Amore* shrine.

Interestingly, however, Fellini films this episode at the shrine in such a way that, in fact, it seems a sign of spiritual strength that Cabiria *not* have an experience of conversion there. The absence of establishing shots, the tight, over-crowded compositions, mostly photographed from above and in claustrophobic medium shots, the noisy soundtrack, full of the shouts of confused pilgrims, aggressive souvenir sellers and the strident tones of a preacher, create an almost surreal, nightmare atmosphere,[41] suggesting perhaps the Temple of Jerusalem from which Jesus expelled the money changers. The final effect of the *Divin' Amore* episode is to reassert Cabiria's basic goodness and sincerity, her spiritual integrity over against all that would crush her. Already, we begin to perceive some christological dimensions in Cabiria's existence.

It is, however, behind these sordid events, implicit in her reaction to them, that Cabiria can be understood and analyzed as embodying aspects of a Christ-figure, albeit in a very particular way. First of all, in a world characterized by violence, cynicism and fraud, including the religious variety, Cabiria's naive faith in humankind, her "persistent optimism,"[42] her mission to love, simply and without conditions are certainly Christ-like attributes. So is her manner of responding to failure, rejection, and betrayal, with hope: "even in her ugly degradation . . . [Cabiria] is an affirmation of life."[43] In her radical goodness, her unlimited love, her persistent hope, Cabiria "embodies in a very moving way, what the Christ of John's Gospel says about himself; 'I am the way, the truth and the life!'"[44]

It is especially in the conclusion of the film that Fellini reveals Cabiria as a Christ-figure. In the final encounter with Oscar, her betrayer and "executioner," she acts rather as Jesus did before Caiaphas and Pilate: "Cabiria's spiritual and moral power is such that she dominates Oscar during their final scenes . . . forcing him to retreat behind his dark jacket and dark glasses."[45] Facing "death" in her ultimate failure, in the betrayal of her greatest act of love, when her life savings (a neat metaphor for her whole existence) are violently taken from her, Cabiria, in a Christ-like gesture that also recalls Isaac's submitting to Abraham before the sacrifice, kneels before her lover-betrayer-assassin, ready to die, "obedient to the point of death." (Phil 2:8) Once again here, the "spirit of pure love [is] trampled by the realities of human selfishness."[46] But then, as with Christ, Cabiria's "death" is vindicated, becomes a victory as she emerges from the woods to a celebration of life and joy and hope in the singing and dancing of the young people who encircle her and give her "life."[47] "From the depths of her nothingness, Cabiria slowly returns to life; she starts to smile again; soon she is dancing, too."[48] In a marvelous close-up of her face, perhaps "the boldest and most powerful shot in all of Fellini's work,"[49] the director makes it quite evident that Cabiria is aware of the absolute newness that she is living. "Her brave smile a final affirmation of life"[50] and her look full of the "wisdom of experience"[51] both suggest that Cabiria is conscious that she has moved into a new dimension of existence.

Fellini underlines the quality of victory, of liberation, in this sequence of the dance of life by a number of formal, stylistic choices. The pastoral flute music and the lyrical voices of the young people, in contrast to the strident tones of most of the film; the low-contrast, luminous quality of the lighting, in contrast to the heavy, high-contrast lighting of much of the film, the respectful distance of the camera and the open compositions of the shots in extreme contrast to the claustrophobic photography in the *Divin' Amore* episode, all suggest a new and different dimension of life. Clearly here we have an image of the Resurrection, a veritable "Easter-Gospel incognito."[52]

If Cabiria's resurrection-victory is in the conclusion of the film, Fellini pre-announces it in a sequence much earlier, in the burlesque theater, a sequence not much discussed by the critics. Cabiria is on stage, in a hypnotic state; on her head she has a crown of flowers, a "crown of thorns" of ridicule that is at the same time, a crown of victory, and she is making a profound and very touching declaration of her love, the love which then leads to her "death." At a certain point, Fellini has the camera frame Cabiria in a long shot from the upstage area: she is seen backlit, a spotlight from the balcony on her, creating a very curious double effect. The light is so strong that the raucous crowd in the orchestra fades into darkness, and, against the dark background, it becomes a precise, powerful shaft of light illuminating little Cabiria from above. We see Cabiria at her best here, expressing her love freely and in a pure, ecstatic way, and transfigured by the experience and by what is symbolically a kind of divine approval. A brief scene of grace and glory before the final suffering, a sequence which recalls Christ's Transfiguration, it is also a prefiguration of the Resurrection. The Resurrection itself is suggested in the very particular way Fellini has Cabiria awaken from the trance; when she slumps to the stage floor, the hypnotist wants to help her up but "before he can bend all the way down to assist her, she pops up, reawakened."[53]

To return for a moment to the film's conclusion, on one level of meaning, it represents objective fact, Cabiria coming out of the woods and meeting a group of festive young people. The sequence acquires a more profound and more christological meaning when instead it is interpreted as a subjective reality, experienced by Cabiria. The critic Frank Burke suggests that already earlier in the film Cabiria becomes aware of "the redemptive powers that have been growing within her,"[54] and he insists on the powerful spiritual self-awareness, no less than christological, with which she faces "death" at the hands of her betrayer Oscar. She falls to the ground, lying dormant in an image of death which is also the fetal position, "at a moment prior to infancy, prior to birth, about to awaken, to a moral environment so highly evolved that

Oscar and all he embodies are no longer possible."[55] When Cabiria does rise, her "body gives way to spirit, weight to lightness,"[56] and the unusual "lyrical, music outburst"[57] which "*is* salvation: unmotivated, gratuitous, ubiquitous,"[58] and the singing, dancing youths so different from anything else in the film, are a subjective, self-conscious reality.

> Her willingness to keep on going . . . generates the youngsters whose music and dance celebrate their life and hers. They are her own transcendent powers released into the world, her own capacity for resurrection and renewal acting upon her in a spiritual domain.[59]

In this interpretation, Fellini's unusual final shot of Cabiria facing the camera takes on a powerful christological significance: "As Cabiria gazes into our eyes, she is a marvelously unified image . . . The resurrected and revitalized Cabiria carries everything forward in synthesis."[60]

Axel's *Babette's Feast*

Babette's Feast narrates the mysterious experience of conversion lived by the members of a small fundamentalist Lutheran community living in isolation, a conversion occasioned by the presence and activity in their midst of a French woman refugee, Babette. Based on the homonymous novella by Karen Blixen, the film of Gabriel Axel is set in a village on the Jutland coast of Denmark in 1883,[61] though two extended flashbacks shift the narrative into the past. In the first flashback, twenty-nine years in the past, Axel represents the community, a "stern Lutheran brotherhood,"[62] as united, devout, well-disciplined, thanks to its strong-willed Founder and Pastor, who is aided in his work by his two daughters, Philippa and Martina.[63] Though puritan, ascetic, and exclusive, the community prospers and does much good. During this period, two visitors from the outside world, a young army officer and a French opera *divo*, fall in love with the daughters, but the moral authority of the Pastor prevails, the visitors leave and life goes on undisturbed. In the second flashback, set twelve years in the past, the Pastor has died and the daughters carry on his mission. One stormy night they give shelter to *Madame* Babette Hersant, an unfortunate refugee from the tragic events of the Paris commune. She remains with them as their cook, a profession she exercised in Paris, and in a short time, her presence begins to have surprising, positive results.

In the present time of the film, the situation of the community has changed: "the brothers and sisters of the minister's little sect have fallen out of grace with one another."[64] Some have died and resentment, fear and guilt, "unspoken jealousies and bridled passions"[65] threaten to destroy the remaining community. On the occasion of the centenary of the birth of the Founder, Babette, who has won a lottery in France, prepares a meal – "*un vrai diner français*," she says[66] – for the community. During Babette's feast, the members of the community, at first terrified of spiritual tragedy and determined to resist, miraculously rediscover forgiveness, peace and hope.[67] "Food proves to be the music of love,"[68] and through Babette, outsider-artist who does "exactly what she does best in the world,"[69] salvation comes to the people of God.

Differently from the two Fellini films we have just discussed, and from *Out of Rosenheim* which we will discuss below, in *Babette's Feast* the religious dimension is explicit from the beginning and at many levels of the five-part structure of the film.[70] In the brief four minute prologue, Axel sets the religious tone by placing us *in media res*, at a prayer meeting. He reinforces it with talk of priesthood and prophecy, of Luther and Melanchthon, and with the theme-hymn of the film, "Jerusalem, Jerusalem."

The first section of the film, a flashback, lasting twenty-five minutes, begins with a liturgy presided by the Founder of the community and includes two other prayer meetings. It chronicles the old man's determined prayers and practical efforts to maintain the spiritual integrity of his flock and the repeatedly-sung hymns lyrically underscore this religious thrust. The second section, also a flashback, lasting eleven minutes, representing the arrival of Babette, broaches the theme, which is important later, of the divine origins of the giftedness of the artist.

In the fourth section of the film, the longest at fifty-four minutes, Axel punctuates his narrative of Babette's activities in the community and especially of her festive meal with an overabundance of explicit religious references, which become denser as the events move towards a conclusion. He includes: prayer meetings, public and private; solemn religious promises; "Jerusalem, Jerusalem" sung twice and played musically; references to the Bible and the eloquent speech of General Löwenhielm on the miracle of divine grace. The density of the religious imagery is Axel's way of creating a spiritually dynamic background for the event of grace and salvation represented in this part of the film. Then in the three minute epilogue the sisters praise Babette by recognizing the eschatological promise of her God-given artistic talents.

If the religious dimension of *Babette's Feast* is incontrovertible and explicit, the christological identity and function of the protagonist is not so immediately clear. Any discussion of Babette as a Christ-figure must be situated within the wider framework of an understanding of the film as having a biblical theme and specifically, of the structure of the film as corresponding to the structure of salvation history. In such an analysis, the first part of the film, which represents the golden years of the Lutheran sect, corresponds to the Old Testament, the first covenant between God and humanity, the Old Law. Under the guidance of the Founder, referred to with the Old Testament terminology of "priest and prophet," this community of chosen people lives at peace; they are good people, believers, God-fearing. But like the people of Israel, they live isolated from the world, strictly disciplined in how they pray, what they eat, in a world-denying asceticism, surrounded by alien peoples against whose corrupt influence they struggle to protect themselves, their trust in the decisive theocratic leadership of the Founder.

The Founder is a just man, "well respected" but also "a little feared" by his people. He repels all attempts to break the integrity of the community and inspired by him, his followers focus their attention on the other world. The narrator recounts that "in the minister's flock, earthly love and marriage were considered of scant worth and merely empty illusion." Thus the visits of the outsider-suitors, General Löwenhielm, and the singer, Papin, are short-lived. These people pray to a God who is distant; they hope for a salvation that is future, the heavenly Jerusalem suggested by the theme-hymn of the film; and because they have to achieve their own salvation, they live in the fear of "not being ascetic and temperant enough."[71]

In the second part of the film, the salvation history of the community shifts forward with the arrival of Babette, whose coming by night is announced with signs in the heavens: a strong wind, violent rain and a mysterious shaft of white light from above. Her arrival is characterized by some quite clear correspondences to a christological *kenosis*:[72] a foreigner, she cannot speak the language; a refugee, she has "lost everything;" she puts herself at the mercy of Martina and Philippa and asks only "to work for no wages . . . let me serve you." As Babette settles in, her hidden existence acquires aspects of a christological incarnation. She maintains her role as a servant: Martina and Philippa eat in the dining room, while she, alone in the kitchen; she dresses as they do, learns their language and relates well to the people in the village.[73] Perhaps the strongest evidence of a christological-incarnational dimension can be perceived in two details: though Babette was a famous chef in Paris, she, "poor among the poor,"[74] humbly "disciplines herself into patience"[75] and submits to learning the unsophisticated method of cooking cod and ale-bread soup. Shortly after her arrival, her presence begins to have miraculous effects, suggested by the surprising reversal of the precarious economic situation of Martina and Philippa. Axel wants to suggest that in Babette, something new and wonderful, something salvific has entered into this community of believers and is quietly bringing about changes not possible under the old covenant of the Founder. Here a new covenant is establishing itself.

If the low-key arrival of Babette in the second part of the film, in which Babette's humble existence might correspond to the hidden life and early ministry of Jesus, signals a subtle shift in the salvation history of the puritan community, then in the third part of the film, Axel dramatically proclaims Babette's role as a Christ-figure who brings salvation to her people. Axel sets the stage by showing the puritan community, fourteen years after Babette's advent, very much in need of salvation: its numbers are reduced to ten and they are all old. "Its spirituality sapped by age-old grudges and guilts"[76] and "riven by ancient feuds and jealousies"[77] resentment, fear and little schisms threaten the group with disintegration. Evidently the memory of the Founder is not enough. There is a need for a more definitive salvific act.

Axel makes it clear that Babette is aware of the precarious situation of the community. She prays about it, and in a gesture that recalls Jesus grieving

over the hard-heartedness of Jerusalem, she weeps. Her lottery winnings[78] and
the feast of the Founder provide the appropriate context, a kind of *kairos* or
moment of opportunity, and inspired by a seagull (there are no doves on the
Jutland seacoast) as she walks meditatively along the beach, Babette makes
an about-turn, a radical decision, christological in its quality, content and effects. She determines to celebrate the anniversary of the Founder (corresponding to a kind of Passover feast) with a meal (an image of the Last Supper) in
which she sacrifices all she has. It is a meal[79] that mysteriously, miraculously
effects the salvation of the community: "the brothers and the sisters . . . are
redeemed through Babette's surrogate self-sacrifice."[80] They leave the feast
fully satisfied, "their spirits exalted by it,"[81] reconciled, united and no longer
fearful. In the village square, "the little assembly fairly swims in the harmony,"[82] proclaiming blessings and Hallelujahs with little less than Pentecos-
tal fervor.

Axel suggests that Babette's feast is more than simply a meal when he
places twelve people at the table, "like the twelve apostles together at the
Last Supper,"[83] and when he has General Löwenhielm refer to Babette's
"ability to turn a meal into a kind of love affair," which is a good description
of the Last Supper. Nor is this sacred intentionality of Babette's *agape* meal
lost on the critics: one refers to it as "Babette's ultimate act of self-sacrifice,"[84] another, as "a sacrifice . . . a kind of sacrament,"[85] and another says
that the meal makes no secret of its religious symbolism; he explains that
Babette elevates "her role as a generous host to a purely christic value [be-
cause] in the meal, she offers the memorial of what her life in Paris had been:
'This is my body.'" Through the person of Babette and her "eucharistic" sacrifice, the people of God are given a new covenant, a new way of being with
one another and of praising God.

Around this three-part account of the salvation history of the people,
Axel creates a narrative frame which brilliantly highlights Babette's christological significance. In the prologue, which represents a prayer meeting at
the home of Martina and Philippa during which all sing "Jerusalem, Jerusalem," referring, to be sure, to a heavenly Jerusalem, Babette, whom Axel photographs twice from the back, is still a hidden, mysterious presence, waiting
for the appropriate moment to reveal herself as a new earthly Jerusalem, offering salvation here and now. In the epilogue, in a scene which seems to
echo the conversation between Jesus and the two disciples at Emmaus (Lk
24:13-35), Axel has Babette move with the two sisters from the kitchen to the
dining-room table,[87] and there has her interpret for them the significance of
the meal they have just eaten, the meaning of her sacrificial action, the sense
"of the sacredness of self-sacrifice."[88] Salvation has come, Revelation is complete.

Axel proposes Babette's christological identity not only in what she
does but in her manner, her way of being and acting, which gives evidence of
a christological dimension. Babette is open, discrete and respectful of all; she
comes to the people as invitation and no one fears her as they did the Pastor.

Every contact with her is life-giving and liberating. Further, Babette's offer of salvation is anything but conditional or exclusive: welcome at the feast are two outsiders to the community, Mrs. Löwenhielm and her nephew, the General, the latter arriving at the last minute. The feast is even more universal, for it includes the lowly coachman and the kitchen boy, perhaps representing the poor, whose conscious joy and appreciation for sharing in the meal is one of the most profound touches of the film. In a natural and spontaneous manner, they seem to have a privileged experience of the wonder of the event. Being in the presence of Babette, they see her grace and artistry better than do the guests.

Finally, like the salvific approach of Jesus, Babette's approach knows no bounds, no limits. Something self-evident, this, in the extreme prodigality of her sacrificing all her winnings – "the price of a life"[89] – for the meal, and in the lavishness of the meal itself, it is also evident in two small gestures of Babette towards General Löwenhielm: the instruction to the kitchen-boy-waiter to fill his glass with champagne as often as the General wishes; and at the end of the meal, to leave a full bottle of *Clos-Vougeot* at his place when he asks for a glass.

Axel proposes Babette as a Christ-figure not only through her own actions which are efficacious for the salvation of the people, but also in the brief speech that Löwenhielm delivers towards the end of the meal. Transformed by Babette's meal, by the "holy moment"[90] that was her "giving the best of herself," the General speaks of the divine gift of grace,[91] describing it as infinite and unconditional: "Everything we have chosen has been granted to us. And everything we have rejected has also been granted." On one level, he is referring to his own past life and choices, but on a deeper level, his words refer to the meal they have just eaten, Babette's "eucharist," Babette's Christ-like gift of herself. The infinite and unconditional grace experienced by the guests, which has brought them salvation and for which they proclaim "Hallelujah," is Babette, and in this, she is unequivocally a Christ-figure.

Babette's identity as a Christ-figure is reinforced by a series of double *leitmotivs* running through the entire film; in each pair, a contrast is made between the old and the new, and in each pair, the spiritual impact of Babette provides the turning point. First of all, Axel creates two distinct worlds. There is that of the Pastor-Founder and his followers, a tough, culture-denying, exclusive world, where asceticism and self-discipline provide the only hope for salvation, where "moral rigidity creates a barrier against the rigidity of the cold."[92] Then there is the world represented by Babette as embodied in the actress Stéphane Audran, about whom the director of the film says: "She's French. She walks like a Frenchwoman, closes a door like a Frenchwoman. Everything she does is gracious, whereas the Danish women are wearing clogs."[93] Babette's is an open, sensual, culture-affirming, inclusive world, where spirit-incarnated-in-matter leads to salvation, a world which does not repudiate or deny the other world. In a very christological way, it enters into that world, liberates and redeems it, bringing it to fulfillment.

Also contrasting throughout the film are two models of priesthood. That exercised by the Pastor, an eminently masculine model, is based on power, control, the exercise of fear. This is perhaps most evident in the dispatch with which the Pastor gets rid of his daughters' suitors and the almost sadistic glee he expresses when he ends Papin's relationship with Philippa. The priesthood of Babette, a more feminine model, continues the ministry of the Pastor but transforms it, as Christ transformed the Old Testament ministry, into a ministry of the praise of God and human salvation through joy, charity, healing, creativity and beauty, a ministry which imposes no demands from God but rather awakens desire[94] for peace and reconciliation. Babette's priesthood, in the sign of Christ, fulfills and transcends that of the Pastor and succeeds, where his fails, in creating a new covenant between the people and God.

Parallel to these two models of priesthood, Axel represents two models of liturgy. The Pastor's, continued after his death by his daughters, is a liturgy of the Word, using Old Testament readings, and whose promise of future salvation remains somewhat disembodied, abstract; evidently, it is not sufficient to nourish the people. Babette's liturgy, her festive meal, is a liturgy of the Word (the General's speech about grace), of Sacrament (the meal as an efficacious sign of grace) and of Sacrifice (Babette's prodigality). It is celebrated in the framework of the old liturgy (the meeting for the anniversary of the Founder) but transcends and fulfills it in a definitive way, becoming "a real moment of communion, spiritual as well as physical."[95]

There are also two models of prayer proposed in the film. One is of the other-worldly prayers and hymns of the puritan community, whose constant theme is that of future deliverance.[96] The other model is of concrete, emotional, sensual prayers, connected with specific this-worldly events, for example, the prayer of Papin when he first hears Philippa's marvelous voice: "Almighty God . . . Thy mercy ascends to the heavens," as well as two prayers uttered by Babette herself: when she wins the lottery, she exclaims "*Seigneur tout puissant!*," "Lord Almighty!,"[97] and when the supplies for the feast arrive from France, "Praise the Lord! All the goods arrived safely."

Related to these contrasting forms of prayer are the two versions of "Jerusalem, Jerusalem" heard in the film. First, it is sung three times during their prayer meetings, and seems to express the desire of the community to remain separated from the real world of human events: a rather disincarnated hymn. But then Axel suggests that even this hymn is redeemed by Babette. He inserts brief excerpts of the musical version of "Jerusalem, Jerusalem" behind very concrete events that have to do with Babette and her christological gift of grace: General Löwenhielm's moment of self-awareness at the mirror as he prepares for the meal; while Babette celebrates her culinary liturgy in the kitchen; when the General, at the meal and under the influence of grace, quietly, silently, offers a toast to Martina; and again in the kitchen, when the coachman thanks Babette for his sharing in the feast. Axel is suggesting that the new Jerusalem, the gift of salvation, is here and now and concretely present in Babette, Christ-figure.

Axel also represents the contrasting worlds in the *leitmotiv* of meals, of which Axel represents two models. There are the simple meals of cod and ale-bread soup, tea and biscuits, served to the poor and eaten by Martina and Philippa. In an exercise in self-denial, these people presume that food and drink are not meant to give pleasure; meals that are anything more than basically nourishing are morally perilous. Their attitude towards food is well-expressed by one of the guests as he fearfully approaches Babette's lavish meal, determined, as they all are, not to enjoy it: "Like the wedding at Cana, the food is of no importance." Is he perhaps confusing Jesus with John the Baptist? In contrast to these ascetic meals, there is the food prepared by Babette who, in a fine example of the new law fulfilling the old, begins by cooking cod and ale-bread soup. Then perhaps in anticipation of the feast, she gradually adds other ingredients, cheese and onions, making the food more tasty, more pleasurable to the poor. Further, there is the feast, the *vrai diner français:* foreign, rich, luxurious, it represents all that is most feared by the community. Yet they eat, and subtly, silently, they begin to enjoy the experience, to live it fully, with neither fear nor guilt. The little woman, who earlier makes the reference to the feast at Cana, by the end of the feast prefers champagne to water and sensually licks her finger after devouring a fresh fig. Under the creativity of Babette, artist and Christ-figure, food and the pleasures of the senses reveal themselves as spirited, as incarnated grace, and become for the guests an experience of conversion and salvation. "Hallelujah!"

If Babette is a Christ-figure and if the film treats of the Christian experience of salvation, then at some point Axel should represent the cross. He does, indeed there are two crosses, and in this most Christian of symbols, Axel suggests how Babette, Christ-figure, is the fulfillment of a promise. The first cross, a life-sized, polychromed wood crucifix, is seen twice in the Pastor's church, pictured dramatically behind him during a sermon and to which he makes no reference: it is a formal, institutional cross. The other is a tiny gold crucifix worn by Babette, but Axel does not put it on her when she first arrives: her mission has not yet begun. Only in the present time of the film does he have her wear it, as a sign of the salvific mission she has at that point undertaken and which reaches its fulfillment in her *agape* sacrifice. Axel seems to be saying that Babette symbolically carries the cross on and in her person, that "she is in essence offering herself,"[98] and it is this more than all else that makes her an efficacious Christ-figure.

What Axel suggests about Babette intradiegetically, within the content of his film, he also underscores extradiegetically with a number of formal and stylistic elements. Perhaps the most obvious of these is his use of color. In the first part of the film and in other scenes where Babette is not present, the dominant colors in exterior shots are grey and brown, giving a very somber tone to the already hostile coast of Jutland. Interiors also are dominated by grey and brown, tending towards darker tones and shadows, and the illumination is limited either to the cold tones filtering through the windows or the weak light of the occasional candle. Into this dark world comes Babette, to whom Axel associates very different colors: when she is outside, the grass is a rich green, the water, deep blue, the sky, either bright blue or the warm orange and red of sunrises or sunsets. It is especially during the festive meal that Babette's presence evokes an explosion of rich, deep and varied colors, of the food, the wine, the candles, the crystal, and the striking red and gold colors of the dress-uniform of Löwenhielm. Babette, Christ-figure, is light and color in the darkness.

The contrasting interface of intradiegetical hymns (notably "Jerusalem, Jerusalem") and extradiegetical music is another technique used by Axel to suggest Babette's christological intentionality. For the little Lutheran community, music is always associated with liturgical hymns: such is the case for "Jerusalem, Jerusalem" the three times it is sung; music is for the service of religion and it must remain quite distinct from concrete, everyday life. This is precisely why the love duet from Mozart's *Don Juan*, sung passionately by Papin and nervously by Philippa, signals the abrupt end of their relationship. Axel suggests that Babette transcends this exclusive approach to music: for her music is a spontaneous and integral part of everyday life. Twice, Axel has Babette hum as she goes about her tasks and, at one point, she actually hums the dangerous "*L'amour nous unira*" verse of the *Don Juan* that has so terrified Philippa. Axel also has the music of "Jerusalem, Jerusalem" punctuate her activities as she prepares the festive meal. Babette, artist and Christ-figure, redeems food, she redeems color and she redeems music.

In the design of his film, Axel proposes a number of interesting details that are not mentioned in Blixen's novella. For instance, in the background of several scenes in the house of the Pastor, both in the past and in the present, a white ceramic statue of Christ is clearly visible on a high cabinet: a rather curious item in the house of a puritan Protestant preacher. But Axel never shows the statue of Christ in a composition with Babette: is it perhaps because he wants to avoid redundancy? Or because he wants to suggest that Babette is a living figure of the Christ represented in the ceramic figure? Babette's gold crucifix is not mentioned in Blixen's novella, nor is the large well in the village square from which Babette takes water and around which the departing guests dance in a circle. Does Axel want to suggest Babette as a source of living and saving and unifying water? At the very end of the film it snows,[99] snow which is barely glimpsed through a window in the dining-room at the precise moment that the two sisters come to understand the extent of Babette's salvific sacrifice. Is Axel perhaps creating, in the snow falling from the heavens, a metaphor of the grace that has come from above in the salvific event of Babette?

In Axel's film, if the christological and soteriological sacrifice of Babette is transparent, then the motif of the Resurrection is only slightly less evident. Insofar as the Resurrection signifies a final victory of life over death, of peace over conflict, of hope over hopelessness, of wholeness over disintegration, then the power of the Resurrection is clearly present in the conclusion of the film. Concretely the force of Resurrection is active in the film's narrative structure: just as the tragedy Babette faced in Paris, her leaving the *Café Anglais* and coming as a refugee to Denmark is a death, so the *vrai diner français* she prepares is a resurrection. Then there are two indirect but rather clear New Testament Resurrection references in the film. The epilogue, as we have already seen, reflects the conversation of the disciples with the post-Resurrection Jesus at Emmaus. Then the earlier scene of Babette in the kitchen during the feast, "absorbed, transformed,"[100] and observed with fascination and devotion by the two disciples, the coachman and the servant, suggests something of the Transfiguration of Christ, itself a prefiguration of the Resurrection. Finally, in the several shots of Babette alone and pensive at the end of the meal, Axel seems to impute to Babette full consciousness of the significance of what she has done, of the salvific act she has accomplished, the christological wisdom that "it is in death that resurrection is accomplished."[101]

Adlon's *Out of Rosenheim*

Made in the United States by a German, Percy Adlon's *Out of Rosenheim*[102] is a film in eclectic style, combining elements of the western, musical comedy, psychological drama and romance, with a dash of surrealism. It tells the singular story of a German tourist, lost in the Nevada desert, who ends up at a truck-stop-motel called the Bagdad Cafe, and of what happens when she decides to stay for a while. Despite its exotic name, with "echoes of the tales of a thousand and one [Arabian] nights,"[103] the cafe-motel is run-down. Its frustrated inhabitants, "a colourful collection of misfits,"[104] live at loggerheads with one another. The "oasis" is more of a wasteland than the desert that surrounds it. But the presence of Jasmin Münchgstettner, with her vulnerability, goodness and generosity, her mysterious powers, begins almost immediately to make a difference, and by the end of the film, she has brought life and hope back into the lives of both the locals at the cafe and the wider community they serve. Bagdad Cafe is once again an oasis in the desert and Jasmin[105] is revealed as a Christ-figure.

If in *Babette's Feast* the christological and soteriological patterns are rendered more explicit by the biblical references, in *Out of Rosenheim* these patterns are more implicit.[106] Of course, the film "works," has meaning on a first level of reflection, that is as a story of healing friendship "finally possible"[107] and of selfless love, but as in other films we have considered, there are too many "signals" pointing beyond this first level reading to be ignored.

The overall spiritual dynamic of the film, as a story of salvation – restored harmony – through self-sacrificing love, has a transcendental reach that is biblical in scope and its overall structure clearly reflects the Christ-event. Then, within the narrative of the film, there are events, actions and words that reflect elements in the Gospel narratives. Finally, there are extradiegetical elements, on the stylistic and technical level, that clearly underline the transcendental evangelical reach of events in the narrative and that identify the protagonist Jasmin as a Christ-figure.

The christological meaning in the overall structure of the film is already evident in the prologue in which, before the opening credits, Jasmin leaves her irascible and violent husband, wanders alone in the desert and arrives at Bagdad Cafe, tired and discouraged: clearly a kenotic incarnation is suggested. Then the first of three movements in the film, each lasting thirty minutes, shows a community in need of salvation, and on the other hand, reveals the commitment of the newly-arrived Jasmin to that community and the first opposition of its members to her presence and action. The second movement of the film details Jasmin's first minor successes, the ongoing resistance of the community and in the end, it celebrates the establishment of an alliance-covenant between Jasmin and Brenda, the leader of the community, which ushers in the "Kingdom of Harmony,"[108] a covenant sealed by a rainbow in the desert, an obvious reference to the biblical covenant between God and Noah.

The final thirty minutes of *Out of Rosenheim* are dense with evangelical significance. Led by Jasmin, the Kingdom of Harmony under the new covenant begins to grow and prosper. Then she is betrayed and sent back to Germany, perceived by all as a kind of death. At first the community languishes but then it celebrates the memory of Jasmin in thought and deed, and at that point, the mysterious Jasmin returns, dressed in resurrection-white, and renews the hope and joy of the community. In the epilogue, an expanded Kingdom of Harmony lives a kind of Pentecost event, an unbridled celebration of creativity and harmony beyond anything seen in the film. At the center of it all is Jasmin, now sharing her gifts and power with all the members of the community, who are living fully their experience of salvation.

Two *leitmotivs* run through the whole film, that of disorder, confusion and that of harmony, and these become the principle metaphors, respectively, of a world in need of salvation and incapable of achieving it on its own, and of the grace of salvation brought by Jasmin, moving and establishing itself in that world. The *leitmotiv* of disorder is announced in the very beginning of the film: a violent argument between Jasmin and her husband, a menacing desert wasteland, its horizon rendered "doubly claustrophobic"[109] by Adlon's oblique camera angles, a mournful theme song: "A desert road from Vegas to nowhere." The disorder becomes even more obvious at Bagdad Cafe: a squalid collection of ramshackle buildings, clouds of dust following every movement, the depressive atmosphere of a restaurant with no clients and, the theme song continues, "a coffee machine that needs some fixin'," a motel with no guests, a neon sign with letters missing, and the constant oppressive buzz of traffic outside.

Adlon expresses the major manifestation of disorder in the lives of the people living at the cafe.[110] First there is Brenda, the "head" of the community, abandoned by her husband and afflicted by "a definite case of loser's blues."[111] She is no longer able to control her children and communicates mainly by screaming; angry, suspicious, desperate, nervous, Brenda lives on the edge of a breakdown. Her teenage son, Salomo, sullen, saddled with an illegitimate child, is dedicated to Johann Sebastian Bach, but he seems unable to play more than a few bars at a time at his piano. The daughter Phyllis lives isolated by her headphones in a world of rock music; she neglects her homework and thinks only of going for joyrides with truckers and motorcyclists. There is a scenery painter in exile from Hollywood, played with marvelous irony by an unlikely Jack Palance,[112] "a Gauguin in search of exotic fleshly inspiration in some South Sea island of the mind."[113] And finally, with a sad, lethargic barman and a strange female tattoo-artist-prostitute, the picture of disorder, of moral paralysis, is complete.

If the theme-song of the film announces the need of salvation in the disordered world of Bagdad Cafe, more importantly, it announces the advent of that salvation: "A change is comin', just around the bend." The words, sung as Jasmin who is shot in slow motion as she approaches the cafe, clearly suggest that she will be the source of the "sweet relief," an experience of salvation that Adlon represents in an ever-greater order that overcomes the chaos of Bagdad Cafe. When because of the presence and activity of Jasmin, Salomo, begins to play the piano again, Adlon has him play Bach's *Well-tempered Clavier*, appropriate music for "it is precisely from the hearing of this piece that harmony will be born in the cafe."[114] Phyllis curtails her "outside activities" and helps in the restaurant, the barman learns how to make coffee and Rudy, the artist, begins to paint again. The harmony established in the lives of the inhabitants of Bagdad Cafe reflects itself in their relationships – no more screaming, they work together – and in the reality of the Cafe and its activities. The office is spruced up, the coffee machine is repaired, customers begin coming once again and within a short time, the "Bagdad Gas and Oil Cafe" becomes an oasis of good food, good music and song, and good community. Over the community, as a further sign of harmony, a boomerang swings in its ordered flight. Its winged shape, its sound like a hovering dove, seem to suggest a spirit of harmony and peace. All this is due to the soteriological identity and action of Jasmin.

Beyond the more global evangelical parallels already suggested, the christological identity of Jasmin is pointed to within the narrative of the film by transparent parallels to the Gospel narratives and to the Gospel spirit. Echoing the sense of the Incarnation, Jasmin, "a being apart,"[115] comes from outside and enters fully into the lives of the people, making herself their servant. One of the most significant moments of the film is when she begins to serve table in the cafe. Like Jesus, she is first accepted by the children. Her magic tricks, largely responsible for the healing effects of her presence at Bagdad Cafe, are transparent metaphors of Jesus' miracles and in moments of crisis, usually at night, she retreats into meditative-prayerful states. Like Jesus, her mission of healing-harmony gets her in trouble with the law, which removes her from the cafe, a kind of death, which is suggested also by the harshly interrupted flight of the boomerang; and after her exile-death, Jasmin returns, more powerful than before, to stay "forever," clearly echoing the promise of the resurrected Jesus in the final verse of Matthew's Gospel: "I am with you always, to the end of the age" (Mt 28:20).

A further correspondence between Jasmin and Jesus can be perceived in the way Adlon represents the reception of the message of liberating harmony-salvation that she brings, a reception in which there seems to be a parallel to the Gospel parable of the sower and the seed (Mt 13). In Salomo, who is already playing Bach when Jasmin arrives, and especially in Rudy Cox, who already paints, Jasmin's message is quickly welcomed. In them, grace is already at work. Her message of salvation arrives late to Sal, Brenda's estranged husband who, having observed events from afar, enters the Kingdom of Harmony at the last minute. Two people reject the salvation she offers: her husband, from the very beginning, and Debbie, the tattoo artist who, after resisting Jasmin through the whole film (she moves around her like a snake), rejects her at the end. Debbie leaves the Kingdom after the resurrection-return of Jasmin because, she explains, in the world of Bagdad Cafe there is now "too much harmony."

It is from Brenda, the "neurotic owner-manager"[116] of the motel, that Jasmin experiences the fiercest resistance. In spite of the words of the theme-song, "I am calling you, can't ya hear me," which could be Brenda's expression of her need for salvation, the woman "senses that the newcomer from Rosenheim will disturb their sleepy way of life"[117] and so she treats Jasmin with suspicion and fear. Brenda is confused by the mystery of Jasmin: "She shows up outa nowhere, without a car, without a man. . . . It don't make no sense at all!" At one point, in a parody of a western movie, Brenda even threatens Jasmin with a rifle. Finally, two thirds of the way through the film, after a violent confrontation in which Brenda faces head-on the issue of Jasmin's identity – "Now just who the hell do you think you are, lady? Huh! Just what is your game?" – and in response to Jasmin's transparent self-revelation, Brenda accepts her. In a "spectacular reconciliation . . . the shrew is finally tamed."[118] Adlon ratifies this new covenant of friendship-love-salvation with two shots of a rainbow over the desert, newly-blessed by a refreshing rain.

A further dimension of Jasmin's christological identity is the evangelical style in which she comes and brings the message of harmony-salvation. Jasmin's approach is gentle, discreet, respectful; she comes to serve, to teach, to help. The perfect *bayerische Putzfrau*, she cleans up Brenda's office with "Teutonic thoroughness"[119] because "I thought it would make you happy," and she humbly, patiently accepts Brenda's violent negative reaction. Like that of Jesus, Jasmin's liberating, harmonizing love is absolutely unconditional. She affirms and inspires the best in others, leaving them free to accept her or not and recalling a phrase from *Babette's Feast*, by her sacrifice, her "giving the best of herself," symbolized in the magic show, she restores life to the community. In the end, after her "resurrection"-return, she shares her power with the others in a celebration of life and freedom and harmony nothing short of a universally salvific Pentecost. Brenda's self-exiled husband, observing from afar and commenting on the number of participants in the feast, exclaims, "Thirty-seven trucks! Goddamn!" (more a prayer than a blasphemy), and he too joins the feast.

Adlon repeatedly points to the mysterious transcendent nature of Jasmin's identity and mission with extradiegetical devices from the opening moments of the film. As Jasmin wanders in the desert, Adlon combines the use of red filters, slow motion, a strange light-effect in the sky, clearly noticed by Jasmin, and repeated at crucial moments during Jasmin's mission, and the words "I am calling you, I know ya hear me," repeated twice. The suggestion is that of a surrealistic vocation experience. A few moments later, when Jasmin walks up to Brenda, another lighting effect, a blinding sun shining directly into the lens, accompanies her appearance. When later Jasmin is cleaning Brenda's office, Adlon edits into this sequence three surrealistic (in content, angle, and color) shots of Jasmin cleaning the water tower, the roof of the motel, the "MOTEL" sign: in this striking montage, Adlon suggests that Jasmin's housecleaning points beyond itself to a wider experience of spiritual purification.

Towards the end of the film, Adlon includes a long and very static scene in which he represents Jasmin, sitting, eyes closed, appreciating profoundly a long piece of Bach that young Salomo is playing. The yellow-gold tones, the strange suffused light that permeates the scene, the dynamic stillness of the composition, all point to a Jasmin transfigured into another dimension, a transcendental reach confirmed by Adlon in the shots of Rudy Cox who approaches this scene reverently, in awe and falls to his knees, echoing the gesture of Peter and James and John at the Transfiguration of Jesus.[120]

Immediately after this "transfiguration" scene, Adlon edits into the narrative of the film a series of brief and very dynamic shots of Jasmin's magic show, the essence of her ministry of harmony. Into this sequence, he inserts a series of shots of long duration of Rudy Cox, who has rediscovered "his artistic inspiration,"[121] painting Jasmin, and very static shots of Jasmin, whose contents, colors and composition clearly suggest sacred icons, and so, confer a sacred, transcendental quality to Jasmin and her salvific activity. Adlon depicts Cox working on six paintings[122] in a primitive style "halfway between Dounier Rousseau and Grandma Moses,"[123] and for each of them, he shows Jasmin sitting against an abstract background and in several cases, the colors are yellow or gold, the traditional colors of sacred icons. In all but one, Jasmin is pictured sitting in a full frontal position, in a balanced formal pose, with a hieratic expression. Not only is Jasmin pictured as a sacred figure – in two of the finished paintings, she even has a halo – but as a female sacred figure, with bulging breasts and holding female-symbolic fruit in one hand, and further, as a sacred figure in the process of revealing herself, for in each successive shot, she is pictured in "a progressive state of *déshabille*."[124] Though these iconic shots are sufficiently significant in themselves, the fact that Adlon edits them into the dynamic sequence of the Jasmin's soteriological magic show, seems to further justify interpreting her as a female Christ-figure.

Robbins' *Dead Man Walking*

Tim Robbins' recent film, *Dead Man Walking*, is an extraordinary piece of work for a number of reasons. It is a highly successful commercial film, and one which has been praised by the most secular film journals for the very unusual reason that in it, "religious sentiments and Christian values have a remarkable importance."[125] A film about the salvific friendship between a Catholic nun and a murderer condemned to death, it avoids the sentimentalism, the violence, the sexual and ideological subtexts and the various manipulative exaggerations in style and content, normally elements of this genre, and very popular among audiences today.[126] In spite of this, *Dead Man Walking* won a Silver Bear at the Berlin Film Festival and an Academy Award in Hollywood.[127]

Perhaps the most extraordinary thing about *Dead Man Walking* is that its portrayal of the protagonist, Sister Helen Prejean, masterfully played by Susan Sarandon, is the most honest, authentic, balanced and hopeful representation of a nun in recent cinema. In Robbins' filmic account of the brief encounter of this woman with the condemned man, which he could certainly have represented in a secular key, focussing exclusively on important and valid immanent questions of human justice, human psychology, human emotions, the director represents instead all the transcendent dynamics the central tenet of the Christian faith, the mystery of human salvation in the incarnate love of God in Jesus.

The film fairly vibrates with clear allusions to a variety of elements of the Christian Gospel and of the "search for salvation."[128] In his narrative, in the paradox of Helen Prejean, a woman in a world of men, a simple nun in the complex, violent (male) structures of the penal system, a consecrated virgin vulnerably facing a sexually violent murderer, Robbins creates a metaphor, a figure of the paradox of the Eternal Word become human and vulnerable in a violent and oppressive world. In synthesis, Helen Prejean is a Christ-figure, and only when the film is viewed through this hermeneutic, does it yield up the full riches of its significance.

Dead Man Walking, made in the United States in 1995, is based on the true story of Helen Prejean, a religious of the Congregation of St. Joseph (CSJ), as told in her homonymous book. Set in Louisiana more or less in the present day, it is the account of the meeting of the nun, who at the time was living and working in a poor black neighborhood of New Orleans, and Matthew Poncelet, played by Sean Penn, convicted rapist-murderer on death row in the Angola Penitentiary some distance away. The film covers the week or so before the execution by lethal injection of Poncelet, during which time Prejean agrees to help him, becomes his friend, and when the appeals for clemency fail, remains his spiritual advisor. In the final days, she accompanies him until his death.

Clearly *Dead Man Walking* represents many of the themes typically associated with such a story. It considers the intellectual, cultural and moral differences between the nun and the criminal. It represents the education and maturing of the nun, as she deals with the obstacles put in her path by the structures of the prison. It portrays well the tensions that the nun's commitment to the condemned man create in her, and between her and her family, her community, and the families of the victims of Poncelet's crime. Robbins' film deals in a balanced way with crucial public issues of justice and morality, and with more personal issues of human suffering, the limits of guilt and responsibility, the wide-ranging effects of a brutal murder and the meaning of forgiveness. Tim Robbins' film is well-made and multileveled. It works on a first level of meaning, as the straightforward narrative of crime and punishment, of friendship and trust leading to confession and forgiveness, all on a purely human level. At this level it assumes the quality of a well-made social and moral critique of capital punishment

Robbins' is a contemporary film *auteur*, who both wrote and directed *Dead Man Walking,* and who "values ambiguity"[129] and "emotional honesty."[130] In the two principle characters of *Dead Man Walking*, he creates very complex human beings. Rejecting "polemic and sentimentality,"[131] he makes Matthew Poncelet a nasty character with few redeeming characteristics. His past is marked by his poor white trash background, petty crime, racism and drug abuse, and then by his atrocious crime. Even in the present, he remains an arrogant and brutish young man, persisting in his racism, his self-pity and his aggressive and vulgar sexism. It is exaggerated, however, to say that "at no moment can we experience sympathy for him,"[132] for Robbins keeps him from being a "repellent monster,"[133] especially towards the end of the film as he comes to understand and admit the gravity of his actions.

Neither is Helen Prejean a one-dimensional character. In fact in many ways, she is more complex than Poncelet. Though she is fundamentally a good and deeply committed woman, Robbins allows Prejean, a woman on the edge of middle age, to be at times a bit naive and uncertain, to hesitate. She is hurt when the people with whom she works in the parish react negatively to her helping Poncelet. She accepts to help the convict but clearly she does not believe in his insistence that he is innocent and she "is repelled by [his] cocky arrogance."[134] Prejean speaks honestly to him about her fears, gaining his respect but at the same time, she strongly opposes his racism and when he tries to seduce her, she firmly resists but without humiliating him. Prejean is well-adjusted in her commitment to celibacy, able calmly and eloquently to defend her choice to Poncelet, and at the same time able to joke about it with a member of her community.[135] Robbins keeps her from becoming an idealized do-gooder, having the father of one of Poncelet's victims justly accuse her of subtle arrogance, a criticism she accepts. She learns to live with failure, to share her life with Poncelet, to laugh with him and to cry with him.

If Robbins creates moral complexity in his film by making the two principle characters rich and variegated personalities, he does it also by absolutely refusing all the usual clichés of the prison film genre. The penitentiary is not a dark, oppressive fortress: in its very ordinary architecture, pastel colors and flat lighting, it is clinical and banal. The guards are not sadistic monsters, but ordinary people trying to do an unpleasant job. The prison staff show no hostility towards Prejean, in fact they seem to be vaguely interested in what she is doing. Nor is there anything in Robbins' filmic representation of this prison reality that suggests violence: no strong dramatic music, no aggressive camera angles or movements, no manipulative editing, all of which techniques are used in the typical prison film to create sympathy for one side or the other and to heighten the emotional experience.

Without a doubt, one of the reasons for the surprising intellectual and emotional balance of *Dead Man Walking* is the virtuoso editing job by which, even as the condemned killer begins to open up to Prejean, begins to reveal dimensions of humanity and vulnerability, begins therefore to gain our sympathy, Robbins never permits us to forget the horror of his crime. Whenever events move our sympathy to the side of Poncelet, Robbins attenuates this sympathy by editing-in scenes of Prejean's conversations with the parents of the victims, revealing and the ongoing destructive power of Poncelet's crime, and especially by periodically inserting flashbacks of the scene of the killing. At first, the flashbacks to the crime are unclear, but as Poncelet's contact with Prejean brings about a slow, laborious awakening of his conscience, the flashbacks become clearer, revealing more of the horror of the crime each time.

Robbins' film is a dense compendium of Christian themes, the clearest of which is that of love. Helen Prejean's love for Poncelet is radically Christian and thus radically different from any experience of love he has ever had. Her love is given in freedom and it frees him. It is not manipulative love, a quality revealed in the firm but gentle way Prejean responds to Poncelet's attempt to seduce her. She realizes this is the only way he has of expressing himself, and her patient response reveals her as the mystery of love to him. Like God's love for humankind, Prejean's love for Poncelet is unconditional. It is not based on his being loveable nor on his being able to respond. It is not judgmental. Prejean's insistence that the boy confess his responsibility for the murders is not for her own satisfaction or gratification; it is for him, so that he might be free.

The first and most important effect of Prejean's love for Poncelet is that it breaks down the high walls of self-isolation within which he is hiding from himself, from Prejean, from God. Robbins creates a marvelous *leitmotiv* of this breaking down of barriers – of fear, of hate, of self-hate, of sinfulness – by showing Poncelet physically separated from Prejean by a series of barriers which gradually become less oppressive as their dialogue progresses. In their first meeting the director separates them by a fine-mesh grille, and then shifts the focus of the camera lens, "sometimes making it an opaque barrier, at others, near transparent."[136] Later he separates them by a thick plastic window, which makes the conversation difficult; and again by widely-spaced iron bars. It is at this point that Prejean insists, urgently, her face pressed against the iron bars, that she will accompany Poncelet to his death because it is important that the last thing he see as he is dying, is "the face of love." Then towards the end, there are no more barriers: Poncelet meets his family and Prejean in an open room, but they have to keep their distance, no touching allowed. Finally, as he walks to his death, she puts her hand on his shoulder. Love knows no more barriers. As he is attached to the cross-shaped execution table, they are again separated, by a thick glass, but it is of no import. With her hand extended to him and her lips saying "I love you," no real barrier can exist.

If salvific love is the primary Christian theme of the film, the theme of Christian courage is not far behind. Prejean demonstrates great courage in accepting the very difficult mission of accompanying Poncelet, one for which she is, as the chaplain points out, singularly unprepared, and as a woman, says he, not adapted. Yet she has a strong conviction that this is God's will and she persists, against the structures of the prison, the protests of her family, the failure of the appeals and especially the brutish behavior of Poncelet. One of the crucial moments of breakthrough in their dialogue, a moment of grace for Poncelet, is when Prejean, showing great courage, sings "Be Not Afraid" to him. Oppressed, by the brutality of the situation, as the prison staff coldly prepare the execution, she courageously sings to break the cycle of violence. "Against these images of violence can be set nothing but Sarandon's [Prejean's] singing the hymn 'Be Not Afraid' in a cracked, tuneless voice, and offering herself as the 'face of love' for Matthew to see as he dies."[137] The hymn, of the St. Louis Jesuits, and based on Isaiah 43:2-3, says "Be not afraid. I go before you always. Come follow me, and I will give you rest."[138] As she sings, Prejean becomes the voice of God for Poncelet, and her courage becomes his courage.

The courage Poncelet acquires from Prejean leads his repentance, confession and conversion, clearly a Christian theme and a crucial experience for the condemned man. Prejean struggles desperately with Poncelet to get him to come to this point, because his admitting the truth to himself and to her, to God, is an act of self-liberation necessary for his salvation. The very Christian theme of peace, obtained by surrendering to violence, that paradoxically breaks the cycle of violence, is clear in the film, especially towards the end, as is the fundamental Christian paradox that it is in death that we achieve the fullness of life.

Robbins represents these Christian themes not in abstract symbols but in the concrete and unequivocally christological context of the person and behavior of Sister Helen Prejean. It is in her moral and spiritual stature and in her actions in favor of Poncelet, that she is the face of love, the face of Christ, the incarnate Love of God, for Poncelet and for us. As such, she is Christ-figure. Robbins suggests Prejean's christological identity by bracketing her experience, and our experience of her, between two crosses. Early in the film, she shows the cross she is wearing during a security check at the prison: a small cross which identifies her as a nun and signals her as a Christ-figure, announcing the passion she will live in this place. At the end of the film, Robbins has her stretch her hand out toward another cross, the one on which Poncelet is dying, a cross on which she too, in a real sense, is participating in his death.

As a nun, a woman consecrated to God in religious life, Prejean is an *alter Christus* for the people to whom she is sent, first her community and then for Poncelet. Parallel to the disturbing, nightmarish flashbacks to Poncelet's double crime of rape and murder, Robbins edits in a series of flashbacks, very different in tone and texture, to the joyous occasion of Prejean's entrance into religious life. She is dressed as a bride, and in the simple, almost naive home-movie shots of her, evidently ecstatically happy to be a bride of Christ, Robbins is suggesting a Christian counterimage of love to the violence of the other images: the image of Christ opposed to the image of hate.

Beyond the christological significance implicit in Prejean's identity, Robbins suggests that in a variety of ways, the dynamics of her experience of Poncelet follow the pattern of the life and mission of Christ. In the story of the development of Prejean's vocation, from home and an economically well-placed family, she leaves to live in poverty in community – the furnishings of her austere apartment are in strong contrast to the elaborate and rich home of her family – and with the poor. Being with the poor, she empties herself ever further, to move into the vulgar and violent low-class world of Poncelet and his family and of death row in a prison. This movement downward, this self-emptying in order to bring salvation clearly reflects the christological mystery of *kenosis*: the Word of God "leaving behind" the privileges and power of the divinity in order to enter the human experience and bring salvation to it.

In Prejean's entering so fully into the world she is sent to, the poor black neighborhood, the prison, the world of Poncelet, Robbins represents the mystery of the Incarnation, suggested first of all by the fact that Sister Helen does not wear a nun's habit, which would set her apart. Prejean identifies with Poncelet, suffers with him, enters his family, never putting any restrictions or conditions in the way. She shares the man's experiences, the horror of his crime, his fears, his suffering, his struggle to achieve freedom, inculturating herself so fully into his world that she symbolically becomes a member of his family when Poncelet meets with them before his execution. When in a horribly vulgar conversation, the condemned man and his brother reminisce about their amorous conquests in high school, rating various girls in an obscene way, Prejean listens quietly, as does his mother, and even laughs with them. She understands and appreciates the human communication and communion going on beneath the vulgarity.

In various specific moments of Sister Prejean's contact with Poncelet, her experience takes on dimensions of several biblical parables and incidents, in all of which Prejean has the role of the Christ- or Savior-figure. In Prejean's leaving the community in which she is already a shepherd to help Poncelet, to save this murderer who is about as far "from the fold" as possible, Robbins clearly suggests the parable of the lost sheep (Lk 15:1-7), an identification then underlined by the urgency with which she seeks to save him. As Poncelet walks to his death, with her hand firmly grasping his shoulder, Prejean reads to him Psalm 23, "The Lord is My Shepherd." Clearly for Poncelet, the shepherd he experiences, leading him through "the valley of the shadow of death," is Prejean, the incarnation for him of the salvation offered in Jesus Christ. Then as we have already noted, when Prejean sings "Be Not Afraid" to Poncelet, she is assuming the role of God speaking to Isaiah (Is 43:2-3), giving him courage, offering him protection, assuring him of victory. Perhaps the most striking of these specific christological-soteriological references is to be recognized in the courageous determination of Prejean to have Poncelet face and speak openly the truth about his crime and therefore about himself. The reference is to the long conversation of Jesus with the woman of Samaria: only when the truth is openly spoken is salvation possible, and in speaking the truth, the person is set free and given life (Jn 4:7-42).

The christological motifs connected with Prejean become denser, more significant, in the final minutes of the film, and take on the undeniable aspect of the passion, of "a Way of the Cross."[139] One critic recognizes the passion-motif, interpreting Poncelet as the good thief being crucified and Prejean as one of the pious women of Jerusalem at the foot of the cross. He adds that "Jesus is not visibly present but his spirit is at work."[140] A more valid interpretation is that Jesus is in fact present, metaphorically, as a Christ-image, in the person of Sister Prejean. Robbins begins the passion analogy in the scene where Prejean, stressed to the limit by the horror of the beginning of the execution protocol, seeks refuge in the ladies' washroom and, pounding her fists against the wall, shouts in agony a desperate prayer to God, asking him to give her strength, not so much for herself but so that she can help Poncelet. The parallel to Jesus in Gethsemane, asking God to strengthen him, so that he can complete the mission of human salvation, is clear.

Prejean's walking behind Poncelet down the corridor to the execution chamber, reading to him, in his place, "the Lord is my shepherd," becomes also for her a way of the cross, for she participates in his suffering, and in his death. But perhaps the clearest point of identification of Prejean as a Christ-figure is during the carrying out of the death sentence. Like the good thief, having publicly confessed his sin and asked for forgiveness, Poncelet is "crucified,"[141] and dying.[142] He turns his head and looks towards Prejean, the "face of love," whose hand is outstretched towards him. She is mouthing the words "I love you" over and over. Though dying, he obviously experiences a "great sense of peace . . . the grace of God."[143] The analogy is clear: the good thief did not receive consolation from the women of Jerusalem, but rather from Jesus himself, towards whom he looked and from whom he received words of love. Helen Prejean is at her strongest and most eloquent here as a figure of Christ, actually carrying out the salvation of a human being.

After the burial of Poncelet, Robbins concludes his film with a very slow zoom away from the gothic window of a church. Through the window he lets us see two figures kneeling side by side in silent prayer; one is Prejean, the other is the father of one of the victims of Poncelet's crime. His name, not by chance, is Delacroix, "of the cross," and he too is living through a passion: his daughter brutally murdered, his marriage failed. The significance of this very low-key closing image, which creates "a genuine sense of consolation, fragile but profoundly moving,"[144] is clear: Prejean, the face of love for Poncelet, now has become the face of love for Delacroix. Love multiplies itself, salvation goes on. The image, suffused by a warm sunny light, and framed by the bright green leaves of a tree, is clearly paschal. It speaks quietly but strongly of the Resurrection.

By way of conclusion, a brief note about the title of the film. The phrase "Dead man walking!" as it is shouted by a prison guard at the end of the film, has one meaning, cruel, almost sadistic. It announces the walking of the condemned man from his cell to the place of execution. But the same phrase, and so the title of the film, has another much more positive, Christian meaning. In the context of the themes of the film and in particular, the theme of Sister Prejean as a Christ-figure who brings salvation to the "dead man," "Dead man walking!" becomes an Easter proclamation, a declaration of the great Christian paradox alive in Poncelet in that moment. He is dead that is, he is about to die, physically. But he is walking, that is he is alive, he is saved. As he gazes on the face of love, the face of God, he is entering eternal life. "Dead man walking!" heralds that victory. More than making a film about philosophical-moral issues of human justice, "Tim Robbins films the triumph of the Holy."[145] That is its remarkable accomplishment.

3

The Hero of the Western as a Christ-Figure: *Shane*

The western, a most American *genre* of cinema, provides a remarkably apt and interesting context for the development of the cinematic Christ-figure. Almost as old as the film art itself, and carrier *par excellence* of the American myth, the western has developed a highly conventional structure, value scheme and repertoire of imagery. In synthesis then, the western propels the spectator *in media res* of a conflict between two groups of people, one of which is clearly in the right, and the other in the wrong. Rapidly the conflict escalates and the "good guys" seem about to lose out to the "bad guys." Into this conflict, this moral crisis, a mysterious and powerful "stranger" comes, who identifies with the forces of good, fights the evil forces and wins, and then almost immediately rides off, "into the sunset." This hero is a *deus ex machina*; his origins, his arrival, his powerful goodness and his departure and destiny, are, by and large, unexplained, and often defy the logic of the rest of the film. Little or nothing is revealed of his thoughts and feelings. He does not incarnate himself or put down roots in the "world" he came to save and his coming, his heroic action, his leaving, in fact cost him little.

In some westerns, the conflict is between the settlers and the Indians: the settlers, civilized, law-abiding, religious, are in the right; the Indians, savage, cruel, lawless and pagan, represent the forces of evil. In some few westerns, such as Kevin Costner's recent *Dances with Wolves* (1990), the Indians are good, and the white military, the government and the settlers, represent the forces of evil. In some westerns, set in southwest Texas, the good, English-speaking settlers are up against Spanish-speaking "outlaws," who maintain that the territory claimed by the "Yankee gringo" settlers is, in fact theirs.

In other westerns, the conflict is between whites, that is between on the one hand, a group of homesteaders, small ranchers and their families, and behind them the government and its laws, and on the other hand, "outlaws," that is the first-arrived on the frontier who forcibly, violently took the land from the Indians. These are big ranchers, who have claim to huge tracts of land and move cattle on the open range. The law wants them to give way to the structures of civilization represented by the homesteaders: families, homes, schools, churches, normal commercial and social activities. They of course resist as long as they can, and often in any way they can. At this point enters the "institution" of the hired gun, the private mercenary, a "bad guy" *par excellence*. A loner, he shoots well, has no scruples and functions completely outside the law. He provides the villains with a way to get rid of their enemies without directly dirtying their hands. The job done, he rides off and the local "bad guys" get off scott-free.

In some later westerns, the social-legal-governmental structures are well-established: there is a town, a sheriff, a jail, perhaps even a courthouse and judge, a school, a bank, a church, and a hotel-saloon. The stagecoach arrives regularly and later the railroad and communications via post and telegraph are easy and quick. In this version of the western, those living outside the law are up against a great deal: obliged to conduct hit-and-run operations, they rob the bank, the stagecoach or the train, take off and hide out. After them rides the sheriff, often with deputies and a posse and there follow, usually in rapid succession, arrest, trial, jail and sometimes hanging.

George Stevens situates his western, *Shane*,[1] rather early in the historical period of the settlement of the Old West. He has the villain insist that, since he and his gang fought the Indians, "We made this country."[2] The homesteaders then are the second wave of settlement. No specific geographical coordinates are given in the film, other than the almost constant visual reference to the Rocky Mountains. The only specific historical coordinate is the several references to the Civil War, one of the homesteaders being from the South, but there is a clear allusion to "the Johnson County range war in Wyoming in 1892."[3] The homesteaders live at some distance from each other – one house is not visible from another – and far from town.

The settlement is a primitive and "lonely row of buildings calling itself a town"[4] in the middle of a valley: a general store-saloon, a stable, another building and a tent. On a hill nearby is the cemetery which seems to have more inhabitants than the town. "A tiny isolated community, cut off by a towering mountain range,"[5] the town has no school, no church: these are a dream for the future.[6] There is no stagecoach and no telegraph, the homesteaders are closed off from the outside world, and most importantly, there is no one to protect them. Caught in this lonely situation, these homesteaders live "not with single-minded determination but in fear and uncertainty."[7] In the film, Stevens makes reference to laws, to the fact that the government has given homesteaders the land they are on. But "the Marshall is a hundred miles away," and thus at the beginning of the film, the "bad guys," though they are about to be eclipsed, still rule the region with impunity. Their purpose is to persuade the homesteaders to leave, thus consolidating their land and their power. ("Your kinda days are over," the hero tells them before the final showdown.")

Stevens' western, "a paragon of the pattern"[8] and recognized by many "as the greatest of all westerns,"[9] tells the story of the complex salvific relationship established between a mysterious stranger, drifter, ex-gunfighter, Shane, and the family of a homesteader, Joe Starrett, who is desperately trying to survive and build a life, a future, a society, in the far west. The Starretts and their homesteader neighbors are being threatened by an aging cattle baron, Ryker, a man without a family,[10] a law unto himself, who does not want to accept that his way of life is on the way out, that a new age is beginning, that he has to give up his absolute power over the land that he himself conquered from the Indians years before.

One day Shane rides down into the valley and, having identified himself to the Ryker gang, who pay a threatening visit to the Starrett homestead, as Starrett's friend, he accepts the latter's hospitality. To the delight of Joey, Starrett's small son, and of his wife Marian, Shane decides to stay on and help Joe work the homestead. As a sign of his decision "to cut out [of his violent past] and win a new life for himself as a law abiding citizen,"[11] Stevens has his hero doff his buckskin outfit and his six-shooter and adopt store-bought work clothes. Shane reveals nothing about himself, but his past as a gunfighter becomes evident to the Starretts early on. Several times he reacts nervously to sudden noises by going for his gun. Even little Joey intuits the truth, saying to his father about Shane's gun, "It goes with him though."[12] The Starretts respect his secret, and from the beginning, are much attracted by Shane's mysterious kindness and generosity. The good stranger is particularly solicitous of Joey, and the boy responds wholeheartedly, as he confesses to his mother at bedtime, "Ma, I just love Shane. . . . He's so good."

Through his relationship with the Starretts, Shane gets drawn into the conflict between the homesteaders and the Ryker gang. He meets them in the opening moments of the film on Starrett's property and the next day in the saloon, he is ridiculed by them as "a new sod-buster" and has whiskey thrown on his new work-shirt so that he will "smell like a man." Several days later when he accompanies a group of homesteaders into the general store to buy supplies, the conflict erupts into a free-for-all fistfight,[13] between Shane and all the Rykers, sparked by an insult to his honor and that of Marian Starrett. When the good stranger seems about to lose, Joe Starrett joins in and together they win the day.

Though Shane's presence among the homesteaders is very reassuring, both to them and to himself, when Ryker offers him a job, Shane refuses, insisting, "I like working for Starrett." Marian intuits the ambiguities and dangers ahead, advising her son, "Don't get to liking Shane too much . . . he'll be moving on one day."[14] She also objects to Shane's teaching Joey how to shoot. The homesteaders' Fourth of July celebration, also the Starretts' tenth wedding anniversary, complete with fireworks, dancing and a huge American flag, is a moment of moral strength and consolation for them. But it ends on a negative note when the news comes of the arrival in town of a gunfighter, "kinda lean, he wears a black hat;" Shane suspects it is Jack Wilson, a gunfighter out of Cheyenne. Hired by Ryker, Wilson reveals his professionalism by drinking not whiskey but only coffee, "no doubt to add to his evil sharpness."[15] He goes to work immediately, provoking and killing one of the homesteaders, Torrey, in cold blood. The Christian burial of Torrey, with a hymn, "In life, in death, Lord, abide with me," and the Lord's Prayer, becomes another moment of solidarity among the homesteaders. They are discouraged, demoralized, but Starrett and Shane together make an eloquent *apologia* for staying on:

> We can have a real settlement here, a town and churches, a school . . . a place where people can come and bring up their families . . . to grow 'em good, to grow 'em up strong . . . it's up to you people to have nerve enough to not give up.[16]

Ryker's gang raises the stakes of the conflict by burning down the home of one of the homesteaders, at which point Joe Starrett, to the horror of Marian, vows to "have this out with Ryker . . . if I have to kill him." Ryker and Wilson set a trap for Starrett, convoking him to town for a discussion of peace, on which occasion they plan to kill him. When one of the Ryker gang, the only one with a conscience, reveals the truth to Shane, Shane decides to go in Starrett's place. Shane subdues Starret, who insists this is *his* fight, by fighting him and finally hitting him on the head with his gun. Having bid farewell to Marian, who again intuits that "we'll never see you again," and being followed by little Joey, Shane rides into town. The final showdown takes place in the saloon by night and with the boy Joey watching on. Shane speaks words of truth to Ryker, "You've lived too long, your kinda days are over," and then facing the evil Wilson, clearly his "antithesis,"[17] Shane deliberately provokes him, "You're a lowdown Yankee liar." In the ensuing gunfight, Shane kills Wilson, Ryker and then, warned by Joey, Ryker's brother, himself sustaining a wound to the hand. Shane bids farewell to Joey, "Now you run on home to your mother and tell her . . . there are no more guns in the valley." His hand on the boy's head, he pronounces a farewell blessing on him: "Grow up to be strong and straight," and then he rides up into the mountains whence he came.[18]

From the above description of the story, some of the elements of the Christ-figure embodied in Shane will already be evident, but let us begin our more precise analysis with a consideration of the world that Shane comes into, the world which, in a certain sense, gives him his *raison d'être* both as the hero of this western film, and as a Christ-figure. In the opening images, George Stevens gives the world of his film the aura of an earthly paradise, a new garden of Eden. The wide expanse of blue sky, the power and magnificence of the mountains, the lushness of the valley, the freshness of the flowing river, all filmed in bright, vivid colors, are enhanced by appropriately pastoral music. The shots of a deer peacefully drinking and grazing near the Starrett house as Joe Starrett works at removing a stump from his yard, suggest a balanced relationship between nature and the human presence.

Starrett and his family are the archetypal settlers in this paradise. Their names, Joe and Marian, "echo the Holy Family and signify purity, faithfulness, hard work, domestic fruitfulness and godliness."[19] They are good, hopeful and caring people, gentle and loving with their son, and clearly committed to building a new and just society, along with other homesteaders, who have the same values as the Starretts, and in harmony with nature. They all support and help one another and have a strong sense of justice. They come together to celebrate the good times and the bad, and they recognize the supreme authority of God over their lives.

But in this new creation, the Rykers, with their harassment and terrorizing of the homesteaders, revealed by Stevens already in the opening minutes of the film, are a threat, a presence of evil. Ryker, as Starrett explains to Shane early on, "thinks the whole world belongs to him," and he acts accordingly. Ryker's stampeding cattle ruin their wheat fields, Ryker's men burn down their houses and every visit to town runs the risk of trouble and even tragedy. Already some homesteaders have left, others are planning to, and Joe Starrett, as strong a moral leader as he is, is running out of arguments to persuade them to stay. Further, Stevens makes it clear that Starrett himself, his family, his home, are under immediate threat and danger from Ryker. His little son, who carries around an empty rifle, says to Shane the morning after his arrival: "I'll bet you wouldn't leave just because it's too dangerous around here."[20]

The specific physical evil represented by the Rykers is compounded by the related moral evil of discouragement, the loss of hope, on the part of the homesteaders. Their solidarity, their moral resolve, is weakening and that interior evil, eating away at their Christian hope and resolve, is indeed most dangerous. If Stevens allows even the remote possibility that the homesteaders might be able to overcome these two levels of evil in their lives (though when Shane arrives, they are not doing too well at it), in his introduction of the professional gunfighter, Wilson, "a vicious, pale-faced, smiling villain,"[21] he is raising the power of evil in the film almost to the metaphysical level.[22] Against this kind of consummate evil, Starrett and the homesteaders are helpless. Stevens has Shane allude to this before the final showdown in the film, when he says to Joe: "Maybe you're a match for Ryker, maybe not, but you're no match for Wilson."

To meet and defeat this level of evil which threatens individuals, society and a whole civilization, a particular moral hero is needed, a redeemer, a restorer of order, a bringer of grace and freedom, one who not only has the ability to act, the skill, the power, but also the moral courage, the spiritual freedom to risk all, to offer himself in redemptive sacrifice. The quadruple trumpet blast on the soundtrack when the newly-arrived stranger says to Starrett as they shake hands, "Call me Shane," is Stevens' signal that the much-needed hero is Shane.

From the time he arrives on the scene, Shane acts in favor of Starrett and through him, the homesteaders, and in these external actions he takes on aspects of the hero. Though perhaps not yet explicitly actions of a Christ-figure, all of Shane's actions and attitudes at this level are entirely compatible with that identity and function as we shall analyze it further below. First of all, Shane helps Starrett in his work of homesteader, of domesticating the earth. The strong images, reinforced by dramatic music, of the two men working together, pushing the tree stump out of the ground – they do not use a team because, as Joe explains, "Sometimes there ain't nothing'll do but your own sweat and muscle" – have archetypal significance.[23] Twice, Shane identifies himself as working for Starrett and when Ryker offers him better pay, he insists, "I like working for Starrett."

Shane serves as a friend and companion to Joe Starrett, a trusting friendship so solid that towards the end of the film, Joe indicates to his wife his conviction that Shane would take care of her and the boy should anything happen to him. More than once Stevens indicates the importance of this relationship to both men, by showing them exchanging knowing smiles.[24] The good stranger is also a companion to Marian, sharing ideas and feelings with her, achieving a remarkable degree of moral and spiritual intimacy with her, of which Stevens creates the wonderful metaphor of their ordered dancing together on the Fourth of July. But perhaps most importantly of all, Shane becomes friend and teacher to little Joey from the very first moments of the film. Joey is profoundly affected by the presence of this strong spiritual guide in his life, something his father, though a strong positive force, has neither the time nor the inclination to be. Shane teaches Joey how to use a gun, and how and when not to. When the boy asks Shane why he never wears his six-shooter, he replies, with a patient smile, "I don't see as many bad men as you do." The boy's declaration to his mother, "I just love Shane," comes as no surprise.

Shane repeatedly stands as companion and helper between Starrett and the homesteaders and the Ryker gang. At Starrett's, the evening of his arrival, he is a quiet positive presence when the rowdy Rykers ride up. Later, after the Fourth of July celebration, again at Starrett's, he helps his friend face the Rykers and Wilson. He states publicly, in the general store, that he's on Starrett's and therefore, on the homesteaders' side. In response to the public insinuations of Ryker, he defends Marian's honor and on the Fourth of July, he helps the homesteaders understand who Wilson really is. Perhaps the high point of Shane's role as moral support to the community of homesteaders is when they gather, discouraged, demoralized on the occasion of the burial of Torrey: Joe Starrett does his best to encourage them to stay, but he runs out of words and it is Shane's eloquence on this occasion which gives renewed hope to Starrett and the whole community. The community recognizes and appreciates this role of Shane in their midst. When the planning of the Fourth of July feast begins, one woman says, "We want you to come too, Shane;" when the Lewis family's house is burned down and Starrett exhorts, "If we all stick together, we can put that place right back up," Marian adds, "Shane will help." She senses that Shane's participation in any project is beneficial. In the end, when the menacing power of the Rykers is amplified by the presence of the evil Wilson, a threat against which Starrett and the homesteaders have no defense, it is Shane who steps into the breech and redeems the situation.

Shane is friend, helper, confidante; he is moral support and encouragement; he is educator, protector, defender; Shane promotes good and opposes evil; he restores order and hope in a world profoundly vitiated by evil, disorder, despair.[25] If then in Shane's external actions on behalf of the community, Stevens suggests elements which reflect the salvific presence and action of Jesus Christ within the Christian community, then he underscores this Christ-like identity in several elements of Shane's personality, his way of being and acting with people, elements which make of Shane an altogether exceptional person. First of all, his physical presence set him apart: well-built, good-looking, graceful of movement, with blue eyes, smooth golden skin and silky blonde hair, captivating smile, a voice both strong and tender. He seems to be the only man in the film who is always clean shaven, though Stevens never shows him at this morning ritual. Whether in his unique light tan doeskin suit, which identifies him with the powers of nature, or in his work shirt (the only sky-blue shirt in the film) and slacks, he is always neat; with the homesteaders, he is well-mannered, always speaks politely, respectfully and, distinct from both the homesteaders and the Rykers, in clear and correct grammatical form. In short, Stevens makes Shane a man full of "wisdom and grace."[26]

Shane is a mysteriously attractive man. His "sun-god appearance,"[27] his goodness and natural grace touch the people with whom he comes into contact. Even one of Ryker's men, Chris, after coming into conflict with Shane, has a conversion experience. All the homesteaders relate well to him[28] and the women, especially, sense his exceptional qualities. If his rapport with Joey Starrett is any indication, Shane has a particular gift for communicating with children: Stevens makes Joey's pure wide-eyed wonder at the first appearance of Shane, and his immediate whole-hearted discipleship (He wants Shane to "teach" him.) which soon becomes love, a major theme of the film. This "mentor/teacher"[29] role of Shane, "common to many westerns,"[30] also involves Marian (his balanced comments about the use of guns) and the whole community (his eloquent exhortation to courage after Torrey's burial). An important aspect of Shane's attractiveness is that he is a spiritually free, well-integrated man. He relates well to both men and women, inspires trust in everyone, is free from attachments that might hinder his effectiveness. In this vein, the critic Jon Tuska speaks of Shane as "a savior, a man less in need of anything than the other characters, less attached to anything, and therefore incredibly free and self-possessed."[31]

Shane is celibate, a dimension of his existence and experience that oddly enough none of the critics notes. His celibacy, not only physical but moral and spiritual, is perhaps what most underlies most his freedom. Whatever its origins may be, Stevens raises Shane's celibacy to a high level of human nobility in his relationship with Marian. Clearly there are strong feelings between them, a profound openness, understanding, sympathy, care and communion. There is love, "unquestionably the purest relationship presented on the screen."[32] Stevens makes this particularly evident several times in the film. When Shane wants to avoid talking to Joey about his past, as a gun-fighter it would seem, saying "It's a long story, Joey," Marian looks straight

at him and says, very calmly but full of feeling, "I think we know, Shane."
That Marian is conscious of the significance of what she is saying here, is
made evident by the pause in her comment: she is about to say "Mr. Shane"
but changes her mind and uses the more intimate form. Later when the two of
them dance at the Fourth of July feast, a dance marked by a calm, ordered
movement in which the two of them unselfconsciously face the camera and
Joe Starrett most of the time as if to say, "We have nothing to hide," Stevens
is suggesting a profound communion of spirits, characterized by great freedom on Shane's part and on Marian's and by a total respect for her commitment to Starrett and Joey.[33] Stevens seems to be saying that, like the
Starretts' marriage commitment, Shane's celibacy frees him to love and to
love freely.[34]

If Stevens allows the possibility of some degree of christic identification
in Shane because he acts as friend and defender of the downtrodden, as
teacher and protector of the innocent, and because he is free man, giving and
inspiring trust and love, then he certainly pushes this possibility further by
creating around his protagonist an aura of mystery, both for the other characters in the film and for the viewers of the film. Shane arrives as if out of
nowhere, not even a pack on his horse. His origins and recent past remain
almost a total mystery for the entire film, though Marian and others intuit that
he has been a gunslinger. His good looks, his intelligence and sensitivity, his
balanced manner of speaking and acting, set him mysteriously apart from all,
as does his astonishing degree of freedom, generosity and selflessness. He is
clearly a man for others. His future, his destiny and concretely, his departure
at the end of the film, having completed his mission of redemption, riding
back up into the mountains whence he came, remain a mystery. The critic
Geoffrey Hill seems to address and interpret this mysterious quality in Shane
when he says of the hero of the western: "He is like a lone, quiet god come
from out of time as an answered prayer to those within time."[35] Hill's words
are very close to being a good description of the Christian understanding of
the Incarnation: the Eternal Word of God, from out of time and space, enters
time and space, to satisfy the yearning, and the prayers of the people of God
for the Messiah and for salvation.

One could object that all these characteristics of Stevens' hero are
merely typical of the hero of the western, as described in rather summary
fashion at the beginning of this chapter. Since it is distinctive of the traditional western to mythologize situations and people – the "good guys" are
always very good, the "bad guys," well nigh irredeemably bad – then one
might conclude that Shane, who he is and what he does, is merely one more
hero of the *genre,* little more than a caricature of what in "more serious,
dramatic cinema" is treated very differently, with more complexity, subtlety.
In response to this hypothetical objection, one can say that on a first level of
reflection, it is possible to appreciate *Shane* as a good western, and understand its protagonist as typical hero of that *genre*, though certainly raised by
Stevens to a mythical level. However a more careful, second-level reading of

Shane yields a much richer and more complex image of the hero of the western, and moves us closer to the possibility of considering the man Shane as a Christ-figure. The point of departure for this second level reading of the film is precisely the traditional western of which we have just spoken, a precise *genre* with a standard structure, stereotypical situations and characters.

The basic point to be made here is that, in a number of ways, Stevens' film evades the usual stereotypical approach of the western. An "unromantic and entirely convincing evocation of the period [. . . without] the horse opera ingredients of the *genre*,"[36] *Shane* has a complexity, a rich ambiguity that defies a facile interpretation. For example, in the typical western, the "bad guys," the villains, are two-dimensional caricatures of various vices who inspire little sympathy in the viewers. Stevens makes his "bad guys" more human, more interesting. One of the Ryker gang, Calloway, after the arrival of Wilson, undergoes a gradual conversion and towards the end of the film, he makes possible Shane's salvific intervention. Ryker himself is not totally devoid of humanity: Stevens gives him a certain degree of self-awareness, noted especially in his conversations with Grafton, the saloon owner, on whose respect he counts. Then his two conversations with Joe Starrett, the second of which is a kind of sad *apologia pro vita sua,* are most telling. We begin to sense Ryker's human struggle to deal with the fact that, as Shane tells him before the final showdown, he is getting old, that his "kinda days are over," that his hard work of a lifetime against the Indians, the land, the elements, to create a cattle empire, has now to give way to a second generation of settlers who have different ideas. He even has to bring in an outsider to fight the battles he is no longer able to win.

It is true that Stevens creates in the gunfighter Wilson a mythologized incarnation of an almost metaphysical evil: his black vest and hat, the black glove he methodically puts on his pistol hand before each showdown, the dissolve and jump cut (unique in the film) by which Stevens has Wilson "appear mysteriously" in the saloon, the poor saloon dog who twice quits the premises when Wilson enters. But at the same time, Stevens gives Wilson some interesting human qualities. His drinking coffee, for example, instead of whiskey, suggests a human, learned discipline. He is defeated in the end because he made the very human error of reacting to Shane's insult, tragically forgetting that this is the very trick he used to provoke Torrey earlier in the film. It is, however, in a brief comment that Stevens has him make to Ryker that the humanity of Wilson is best revealed. Exasperated by Starrett, Ryker vows, "I'll kill him if I have to!" Wilson, coffee mug in hand, calmly, with conscious irony, responds: "You mean *I'll* kill him if *you* have to." In that moment of public self-consciousness, Stevens is suggesting that Wilson knows how he is irrevocably trapped in an identity, a destiny of which, it would seem, he might prefer to be free.[37]

Also in the Starretts, Stevens creates much more than an idealized Joe and Marian, a two-dimensional couple in their Old West Garden of Eden.[38] Joe Starrett's behavior at the Fourth of July dance, already referred to, suggests his complexity. The big man first steps aside to have his wife dance with his friend Shane, and then realizes how far his friend surpasses him in goodness or perhaps sadly, that this friend will one day leave. But it is especially in Starrett's comments to Marian as he prepares to go to town for the final showdown that Stevens shows his deep and very human goodness. In a quite remarkable, yet utterly convincing, statement, Starrett first confesses his limits, admitting "I know I'm kinda slow sometimes, Marian," but then he indicates a sensibility to what is happening around him: "I've been thinking a lot, Marian . . . I see things." He is saying here, with calm and trust, that he has sensed the positive dynamic of friendship, of love, that has flowered between Marian and Shane. He adds, repeating it twice, as if he finds it difficult to say, "I know that if . . . if anything happened to me [he means in a gunfight with Ryker and Wilson] you'd be took care of, you'd be took care of better than I could do it myself." Then, to indicate how much it has cost Starrett to say this, to suggest in this big, burly farmer, deep levels of self-awareness and ambiguity, Stevens has him conclude very convincingly, "I never thought I'd live to hear myself say that."

Stevens creates also in Marian Starrett interesting levels of complexity. She is the first to intuit not only Shane's secret past, but also the pain, the moral ambiguity, this inescapable past imposes on Shane in the present. The words and the tone of her comment, "I think we know, Shane," reveal her delicate sensitivity and respect for the guest. Stevens suggests the intensity of her feelings towards Shane in the tender care with which she cleans his wounds. Once Shane leaves the room, in Marian's gesture of going to her husband and saying "Hold me. Don't say anything, just hold me tight," Stevens creates a profoundly meaningful gesture of human freedom, of marital fidelity, of chastity. When Marian bids farewell to Shane, her words suggest not only an appreciation of his gesture of self-sacrifice, but of her own feelings towards him, all tempered – as she says, "Please, Shane, take care of yourself" and shakes his hand – by the chastity and conjugal fidelity already noted above.[39]

Stevens makes of the boy Joey a far more complex creation than at first one might think. Beyond the blond hair, the sweet, angelic face, the wide-open eyes with which he marvels – "Gosh almighty" – at the realities around him, Stevens gives him a complex double role to play in the film. On the one hand, within the diegesis of the film, while being himself, Joey helps focus attention on certain crucial issues. In his oft-repeated plea to be taught to shoot, first by his father and then by Shane, countered by his mother's wish that he not learn how to shoot, Stevens situates very clearly, within the narrative of the film, the issue of violence versus pacifism as a solution to problems and as a way of life.[40] In the boy's great sensitivity to Shane, expressed quite openly, innocently, in looks, words, gestures – "It [the six-shooter] goes with him though"; "Ma, I just love Shane. . . . He's so good" – Stevens is modulating our ongoing response to Shane. In the boy's very frank comments to his friend – "Pa wishes you'd stay too"; "I know you ain't afraid"; "Pa's got things for you to do, and mother wants you" – Stevens has him communicate to Shane, and to the viewer, crucial information that would otherwise be awkward to convey.

At the same time as Joey has this complex function *within* the diegesis or narrative of the film, Stevens gives him and even more complex role *outside* its diegesis, that is on a stylistic-technical level. He makes the boy into the creator-modulator of the point of view of the viewers of the film: "as a point of view character . . . nearly everything that happens is seen through his eyes."[41] Perceptive viewers of *Shane* note that during number of crucial scenes in the film – gunfights, fistfights, Shane's shooting lesson to Joey, the final showdown – the dramatic intensity of the action seems to shift upward. They may also note that the boy Joey is present at these scenes and that Stevens shows him from time to time in close-up, his eyes open wide. A careful analysis shows that we viewers see and hear what "happens" in these sequences from the very subjective, and very particular point of view of Joey, filtered through his acute sensitivity. Fistfights go on for the longest time, and the grunts and groans of the participants are loud, firing pistols are very loud and produce an exaggerated amount of smoke.[42] In these conflict scenes, the adult participants, Shane in particular, become giants. Stevens places the movie camera at the eye-level of Joey. It becomes his eyes, and so we "see" the reality of the event as he sees it. Stevens suggests the intensity of the boy's identification with Shane and of his participation in the action, by editing in "a close-up of Joey biting down on a peppermint stick each time Shane gets hit in a fight with the rangers."[43]

This effective technique of Stevens reaches a quite exceptional point during the scene of the final showdown in the saloon. As might be expected, since Joey is observing the action, Shane looms large, the shooting is loud, the smoke billows and the ultra-villain Wilson ends up ignobly under several empty beer barrels. But then, lo and behold, Joey himself begins to participate in the action. He shouts to Shane that Ryker is about to shoot him from the upstairs landing. Another explosion of sound and smoke, and Shane walks away tall. As he steps out of the saloon, Joey, rather small now in the doorway, whispers, "Shane, I knew you could, Shane, I knew it." Shane, surprised, says, "Joey, what're you doing here?" Why does Stevens have the boy whisper? Why Shane's surprise and question, if the boy, in fact had shouted a warning and saved his life? Stevens is adding complexity to the character of the boy Joey by suggesting that his warning and his saving Shane's life, which we the spectators have seen, are, in fact, Joey's imaginative reconstruction or experience, of the reality. Joey's presence, then, determines not only how things are seen, but also, in the end, what is seen.[44]

If Stevens, in the "good guys" and the "bad guys" of his film, creates characters who transcend both the stereotypes of the typical western, and also the strict limits of the heightened, "mythologized" version of the *genre* that he wants to create in *Shane*, then we can expect that he will do no less in the protagonist of his film. Clearly Shane, while sharing some of the qualities of the typical and the mythological western hero, as we have reconstructed it, transcends these limits in the direction of a full incarnation of the god-like hero in human flesh and human experience. Thus, Stevens prepares the way for a second level reading of Shane that understands him as a Christ-figure.

Stevens has Shane's kenotic incarnation begin the very evening he arrives at the Starretts' homestead: he shares a meal with them. Afterwards, he removes his buckskin shirt and works, indeed sweats, bare-chested. He puts aside his pistol and uses his hands. The next day he rides into town on a wagon, not on his horse, and buys and immediately dons simple work clothes, putting aside his distinctive buckskin suit. That these kenotic incarnational gestures are choices, and not particularly easy, for Shane, Stevens suggests in his nervous, instinctive reaching for his pistol twice, and in his awkwardness in the general store: he says, almost apologetically, "It's a long time since I got store-bought clothes."[45] Yet when, in the same general store, Shane announces his *kenosis* from the identity of gunfighter and his incarnation in the world of the homesteaders – "Yes, I'm working for Starrett" – he says it easily, with satisfaction with his new reality.

Full incarnation involves humiliation, and Shane seems to experience it from all sides. One of Ryker's gang makes fun of him in the saloon when he orders a soda pop for Joey, refers to his smelling like a pig and spills whiskey on his new shirt so that he will "smell like a man." Again here, Shane could, and evidently would like to, defend himself but he chooses to accept the humiliation, to live fully his incarnation. As he does again that same evening, but this time from his own people, who during the meeting at Starrett's place, describe the earlier events in the saloon and accuse Shane of being a coward, saying, "Ya can't count on him."

Stevens does not limit Shane's kenotic incarnation to external aspects of his life. Also in his interior life, Shane, gunfighter, self-sufficient outsider, comes to experience the tensions, the ambiguities and the joys of the people he has come to be with and eventually to save. His commitment to Starrett is reciprocal. They work together, and when Shane is about to lose the fight in the saloon, for his and Marian's honor, Starrett joins the fray and together they prevail. Stevens includes a closeup shot of Shane and Starrett, fighting back-to-back, as they look at each other and smile triumphantly. Evidently Shane enjoys this very human fellowship, as he also enjoys eating with the Starretts and being invited to the Fourth of July celebration. Shane becomes a man who depends on others.

Stevens makes Shane both capable of loving and capable of receiving love: he responds positively to the declared love of Joey and to the undeclared but no-less-real loving care and trust of Starrett and his wife. He enjoys this experience of love, thrives on it – his dancing with Marian makes this clear – and perhaps derives the strength to make his ultimate sacrifice from it. Shane loves chastely, in a celibate way: he remains a respectful guest in the Starrett home. But this choice is not without struggle or cost for Shane. Repeatedly Stevens suggests his hero's yearning for love, domestic love, a wife, a son. Shane's downcast, reflective eyes when Starrett says to him, "Take care, Shane, you get a wife that's worth waiting for," or when Joey says to his mother, "I just love Shane," are eloquent testimony to this very human need.

This question of Shane's yearning for domestic realities, which is nothing other than a particularly radical incarnation into the world he comes into,[46] reveals a further dimension of the human complexity of Shane: his high degree of self-consciousness. We have already noted how Marian and Joe, and even Ryker and Wilson, demonstrate evidence of self-awareness, which, of course, makes them more roundly human, less caricatures. Stevens gives to his protagonist the highest level of self-consciousness in the film. From the beginning of the film, Stevens makes Shane a thoughtful man, who reflects on events taking place around him and on his own role in these events. The smiles, the alert, appreciative glances at people – his look at Marian when she indicates she understands his secret is full of meaning – the reflective eyes which signal a moment of interior struggle, particularly towards the end of the film as the call to self-sacrifice becomes clear. All point to a man with a high degree of self-awareness, a strong sense of the ambiguity of the human condition which he has entered, to which he has committed himself, and which he chooses to live fully.[47]

Stevens creates a further and fascinating dimension of Shane's complex self-knowledge in the curious, and very uncharacteristic fact that on two occasions he has Shane consciously de-mythologize himself. When Joey, who idolizes his friend, predicts he will not say anything when Marian disinfects his wounds, "no matter how much it hurts," Shane purposely says very clearly "ouch." The smile on his face reveals his motivation. Then after the final showdown, as if to redimension it and himself before the boy, Shane speaks very frankly, more than ever before, about himself, his hopes, his failure: "A man has to be what he is, Joey; I can't break the mold. I tried but it didn't work for me." Shane realizes it is not good for the boy to idolize a gunfighter and, because he loves the boy, he reveals himself as he is, he shows his limitations, he breaks the myth.

The extent to which Stevens has Shane live his fully-human incarnation becomes most clear in the ultimate sacrifice that the protagonist makes in order to render life possible for his people, the homesteaders. Shane's sacrifice will be discussed below, but here let us recall that central to the notion of sacrifice, of sacrifice as a purely human experience, before any christological considerations, is the element of self-giving, self-denial, of *passio* or submission to the will or the actions of another. Clearly, for the typical hero of the western, conscious sacrificial self-denial or submission to the will of another is not part of the vocation. At the end of the film, this typical hero rides off into the sunset, triumphant, more self-assertive, more than ever in control of reality and of himself. It is not so with Shane.

By giving Shane the character traits just now discussed, his kenotic incarnation into the world of the homesteaders, his full humanity, his self-awareness and self-sacrifice, George Stevens moves him out of the ken of the mythologized hero and thus, points to the possibility of our considering him a true Christ-figure. Then in a number of other ways, Stevens specifies this christological correspondence in his hero.

Perhaps the obvious place to begin is by considering Shane's mysterious origins and mysterious past, and with the fact that he arrives into the world of the homesteaders from above, "like a messiah,"[48] coming down from the mountains, the majestic mountains which serve as a backdrop to most of the film, their summits mysteriously shrouded in cloud. Stevens makes Shane's destiny equally mysterious, and has him depart by going back up into those same mountains, a departure lived with a sense of loss by the boy-disciple Joey. In these elements, exclusive to Shane in the film, because no one else comes down from, or goes up into the mountains, Stevens is alluding to the Incarnation-descent of Christ from on high and his return to the Father in the Ascension,[49] a departure experienced with confusion and sorrow by the disciples.[50] Shane's arrival at the Starrett homestead, where his mission begins, by crossing a river, seems to be a further biblical allusion, this time to the Jordan where Jesus was baptized and began his mission. Crossing the river represents for Shane a kind of irrevocable commitment, rather like the Incarnation for the Word of God. Shane never goes back across that river.[51]

Like the Word of God, Shane takes his kenotic incarnation seriously. When he removes his gun belt, he leaves behind his power over life and death, a power he reassumes only when his mission of liberation obviously requires it. Like Jesus, Shane lives the ideal of evangelical poverty: he has no pack and nowhere to lay his head but relies on the goodness of others for everything. Like that of Jesus, Shane's ministry, of helping, teaching, liberating the people, is gratuitous, a grace, that Ryker, for one, cannot understand: "What are you looking for?" he asks Shane, who answers perhaps enigmatically, "Nothing."[52] This gratuitousness, this grace, characterizes in a particular way Shane's very human and in a sense very divine way of loving. Like that of Jesus, Shane's love is chaste, selfless, life-giving, liberating. His love enables Joe Starrett to be the good husband and father he is capable of being. It fosters and strengthens Marian's fruitful love for Joe and their son in a world of peace. It is the blessing of a "strong and straight" future for the boy.

Like the Incarnate Word of God, Shane undertakes a monumental struggle with the powers of evil as they are incarnated especially in Wilson. The raw violence of the early fist-fight, and of the final gunfight in the saloon, adds a note of ambiguity to Shane, which does not however negate his being a Christ-figure. Geoffrey Hill explains: "the Prince of Peace in the Christian Bible is painted as one with an awesome sense of peace and passive acceptance of violence on one hand, and as an angry vandalizer of the corrupt temple on the other – a man of ambiguity."[53] Like Jesus, Shane accepts violence on himself passively; when the violence is aimed at others, he fights it; to paraphrase for Shane the words of the devout man of God, Simeon, regarding the child Jesus, "The stranger is a sign of contradiction."[54]

The highest point of the kenotic Incarnation of the Word of God in Jesus is his sacrificial death on the cross for love of humankind. The highest point of Shane's mission of liberation is his final sacrifice for love. Like Jesus, Shane conquers death, represented by the Rykers and Wilson, by dying to himself, to his own hopes for a different kind of life, a different future.[55] Like Jesus, Shane brings salvation to his people by "violent sacrifice."[56] He sheds his blood so that there might be peace – "no more guns" – in the valley. To underscore unambiguously the association of the sacrificial act of Shane and the sacrificial-salvific death of Jesus, Stevens brackets the scene of the final showdown in the saloon with two particularly dramatic shots of a cross, a specifically Christian cross at a grave site in the cemetery, seen earlier in the film.[57] As Shane rides into town, Stevens edits into the film a traveling shot of him on his horse, superimposed over a still shot of the cross, and holds this curious composite shot for five full seconds. The association is clear. Then once the showdown is over, the victory of good over evil confirmed, and Shane's final sacrificial act of leaving his people and returning into the mountains fulfilled, Stevens closes his film with an absolutely clear visual reference to the fullness of the Paschal mystery, the death and Resurrection of Christ. Shane goes up into the mountains and as he rides through the cemetery, Stevens has him go past the same cross, and continue towards, not the setting sun, so typical of the classical western, but the rising sun, in a splendid image of dawn, a new day, a resurrection.

4

A Christ-Figure
in Two Films of Kieślowski

A Short Film About Love,[1] a film by the Polish director Krzysztof Kieślowski, offers the exceptional opportunity of observing the thought of a director shift and change as he creates his film. Contemporaneously, Kieślowski shot and edited two versions of the same film, one for television, fifty-five minutes long, and one for the cinema of ninety minutes. Both films are part of a wider project of ten films collectively entitled, *The Decalogue.*[2] Because of that, and because in this chapter we will consider both films, though we will focus mainly on the longer version, it is important to analyze, even if briefly, the *Decalogue* project.

For the viewer who is conscious of the title of the overall work and of the titles of the individual films, *Decalogue One, Decalogue Two* and so on, the Judaeo-Christian *Decalogue,* the Ten Commandments given by God to Moses on Mount Sinai, hover in the background of the films, creating a kind of moral ambience or atmosphere. For Kieślowski and his friend and scriptwriter Krzysztof Piesiewicz, "the intention was not at all that of simply illustrating"[3] the commandments, but rather that of exploring some crucial dimensions of life in the postmodern world, as it confronts human beings with a variety of difficult existential situations and "complex ethical questions,"[4] often full of ambiguity: "knots in the daily effort to live."[5] In each film, the existential situation of the protagonists, the moral struggle, the human imperatives and choices they face, are rendered more clear, more sharp, more significant against the background of the biblical Commandment. Emanuela Imparato explains well how Kieślowski forges a new approach:

> Kieślowski in his *Decalogue* seems to have rewritten in the flesh of everyday human experience, the divine Commandments inscribed in stone; reversing the Law of the Other, from the beginning experienced as inhibitory, he transforms it into a norm that is civil, social and profoundly human.[6]

Kieślowski says, perhaps a bit ironically, about the *Decalogue* project:

> The films should be influenced by the individual Commandments to the same degree that the Commandments influence our daily lives. . . . No philosophy or ideology had ever challenged the fundamental tenets of the Commandments . . . yet they are nevertheless transgressed on a routine basis.[7]

The films of *The Decalogue* have as their protagonists middle class and upper-middle class men and women, more often than not professionals – a doctor, a lawyer, an artist, a student, a taxi driver, a couple of university professors – and their setting is the Stowki residential suburb of Warsaw and specifically, the complex of condominium apartment towers or *"bloki"* that dominate the district. The specific setting, however, is not meant to be restrictive:

> These condominiums and the open space in which they are become a kind of stage of the world for the "human comedy" of Kieślowski and Piesiewicz. It's not by chance that the original title for the cycle was to be "The Human Condition" or "On the Ten Commandments."[8]

In this microcosm, the "men and women of the Condominium Earth"[9] live and work, cross paths and touch each others' lives.[10] Some die, some begin their lives again, some forgive and others are freed by forgiveness, some deny God, some discover God, and for others, God remains an unresolved question. Some fall in love, even for the first time, and others, having refused or resisted love, rediscover its greatness. Each of the films can be viewed independently of the others. Each episode tells its own story but never entirely separate from the others. Kieślowski creates a thick net of meetings, connections, parallels, among characters, events and themes – often the protagonists of one episode appear briefly in another and one mysterious figure is even seen in eight of the ten films – which along with a variety of stylistic parallels reinforces the universal reach of the individual themes and of the common exploration of *The Decalogue*.[11]

Regarding Kieślowski's style, there are many formal elements common to all the episodes. In general, his style is intense, pure, "hard as a blade,"[12] in the photography, in the strong but controlled acting style, in the choice and use of music, and particularly in the editing. Even though Kieślowski uses a different cinematographer in each episode with quite different specific effects, he insists that "the films are [surprisingly] similar."[13] In addition, Kieślowski privileges the close-up shot, often held for the longest time: of faces, to reveal human interiority, "the cry of the soul,"[14] and of objects, which under Kieślowski's lens acquire profound moral-spiritual significance. A curious aspect of his approach in *The Decalogue* is the self-conscious use, in the same and successive episodes, of similar objects, creating fascinating *leitmotivs* which fairly vibrate with meaning: glass and reflections on glass, through which reality is both hidden and revealed, telephones which both permit communication and prevent it, photographic images, doorways, milk and tea, and, of course, the already-mentioned mysterious man in white, strikingly and significantly present in eight of the films. Commenting on the device of the stranger, and in general on Kieślowski's technique of making simple objects into complex metaphors, the critic Gina Lagorio suggests that the many curious signs in the films are a means by which Kieślowski approaches "the mystery of the human condition," and she goes on to speak of a "metaphorical tension that becomes metaphysical tension," in the sense that it permits the viewer to see the protagonists "facing situations that go way beyond them,"[15] situations, in other words, that reach towards the Transcendent.

In *A Short Film About Love*, the cinema version of *Decalogue Six*, Kieślowski examines the very particular relationship that is hoped for, established and then develops between a young man, nineteen years of age, and a woman, perhaps ten years his senior. Tomek is a shy, withdrawn, awkward young man, by his own admission "still a virgin,"[16] who "projects a graceless ordinariness made vulnerable by innocence."[17] An employee at the local post office, he studies foreign languages in his free time. He has no friends and being without a family, he rents a room in the apartment of the mother of a friend. The woman of Tomek's attentions is rather different from him. Very attractive, extroverted, an artist, she has her own apartment several floors below that of Tomek, in the condominium tower facing his, an apartment in which she entertains men – clients, lovers, business partners – regularly. Every evening when the woman comes home, with or without men, Tomek observes her through a small telescope that he has set up in his room. When the amorous activity goes beyond a certain limit, Tomek stops watching[18] and on one occasion, on the pretext of the odor of gas in the corridor, has the gas company men come and interrupt the amorous activity. Occasionally, he makes anonymous telephone calls to her.

In the hope of meeting the woman even briefly, Tomek sends her false notices of payments to her postal bank account and then takes the early-morning job of delivering milk in the condominium.[19] One night he witnesses a fight between her and a man in the parking lot, and then observes her crying in the apartment. He, too, cries. The next day at the post office, when Tomek's ruse backfires and the woman is insulted by the supervisor who detects the false notices, the boy follows her out and confesses that he sends the notices because he wants to meet her. The woman walks away indignantly, Tomek blurts out "I saw you crying last night,"[20] and then, of course, he has to tell her that he observes her from his room. That evening, moving her double bed into full view, she puts on a show for him. When her partner finds out what's going on, he storms into the courtyard and challenges Tomek to come down and defend himself. The boy ends up with a black eye and a bloodied nose.

The next day, when Tomek courageously delivers her milk, the woman, curious about this strange young man, tries to seduce him. He resists, insisting repeatedly that all he wants is to love her. Ever more curious, she agrees to go out with him and the boy, triumphant, ecstatic, runs through the courtyard shouting, "I'm in love." After the ice cream parlor date, during which Tomek reveals much about himself to the woman, she has him come into her apartment and, after confessing that she is no good and insisting that he is wrong, that love does not exist, she "treats him as if he were one of her usual partners,"[21] and tries again to seduce him. Almost before he realizes what is happening, Tomek, still fully dressed, has an orgasm. The woman ridicules him, saying, "There, that's all it comes down to, *your love*." The boy, humiliated, ashamed, betrayed, runs violently out of her apartment and at home goes into the bathroom and cuts his wrists.

At this point, two-thirds of the way through the film, the attention shifts to the woman. She immediately realizes the gravity of her gesture and tries, without success, to contact the boy by displaying an apology message in her window, then by speaking to his landlady, who says only that he is in the hospital. The postman, however, reveals to her that Tomek has "cut his wrists out of love." At the same time, mysteriously, without any apparent conscious decision in the matter, things begin subtly to change in the woman's life. Her makeup, hairstyle and clothes become less sexy, she turns away men from her apartment, her only interest is to find Tomek and tell him, as she says into the telephone one night, thinking Tomek is on the line, "You were right [about love]." Clearly she has changed, and drastically. When Tomek does return, she immediately goes to find him. He is sleeping, his bandaged wrist outstretched, but the landlady will not let the woman touch him. The woman, at first disappointed, troubled, then turns to the small telescope still focussed on her apartment. Looking into it, she "sees" herself the night she cried at the table, and more importantly, now closing both eyes, she "sees" Tomek appearing by her side and consoling her. Finally satisfied, she smiles.

Interpreting *A Short Film About Love* on a first level of reflection, taking the events of the film's narrative as described above at face value, one might be tempted to conclude that the film tells a strange and rather sordid story of obsession, robbery, voyeurism, prostitution, or at least promiscuity, violence, seduction, suicide. An immature young man, "jealous, puerile, prankish, and frustrated,"[22] sexually confused and repressed; a promiscuous woman who uses her body as an instrument to control others and ends up hurting others and herself; a botched seduction scene; a botched suicide in a "a rash attempt to blot out his over-intense shame;"[23] a man and a woman of Stowki and of "Condominium Earth" locked into a desperate no-exit situation in which all "attempts at love must be neurotic:"[24] interpreted this way, Kieślowski's film becomes "a sad apologue on the impossibility of communicating in our contemporary world."[25] If the film has to do with the Sixth Commandment, then on a first level of reflection, it seems to want to illustrate the hell-on-earth that people who violate the commandment create for themselves and others. The title thus becomes an ironic comment of the director, a little like the bitter comment of the woman to Tomek after the seduction attempt: "There, that's all it is, *your love*." Some viewers and even critics do not go beyond this first level of interpretation. Clearly and understandably, they are not satisfied by the film.[26] Clearly too, and understandably, on this level of reflection *A Short Film About Love* is far from embodying anything like a Christ-figure.

Yet there are a number of elements in *A Short Film About Love* that oblige the serious viewer to go beyond this first level interpretation and thus to encounter a very different film, more significant themes, more positive and more interesting protagonists, and in particular a more satisfactory conclusion. To speak first of Tomek, the obvious protagonist of the first part of the film, a closer examination permits us to reject on a number of counts the idea that he is a voyeur, a Peeping Tom: "If anyone in the story is innocent, it is Tomek."[27] The classical voyeur is interested in himself and his own sexual gratification; Tomek is interested in the woman, and his motivation for watching her is not sexual excitement, rather the opposite – "his act of looking is never stained by impurity"[28] – since he turns away whenever the action goes beyond a certain point. The classical voyeur never reveals himself, Tomek does. The classical voyeur does not accept responsibility for his actions, Tomek does, even though it means a black eye. The boy's interruptions of her amorous activities, interpreted erroneously as "the dark side of love, jealousy,"[29] can be seen as an expression of his desire to protect her from herself, to keep her from getting hurt. He proclaims his love for the woman,[30] a true, sincere, pure and responsible love, and he is willing to suffer for it.

Tomek's suicide attempt could seem to be further evidence of the weakness of his character and the sordidness of his involvement with the woman. Rejected in love, humiliated, he seeks to escape further responsibility by slashing his wrists. But a closer analysis of the film seems to yield quite a different conclusion. Kieślowski carefully sets the so-called suicide attempt in the context of two other shedding-of-blood actions involving Tomek. The first takes place after the boy sees the woman crying alone in her apartment. After discussing the matter with his landlady, who tells him that people cry "when they can't stand it anymore . . . living," he goes to his room, plays a game of risk striking the desk with a pair of scissors between his fingers. Kieślowski makes his cutting himself a kind of sacrifice by which, through his pain, he participates in her pain, clearly a manifestation of "love in its essence."[31] The second blood-letting is when Tomek ends up with a bloodied nose and lip after the woman's indignant lover strikes him. Again here, in a certain sense, Tomek suffers for love. He freely offers himself, he offers his blood, in order to be responsible for his actions, for what he later reveals to be his love for the woman. In this context, Tomek's cutting his wrists acquires the significance of a ritual sacrificial gesture by which the boy, recognizing the tragic situation of his loved one, who is incapable of loving and being loved, offers his blood in the hope of bringing about healing in her.[32] This interpretation is justified by the curious fact that Kieślowski does not actually show the slashing of the wrists,[33] but rather only the subsequent pouring out of Tomek's blood.

It is equally erroneous to limit an interpretation of the woman to that of her being a sophisticated, selfish, skeptical, somewhat promiscuous *bourgeoise,* "connected to a pseudo-artistic world,"[34] who cruelly abuses the naive Tomek and afterward seeks him out merely to assuage her guilt feelings: "an empty woman, almost absent . . . perhaps incapable of loving."[35] Kieślowski makes her a much more complex and interesting, much more mysterious figure than that. Though in the beginning, she is closed in "the solitude of the person who has made love an activity without a soul,"[36] the woman shows a peculiar interest in the goodness of Tomek from their first contact. Even as she violently rejects him outside the post office and he sadly walks away, she turns and looks at him quizzically as if somehow troubled by him. Later in the ice cream shop, she calmly accepts his embarrassed description of her as "S.S.I.A. [which means] She spreads it around" and continues to ask him questions about his origins, his interests, something she probably does little with other men; evidently "something in the innocence of those eyes that look at her adoringly, disturbs her."[37] Even before this at the door of her apartment, she is clearly incredulous of his insistence that he does not want to come in and make love to her, that he only wants to love her. The shot of the two of them standing in the corridor, framed by the red glass window, is one of the strongest and most beautiful, most profound moments in the film: Tomek, full of integrity, who knows "much more about love than the provocative and skeptical"[38] woman, she obviously struggling mightily with something moving in her heart, in her soul, old categories, new categories. Then there is her strange, inexplicable confession – "I'm not good. . . . You know I'm not good" – before the seduction scene, almost as if, in revealing herself, she hopes to be rejected, as if she hopes to protect his innocence.

After this scene, as Tomek blunders out of her apartment, Kieślowski makes it very obvious that the woman realizes immediately that she has done something terrible, something she has never done before. Thus, she who has always been pursued by men, now begins her own search, significantly using opera glasses, the instrument with which Tomek has searched for her in the beginning. Her complex, mysterious reaction is more than a psychological guilt reflex. The woman senses that in Tomek and the events around their meeting, she is before something that goes beyond her previous experience of men, beyond even her capacity to understand. This is seen particularly in the fact that, as already noted in our description of the narrative, the woman begins to change. At first, there are subtle changes, of clothes, hairstyle and makeup, that she may not even be conscious of. Later there are major changes in her longstanding behavior patterns: she does not resume her artwork and she stops entertaining men, indeed she rejects them when they telephone and come to her door. The woman seems to submit all else in her life to the search for Tomek. Gone is the cold scepticism, the angry bitterness, the self-destructive promiscuous behavior; it is almost as if she feels called to chastity and is at peace in that calling.

Perhaps the most important statement the woman makes in the film is into the telephone when she thinks Tomek may be on the line. She blurts out "I've looked for you everywhere . . . to tell you you were right. Do you hear me? You were right." What in effect she is saying is "I was wrong. You know more about love than I do. Love exists. You have shown me the way." It is significant that Kieślowski never has the woman say to Tomek, "I love you."[39] He wants to avoid the merely sentimental and he wants to make it clear that the "love" experienced by the woman in Tomek and to which she is doing her best to respond is on an entirely different level than the "love" to which she is accustomed. Tomek remains a somewhat gauche, badly dressed, nineteen year old with little sophistication and urbane charm, not at all what the woman is used to in her male companions. But he has given the woman love and what Kieślowski shows in her is "an authentic and true osmosis of love."[40]

Therefore, to summarize an interpretation of the film on this second level of reflection, it would appear that Kieślowski is presenting us with a love story, a rather peculiar love story, skirting the limits of normalcy. It is the story of the meeting of two solitudes: "the solitude of the person who has made of love an activity without a soul [and] the solitude of one who has such a high ideal of love that it becomes a kind of armor that separates him from the rest of reality."[41] But Kieślowski has Tomek break out of his armor, enter reality and suffer for love. He also has the woman, clearly wounded in the past by love-gone-wrong, perhaps seeing an earlier, more innocent self in Tomek's goodness and idealism, respond to his sacrifice, and begin to love again. Kieślowski is saying that in the urban desert of Stowki, love is still possible; there is hope for "Condominium Earth."

In this second level interpretation of *A Short Film About Love*, there is nothing specific that leads necessarily to the recognition of a Christ-figure. Yet this reflection, while basically satisfactory, has not accounted for all the significance of the film. A number of details, rather evident in their presence but at the same time, mysterious, troubling in their meaning, seem to be signals from Kieślowski calling us to another level of understanding of the film. The prologue for example is a rather mysterious montage in which Kieślowski shows us a woman's hand reaching for a bandaged wrist, the face of a young man (Tomek), sleeping, the woman playing solitaire at the kitchen table and walking about her apartment, and then a scene in which the same Tomek, having shattered a window off-camera, drops into the frame from above, looks around and proceeds to steal a telescope. The epilogue, already described, is equally enigmatic: the woman "sees," in slow motion, the crying scene and Tomek consoling her, and she smiles. There remain many unexplained details about Tomek: his origins are unknown, his study of foreign languages is odd, his awkwardness and his idealism (about love) are, on the whole, unjustified,[42] the variety of messages he sends the woman, by post, by telephone, in person, without asking for anything in return, is unusual.

When, however, attention is paid to a very specific hermeneutical clue that Kieślowski provides about two thirds of the way through the film, these details and a number of others are given significance, and the film as a whole leaps onto another level of meaning. Several days after the botched seduction scene, the woman is awakened during the night by a ringing telephone. She answers and presuming the silence at the other end of the line means that it is Tomek, she excitedly confesses: "I've looked for you everywhere . . . to tell you you were right. Do you hear me? You were right." Kieślowski is having her do nothing less than confessing her error, her "sin" of having denied the existence of love, a sin that is the basis of her self-destructive behavior.

When there is no response, she hangs up. A few seconds later, the telephone rings again, she picks up the receiver, a man's voice says: "Mary Magdalene?" and she answers, "Magda."[43] With this little dialogue, so subtle and understated that many viewers miss it completely, Kieślowski is not only providing the key to a number of questions that remain unanswered but he is also moving the meaning of the entire film to the level of a biblical parable. If the woman is Mary Magdalene, then we have to conclude at least by way of hypothesis to be verified by testing, that Tomek, whose pure love, whose suffering and sacrificial "death" have brought about a radical change, a conversion, in Magda's life, is Christ or rather a Christ-figure.[44]

Perhaps the best place to begin such a hypothesis-testing, before getting down to details, is by applying the suggested Christ-Magdalene pattern to the basic dynamic of the relationship between the boy and Magda. Tomek loves the woman unselfishly, unconditionally and responsibly. He reveals himself, speaks the truth and invites Magda to another way of living and loving. He suffers for her, is rejected and betrayed. He sheds his blood, symbolically dies and then returns from the dead, all for love of her.[45] On her part, Magda, a sinner, is attracted by Tomek's goodness. At first she resists but then responds to his invitation. She listens to the truth he tells her about herself and she then confesses the whole truth to him. Struggling desperately to understand what is happening in her, confused by this presence of goodness and moral strength in her life, Magda betrays Tomek. Deeply and mysteriously moved by his sacrifice, she is converted. She learns to love and in the end, when she finds him once again alive, accepts his revelation and, "carrying him within herself,"[46] she comes to "see" more profoundly than ever before how he has moved in her life.

This description of the dynamic that takes place between Tomek and Magda is also transparently the description of the dynamic of the relationship of Jesus Christ and the sinner in general, and to express it in biblical terms, of the relationship between Jesus and Mary Magdalene with some allusions to the conversation of Jesus with the Samaritan woman at the well, to the post-Resurrection appearance of Jesus to Mary Magdalene, and to the meeting of Jesus with the disciples on the road to Emmaus.[47] Against this christological-soteriological pattern, one can understand the motif of Tomek's many communications as a metaphor of the mysterious invitation of divine grace to conversion, to the encounter with God in Christ. Tomek's communications are always by way of invitation, respecting the liberty of Magda to respond or to reject. The invitation of grace to encounter with Jesus Christ always shows absolute respect for the freedom of the person, as, of course, did Jesus' invitations to Mary Magdalene, to the Samaritan woman and to the disciples. A further note regarding the meaning of the several telephone calls Tomek makes to Magda in the course of the film. On one level of meaning, they are actual calls, and the telephone is real. Yet there is a curious bit of evidence in the film that on this deeper level of meaning, Kieślowski means Tomek's telephone calls to Magda more as spiritual communications than actual telephone calls. When Magda, after visiting Tomek's room, during which scene Kieślowski has us see the telephone on Tomek's table, asks his landlady for the telephone number, the latter calmly responds that she has no telephone. Kieślowski is suggesting here that Tomek-Jesus' invitations to the woman are of a different, a spiritual order. Seen by Tomek and by the viewer, the telephone is the carrier, the metaphor of this spiritual significance.

Kieślowski creates in a wide variety of glass objects a series of metaphors of the way salvation history in Jesus Christ moves in the lives and experience of human beings. Kieślowski has Tomek replace the opera glasses with which he has observed Magda with a small telescope. In the script he even has Tomek then consider replacing the small telescope with a larger one (160). Here, glass and lenses reflect the way God approaches us in love, observes us carefully, without interfering with our freedom. Kieślowski places a peculiar concave glass lens on the window of Magda's living-room-bedroom, a lens of which Magda seems totally oblivious, but through which Tomek, and we, see her repeatedly. With its extreme wide-angle effect, it seems to provide "a deformed perception of the reality of the protagonist . . . distorted and displaced,"[48] but metaphorically, it shows Magda the way the love of God in Christ considers the sinner, seeing both the details and the "wider picture," the present and also the past and especially the future. Then, in the glass window of the post office, Kieślowski creates a brilliant metaphor of the way we see God and the way God sees us. When he shows Tomek from Magda's point of view, that is, God "seen" from the point of view of the human being, the glass reflects Magda's face and in a couple of instances, her face is precisely superimposed over his. In short, often our notion of God is a projection, a reflection, of ourselves. When, however, Kieślowski shows Magda from Tomek's point of view, there are no reflections on the glass, Tomek sees Magda clearly without a trace of egoism or distortion, the way God sees us, as we are, for who and what we are.

Kieślowski makes milk a major *leitmotiv* in his film, a repeated metaphor that has christological-soteriological significance. Clearly milk has value as a symbol of physical nutrition, but there is a tradition, particularly in eastern-European iconography that gives to milk the valence of spiritual nutrition: it becomes a symbol of grace. In the film of Andrei Tarkovsky, *The Sacrifice* (1986), in a moment of profound spiritual crisis for the protagonist, a large glass pitcher full of milk which strangely enough has been plainly visible on the mantel, crashes to the floor. It is a moment of grace, because from that moment on the protagonist begins to understand what he must do. In *A Short Film about Love*, Kieślowski associates milk with Tomek's love for Magda. One of the most striking moments in the film is when the boy, having obtained a date with Magda, in an "explosion of joy"[49] runs in circles through the courtyard of the condominium, dragging behind him the cart full of milk bottles. Kieślowski has Tomek deliver milk to Magda several times. He has her drink the milk – Tomek interestingly enough drinks only tea – and in her moment of greatest crisis Kieślowski shows her, from Tomek's loving point

Intolerance: Jesus solemnly presides at the wedding at Cana (MOMA)

Ben-Hur: Jesus is hidden from the camera as he meets Ben-Hur and his family on the way to Calvary (MOMA)

Three Versions of the Last Supper

The King of Kings:
An intimate meal

*The Greatest
Story Ever Told:*
Da Vinci revisited,
but very statically
(MOMA)

King of Kings:
The bizarre Y-shaped
Table (MOMA)

Jesus Christ Superstar: A black Judas, strong and attractive, berates an uncertain, wimpy Jesus (MOMA)

Godspell: Jesus is baptized in Central Park (Photofest)

Godspell: Jesus (center) as "Lord of the Dance" leading his disciples (MOMA)

The Last Temptation of Christ: A neurotic Jesus lifts the cup of blessing (MOMA)

Jesus of Nazareth: One of the few shots of Zeffirelli's sanitized crucifixion (Photofest)

The Gospel according to Saint Matthew: A happy, smiling Jesus surrounded by children (MOMA)

The Gospel according to Saint Matthew: At times, Pasolini isolates Jesus from the people (MOMA)

Jesus of Montreal: Daniel in his final agony is supported by Mireille and Constance (MOMA)

A Short Film about Love: Tomek with his wounded finger sends a message of love to Magda (MOMA)

Babette's Feast: Early in the film, Babette eats a simple meal alone (MOMA)

Babette's Feast:
Later, Babette, with
a gold cross,
prepares her
sacrificial feast of
love (MOMA)

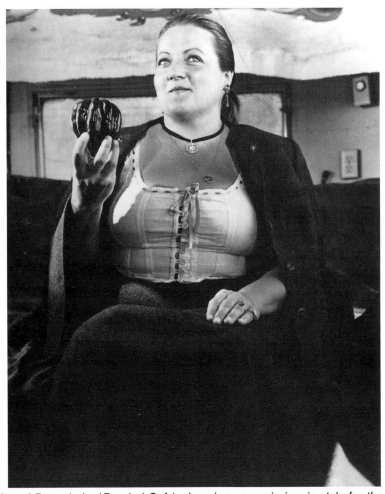

Out of Rosenheim (Bagdad Cafe): Jasmine poses in iconic style for the painter Rudy (MOMA)

Dead Man Walking: In the conclusion, Helen Prejean, her hand on Poncelet's shoulder, prays Psalm 23 (Photofest)

Shane: The "solar" hero Shane arrives at the ranch and meets Joey (MOMA)

Au hasard Balthazar: Balthazar submits to his torturers (Photofest)

Au hasard Balthazar: Balthazar dies surrounded by sheep (MOMA)

12

I Confess: Father
Logan ringed in and
threatened by his
accusers (MOMA)

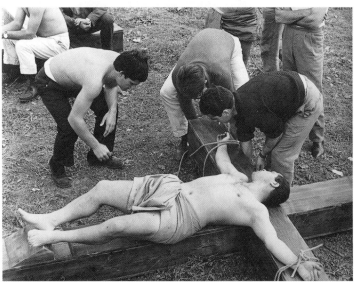

La ricotta: The beginning of Stracci's passion (MOMA)

Giant: Jett Rink "crucified," with a famous Magdalene at the foot of the "cross" (MOMA)

Raging Bull: A young and defeated Jake LaMotta in a crucifixion composition (MOMA)

The Trial of Joan of Arc:
Joan, cross in hand, goes
to her death
(MOMA)

The Passion of Joan of Arc: Joan
ridiculed with a crown of straw
(MOMA)

The Passion of Joan of Arc:
The multiplication of
crucifixes that Joan sees as
she dies (MOMA)

The Diary of a Country Priest: The priest is isolated in a hostile nature
(MOMA)

Stalker: The Stalker at the beginning of his mission (Photofest)

of view, knocking over the bottle of milk. After zooming into a closeup of the spilling milk, Kieślowski shows Magda from behind crying and as she slowly, deliberately moves her hand to and fro in the spilled milk, she stops crying. In the epilogue of the film, which we shall discuss below, Kieślowski renders explicit what is implicit in this scene, namely that in the depths of her desperation, the grace of salvation begins to move in Magda's experience.

Both the prologue and the epilogue of the film can also be considered as important elements for an interpretation of the film as a christological-soteriological parable, and of Tomek as a Christ-figure. In the prologue, then, the brief shot of the hand of Magda reaching out to touch the bandaged wrist of Tomek becomes a fascinating analogy of Mary Magdalen's meeting with the post-Resurrection Jesus Christ: she reaches out as if to possess him and Jesus stops her saying "Do not hold onto me" (In 20:17). Three closeups of Tomek's face, half-shaded as he sleeps, edited between the shots of Magda, seems to suggest he is thinking or dreaming of her. A shot of Magda (from Tomek-Christ's point of view) playing "solitaire" at the kitchen table where she will later encounter salvation, suggests her existential, spiritual isolation, her sinfulness, out of which salvation (the meeting with Tomek-Jesus) will lead her. A shot of her, again from Tomek's point of view, behind the concave lens on the window, seen in "double" (in detail and in wide angle), suggests the in-depth perception of her that Tomek will have. But it is the final sequence of the prologue, that of Tomek's stealing the telescope, that explodes with christological-soteriological meaning. Tomek's stealing the instrument which permits him *to come closer to* Magda and thus to effect her salvation, is analogous to the Word of God's assuming, that is "stealing," a human nature, a human existence in order to come closer to humanity and effect human salvation. This image of the Incarnation is supported by another, immediately preceding it and perhaps even more striking in its originality and power. The sudden, mysterious shattering of glass[50] *from above,* represents the breaking of the barrier between God and humanity, and the leaping *from above,* into a circle of light coming *from above* of the mysterious figure who will carry out the salvific action, represents the Eternal Word of God leaping "from above" into time and space and human experience. In this shot that lasts forty-two seconds, and that has clear significance on the first two levels of interpretation of the film – Tomek's breaking into a school to steal a telescope – Kieślowski quite audaciously creates an original and most powerful metaphor of the absolutely crucial moment of salvation history, that is the *kenosis*[51] of the Word of God and its Incarnation into human experience, and the boy Tomek represents that Incarnation, and is thus a Christ-figure.

The epilogue of the film concludes and consolidates well the representation of a Christ-figure in Tomek by depicting the post-resurrection experience of Magda-Mary Magdalene, already alluded to in the prologue, in which the woman is prevented from touching Tomek, her Savior, who is not dead but living. But it represents especially, the spiritual assimilation of that experience – "I have seen the Lord" (Jn 20:18) – in Magda as she "looks at herself" through Tomek-Christ's eyes (the telescope) and sees, understands and appreciates her conversion and the grace-filled presence of Tomek-Christ in that experience.[52] The fact that Kieślowski films this scene in slow motion removes it from the logic of the objective narrative. That it is the repetition of a scene seen earlier in the film suggests the imminent revelation of something new or beyond the mere narration. That Magda, at the telescope, has both eyes closed and then both eyes open, suggests that the telescope, the vision, the whole experience, are more spiritual than physical. Then the appearance in her vision of Tomek-Christ-consoler beside Magda is clearly a moment of spiritual revelation and understanding, recalling the parallel post-Resurrection experience of the two disciples when they meet Jesus on the road to Emmaus (Lk 24:13-35), and especially the experience of his interpretation and of their insight: "Then . . . he interpreted to them the things about himself in all the scriptures. . . . And their eyes were opened and they recognized him." (Lk 24:27-31) Kieślowski closes his film with a close-up of Magda at the telescope, both eyes open, calmly, peacefully smiling, perhaps for the first time. He is suggesting that she is no longer desperate to find, touch, possess Tomek, her savior, that she knows now more than ever before that he is alive and moving in her life, and that she is finally and definitely liberated.

Decalogue Six, while maintaining essentially the same story line, theme and style of *A Short Film about Love,* is different from the longer version in a number of significant ways. The opening of the film, not so clearly a prologue as that of the other version, takes place in the post office, *in media res*, with Magda bringing a notice of payment to Tomek, announcing immediately the motif of invitation-response that will mark the entire film. Then, as the titles appear on the screen, we see a series of shots of Tomek breaking into the school and stealing the telescope but differently from the longer version, Kieślowski edits into this scene three shots of the woman walking nervously about her apartment, eating a piece of bread and working on a tapestry. Evidently he is suggesting the relationship that will develop between these two, and linking it with the telescope being stolen.

The shorter version of the film omits two other sequences present in the longer version and particularly significant for an interpretation of Tomek as a Christ-figure. The conversation between Tomek and his landlady after he observes Magda crying and the boy's sacrificial gesture of blood-shedding afterwards as a participation in her suffering are cut from the shorter version. The absence of these two scenes which, in *A Short Film About Love*, provide a hermeneutic of sacrifice for the interpretation of Tomek's more dramatic blood-letting later, somewhat reduce the force of the christological-soteriological interpretation of the film. Kieślowski makes a more serious cut later in *Decalogue Six*: the woman's name, pronounced by the man's voice on the telephone after her confession (that Tomek is right about the existence of love) is not the unequivocal "Mary Magdalene?" of the longer version, but the simpler and less-clearly biblical "Magduśka?"[53] This change does not deny the Mary Magdalene-Christ analogy but it renders it a little more opaque.

Kieślowski makes the conclusion of *Decalogue Six* considerably different from that of the longer version. Magda does not go to Tomek, she does not reach for his wrist, she does not relive that crucial moment of his "presence" in her past, and thus "see" and appreciate his role as comforter and savior in her moment of desperation. But the conclusion is not so different as to deny Tomek's salvific role in her life. The scene begins the morning after Magda realizes that Tomek is back as she returns to the post office. Without makeup, she looks more free, more innocent, more wholesome than anywhere in the film. Already from outside the building, she sees Tomek. He turns towards her as if he feels her presence and they make eye-contact. Shown in close-up by Kieślowski, illuminated by warm tones, Magda is smiling shyly. There is a transparency, a simplicity, a joy in her look that certainly was not visible in the post office scenes at the beginning of the film. Kieślowski then frames Tomek in close-up, a rather intense expression on his face, as he says to her "simply,"[54] in a matter-of-fact voice, "I'm not peeping at you anymore," and almost smiles. The camera then repeats the previous shot of Magda; she no longer is smiling, but continues to look calmly and seriously at Tomek.

Kieślowski says justly of this conclusion: "the television ending is very dry, laconic and also very simple."[55] There is no doubt that the ending of the shorter version of the film is simple, succinct, perhaps even less sentimental than the other. Yet the biblical exegete Gianfranco Ravasi is wrong when he interprets Tomek's words as a rejection of Magda: "But by now the fire of love has gone out in Tomek, who says to her coldly, 'I don't look at you anymore.'"[56] First of all, Tomek's tone of voice is not "cold," nor is his look, and neither he nor Magda live the experience of meeting as a rejection. Besides, Ravasi's interpretation does not recognize the sense, the power, the transcendent thrust of the boy's love for the woman. If he loves her enough to suffer for her, to shed his blood for her twice, then it is not likely that, in the very moment when she indicates a positive response to his love, he would reject her.

Another interpretation of Tomek's words and of the meaning of the scene is possible and more satisfactory. First of all, it is important to note that the boy does not say "I don't love you anymore," and neither his words nor his look imply that. In as much as his "peeping" is an invitation from Tomek, an expression of his hope that Magda might be liberated and learn to love in another way, now that she has accepted and internalized his invitation, now that she is free and loving in a new and liberating way, Tomek's "peeping" is no longer necessary. In terms of Tomek as a Christ-image, now that Magda has accepted the offer of salvation and is capable of "looking at herself," as indeed she does in the cinema version of the conclusion, Tomek-Christ calls her to another level of relationship. Here, Tomek is acting like the Christ of John 20, who tells Mary Magdalene not to "hold onto him," as she may have done before the Resurrection. Tomek-Christ is telling Magda not to hold onto the old way of relating. He is calling her to mature spiritually, to live fully the liberating love he is offering her.

5

An Exceptional Christ-Figure:
Au Hasard Balthazar

Among the many films considered in this book, *Au hasard Balthazar* is an exceptional film, and this for several reasons. It is exceptional because it is the work of Robert Bresson who by all accounts is an exceptional film-maker: "the most demanding, the most daring *auteur* of all of French cinema (and perhaps of cinema *tout court*)."[1] It is exceptional also because, preceded by six films and followed by six, it is the central "and most complex film"[2] of Bresson's long career as an artist, "the most ecstatic of his films,"[3] the culmination of all his previous work. Speaking with Jean-Luc Godard, Bresson said about *Au hasard Balthazar*: "It is possible that in the other films [made before] you can find what it *[Balthazar]* was or would be. . . . It seems to me to be the most free film I have made, the film in which I put most of myself."[4] The film is exceptional too because it is one that Bresson wants "more stubbornly than all the others,"[5] a work that is in the making, at least in the mind of its *auteur*, for many years: "It is a film I thought about for fifteen years, a project which I had abandoned and resumed, and again abandoned and resumed because of problems in the composition."[6]

Au hasard Balthazar is exceptional because it is "a difficult and mysterious film,"[7] one not easily accessible either to the general public or even to a more specialized audience. This is due in part to the theme and content of the film whose moral focus, speaking very generally, is that of the conflict between good and evil, the radically "theological" confrontation between sin and grace, and whose protagonist is a donkey. The critic Jean Collet muses rather rhetorically about this apparent drastic shift in Bresson's approach:

> A donkey. Yes, it is strange. It seems bizarre that a film-maker as important as Bresson would all of a sudden leave behind his family of heros, the country priest and Joan of Arc, the man condemned to death and the pickpocket, the ladies of the Bois de Boulogne and the nuns of Giraudoux. It seems bizarre that Robert Bresson would be interested himself in depicting the misfortunes of a donkey, the dismal existence of a peaceful animal.[8]

Collet further qualifies the film, making a connection between the protagonist and the texture of the film, and at the same time giving some hope to the timid viewer: "*Au hasard Balthazar*, in the image of its hero, seems to me a film of considerable opacity. . . . But it is an opacity that tends little by little toward transparency."[9]

The apparent or rather initial inaccessibility of *Au hasard Balthazar* is also clearly a function of Bresson's very particular inspiration and style of

film-making.[10] His style is referred to variously as intense, meditative, contemplative, even transcendental, opaque, allusive, elliptical, poetic, spiritual
and even theological. It reveals, among other things, a conscious desire and
effort of the director to develop a "'pure' cinema uncontaminated by literary
or theatrical effects"[11] so typical of most film language and style to which the
average and even above-average film viewer is accustomed. This self-
conscious experimentation of Bresson in film language and style gives the
impression, in *Au hasard Balthazar* and in other films as we shall see in the
final chapter of this book, that in fact questions of theme and content are
secondary. Bresson himself does little to dispel the impression. In fact, he
seems to encourage it when he says: "The subject of a film is only a pretext.
Form much more than content touches viewers and elevates them. . . . I am
more occupied with the special language of the cinema than with the subjects
of my films."[12] We shall resume the analysis and discussion of the style of *Au
hasard Balthazar* later in this chapter. For now, suffice it to say that Bresson's words, spoken in the context of a discussion of cinematographic style,
should not lead to the conclusion that he is not interested in content. Rather
just the opposite is the case.

Recognized as one of the greatest film-makers in the history of cinema,
Robert Bresson, in his thirteen major works,[13] has created a canon of film-art
that no serious student of cinema can afford not to consider. Recognized as
one of the most spiritual, intelligent and Catholic of film-makers, from the
very beginning of his career he has explored with exceptional courage, honesty and coherence, the major themes and mysteries of the Christian faith
experience to which he is explicitly and radically committed. Usually Bresson
embodies his exceptionally sensitive exploration in the lives and radical struggles of women and men in a wide variety of original existential situations. *Au
hasard Balthazar*, from this point of view, is an exception. In this his "most
original and most moving film,"[14] he tells the story-parable of the life and
struggle and death, not of a human being but of a donkey, the Balthazar of
the title. The critic René Maurice, touching on these preferred themes of the
French director, justifies well our interest in this film:

> Bresson, pursuing and deepening the design he has been stubbornly ex-
> ploring for more than twenty years, offers us a new parable of the mys-
> tery of grace and of the communion of saints, a new fragment of the
> struggle between God and Satan, invisible protagonists of a film of rare
> artistic perfection and at the same time, of an extraordinary spiritual den-
> sity.[15]

The complex genesis of *Au hasard Balthazar* in the mind of Bresson
suggests the profoundly spiritual, biblical and Christian heritage of his inspiration and thought. Already in its genealogy and title, the film begins to move
toward the theme of the Christ-figure. Bresson himself speaks of his original
inspiration:

@QUOTE = My film started from two ideas which come together.
First: to show that the stages in the life of a donkey are the same stages as in

the life of a man. Childhood: caresses. Maturity: work. Talents or genius: the wise donkey. The mystical period that precedes death: the donkey who carries the relics. Secondly, this donkey passes through the hands of different masters, each one representing a human vice: drunkenness, laziness, pride, etc. He suffers in a different way from each of these.[16]

In another interview, Bresson adds a detail crucial for the development of the Christ-figure motif, saying that the donkey "must suffer from what makes us, ourselves suffer."[17]

The title of the film is precisely the motto from the coat-of-arms of the Counts of Baux in Provence, and means "By chance, Balthazar." The noble family of Baux believed they were descendants of the Magi-King Balthazar, one of the three Wise Men who visit the child Jesus.[18] Bresson insists on the biblical connection: "The title comes from, first of all the fact that I wanted to give my donkey a biblical name" and he adds mysteriously and enigmatically but typically for him, "I like the rhyme."[19] Bresson leaves no doubt as to the biblical connotations of the figure of the donkey when he says with rhetorical hyperbole: "The donkey is the entire Bible, Old Testament, New Testament."[20] The New Testament connection is rather clear. Christian folklore places a donkey in the stable at Bethlehem, as a mute witness to the kenotic Incarnation and birth of the Word-made-Flesh, a pious tradition which find its roots in a verse at the beginning the Old Testament Book of Isaiah: "The ox knows its owner, and the donkey its master's crib" (Is 1:3). Clearly more significant is the association to the donkey who carries Christ triumphantly into Jerusalem on Palm Sunday at the beginning of his redemptive passion: "Jesus chooses the humble and peaceful mount of the ancient leaders of Israel, and in particular, of David."[21] In that reference, to an event attested to by all four gospels[22] and symbolically reenacted, as we shall see, in the penultimate episode of the *Au hasard Balthazar*, Bresson creates a series of dense associations between his little Balthazar and the biblical prophecies that vibrate with messianic meaning all the way from Genesis:

> The scepter shall not depart from Judah,
> Nor the ruler's staff from between his feet
> until tribute comes to him;
> and the obedience of the people is his.
> Binding his foal to the vine
> and his donkey's colt to the choice vine. (Gen 49:10-11)

to the Book of the prophet Zechariah:

> Rejoice greatly, O daughter Zion!
> Shout aloud, O daughter Jerusalem!
> Lo, your king comes to you;
> triumphant and victorious is he,
> humble and riding on a donkey,
> on a colt, the foal of a donkey. (Zech 9:9)

There is also in Balthazar a veiled reference to the scapegoats of the Old Testament, animals "loaded by the High Priest with the sins of the people and carrying these sins out of the city into the deserts,"[23] a tradition related to Jesus Christ in the New Testament Letter to the Hebrews, about which we shall speak more in detail below. Bresson himself admits a further biblical allusion in his donkey: "I thought of the female donkey of Balaam. It sees an angel on the road. Its master beats it, but it does not move because of the angel."[24] This reference to the prophet Balaam in the Book of Numbers (22:22-35) is particularly significant because its suggests the donkey is a wise animal, with a spiritual intuition and a vision nothing short of transcendental.

Echoing the biblical allusion to Balaam's wise she-donkey is a reference to the spiritual adventure of Saint Ignatius of Loyola and his mule, of which Bresson, who was to make a film on the life of Ignatius, knew full well. "St. Ignatius wanted to kill a Moor who had offended the Virgin Mary. But then he has a scruple, he hesitates in his pursuit. . . . In his doubt, it is the mule who decides. And the animal chooses the route of clemency, not of chastisement."[25] Further, in the realm of the spiritual-ecclesiological, there is the omnipresence of donkeys conspicuously sculpted into the facades of so many medieval cathedrals and finally there is the donkey of the medieval "Feast of Fools," at Notre Dame de Paris which carried the archbishop facing backward, sitting on its back.[26]

There are two further references, both of considerable significance for an understanding of the multilevel complexity of Bresson's Balthazar. The first is a painting of Watteau, entitled "Gilles," in which one cannot help but note in the background a donkey resting its head on the hillside, "observing the passersby with a contemplative eye."[27] If there is one feature of his little Balthazar that Bresson emphasizes repeatedly, it is precisely his very contemplative eye, through which Bresson makes it clear that "the donkey understands. And that's what makes it interesting."[28] Finally there is in Balthazar an allusion to the noble donkeys of two novels of Dostoevsky, *The Brothers Karamazov* and *The Idiot* and in particular, to the passage in *The Idiot* where Prince Mishkin recounting his trip through Switzerland, "affirms that the braying of a donkey [in the market at Basel] was responsible for the sudden enlightening of his spirit and the vanishing of the feeling he had of remaining a 'stranger' in a western country."[29]

Set in the countryside and a village in the foothills of Pyrenees in the present time (1966), *Au hasard Balthazar* recounts certain events in the life of the donkey Balthazar. It begins shortly after his birth in a mountain meadow as he feeds from his mother, and is bought and leaves with two children and their father, and it ends some twelve years later, as he dies in a mountain meadow, victim of the bullets of border police who have shot him in an attempt to stop the smugglers who were using him to transport contraband goods. The narrative, extremely linear, episodic rather than dramatic, and "totally elliptical,"[30] details the stages in the life of the donkey, a life lived to a great extent in the shadow of events in the lives of those around him. In the second scene of the film, he is christened "Balthazar . . . in the name of the Father and of the Son and of the Holy Spirit"[31] by the children who then play with him in the straw. Then he witnesses the tender friendship that develops between Marie, the daughter of the schoolteacher, and Jacques, the son of the land-owner. During the latter part of this scene, music is heard on the sound-track.[32]

Twelve years later – a subtitle reads simply "The years go by" – the donkey is being treated badly by different owners. One day, when the hay wagon he is pulling overturns, Balthazar escapes and returns to the farm where Marie's father works the land for the owner. Marie, now sixteen, is happy to see him [music]. Balthazar, who pulls the family carriage, and Marie are ridiculed by a group of delinquent young men, led by Gérard, who then spy on her one night as she crowns the donkey with flowers and kisses him. Then, after she enters the house, they cruelly beat Balthazar. A misunderstanding develops between Marie's father and the landowner. When his son Jacques comes to settle the problem and to renew his friendship-love with Marie, Balthazar watches as he receives a lukewarm reception from Marie and is sent away by her father. The father then in frustration determines "to get rid of this retrograde and ridiculous donkey."

Now working for the village baker, Balthazar is sadistically beaten and burned by Gérard [music], who also works for the baker. When Marie stops to comfort the donkey, Gérard takes advantage of the situation and, while Balthazar watches, he seduces her. Afterwards, she goes to Balthazar [music]. The baker's wife favors the young man, but is jealous of Marie. In spite of this Gérard searches out Marie again, and in an abandoned shack has his way with her. Balthazar, witness to this, brays. Gérard and company are investigated by the police and the baker's wife proposes to help him escape by night. He responds by beating up the village vagabond, Arnold. Marie tries to defend Arnold but is treated violently by Gérard. Left unsheltered in the rain and snow, Balthazar is deathly ill and about to be put out of his misery by the veterinarian, but Arnold intervenes and takes him home.

Arnold cures Balthazar and uses him and another donkey to transport tourists on mountain outings. An alcoholic and given to fits of anger, Arnold beats the two donkeys and on the second such occasion, Balthazar runs away. He ends up next in a circus, where he performs a "multiplication" number. Once during a performance, Balthazar sees Arnold come in with bottle in hand, and braying, he tries to escape but Arnold reclaims him. When the vagabond inherits a fortune, he hosts a party in the village bar, during which Marie defends her liaison with Gérard to her mother, insisting she loves him and refusing to come home. Gérard treats her badly, dancing with another girl. On the road that night, inebriated, Arnold falls off Balthazar, hits his head and dies.

Next Balthazar is bought at a fair by the grain merchant, who makes him work hard at a well in the hot sun and whips him mercilessly to the point where the donkey refuses to accept water from him [music]. One night, Marie seeks refuge from a thunderstorm in the merchant's barn, and while her clothes dry by the fire, she treats the man rather cruelly, offering to make love to him, insulting him, taking money from him and insisting that she needs "a friend who will give me the help I need to run away . . . I have always wanted to run away." Shortly after, she runs off, leaving Balthazar in the stable. The next morning her parents come looking for her and they return home with the donkey [music].

Jacques comes to Marie wanting to repay her father the money he lost unjustly in their lawsuit; Balthazar brays [music]. With Balthazar listening, Jacques speaks of their love and when she explains that she cannot marry him because of her liaison with Gérard, Jacques insists he still wants to marry her. She blurts out: "Our vows of love, those childish promises that we made, they were in a fantasy world. Not in reality . . . Reality is something very different." Later in the stable, in front of Balthazar [music], she says "I will love him, I will love him."

Gérard and his gang beat up Marie in a deserted building and, leaving her locked inside, scattering her clothes on the road. Marie's father and Jacques arrive, break a window to get into the building and take Marie home on the wagon pulled by Balthazar. When sometime later, Jacques comes looking for Marie, her mother announces, "Marie is gone . . . she will never return." When Marie's father is dying, the village priest comes and reads a passage from the Book of Lamentations. Standing near Balthazar, the mother prays desperately: "My God, do not take him too. He's all I have left." The husband dies. Later Gérard and company want to borrow Balthazar from the widow. She refuses, saying, "He's a saint." Balthazar carries sacred relics in a religious procession, and is blessed with incense.

By night Gérard and a companion in crime remove Balthazar from the stable, load him with contraband, beat him [music] and lead him roughly through the woods and up into the mountains. Shots are fired, Balthazar is wounded and the delinquents flee. Balthazar stands still. The next morning, bleeding, he continues climbing up the mountain. A flock of sheep arrive, the sound of their ringing bells dominating the sound track of the film, and as Balthazar sits down, they surround him. The sheep move away and Balthazar, extended on the earth, dies.

From this necessarily brief description of the plot of *Au hasard Balthazar*, several things are evident. First of all, the episodic construction of the plot of the film, reflected in the episodic quality of the summary, a mysterious nervous quality that is then augmented by the many ellipses. Bresson has things happen when they should not happen, or at least when we do not expect them to happen; and most of the time, he does not explain or justify sudden shifts in location, action or character. Often for example, he presents the effects of some action without describing its cause and at times without even suggesting a cause. Bresson succeeds in creating a strange often incomprehensible world, characterized by a "sense of mystery,"[33] an enigmatic world, vaguely off-balance, darkly menacing, a particularly apt spiritual-psychological environment for the events which take place in it.

Evident also is the tension between good and evil that, from the beginning of the film, makes itself felt in the lives and particular experiences of all the major characters. One side of this situation of tension is represented by the consummate evil that manifests itself in Gérard and his delinquent friends, an evil that has none of the usual psychological or sociological motivations. Gérard's is an evil that, on the one hand, seems undramatic, banal. This ordinary quality is best represented by the small motor-scooters the gang uses to get around and by Gérard's rather pathetic little transistor radio whose tinny sound accompanies his seductions of Marie. On the other hand Gérard's evil is deadly and deadly serious. His cruelty with individuals seems boundless, total; his public destructive power, represented in his spontaneous wrecking of the village bar during the dance, is quite terrifying.

If from his very first appearance, Gérard represents evil, most of the other characters are in the beginning good, or at least demonstrate a potential for good. Rather early in the film however, Bresson makes it clear that in this situation of moral tension, evil has the upper hand: the malice of Gérard becomes an inexorable destructive force that insinuates itself directly or indirectly into the lives of the other characters and destroys them. Marie is the most dramatic, most tragic of these victims, but she is not alone.

Into this unstable, unbalanced, treacherous situation of moral-spiritual tension, Bresson introduces the innocent donkey christened "Balthazar." As suggested in the above description of the plot and of course, in the genesis and background of the film, Balthazar is "clearly the keystone of the narrative,"[34] both because of what happens to him, his story from birth to death which literally frames the entire action of the film, and also because of his quiet but intense presence, his witnessing, his participation in the experiences of the other characters. Balthazar suffers from the cruelty visited on him by the various masters, who "represent the capital sins,"[35] and by the situations in which he find himself and, recalling Bresson's statement that the donkey "must suffer from what makes us, ourselves suffer,"[36] Balthazar is literally and mysteriously present in the moments of cruelty and suffering visited on others, and so participates in that tragic and often incomprehensible suffering.

To anticipate the second and more analytical part of this chapter, it is precisely in this double experience of Balthazar, as sympathetic participant in the evil visited on others and as victim of the same evil, that he acquires significance, that he becomes a Christ-figure and in fact, one of the most theologically-complex, biblically-verified, spiritually-moving and memorable Christ-figures in the history of the religious film. It behooves us at this point to take up again the question of evil in the film, to do a more precise analysis of just how pervasive this evil is, of how much it affects all the characters in the film, and of how and with what effect Balthazar as Christ-figure enters into this situation of tension. The most basic thing to say about evil in this film is that it is of cosmic proportions, not in the sense of the superficially

terrifying dramatic representations of the "cosmic" evil in so many Hollywood horror movies, but rather in a low-key, invisible, insidious and all-pervasive way. It is thus a much more terrifying representation than that of evil,
for example, in the *Exorcist* or *Alien* cycles of films.

The French philosopher, Xavier Tilliette, suggests that the pervasive
evil in *Au hasard Balthazar* reflects "our world in all of its fundamental deso-
lation and distress, as the Prophets described it. It is the kingdom of evil, the
place of [moral] decay."[37] He specifies further, speaking of this world as "the
prison of solitudes. No one understands anyone, no one puts themselves 'in
the place of the other,' and more to the point, everyone strains eagerly to get
away."[38] The microcosmic world of *Au hasard Balthazar* – Jean-Luc Godard
says, "This film is really the world in an hour-and-a half"[39] – is marked by
"pride, cruelty, humiliation, folly, violence and sensuality"[40] and "even by a
sort of sadism."[41] It is an evil which dominates individual events and which
seems by all accounts to be out of control: "This procession of disasters takes
on the aspect of incarnate evil in an insane liberty of movement."[42] One
critic, unfairly severe, as we shall see later, speaks of the experience of the
people of the world of *Au hasard Balthazar* as "marked by a suffering without redemption, to which there is not the least suggestion of liberation."[43]

Perhaps the most concrete manifestation of this inexorable evil on the
move in a "world from which grace is withdrawn,"[44] is the presence of death
in the film. In its opening minutes, the little girl present on a stretcher at the
christening of Balthazar, dies. Bresson provides no explanation: her death remains mysterious. She is a "victim as innocent as Balthazar, and whose destiny prefigures that of the donkey."[45] Later Arnold the vagabond dies, again
in vaguely mysterious circumstances. The father of Marie dies and once
again, the precise reason is uncertain: a broken heart? a depression? Bresson
maintains an aura of sinister mystery around the event as he also does around
the disappearance "never to return" of Marie: death by suicide probably –
anticipating the gesture of Mouchette, the protagonist of Bresson's next film,
Mouchette (1967) – but it is not certain, and that makes it more terrible.
Finally, of course, there is the death of the wholly innocent Balthazar.

The roots of this relentless evil in the film are, and remain largely mysterious, but Bresson does give one clue: "the origins of evil are profoundly
rooted but not indecipherable . . . in *Balthazar* money governs indirectly, but
with absolute determination, the destiny of the personages."[46] The innocent
and good relationship between Marie and Jacques ends to a great extent because of the financial problems between their fathers. The failure of Marie's
father, a good, hardworking, loving man, has indirectly to do with a lawsuit
and finances; the grain merchant is a pathological miser, which determines
the way he deals with Marie. The ruin and death of Arnold is due to the
money he inherits, the destructive relationship of the baker's wife with
Gérard involves money, and as we shall see in more detail below, one dimension of Gérard's monumental evil, that which leads directly to the death of
Balthazar, has to do with money.

If this cosmic, all-pervasive evil in the film, its roots somehow connected to money and its effects most visible in the moral destruction and death visited on so many of the characters, remains to some extent mysterious and obscure, there is one character in whom its power seems to be concentrated and in whom its vigor never seems to abate: Gérard. René Maurice is very clear in his judgment of Gérard: "He is a negative being, who knows only how to destroy, soil, betray. . . . That Gérard is an 'incarnation' of Satan, all of his actions, through the entire film, proclaim it."[47]

As we have already suggested above, there is little *visibly* dramatic or shocking about the evil incarnated in Gérard: he is of average looks and build, speaks little and when he does it is more of a mumble. His interest in motor-scooters and pop-music seem ordinary. But behind this rather banal exterior, Bresson reveals a force of evil perhaps unequaled in all his other films, perceptible in Gérard's eyes, cold, calculating and seductive and in the aggressive look on his face pressed against windows several times in the film as he observes the results of his cruelty on his victims. Gérard is leader of a gang of four or five delinquents who become organic extensions of his evil: their "squalid and automatic brutality"[48] is gratuitous, rendered even more perverse by the strange fact that not once in the film does Bresson show Gérard giving orders or instructions to his companions in delinquency. Theirs is an evil transmitted intuitively, by a kind of silent, perverse osmosis.

The evil in Gérard, the evil that *is* Gérard, touches all those with whom he comes into contact. He betrays the parish priest who tries to help him, he steals from the baker who gives him work, he sadistically takes advantage, economically and emotionally, of the baker's wife. With the vagabond Arnold, he is particularly cruel, ridiculing him, beating him, trying to frame him with the police, spending his money at the dance, and in the end sending him off to his death with a Judas-like kiss, "My dear friend, Arnold."[49] If Gérard's evil is most of the time focussed on individuals, there are times when it lashes out blindly with a kind of mad destructive frenzy, for example, the purely malicious scene at the beginning of the film where he and his pals, without speaking a word, spread oil on the road and watch a car go sliding into the ditch. Then they calmly ride away as a second car crashes into the first one. Perhaps more indicative of this uncontrolled evil incarnated in Gérard is the incredibly violent scene towards the end of the film in which he, without the least motivation, singlehandedly wrecks the dance hall bar. No one interferes and tries to stop him, no one even notices. They continue dancing and at the end of the evening, the town notary inexplicably pays the bar owner for the damages with Arnold's money.

Gérard's most subtle and maleficent evil is reserved for Marie, the most mysterious and drawn out exercise and experience of evil power in the entire film, apart, of course, from that lived by Balthazar. Marie, the innocent, and yet "the most complex young woman in all of Bresson's films,"[50] who at the beginning of the film holds the lighted candle at the christening of Balthazar and who has so much hope in the love offered her by the good and sincere

Jacques, clearly intuits the powerful evil in Gérard. The glance she gives him in church as in the choir loft he sings the "Panis Angelicus," a glance met by his intense, knowing, sadistic smile, is full of apprehension, creates a blasphemous, chilling moment. Gérard's seduction and abuse of Marie is rendered more terrifying by Bresson in the almost total silence that characterizes their encounters: in the car, on the road, in the first shack. During his cruel abuse of her in the dance hall he dances with another while she awkwardly and tragically defends her love for him to her desperate mother: "I love him. . . . He says, 'Come,' and I go, 'Do this' and I do it. I'd follow him to the ends of the earth." Finally in the abandoned shack towards the end of the film, her destruction seems complete.

Marie's physical destruction is merely an external manifestation of the moral-spiritual destruction that Gérard wreaks in her. The seduction is mental, moral, psychological, clear in her words to her mother: "And if he asked me to kill myself, I'd kill myself." Gérard's evil moral power over Marie is complete. It makes her reject all that is good in her life, all that offers hope. Bresson renders this most evident in a scene towards the end of the film: the good Jacques returns and insists he wants to marry Marie, that all that has happened to her makes no difference, "We'll get married anyway. We'll be poor in the beginning, but I'll work twice as hard." Marie first protests, saying to him, "Our vows of love . . . they were in a world of fantasy," but then, later confiding in Balthazar she seems to respond positively: "I will love him!" Bresson cuts to their running through a field: Marie falls, Jacques helps her up (an effective metaphor of the spiritual sense of the scene-in-progress), Marie insists that she wants to make a clean break "once and for all" from Gérard. Jacques, intuiting the danger, pleads that she not go back to him, even to make a break, but Marie walks away, is pulled into Gérard's trap and it means her final and total destruction.

The inexorable evil power let loose in the film afflicts with a particularly tragic ferocity the donkey Balthazar. As we have already suggested, Bresson gives two dimensions to the contact of Balthazar with evil: simultaneously and throughout the film, he has Balthazar accompany the other victims of violence in their suffering and he has Balthazar become victim in his own right of the unleashed violence, of Gérard in particular, but of a whole variety of evil people – the "panorama of the vices . . . pride, anger, licentiousness, laziness, gluttony, drunkenness, avarice, rage"[51] – that surround him.

Quite consistently, Balthazar's innocent, humble, quiet presence expressed typically by Bresson in a low-key way – often he shows only Balthazar's shadow, his front feet or his wagging tail – accompanies the moments of greatest suffering of all the victims in the film. Bresson boldly announces this accompaniment in the opening of the film, in which the donkey is christened in the sign of the cross in the very room in which the sick girl dies a few moments later. It is a bold move because in this scene Bresson announces though rather obliquely his Christian strategy for the whole film, creating an intricate interplay of human suffering and death and Christian sacramental significance with baptism as a dying and rising with Christ and with the symbolism of the Incarnation and cross. This connects the whole of this scene, though we do not realize it yet, to the salvific passion and death of Jesus Christ, and to Balthazar, the Christ-figure, who at the end of the film will himself suffer a similar sacrificial passion and death.

Balthazar is also present during the several experiences of humiliation of Marie's father, a good man who is injured and eventually destroyed by the jealousy and evil of his neighbors, by humiliations at the hands of Gérard and his boys as they ridicule the donkey pulling the wagon and at home when Jacques attempts to make peace and later at the courthouse. The donkey is nearby in the two occasions when Jacques proclaims his sincere love for Marie and his desire to marry her, to save her from the destruction that awaits her, only to be rejected in a terrible way as she cries, "You bore me! You bore me!" Balthazar is also there when Jacques witnesses the full horror of Marie's destruction as he and her father find her in the abandoned shack. Balthazar is quietly waiting outside the dance hall during the insane destructive rampage of Gérard and it is he who carries poor Arnold to his death. Balthazar waits outside during the final agony and death of Marie's father and he stands quietly beside the widow as she mourns.

At this point, we might consider Balthazar's way of being with the other characters in the film, both in the good times (of which there seem to be precious few), and in the bad. Balthazar's is a way of being and of communicating represented with originality, sensitivity and consummate skill by Bresson. The typical approach to animals in film is to treat "the animal world with the most naive anthropomorphism,"[52] either by actually making them talk by dubbing, or by suggesting human reactions via careful editing techniques. This latter approach is best represented by Walt Disney "who does it unscrupulously,"[53] and by his many imitators both in film and more recently on television. Bresson includes animals in many of his films: a cat in *Les anges du péché* (1943), barking dogs and a crowing rooster in *The Diary of a Country Priest* (1951), the very strange, and yet very normal, appearance of a dog and two pigeons at the end of *The Trial of Joan of Arc* (1962). These animals simply do what they normally do, but precisely because they are presented in all their "animal-ness," they also seem to have some sensitivity to deeper forces in human events: "animals have an awareness that something unusual is happening."[54]

Bresson treats his animals with respect. "He succeeds in moving us, without resorting to anthropomorphism. We are moved at the end by the death of the donkey only because we see a donkey dying, who remains only a donkey."[55] On-screen he exerts great efforts to preserve the mystery of the animal's world and existence, refusing absolutely to violate it.[56] Perhaps better than in any other film, Bresson suggests this in *Au hasard Balthazar* in the truly remarkable scene in in the circus where Balthazar, the servant, delivering fodder, exchanges slow, intense, deliberate looks with four other caged animals, the Lords of the circus: a tiger,[57] a white bear, a monkey and an elephant. A scene that defies explanation, it speaks of a "reciprocity from which we are excluded [and this] repeated exchange of looks reaches a mysterious depth."[58]

As well, in Balthazar's contacts with human beings, Bresson adopts the same approach: he "does not use montage to violate the mystery of the animal. On the contrary, it is precisely this mystery that Bresson would have us experience, to the point of anxiety."[59] At the same time, the enigmatic quality that Bresson confers on Balthazar's presence in the suffering of the others, avoiding all sentimentalism, gives to this mysterious creature a moral strength and integrity that goes beyond that of anyone else in the film: "The total absence of gestures expressing judgement, the absence of moral expression, contributes to the great dignity . . . of Balthazar in the entire film,"[60] a dignity that clearly is a critical element of his identity as a Christ-figure.

If Bresson has Balthazar accompany all the victims of evil in the film, thus having him share in their suffering, he moves this dynamic to its highest and most poignant level in the relationship between Balthazar and Marie. In a very real sense, Marie, a complex character, is not simply one of the people encountered by Balthazar. Bresson makes her crucial to the significance of Balthazar. The critic Maurice, speaks of Marie's importance, insisting that without her, Balthazar's story would have little sense, would remain a series of sketches: "It is the story of Marie . . . that gives to the work its basis and its continuity, not only on the dramatic level, but also on the spiritual level."[61] Maurice goes on in fact to speak of two interconnected plot lines in the film: "the horizontal line of the donkey's existence who, always true to himself, supports to the death the destiny imposed on him by human beings, and the descending line, alas, of the little Marie."[62]

The privileged relationship of accompaniment between these two begins with the sequence at the beginning of the film of Balthazar's christening at which Marie, holding a lighted candle, symbol of the light of the Spirit and of her responsibility for Balthazar, acts as "godmother."[63] The sequence is, on the one hand a child's game, yet on the other hand, it is dense with spiritual and theological significance: the lighted candle is sign of the victory of Christ over the darkness of Satan, a promise for Balthazar, and for Marie, that does not quite work out. The words "In the name of the Father and of the Son and of the Holy Spirit," in the sign of the cross, vibrate with the sense of the salvific passion, death and Resurrection of Christ, and repeat the traditional symbolism of baptism, that of dying and rising to new life. Both of these characters are headed for such a passion.

The early childhood moment of play in the film is followed by Balthazar's first sufferings, but when he escapes from his first cruel master, he returns to Marie, who is happy to receive him. Their first humiliation in common is when Gérard and his boys ridicule them as Balthazar pulls the cart bringing Marie and her father from church. Shortly after, Balthazar is present when Gérard seduces Marie in the car and on the roadside, and later he comes between them. As Gérard extends his evil control over Marie – the second seduction scene in the abandoned shack, and the terrible scene outside the dance hall where Marie defends her "love" for Gérard to her mother – Balthazar quietly stands by. In the equally frightful nighttime scene at the shack of the grain merchant, when Marie seems as evil as Gérard, Balthazar quietly observes.

Bresson has Balthazar stand by Marie in several moments when her struggle against the evil that threatens her seems to be victorious. He is there both times Marie speaks with Jacques, the good man who offers her love and forgiveness. In the second of these occasions, Balthazar does something quite remarkable. While Marie confesses to Jacques the squalid truth of her relationship with Gérard, Bresson shifts the camera from them and onto a quietly grazing Balthazar, as if he wants to suggest that Balthazar is taking onto himself her sins, the weight of evil she is carrying. Appropriately enough, a few moments later, apparently renewed in spirit, Marie confides to Balthazar "I will love him! I will love him!" Finally, when the end comes for Marie, the horror and the passion of her utter humiliation at the hands of Gérard in the deserted shack, Balthazar is there and he pulls the cart, more a hearse, which brings her home, the last time we, and he, shall see her.

But early in the film, before the tragic destiny and choices of Marie begin to manifest themselves, there is a scene between her and Balthazar, which is surprising, mysterious, an "almost mystical scene,"[64] which has profound spiritual meaning in itself, and "gives meaning to all the other"[65] scenes between them. It takes place in the garden of the farmhouse at night and expresses the deep union of spirits that exists between these two beings. Luigi Bini describes and interprets the scene:

> The "union of life" [between Marie and Balthazar] reaches the highest point of its significance in the night-time "celebration" in which the young girl crowns him with flowers of the field, embraces him tenderly and then sits in front of him in contemplation.[66]

The scene is nothing short of a mystical marriage, in clear contrast to the squalid, perverse, compulsive and destructive sexual commerce that will soon begin insidiously to establish itself between Marie and the evil Gérard, a squalidness already announced in this moment by the obscene suggestions made by Gérard who spies on the encounter between Balthazar and Marie. Further, as a "mystical marriage," the scene carries with it a promise of fidelity, for better or for worse, a promise which Balthazar will keep in spite of the "infidelity" of Marie.

Bresson creates in Marie one of his most complex and ambivalent characters. Perhaps more than all the others, she is representative of humankind, of the moral inferno we find ourselves in. It would be oversimplifying the case to suggest that she is purely innocent victim of Gérard's evil; "Marie is the victim of an interior breakdown of which she is in large part conniving and responsible."[67] Her ambivalence is also very clear in her positive response to the sincere ideal love of Jacques and the conscious submission to the cruel carnality and violence of Gérard. This ambivalence is also clear in her paradoxical "attachment to Balthazar and [her] love for Gérard, the natural and the attractiveness of evil."[68]

In effect, Bresson makes of Marie, more than the other characters, a classic case of St. Paul's analysis of his own situation and that of the weak and sinful Christian, facing the evil of the world:

> I can will what is right but I cannot do it. For I do not do the good I want, but the evil I do not want is what I do. . . . For I delight in the law of God in my inmost self, but I see in my members another law . . . making me captive to the law of sin that wells in my members. (Rom 7:18-19, 22-23)

In doing this Bresson is among other things preparing the ground for a consideration of his donkey as a figure of Christ.

Bresson identifies Marie as a carrier of light at the beginning of Balthazar's life. He has the donkey accompany her, to be a carrier of spiritual light for her, in all the vicissitudes of her brief and tragic life, and he is with her also in the end. "In fact the connection between the young girl and the animal is so indissoluble that, once Marie has definitely disappeared, the destiny of Balthazar also seems to be accomplished."[69] Once Marie is no longer on the scene, things begin happening to Balthazar at an accelerated rate, as if his *raison d'être* is no longer. His end comes very quickly and, as we shall see, very mysteriously.

If Balthazar's privileged positive relationship is with Marie, his most negative relationship is with Gérard in the sense that Gérard, though he is never an owner of Balthazar, exercises more gratuitous violence on him than anyone else does. It is more gratuitous, more sadistic, more perverted and ultimately more tragic, for it leads to his death. Others, his various owners, beat Balthazar at specific moments and for specific reasons: he is slow at his work or they are drunk or frustrated. But in the case of Gérard, from the beginning when he ridicules Balthazar on the road, saying ironically to Marie and her father, "A donkey is cute, he's fast, up-to-date," the cruelty is both unmotivated and exaggerated. Gérard's first beating of Balthazar is without reason. The donkey is following him, loaded down with baskets of bread, but Gérard deliberately stops, punches and kicks the donkey and finally, with quiet deliberation, ties a piece of paper to his tail and sets it on fire. This is pure sadism.

Shortly after, Gérard and one of his henchmen spy on the nighttime meeting, the "mystical marriage" scene of Balthazar and Marie, and the obscene comment he makes to his colleague suggests not only the perversion of Gérard, but even his jealousy of Balthazar, his aversion to the good represented by the donkey: "Balthazar is in opposition to the gangleader of the black jackets, just as good is opposed to evil and the light to the darkness."[70] It is an aversion which is confirmed when Gérard interrupts Marie's contemplation and when, after she runs off, he beats the donkey mercilessly.

If Gérard's final salute to Arnold, the kiss and the words "my faithful companion" spoken with homicidal irony, are a first suggestion of the evangelical Judas-betrayal and the passion of Jesus, Gérard's final contact with Balthazar fairly vibrates with these suggestions. Gérard comes by night through the garden, steals the donkey from the widow, after she has referred to him as a "saint," loads him with contraband, leads him up a mountain, beating him three times, and then abandons him to the death of a criminal. What appears to be Balthazar's final humiliation, his "final calvary and death,"[71] he suffers at the hands of Gérard.

Already in the early part of this chapter, the subject of Bresson's Balthazar as a Christ-figure is broached, or at least some associations were made that could begin to lead to such an identification. In part, the evidence is biblical: Bresson's own biblical intentions and explanations for the name "Balthazar," the references to Bethlehem, to the Magi, to the subsequent slaughter of the innocents thus connecting suffering with the birth of the Messiah. In part too, there is the fact that in most of Bresson's films the protagonists are Christ-figures, recognized as such rather universally by the critics: "It is possible to find in almost all the films of Bresson . . . allusions to the life of Christ . . . a way of the cross, the passion of Christ becoming the common where human beings discover their fulfillment."[72] In this latter part of the chapter, we have considered further levels of correspondence between Bresson's donkey and Christ, namely that in the dominant dynamic of the film, the struggle of good against cosmic evil, Balthazar both accompanies others in their suffering and suffers himself to the point of death.

At this point, and in order to move the analysis of Balthazar as Christ-figure to a deeper level, a couple of qualifications are necessary. If the basic dynamic of the film is that of the monumental struggle between good and evil, and if the world of the film is profoundly ambiguous, vitiated, apparently lost to the forces of evil – Gérard and his delinquent friends escape from the police at the end, presumably to begin another day of evil – it is in this world that Balthazar the Christ-figure must exist and must act. It is this world that Balthazar the Christ-figure has come to redeem.

Our analysis so far has indicated clearly how Balthazar exists in this world, namely, as a victim. But how his actions qualify him as a Christ-figure is more difficult to appreciate, especially if one thinks of the filmic Christ-figures analyzed thus far in this book, which are all very different from Balthazar. Shane, the strong man, saves the day and saves the civilization; his action is clear and definitive, it defeats the forces of evil and brings peace and salvation. The actor-director in *Jesus of Montreal* gives hope to his community, and especially to Mireille; he redeems their lives, he redeems art and even cinema. In Kieślowski's film, the young man Tomek saves Magda, brings about a major change in her life. In *Out of Rosenheim*, Jasmine brings salvation, harmony, fellowship to the community; Babette's sacrificial act initiates a new era of reconciliation and peace in a covenant of love; and Helen Prejean in *Dead Man Walking* brings salvation to the condemned man and hope to one of his victims. In Fellini's two films, Cabiria, because of her great hope and trust in humanity, becomes an image of resurrection hope, and Gelsomina who in her sacrificed life is very much like Bresson's Balthazar, in her death brings about the redemption of the man who makes her suffer.

Balthazar as Christ-figure is very different from all of the above. Clearly, he never takes the initiative,[73] he never strikes back at the cruelty and violence of the oppressors of others. Though "it is not correct to say that the donkey is inert, opaque, an unfeeling brute presence,"[74] he accepts all manner of cruelty visited on himself. In terms of the classical dramatic categories, Balthazar is a kind of "anti-hero."[75] But it is precisely in this "anti-hero" quality of his presence and actions that the donkey is most clearly a Christ-figure. The evidence for this conclusion is first of all external to the film, that is in passages in the New Testament in which Jesus is presented as an "anti-hero" and achieves his glory precisely in this role, and secondly internal, that is in elements within the film which link Balthazar to Jesus as the suffering servant.

First, let us consider the external biblical evidence. In his Letter to the Corinthians, Saint Paul speaks boldly of Jesus the Christ as a sign of contradiction. Instead of a Messiah with power and majesty, a political, military leader, he says: "We proclaim Christ crucified, a stumbling block to Jews and foolishness to Gentiles . . . Christ the power of God and the wisdom of God" (1 Cor 1:23-24). Balthazar, too, like Christ crucified, is "a sign of contradiction":[76] his spiritual power is precisely in the fact that with Marie and the others, he walks the way of the cross.[77] He lives through "a veritable passion because he suffers and dies weighed down by the sins of a humanity to which he as an animal is as much an outsider as was Jesus Christ, for he was the Son of God."[78] Thus analogically Balthazar shares the passion of Christ.[79]

Xavier Tilliette's perceptive analysis of Balthazar as Christ-figure and sign of contradiction makes reference to another book of the New Testament:

> The *Epistle to the Hebrews* is not afraid of the rude parallel [Jesus-scapegoat] when it brings to memory the holocausts of the Old Law, the blood of goats and heifers, and the scapegoat expelled *extra castrum*. . . . The donkey [Balthazar], suffering pain, an expiatory animal, carries with great effort the heavy weight of sin to the heights.[80]

Several citations from the Letter to the Hebrews render more clear Tilliette's analysis and Bresson's intention for his donkey. Like Christ, Balthazar "learned obedience through what he suffered" (5:8). Like Christ he "endured the cross, disregarding its shame" (12:2). Like Christ, Balthazar's own suffering permits him to share the suffering of others: "Because he himself was tested by what he suffered, he is able to help those who are being tested" (2:18). Balthazar, "the incarnation of absolute innocence,"[81] can even be likened to Christ the High Priest: "For we do not have a high priest who is unable to sympathize with our weaknesses, but we have one who in every respect has been tested as we are, yet without sin" (4:15).

By synthesizing the soteriology of the Letter to the Hebrews with the life and death of the innocent Balthazar, and therefore clearly identifying the donkey as a Christ-figure, the critic Maurice says:

> Of this evil, of this sinfulness, of this Satan [in the film], Balthazar is never an accomplice. If he accepts the burden, if he carries it on his back, with much pain, all the way to the top of the mountain – in a difficult climb during which three times he is beaten because, exhausted, he cannot go ahead – it is not because he cooperated in the sinful acts: he takes onto himself only the burden of the suffering. Humble, abandoned, peaceful, he is pure of all this evil that he carries away from humankind, among whom he lived without cheating. He is mercy granted continually.[82]

This external biblical evidence suggesting Balthazar as a Christ-figure is supplemented by Bresson with evidence internal to the film. Some is circumstantial, indirect, such as the fact that at the beginning of the film Balthazar comes down out of the mountains and at the end he returns up into the mountains to die. There is the fact that he is referred to as a "saint," and incensed as a holy person, suggestive of Christ's triumphal entry into Jerusalem. Regarding this "saintliness" of the donkey, four times in the film Bresson repeats a full-frontal shot of Balthazar, directly facing the camera in close-up, that suggests the content, composition and style of classical Byzantine icons, clearly underlining this understanding of Bresson's donkey as a "saint," a Christ-figure.[83] Finally, Balthazar dies a violent death, "a shameful death for a 'saint,' "[84] loaded down with contraband material – perfume, gold, clothes – "the weight of the sins of humankind."[85] Clearly, as Luigi Bini insists, in this context, "a reference to Christ is not at all out of place."[86]

If this evidence were not sufficient to suggest a conscious identification of Balthazar as a Christ-figure, there is a further direct biblical reference that leaves very little doubt. Towards the end of the film, after the mysterious disappearance of Marie, her father is dying. The parish priest comes to assist him and picking up a Bible from the bedside table, he reads a passage from the Book of Lamentations:

> For the Lord will not reject forever.
> Although he causes grief, he will have compassion,
> according to the compassion of his steadfast love;
> for he does not willingly afflict or grieve anyone. (Lam 3:31-33)

Verses about suffering and redemption, one can presume they are meant in reference to the father of Marie. The three verses immediately preceding these however, also verses about the redemptive value of suffering, seem to refer rather to Balthazar:

> [It is good for one to bear the yoke in youth]
> to sit alone in silence
> when the Lord has imposed it,
> to put one's mouth to the dust

> . . . to give ones's cheek to the smiter,
> and be filled with insults. (Lam 3:28-30)

These verses clearly recall the words of the suffering servant song of Isaiah:

> I gave my back to those who struck me
> and my cheeks to those who pulled my beard;
> I did not hide my face from insult and spitting. (Isa 50:6)

Clearly these are words which give profound spiritual, biblical and christological meaning to the existence and the experience of suffering of the donkey Balthazar. Commenting on these biblical references and on Bresson's
reticence to admit precise conscious references to Christ in his donkey, the
critic Maurice concludes: "Whether Robert Bresson admits it or not, these
correspondences lead the believer and even the unbeliever, to discover in the
destiny of Balthazar reflections of the redemptive mystery of the God-man."[87]
Another critic confirms this point:

> The donkey Balthazar seems to be a Christ reincarnated, returned to un-
> derstand the transformed nature of twentieth-century man, and once again
> his knowing involves his taking onto himself what is ours. As the Lord
> was crucified, so Balthazar falls in the end under the strikes of human
> passion.[88]

Before completing the analysis of Balthazar as Christ-figure, we might
recall a *caveat* already made more than once in this book, a clarification that
has to do with the nature of the Christ-figure. We are not saying that
Balthazar *is* or represents *literally* Jesus the Christ. Nor would it be correct to
consider the film an allegory: "the film is a quest . . . an adventure open to
the breath of grace (and of Grace) [not] a heavy allegory."[89] Maurice explains: "To insist on an explicit correspondence between Christ and Balthazar,
to seek out exact equivalences, is to harden, and, in the extreme, to falsify
and pervert the work of Bresson."[90] Several critics speak of *Au hasard
Balthazar* as a parable,[91] and Maurice, speaking in general of Bresson's style,
but certainly also of *Au hasard Balthazar*, concludes:

> He creates parables, in the biblical sense of the word, that is to say, a
> world, a story, a painting, an atmosphere, which in their totality have a
> teaching value . . . in a much more flexible way than does an allegory
> where each of the elements has a meaning and a precise equivalent.[92]

René Gilson calls the film a "poem-parable"[93] and he explains, "the
donkey came among his own and his own received him not."[94] In this christological parable then, Balthazar experiences a Christ-like suffering[95] and
shares the suffering of others. He is the innocent victim of forces of evil both
specific and cosmic, taking onto himself the sins of humankind, clearly a
suggestion of "his role as 'lamb of God.'"[96] In this sense and differently from
the more triumphant Christ-figures of other films, Balthazar as a Christ-figure
represents the fulness of the kenotic Incarnation of the Word-made-flesh, the
fulness of the human nature of God-in-Jesus, the fulness of human weakness,

suffering and failure that God-in-Jesus took onto himself in order to effect salvation.

Some of the critics speak of the futility of Balthazar's sufferings and death, one for example saying, "he dies and redeems nothing,"[97] and another, "he dies like a victim whose immolation is useless."[98] Bresson however seems to suggest, very discretely and very subtly, that Balthazar's contact with some of the characters of the film does have a salvific effect. He is near the schoolteacher, a good man, when at the moment of his death, the man seems to have a moment of peace and reconciliation, saying to the priest: "Perhaps I suffered less than you think." It is Balthazar who inspires the act of kindness and generosity in Arnold when the latter saves his life, and he stands by Arnold at the moment of his death. The donkey's presence in the life of Marie's mother is most significant: she protects him early in the film, and towards the end, when Gérard and his black-jacketed friends want to take Balthazar, she resists. Maurice sees this as a moment of grace for her inspired by the donkey. He describes the moment: "She turns towards us, her eyes in tears, it is the first times we see her cry. Her face is purified, made peaceful . . . She has abandoned herself, and it is precisely in the instant when she confesses that Balthazar 'is a saint.'"[99] Then regarding the most enigmatic, most desperate character in the film, Marie, Maurice adds, "finally, it is clear, Balthazar fulfills in himself what is missing in Marie."[100] Maurice's explanation of this mysterious salvific role of Balthazar, echoing passages in the New Testament's Letters to the Ephesians and to the Colossians,[101] has clear christological overtones and gives a clear christological identity to the donkey.

> Everything happens as if the "holiness" of Balthazar permitted him to bring to completion in himself, the impulses, the aspirations towards the good, or rather the possibilities which exist in the other personages of the drama, but which in them, do not succeed. It is as if Balthazar were mysteriously . . . the "fulfillment" of those whom the rigors of existence or the weakness of their hearts prevent from reaching the fulness of holiness to which they are called.[102]

Recalling what was said above concerning *Au hasard Balthazar* not being an allegory, there remains one more issue to be discussed regarding Balthazar as a Christ-figure, that is the question of the Resurrection. Bresson has Balthazar die where he was born, on the mountainside, the shameful death of a criminal, an apparent failure, an apparent negation of meaning or spiritual significance.

Yet again with typical discretion, subtlety and understatement, Bresson films this scene in such a way that it has clear suggestions of resurrection. The closing scene is parallel to the opening scene of the film. The film has come full circle and Balthazar's death is likened to his birth. In a sense it is a birth, a higher birth. But there is a significant difference. In the opening of the film, the spaces are restricted, the camera focusses in very close on the small donkey; we see only his head, we do not see his mother, the tones are dark, shadowy. We know there are sheep present because we hear their bells and glance them furtively.

In the closing scene, "the most richly evocative sequence in all of Bresson and surely one of the most affecting passages in the history of film,"[103] everything opens up: "The film achieves . . . a lyrical quality, finally set free in its concluding images."[104] The photography of the mountainside favors wide, panoramic shots of the meadow and of the splendid, sun-filled morning sky: "For the death of Balthazar in a rather grandiose natural frame, the image widens: it is the only real 'landscape' of the film."[105] The colors and tones are light, bright; the white sheep – "the biblical reference is unmistakeable"[106] – surround Balthazar. The music of the bells of the sheep, dominating the soundtrack "seems to be calling Balthazar and it continues after he dies."[107] In this conclusion, like the character of Balthazar, the Schubert music "that corresponds to him speaks, in this admirable *andantino*, less of resignation than of courage: a quiet, poignant courage."[108]

All these elements, these visual and auditory images, speak of life and victory, not of death and failure. They express a "thanksgiving for this life which, through so much pain and some little happiness, there is revealed a higher order."[109] Luigi Bini has no doubts about the element of victory in the conclusion, declaring unequivocally, "the death of Balthazar is a definitive entry into peace."[110] Another critic says that "in death, Balthazar celebrates his victory,"[111] and a third speaks of the "serenity of this new birth that is death."[112] And finally, Jean Sémolué says:

> The conclusion of *Balthazar* gives the impression that, in spite of so many incertitudes, so many chaotic appearances, there exists, finally, an order. . . . In this conclusion and in the relationship of this ending to everything that precedes it, things appear to be ordered on a cosmic level.[113]

6

Essential Dimensions and Typical Guises of the Christ-Figure

The profile of the Christ-figure in film can include a number of elements or dimensions, all of which can be recognized on the one hand in the fullness of their meaning in Jesus the Christ, and on the other hand to a lesser extent in the figure of Christ represented in the film in question.[1] At the same time, the filmic Christ-figure assumes a number different guises or forms, each of which serves as an appropriate metaphor of the totality of the Christ-event or of some dimension thereof. So far in this book, we have considered this reciprocal dynamic between the Christ-figure and the Christ figured through the detailed analysis of individual films, in most of which the totality of the Christ-event is represented. In addition, most of these films are recognized classics, masterpieces of the filmic art. In this chapter, which is conceived as a wide-ranging overview of the Christ-figure theme in film, we shall shift our approach. From an attention paid almost exclusively to classic films, we shall here consider a wide variety of films, some classics and many very popular. As well, moving from a detailed and extensive analysis of a limited number of films, in this chapter we shall focus briefly on a larger selection of films, the intention being to suggest how widely and how variously the Christ-figure imagery is diffused in the seventh art.

Some Dimensions of the Filmic Christ-Figure

Since the filmic Christ-figure does not always reflect the totality of the Christ-event, in the first part of this chapter and by looking briefly at a number of films, many of them popular rather than classics, we shall consider how different dimensions of the Christ-event are represented in individual elements or images or sequences of the films in question.

Reflecting the wholly other, transcendental character, or at least origins of the Word-of-God-made-flesh, the filmic Christ-figure often has mysterious origins. This mysterious quality is evident in Pasolini's *Teorema* (1968) where not even the name of the strange "visitor," let alone his origins and destiny, is known: he arrives announced by an "angel-figure," and departs the same way. As we saw in chapter three, the transcendent dimension is also present in the western, *Shane*, in which the mysterious origins and destiny of the enigmatic hero are never fully revealed. Sometimes the Christ-figure comes from outer space as in Stephen Spielberg's *E.T. The Extra-Terrestrial* (1982) or from another time zone, as in Vincent Ward's *The Navigator: A*

Medieval Odyssey (1988) or even from the ethereal, transcendent dimension of the angels, as in Wim Wenders' *The Wings of Desire* (1987).

Jean-Luc Godard's 1985 film, *Hail Mary*, attempts to represent a modern-day analogy of the story of Joseph and Mary, of the virginal conception and birth of Jesus, and thus of the Christian mystery of the Incarnation and of the divine Sonship of Jesus. The complicated and often disturbing, alienating style of the film, and Godard's somewhat obsessive preoccupation with the female body, do not prevent the film from approaching, says one critic, with some "theological daring and originality,"[2] the theme of the divine origins of Jesus, a theme too often treated in a falsely sentimental, devotional manner in Jesus-films, or in an erroneous mythical manner in the Christ-figure film, for example in the first *Superman* film (1978).

Reflecting the actions of Jesus Christ the Master, the protagonists in many Christ-figure films attract a group of followers whom they teach and form and save. Once the masters are gone, the disciples carry forward the mission. This pattern is quite transparent, as we shall see later, in two prison films, Milos Forman's *One Flew Over the Cuckoo's Nest* (1975) and Stuart Rosenberg's *Cool Hand Luke* (1967). The master-disciple dynamic is also operative, as we have seen, in *Shane* and in Arcand's *Jesus of Montreal* and also in Luis Buñuel's *Nazarin* (1958), though with different motivations and different results in each of these cases. In Liliana Cavani's two films on Francis of Assisi, *Francesco d'Assisi* (1966) and *Francesco* (1989), the gathering of followers and the complex dynamic between the disciples and the master are a rich christological dimension. Billy Kwan in Peter Weir's 1982 film, *The Year of Living Dangerously,* acts as master and guide for Guy Hamilton, in the end paying for Hamilton's salvation with his life.

Another motif typical of the Christ-figure is that of the commitment to justice. The protagonist of the film often enters a community or a situation in which injustices are being perpetrated against the people, and one aspect of his mission is to free the people from this yoke. This pattern is clear in many westerns in which the protagonist-heros are Christ-figures, it is crucial in the popular christic hero films such as those of the *Batman* and *Superman* cycles and it takes a very original and interesting form in the Sigourney Weaver character, Ripley, in the later *Alien* films. Archbishop Romero in John Duigan's *Romero* (1989) opposes the social and economic injustice of a military dictatorship, the Stalker in Andrei Tarkovsky's *Stalker* (1979) struggles against Stalinism, the hero of Boris Sagal's science-fiction film, *The Omega Man* (1975) faces the injustice of religious fanaticism, the peasant Battistì of Ermanno Olmi's *The Tree of the Wooden Clogs* (1978) becomes a prophet for the rights of oppressed peasants in still feudal Northern Italy.

Christ worked miracles as a sign of the coming of the Kingdom and the motif of working wonders is common in popular superhero films like *Batman* (1989) and its sequels and *Superman*. It is rather problematic in the serious Christ-figure film, because miracle and mystery are categories not widely credible in the modern and postmodern worlds. Still Dreyer daringly has his

Christ-figure perform a "radical"[3] miracle in *Ordet* (1955), the raising of a woman from the dead; so does Wenders in *The Wings of Desire.*

In the gospels, perhaps the element which creates the most dramatic tension is the conflict between Jesus and the Jewish religious authorities. From the beginning of his public life until his crucifixion, and in a crescendo of violence through which Calvary became ever more inevitable, Jesus found himself in conflict with the Pharisees and through them the Sanhedrin. Also in the Christ-figure film, the conflict between the protagonist and some authority figure or figures is a crucial dramatic element. In *One Flew Over the Cuckoo's Nest*, the protagonist McMurphy is pitted against Nurse Ratched and the hospital authorities, and in Rossellini's *Open City*, both the priest, don Pietro, and the resistance leader are in conflict with the German occupation authorities. In Alain Cavalier's *Thérèse* and Cavani's *Francesco*, rather curiously the opposition comes in large part from within the religious communities to which each belongs, and from the Church authorities. Yet after all, this is not so curious, for Jesus faced opposition from his own religious contemporaries and to a lesser extent even from his own apostles. One of the most powerful images in Arcand's *Jesus of Montreal* is that of the protagonist Daniel in the role of Jesus during a performance of the passion play, standing facing the priest who is director of the shrine, and his two superiors. These three authorities loom in a high triangular composition, and half in light, half in shadow, they strongly suggest the menacing power that will be responsible to Daniel-Jesus' death.

Jesus Christ in his passion and death redeemed humankind. He was the sacrificial victim, the scapegoat, who took onto himself the sins of the world. As we saw in the discussion of Bresson's *Au hasard Balthazar*, in the experience of the innocent donkey-protagonist, there a "deliberate parable . . . an analogy of the Passion of Jesus,"[4] a parable particularly represented in the conclusion of the film in the biblical image of the scapegoat, going out with the sins of humankind on its back. In the conclusion of *Shane*, the protagonist, having in a sense taken onto himself the sins of the people he has saved, rides out of town towards the wilderness, like the biblical scapegoat. The cinematic priest, about whom we shall speak more at length later, in his role as confessor, one who "takes away the sins of the world," is often a Lamb of God-scapegoat image. Father Logan of Alfred Hitchcock's *I Confess* (1953), for example, carries around the sins of the murderer and innocently suffers persecution because of this. *Abbé* Donissan of Maurice Pialat's *Under Satan's Sun* (1987) literally dies in the confessional, a death which shines with the power of the Resurrection.

The gospels tell us that Jesus often withdrew to a "deserted place" (Lk 4:42) to pray. One of the most astonishing and effective moments in *The Gospel According to Saint Matthew*, as we have already seen, is the brief sequence in which Pasolini shows us Jesus kneeling silent in early morning prayer, in communion with God. The image is particularly astonishing because it is so rare in the Jesus-film; in fact, the evidence seems to indicate that the filmic Christ-figure is more often seen in prayer than the filmic Jesus. This film portrayal of prayer, of moments of intimacy with God, of closeness to or mystical union with God, is one of the most significant, if subtle and delicate dimensions of the filmic Christ-figure, one which brings him very close to the Jesus he represents, one of whose regular activities, noted in the gospels, was that of union with God in prayer. A low-key but crucial example of this is in *Cool Hand Luke*, where the director has Luke, as he hides out in the church, awaiting the final showdown and his death, address a very direct and impassioned prayer to God, powerful because it is so familiar in tone: the parallel to Jesus' prayer in Gethsemane is evident. In *Thérèse*, Cavalier has his protagonist pray in a disarmingly simple but most effective way, absolutely void of easy devotional sentimentalism. Once, as she "talks" with Jesus, she places her hand on his picture to add urgency to her words; later on, during her final agony, when she realizes Sister Lucie is quitting the convent, as she prays she races around her bed over and over, recalling the way Pasolini suggested the intensity of Jesus' prayer in Gethsemane.

Two films on Francis of Assisi provide an interesting contrast in the styles of prayer of Christ-figures. In Liliana Cavani's *Francesco*, Francis' sense of total abandonment and his terrible "Talk to me!" repeated over and over as he lives through his dark night of the soul on the edge of a precipice, is clearly parallel to Jesus' sense of abandonment in Gethsemane and on the cross. The prayer of Michael Curtiz' Francis (*Francis of Assisi*, 1961) is in total contrast: formally eloquent, sentimental-devotional, quasi-liturgical in tone, a prayer supported extradiegetically by a symphony orchestra and a choir of angelic voices, and by dramatic gestures, arms outstretched in the form of a cross, and fancy footwork more apt in a ballet. In both films, the prayers of the protagonist are answered by the christological sign of the stigmata, but only Cavani's Francis is a convincing image of Christ crucified. Curtiz's heavy-handed approach makes his protagonist into a sad caricature and the attempt to represent metaphorically Christ at prayer is a risible failure.

In film, not only saints pray but also fools, as in the case of little Stracci in Pasolini's *La ricotta*, whose simple prayer deepens his association with the crucified Christ, of whom he will be an image in his death. Twice, as Stracci runs (comically, in a Chaplinesque fast-motion sequence) to buy the ricotta cheese and on his way back, Pasolini has him pause for a split second at a roadside crucifixion shrine, and make the sign of the cross. As well, perhaps the closest the cinema of Christ-figures comes to represent the profound mystical prayer of Jesus is, as we have seen, in *Jesus of Montreal*, in the experience of the young actor Daniel as he, in the role of Jesus in the passion play, hangs on the cross. In these two quite remarkable sequences, Arcand's Christ-figure comes closest to the Christ he represents or figures.

Jesus in his passion was the fulfillment of the suffering servant prophecy-image of the Old Testament, a figure of whom Isaiah says: "He was despised and rejected by others; a man of suffering and acquainted with infirmity; and as one from whom others hide their faces" (Is 53:3). The protagonist of David Lynch's film *The Elephant Man* (1980), in his life situation, cruelly deformed, reified by men, object of ridicule, of false accusations and injustice, reproduces in his own flesh and experience the situation of the suffering servant. A paragon of the innocent person who accepts the burden of suffering, of whom the Old Testament figure of Job is also a classic example, John Merrick never loses faith in God, a point made by Lynch when he has Merrick, alone in his room, read Psalm 23, "The Lord is My Shepherd."

The shedding of blood, representing the blood of Jesus, shed like that of the sacrificial lamb for the redemption of humankind, is often a dimension of the dynamic of the Christ-figure in film. In the conclusion of *The Omega Man*, the blood of the hero is shed as the price for the freedom and life of the people. The only hope of the people after a war fought with bacteriological weapons, because he has miraculously "healthy" blood, the hero is pursued by evil powers. In the end, he chooses to die in order to redeem the people: his heart pierced, his blood flowing into a fountain of water in which he dies, an abstract sculpture of a tree behind him (a cross, a tree of life), all these are details which point, perhaps too obviously, to his identity as a Christ-figure and more specifically as a "Sacred Heart of Jesus" figure.[5] In *Romero*, the director Duigan has the Archbishop shot at the moment of the elevation of the chalice of consecrated wine, so that in a very powerful christic symbol, the blood of the dying martyr is literally mixed with the sacrificial blood of Christ. Elia Kazan, in *On the Waterfront* (1954), has both the film's Christ-figures shed their blood, as does George Stevens with his Christ-figure in *Shane*. In *Jesus of Montreal*, Arcand, has the Christ-figure not only shed his blood but, as we have already noted, he suggests a Sacred Heart image far more credible and powerful than its bizarre analogue in *The Last Temptation of Christ*.

The *via crucis*, the representation of the suffering Jesus carrying his cross to Calvary, is almost always suggested in a metaphorical way in the Christ-figure film. In two of these films, *Jesus of Montreal* and Jules Dassin's *He Who Must Die* (1957),[6] the Christ-figure actually plays the role of Jesus in a passion play. Thus the "theatrical" *via crucis* has a double significance: it echoes the actual passion of Jesus, and it becomes the locus of the passion of the Christ-figure, the point at which he most closely represents Christ. In *Dead Man Walking*, as we have seen, the nun and Christ-figure reaches out to the good thief-figure on his cross. The gesture is clearly suggestive of that of Jesus on his cross, "reaching out" to the repentant thief.

In four films, Pasolini's *Accattone* (1961), Tarkovsky's *The Sacrifice, I Confess* and *Jesus of Montreal*, the passion of Christ is represented quite directly in music. In the first two, the music and words of Bach's "Passion of Matthew" are heard at key moments and in the Hitchcock film, the "Dies Irae" carries the passion meaning, while in the Arcand's film, the Pergolesi "Stabat Mater," sung intradiegetically in the opening and the conclusion, most effectively frames the christological action of the film. In his *La ricotta*, Pa-

solini has a Gregorian "Dies Irae" played on an accordion during a last supper scene – Stracci, the Christ-figure, having given his food to his wife and
children is not present – which points to where the film's "true holiness is."[7]

After his death, Jesus of Nazareth was recognized as the Christ in his
Resurrection, and as we have already said, a filmic Christ-figure is authenti-
cated when there is some metaphorical representation of the Resurrection. We
have seen how the protagonist of *Nights of Cabiria,* in spite of her suffering
two death-like experiences, the second of which is particularly terrible, lives a
resurrection experience in the film's conclusion. A parallel experience is
given to the diminutive "Professor," the protagonist of Ermanno Olmi's *During the Summer* (1971), again in the conclusion of the film. Locked in a
prison cell, clearly for him an experience of failure and of death, the innocent
little man looks out the barred window evidently discouraged. Suddenly and
gratuitously, the woman he has "given his life for" calls to him from the
street below; he raises his head, his face transfixed with a radiant smile which
beams with Easter victory.

Two other Olmi films conclude with metaphorical images of the Resurrection. In the conclusion of *The Legend of the Holy Drinker* (1988), the
protagonist, Andreas, having completed the mission given him by a mysterious stranger, a God-figure, dies in the sacristy of a church. It is Sunday morning, the church bells are ringing, and Olmi places Andreas on the ceremonial
throne reserved to the Bishop, surrounding him with priests and acolytes. For
Andreas, unreformed alcoholic and derelict, who lives under the bridges
along the Seine, but who finally acquires some self-respect, this death – with
a shaft of sunlight shining on his face – is a Resurrection-victory. In *The Tree
of the Wooden Clogs,* the Resurrection-metaphor is much more subtle. The
big peasant Battistì has risked and lost all to give his son a chance to go to
school. The man undergoes a passion and a kind of death as he is banished
from his community by the angry landowner and moves into the dark night
with his family and all he owns on a wagon. Olmi suggests the victory that
follows Battistì's sacrifice in three elements: in his little boy, who in spite of
the tragedy keeps doing his homework, a hope for the future; in the newly-
constituted peasant family with the "miracle-child" called, not by chance,
Giovanni Battista, John the Baptist; and finally in the lamp hanging from
Battistì's wagon, a light that shines in the darkness (Jn 1:5).

Some Models of the Filmic Christ-Figure

The filmic Christ-figure is embodied in a variety of guises or models, some
traditional and others rather original, some representing the totality of the
Christ-event and others of a more limited scope, only some of its aspects. We
recall that at times the Christ-figure is a dominant presence, with a major
significance for the overall theme of the film and at times it is embodied in a
secondary character or even in a single image, effective only for a brief mo-

ment and with a limited significance in the film as a whole. We recall also Neil Hurley's distinction between the classical Christ-figure and the Jesus-transfiguration, the former being an unequivocal reference to the Jesus Christ of the Christian faith, and the latter, a more narrow reference to the Jesus of history and of human culture.

1. The Saint as Christ-Figure

The New Testament challenges all Christians to be followers of Christ, to model their lives after him, to be Christ-figures: Paul says to the Christians at Corinth: "Be imitators of me, as I am of Christ." (1 Cor 11:1) Evidently, the Christian saint fulfills this challenge to a particular high degree, and thus is more clearly an image or figure of Christ. In film, however, not all saints qualify as Christ-figures, just as not all filmic Jesus representations are valid. Sometimes in cinema, the saint exists only as an excuse for an adventure film or an historical or sentimental drama. Sometimes the treatment of the saint is so devotional-sweet that the salt of the authentic imitation of Christ disappears. As in the case of the Jesus-film, sometimes the style of the saint-film – the presence of major stars, the choice of the epic or spectacular approach, an overpowering music score, a particular historical or ideological bias – distracts from the theme of sainthood as an *imitatio Christi* and renders the protagonist less incisive, less authentically a Christ-figure. In general, if the saint is a martyr, the Christ-image is clearer. In general, in the case of saints who receive the stigmata, the visual signs of the passion of Christ, their representation of Christ is more evident. Yet again here, choices of the director regarding style and content can reverse the meaning and actually negate the significance of the Christ-figure.

Films about saints have been around since the beginning of the film art. Already in 1898,[8] Georges Hatot made a short film, *Jeanne d'Arc*, the first of sixteen films dedicated to the French saint,[9] followed in 1917, after three other minor Joan of Arc films, by DeMille's version, *Joan the Woman*. In 1911, *Il poverello d'Assisi*, the first of nine films on Saint Francis, was made by the Italian Enrico Guazzoni. In 1897, Walter Haggar made *The Sign of the Cross* – it was then remade by DeMille in 1932 – the first of a seemingly endless series of films on the early Christian martyrs, in which series there are six *Quo Vadis?* films, reaching from 1901 to 1985.

Two films which treat of the murder of Archbishop Oscar Romero of El Salvador, now considered a martyr, reveal how in the treatment of different directors, the same saint-figure can reach Christ-figure status or can fall short of it. John Duigan's film *Romero* deals with Archbishop Romero, first as a quiet priest and scholar, living rather distant from the problems of violence and injustice in his country, and then as Archbishop, who becomes in a short time an eloquent spokesman for justice and human rights, and thus a thorn in the side of the governing military regime. As we have already noted, Duigan portrays Romero's murder, early one morning while he celebrates the Eucharist, as a martyrdom, clearly identifying it with the redemptive sacrificial death of Jesus. In his death, Duigan's Romero is a Christ-figure. The director Oliver Stone includes the episode of the murder of Archbishop Romero in his dramatic action film *Salvador* (1986), but in his interpretation, it is neither a martyrdom nor is Romero portrayed as a saint or a Christ-figure. The episode – marked by verbal, physical and visual violence and filmed in an aggressive, violent style – functions in the film not as a thematic or moral climax, but as one of many events of gratuitous violence with which the protagonist, an American journalist and not the Archbishop, has to deal.

1. A. Four Films on Francis of Assisi

In four films dedicated to Francis of Assisi, we can perceive this same pattern of "Christ-figure gained, Christ-figure lost." Michael Curtiz's *Francis of Assisi* is basically a Hollywood formula-style film of adventure and romance, in which "the aura of spirituality is rendered by pregnant pauses, empty stares, unspeakable lines, crucifixes [and] cosmic voice-overs."[10] Inauthentic in its settings – "the only cave it shows us is almost comfortably furnished"[11] – in its costumes, in many of its characters, and especially in its tone and spirit, the film's spiritual sense and impact are minimal, and its protagonist, complete with pre-Spielbergian special-effects stigmata, is a saint only in the most formal, superficial and unconvincing sense, and does not even approach the status of Christ-figure.

Franco Zeffirelli, in his *Brother Sun, Sister Moon* (1971), perhaps anticipating the style of his later *Jesus of Nazareth*, created a hagiographical portrait of the young Francis that, though not as blatantly a studio formula-product as Curtiz's film, suffers badly from a rather pretentious spirituality which lacks incisiveness, and from a variety of stylistic elements typical of a Zeffirelli film: beautiful young men and women, repeatedly shown in self-conscious, lingering close-ups, breathtaking landscapes, flawless compositions and group action scenes, swelling music and angelic choirs, with a conclusion that shamelessly pulls out all the emotional stops. Experiencing no struggle with his disciples, no self-doubt, no stigmata, Zeffirelli's saccharine Francis is more flower-child than Christ-figure.

In her first film about Francis, *Francesco d'Assisi*, Liliana Cavani created an unpretentious, low-key portrait in neorealistic episodic style of a Francis who identifies radically with the poor and protests against injustice and who, supported by the innocence of a little child, lives the final experience of the stigmata and death with a simple and instinctive trust in God. He is a believable saint and a credible Christ-figure. Cavani's later *Francesco* was quite a shift from this earlier film: an international production with a big budget, major stars – Mickey Rourke[12] as Francis and Helena Bonham-Carter as Clare – and wide distribution. Yet the film works admirably. While not neglecting the classical Franciscan issues of struggle against poverty and injustice, in her second film, Cavani considers the mystic side of the saint, portraying him above all as a lover of Christ and of God, which intense and intimate love nourishes and strengthens him in his mission. In this love, in his self-identification with Christ as the Loved One and in the stigmata which he lives as a mystical dialogue with God, Francis is clearly portrayed as a Christ-figure, a synthesis well-supported by the frame Cavani expertly builds around the story of Francis, that of Clare and the other disciples of Francis gathering several years after his death to recall their experience of him and to write it down, suggesting a process parallel to what went on after Christ's death and Resurrection, the development of the oral tradition and the composition of the gospels.

1.B. Joan of Arc in Film: Two Classic Christ-Figures

Probably the first saint-film which deliberately and carefully represents its protagonist as a figure of Christ was Carl Theodor Dreyer's silent classic, *The Passion of Joan of Arc* (1928), whose original Danish title, *Jeanne d'Arcs Lidelse og Dod*, literally *The Passion and Death of Joan of Arc,* already suggests the director's strategy. This film, which remains one of the finest examples of filmic Christ-figure hagiography, proceeds on two levels: that of the story of Joan and that of the passion of Jesus, which Dreyer "wanted to make visible."[13] By means of this "narrative parallelism,"[14] the film becomes a "masterful dramatic symphony of images arranged according to the narrative thread of the Passion of Christ,"[15] and clearly its protagonist is the classic saint-Christ-figure, "a living Imitation of Jesus Christ."[16] Limiting his account to the trial of Joan, which he telescopes into the timeframe of a single day,[17] and to her subsequent burning at the stake, Dreyer clearly structures his film "as a symbolic paraphrase of the Passion of Jesus,"[18] an association rendered transparent in a number of ways. Perhaps the most obvious of Dreyer's techniques is his dominant use of close-up shots of Joan, played powerfully by Renée Falconetti, in whom the director "explores the human face capable of expressing that of Christ."[19] By photographing Joan in close-up against neutral backgrounds, Dreyer makes her face into an "icon of Christ."[20]

The second technique used by Dreyer is the repeated visual references to the archetypal christological symbolism of the cross, references he makes throughout the film and in a variety of ways: "The cross-motif appears first as the chains lashed around the Bible, then as the crosspiece on Jeanne's cell window . . . then as the grave markers and as the crosses atop the churches, and, in the last scene, as the crucifix extended to Jeanne."[21] In fact, towards the end of the film, there is a multiplication of crosses, frame after frame, and often two in a single frame. Dreyer makes his Joan very much aware of these crosses and of their particular significance for her: at one point, in her cell, when Joan sees "a cross on the floor, formed by the shadows of the [window] bars, she smiles through her tears,"[22] and in the end, as she dies at the stake, Joan presses a crucifix to her breast: she presses the corpus – of Christ as High Priest – to her breast and closes her eyes in silent prayer-ecstasy. Beyond the crosses, Dreyer has the soldiers give Joan a crown of straw and a "mock sceptre,"[23] creating an image which "achieves a simple equation of her passion with the passion of Christ,"[24] a factor further underlined by the nailing of the "apostate"[25] inscription above her head on the stake, unequivocally reflecting the I.N.R.I. inscription on the cross of Jesus.[26]

The Christ-image active in Joan is also suggested by her suffering: "the humiliation . . . the scourging, the crowning with thorns, Christ insulted, the *'Ecce homo.'*"[27] As with Christ, Joan's passion is "more than that inflicted by the torturers; it is the silence of her Voices. She no longer hears the Voices of God."[28] At one point during the torture one of the soldiers says, "There. She looks like a daughter of God,"[29] clearly suggesting Joan as a figure of the Son of God, and as she dies, the crowd murmurs, "You have burned a saint," a phrase which in some sense echoes the centurion's reaction to the death of Jesus, "Truly this man was God's son" (Mt 27:54).

Beyond the content, Dreyer augments the sense of Joan's passion by means of several extradiegetical or formal choices. Paul Schrader points out how the architecture of Joan's world literally conspires against her: "Like the faces of her inquisitors, the halls, doorways, furniture are on the offensive, striking, swooping at her."[30] He continues: "Not only is poor Joan being attacked by the judges, the architecture, the lighting, but even the camera movement is conspiring against her. Dreyer's use of camera angle is also unabashed."[31] As well, Dreyer makes visual references to paintings of Christ's passion, especially to the painting of Hieronymous Bosch, "Christ Carrying the Cross" – a painting, as we have already noted, on which Scorsese bases his *via crucis* – and to other paintings in which the "theme is always the same . . . a face of Christ serene in its suffering, surrounded as if crushed by a filthy circle of bestial faces."[32] If Dreyer's Joan reflects the horror of the sufferings of Christ, she also mirrors the serenity which was demonstrated by Jesus in his passion. At one point, for example, she says to her inquisitors, "You are not real judges," which is rather like Jesus' words to Pilate, "You would have no power over me unless it had been given you from above." (Jn 19:11) Later on the scaffold, when a rope falls, Joan picks it up and "hands it to the executioner with a look of divine gentleness."[33]

Perhaps one of the most profound moments of the film, and a crucial turning point, is when Dreyer has Joan become aware that in her own passion, there is an image of the passion of Christ: "When Jeanne sees her crown of straw swept out by the barber, she recognizes both her betrayal of Christ and her likeness to him."[34] Dreyer recreates in Joan's passion the mysterious paradox of the passion and death of Jesus: "Like her Master Jesus, Joan is an incomprehensible 'sign of contradiction.'"[35] He pushes the association even further, suggesting in the failure of the death of the martyr, the profound Christian paradox of ultimate victory: "This is grace in all the bloom of martyrdom with the resurrection triumph coinciding with the act of death itself."[36]

The title of Robert Bresson's *The Trial of Joan of Arc*, like that of the film of Dreyer, announces both the director's narrative-thematic strategy and the way in which the protagonist is a Christ-figure. In general, the Christ-analogy is clear in Bresson's film. Touching on all the main issues of the film, Leo Murray explains:

> One of the things that struck Bresson most about the story of Joan was the analogy of her passion with that of Christ: betrayed to the enemy for a price, she is abandoned by her friends, tried illegally on false charges, tortured and finally put to death. This happened because of her fidelity to a vocation that she firmly believed came to her from God.[37]

In particular, the principal element of the analogy and of Bresson's Joan as a Christ-figure is her trial, which Jean Guitton sees as a illustration of the *imitatio Christi*.[38] Her passion is there, in the doubts, fear and temptations that assail her, and in the courage and nobility with which she deals with her inquisitors.

Bresson bases the script of his film on the actual transcripts of the trial of Joan at Rouen between January and May 1431, a "series of nine interrogations, five of them public in the trial room and four private in the cell":[39] the dialogue holds scrupulously to these transcripts. The style of Bresson's *Trial*, "the most ascetic of all his films,"[40] is anti-dramatic.[41] There is no music to speak off, no dramatic structure, and the actress who plays Joan, Florence Carrez, "simply reads the lines . . . there is no acting at all."[42] The film, without a discernible narrative line is "composed of static, medium shots of people talking; the scenes are the inexorable sequence of [Joan's] interrogations."[43] But within this linear structure and static style, in quite evident contrast to the highly dramatic, almost expressionistic style of Dreyer, Bresson builds a powerful analogy of the passion of Christ and clearly indicates Joan as a Christ-figure.

The basis of Bresson's representation of Joan as a figure of Christ is that of the fundamental christian paradox, that is, in his own words, the "general principle that 'the one who loses, wins.' To win, you have to lose . . . the analogy of *her passion* with the passion of Christ."[44] Then Bresson amplifies the Christ-association in a number of ways. Foremost of these is the courage with which he has Joan speak with her judges. Like Jesus, "Joan answers her corrupt inquisitors with sincerity, forthrightness, honesty, and complete disregard for her personal safety."[45] Like Jesus during his trial, Joan "is superior to her judges, first because she almost dominates them, to the point at times of seeming to direct the debates, and then because she accepts to be defeated and understands the necessity of the martyrdom."[46] As well, some of Joan's comments during the trial clearly echo words of Jesus: "I have come from God and have only to do his will here . . . I ask only to be sent back to God from whom I came,"[47] and again, "Oh Rouen, I have a great fear that you will suffer for my death."[48] Bresson gives his Joan another point of contact with Jesus in her awareness of having a divine call and mission, a conviction of a "supernatural order that makes her live and moves her to offer her life in response to a vocation that is providential,"[49] a certainty that she is doing the will of God, that "she cannot fulfill herself . . . except in free submission to the design of God."[50]

After the trial, Bresson represents the Christ-figure in Joan through a series of details in the final movement of the film which call to mind the crucifixion of Jesus. For example, the many shots of Joan's hands and feet are a reference to the fact that "on the Cross of Calvary, it is precisely in these two parts of the body that the nails were planted."[51] The fact that Bresson has Joan tripped as she moves through the crowd, the director himself explains, "has a certain connection with what happened to Christ when he went to be crucified. I mean the way Christ was mocked and molested."[52] Joan's curious, "almost *scampering* to the stake"[53] – her feet are chained together – suggests her willing submission to this ultimate sacrifice, and Bresson's choice to photograph her movement with a traveling shot creates a dynamic image of "the decisive moment in which the total sacrifice is fully assumed in the springing forth of her spirit finally liberated from fear."[54]

The execution scene repeats the cross-motif on several levels: in the stake as the "upright of the cross"[55] of Christ, image reinforced by the crucifix on the rosary she carries with her to the scaffold, by the simple cross made for her by an English soldier and by the processional cross held up for her by two Dominicans and shown repeatedly by Bresson. Finally, there is sense of a victory over death, of Resurrection victory. Bresson suggests it partway through the film with the sound of church bells ringing for Easter Sunday. Leo Murray insists that the bells tie together "Joan's suffering and the mystery of Easter Sunday which celebrates the victory of Jesus Christ over death."[56] Finally, in the film's conclusion, everything points to the sky above, to heaven: "the ladder that Joan must climb, the rising movement of the camera, the chains falling away to signify a release, and finally the bare stake pointing to the sky."[57] The final shot of the film, of the charred stake held on-screen for thirty-five seconds, becomes "an icon"[58] of Joan's victory, in the words of Jean Guitton, "a spiritual deliverance, martyrdom! Heavenly deliverance."[59]

2. The Priest as Christ-Figure

If the filmic saint is an apt vehicle for the Christ-figure, so is, though perhaps to a lesser extent, the priest or the minister, a character who through ordination is an *alter Christus*, who represents Christ in the celebration of the sacraments and who in his mission represents the pastoral teaching and guiding activity of Christ. Clearly not all filmic priests are Christ-figures. The identification is not automatic for, depending on the film, the priest can serve a variety of functions and meanings, one of which is as a caricature, that is as "the ineffectual support, the hand-ringing moralist, the platitudinous adviser, the remote commander, the plastic or unctuous hand-shaker."[60] For example, Bing Crosby's "warm, humorous, sentimental, common-sense"[61] priest in Leo McCarey's *Going My Way* (1945) and *The Bells of St. Mary's* (1946) cannot really be considered a Christ-figure. Neither can the cold, distant, psychologically-troubled and very secular priest of Nanni Moretti's *The Mass Has*

Ended (1985), who is more an ideological figure than anything else. The priests of Otto Preminger's *The Cardinal* (1963) and Frank Perry's *Monsignor* (1982) are straightforward melodramatic characters, and represent little authentically of the priest and nothing of the Christ-figure. The same must be said for the priests of Fellini's *8½* (1963), *Roma* (1972) and *Amarcord* (1973), all satirical caricatures. The servant-priest of the rich and powerful landowners in Bertolucci's epic film *1900* (1976) is a caricature-pawn of the film's dominant leftist ideology. In contrast, the parish priest of Olmi's parallel film, *The Tree of the Wooden Clogs*, is a bold, imaginative and prophetic figure, a man of charity, an effective pastor and clearly a Christ-figure. In John Ford's film, *The Fugitive* (1947), based on the Graham Greene novel, *The Power and the Glory*, the priest-protagonist is a weak man and a sinner. In the end, however, during a violent persecution of priests and religious, he chooses to stay behind "to serve his flock even though it means capture, arrest, and execution."[62] Ford signals the christic quality of his decision by photographing him in a long shot with three large crosses included in the composition.

In some films, the priest is a negative foil to the authentic Christ-figure incarnated in one of the other characters. For example, in Bergman's *Winter Light* (1962), the pastor-protagonist is a cold man without faith, isolated in his egoism, clearly an unworthy foil to the real Christ-figure, the sacristan, who "stands out in an otherwise secular world because of his key redemptive role."[63] In his intense physical pain carried with quiet patience, the man clearly images the suffering servant of Isaiah, and through him, Christ. The turning point in the film comes towards the end when the sexton, looking at a large crucifix in the church, says to the skeptical pastor "That must have been terrible suffering." Thus, in his persona and in his words, "the cripple puts everything back into place again by echoing symbolically the death of Christ on the cross."[64]

Dreyer in *Ordet* follows the same procedure. The pastor who presides at the wake of the dead Inger, a liberal theologically, is distant and out of touch, and his agnostic faith is in contrast to the pure and effective faith of the little girl and of the Christ-figure, Johannes. In the recent film *Dead Man Walking*, the prison chaplain, with his cautious, skeptical approach to ministry, is a negative foil to the Christ-figure which shines forth in Sister Helen Prejean. An interesting variation on this theme can be seen in Buñuel's *Nazarin*. The priest-protagonist makes great efforts to be a Christ-figure throughout the film, all without success. Only in the conclusion, when on his way to prison, his *via crucis*, he humbly and gratefully accepts a refreshing pineapple from a peasant woman, does the Word become flesh in him.

Interesting in this regard too are the films which feature several priests. The effect is often subtle variations on the Christ-figure theme, different degrees of identification with Christ in each of the priests. In Roland Joffé's *Mission* (1986), for example, "the Church figures vary greatly regarding their resemblance to Christ."[65] There is the transparent Christ-figure of the priest-martyr crucified on the cross going over the Aguazú Falls in the opening sequence; there is the Jeremy Irons-character, Father Gabriel, whose gentle non-violence leads to his death in the conclusion; in contrast to him, there is the Robert De Niro-character, Mendoza, also a priest who at the end of the film reverts to violence as a response to violence and thus negates what there was in him of the Christ-figure. Finally, there is the Papal legate, Altamirano, who is not a bad man but whose compromising compliance with political realities against the simple and poor indios of the mission, keeps him far from being a Christ-figure. On the other hand, Antonia Bird's scandal film, *The Priest* (1995), is fatally-unbalanced by an overload of "crucial" and contentious issues, by an irregular style and by five priests, all of them who are caricatures,[66] and who illustrate, if anything, five degrees of distance from the authentic Christ-figure.

Alfred Hitchcock, in the priest-protagonist of his film, *I Confess*, represents a classic and "explicit Christ figure."[67] Having heard the confession of a murderer, Father Logan is then framed by this same man. Accused by the police of the murder, Logan chooses to respect the seal of the sacrament of confession and to say nothing, even at the risk of being convicted of the murder himself. The spiritual anguish he lives through, his passion, reflects the passion of Christ. This association, clear in the dynamic of the film and in Logan as a priest, is underlined by Hitchcock in a series of visual signals or clues. While Logan climbs by night through the hilly streets of Québec City[68] – "enacting his Calvary"[69] – as he decides how to deal with this impossible moral-spiritual dilemma, Hitchcock composes one of his shots to include both Logan weighed down by the "cross" he is bearing, and a large bronze statue of Christ carrying his cross, part of an outdoor monumental way of the cross in a park. Later in the courtroom, as Logan refuses to give any information that would compromise the sacrament, Hitchcock tilts the camera upward, thus keeping Logan in the frame but revealing behind him a crucifix on the wall.

The priest-protagonist of Rossellini's *Open City,* having helped his people during the Nazi occupation of Rome, dies a martyr to protect those fighting for freedom in the resistance. A Christ-figure in his death, Rossellini gives the priest a kind of resurrection in the group of boys who witness his execution and walk back into Rome. Rossellini has the protagonist of his film supported by the Communist resistance leader, whom he makes into a less typical Christ-figure. Though this man is far removed from the Christian faith, he suffers the same fate as the priest, and for the same reason. During the shocking scenes of his torture and death, the man is shown in one close-up in which "he strikingly resembles the traditional images of the face of Christ on the cross."[70]

Two films have been made based on Georges Bernanos' novel, *The Diary of a Country Priest*. Robert Bresson in his *The Diary of a Country Priest*, a film we shall consider more in depth in the next chapter, represents in his protagonist an image of the passion of Christ. As well, Maurice Pialat, in

Under Satan's Sun, based on Bernanos' *Diary* and another of his novels, makes a Christ-figure out of his priest-protagonist. As we have already noted, as a priest, and in his struggle against evil, *Père* Donissan is an *alter Christus*, and though the film at times is confused and uneven, and is not a spiritual masterpiece like Bresson's, as a healer and a confessor-forgiver of sins, Donissan clearly represents Christ. When he dies in the confessional, with his eyes open and a brilliant light from above on his face, Pialat seems to be suggesting in him a resurrection victory.

3. The Woman As Christ-figure

A good number of films portray women as Christ-figures. As we have already seen in chapter two, Fellini's *La strada* and *Nights of Cabiria* are films in which the protagonist represents some aspects of the Christ-figure, and *Out of Rosenheim, Babette's Feast* and *Dead Man Walking*, have as protagonists women who in their persona and in their activities represent the full dynamic of the Christ-figure. There are also several films in which "canonised women saints are an obvious example of feminine Christ-figures."[71] We have already seen, for example, how the films of Dreyer and Bresson on Joan of Arc are considered to be among the finest examples of cinematic Christ-figures. A careful analysis of Cavalier's *Thérèse* would yield similar results.

Here we will consider briefly Ingmar Bergman's *Cries and Whispers* (1972), an exceptionally beautiful but very difficult film which, in its conclusion, represents in a woman a splendid Christ-figure. The carrier of the image is Agnes, one of three sisters, who in the course of the film suffers a long and painful death. Her sisters are repelled by the spectacle of this horrible death and only the maid, Anna, can approach the dead woman. She takes Agnes into her arms, "like an earth mother [and] cradles her corpse as a dead Christ in 'Pietà' fashion."[72] In a profoundly moving prayer to the dead woman, the Pastor officiating at her burial clearly suggests dimensions of the Christ-figure[73] in her experience. He says, "You have gathered our suffering into your poor body," making her a sacrificial scapegoat (or lamb: *agnus*-Agnes); he continues, "If it is so that you can speak the language that this God understands . . . then speak to this God . . . pray for us," making Agnes a mediator for them before God; and finally, he concludes: "Lay your burden of suffering at God's feet and ask Him to pardon us," thus identifying Agnes as a redeemer-savior.

4. Some Extreme Christ-Figures: The Clown, the Fool, the Madman

One of the most unlikely guises for the Christ-figure in film is the clown or fool, or sometimes, the madman. Michael Graff justifies this strange category of Christ-figure by pointing out that in the Gospel, "Jesus is treated as a clown in his Passion. He is slapped, ridiculed and dressed as a mock king."[74] Reflecting also the suffering servant of Yahweh, "Jesus is a sad clown, a butt of cruel jokes."[75] Typically, the clown, the court jester, reveals the truth, and then is punished for doing so.

Charlie Chaplin in *Limelight* (1952) is a clown-Christ-figure. His name in the film, Calvero, a variation on Calvary, already signals his christic identity, as does the soteriological dynamic of his activity. Though a down-and-out comedian and past his prime, he rescues a woman so desperate that she is about to commit suicide. He cares for her and inspires her to resume her dancing career. When she finally goes on stage, Calvero is in the wings; she does well, but he has a heart attack and dies, happy for her and peaceful. "The way Calvero is carried out is reminiscent of paintings of the descent from the cross."[76] Clearly, the hope that Chaplin shows us in the dancer, her re-birth artistically, is a "resurrection image."[77] Calvero lives on in her. A clown-Christ-figure is also the protagonist of Pasolini's *La ricotta*. Stracci is a comic figure in the manner of Chaplin, and the object of repeated ridicule and cruel jokes on the part of his companions. In his suffering, he reveals some profound truths about human indifference and cruelty, and in the end, he dies, Christ-like, on a cross.

Very different from Chaplinesque figures, and anything but comic, is the character Johannes in Dreyer's *Ordet*. A deeply enigmatic figure, he incarnates both the sacral and delusions, both holiness and lunacy and he represents the great paradox – the sign of contradiction – of the word of truth in the mouth of the madman. In front of two families, "two ways of praying to God, each one jealous of the other and convinced that they are in the right,"[78] Johannes insists to all who will hear him that he is Jesus Christ; he preaches the words of Christ in the fields and to the wind. His claim is as absurd for his people as was that of Jesus for his family, who were convinced that he was out of his mind (Mk 3:21). Considered by some a "pseudo-Christ,"[79] it seems clear that when, in the conclusion of the film, freed of his delusions (rather like Father Nazario at the end of Buñuel's *Nazarin*) and his faith strengthened by the pure faith of his little niece, Johannes performs the life-giving miracle, he is an image of the Word-become-flesh, a true Christ-figure.

A short film produced for the Protestant pavilion at the 1964-65 New York World's Fair[80] was conceived as an extended metaphor of the Christ story. Entitled, perhaps too obviously, *Parable*, its protagonist is a clown in a circus in which a group of human puppets are sadistically manipulated by a villain called Magnus. The clown, seen in a parade riding a donkey, becomes the leader of the victims, and so is persecuted by the authorities. Eventually he frees the human puppets by taking their place. In their place he is cruelly put to death. When the parade comes through a second time, the clown, dressed in white, is there. He is risen. The narrative of *Parable* is so close to the dynamic of the life and death of Jesus that it might more accurately be entitled "*Allegory*."[81]

5. The Outlaw as Christ-Figure

While there is no problem with a Christ-figure represented by a reformed criminal or repentant sinner, there remains the delicate question of whether an outlaw, an unrepentant sinner or a vulgar and brutal man without a hint of conversion, can have dimensions of a Christ-figure. In Pasolini's film *Accattone*, Accattone is a cruel bully and in Scorsese's *Raging Bull*, Jake La Motta is a sadistic prize fighter, but both are pictured in typical Christ-on-the-cross poses. Stracci in Pasolini's *La ricotta* is a petty thief, but he dies on the cross. Of Stracci, Maurizio Viano insists: "a seemingly vulgar man with a gargantuan appetite, is in fact a Christ-figure."[82] In a rather different key, in the bloody conclusion of his early and very violent film, *Boxcar Bertha* (1972), Martin Scorsese has the male lead, the outlaw Bill Shelley, a man with few redeeming features, literally crucified to the side of a boxcar by some railway men who are taking their revenge for his spree of train-robbing and killing. To complete the crucifixion-image, the inimitable Scorsese has the men nail a little notice above the crucified man's head. Finally, there is the famous shot in George Stevens' film *Giant* (1956), in which Jett Rink, played by James Dean, a victim though anything but sympathetic, rests his arms on a rifle slung over his shoulders and bows his head, in a precise visual reference to Christ crucified. A young Elizabeth Taylor kneeling at his feet and looking up at him completes this peculiar Calvary-image.

Michael Graff explains that these far from edifying characters can represent dimensions of the Christ-image because they are "not only culprits but also victims,"[83] and he goes on to explain that "it is not that the outlaw as outlaw represents Christ, but rather that the crucified Christ stands near him. The point is that the cross is always in a crucifixion group [of Jesus and the two thieves]."[84] Neil Hurley suggests a different and interesting justification of the filmic "bad guy" as a Christ-figure, explaining that "the nature of Jesus' death as a criminal, incontrovertible as a historical datum, makes the persecution and death of certain rebels take on a mystical aura."[85]

6. The Child as Christ-Figure

Vincent Ward's film *The Navigator: A Medieval Odyssey* is one of the few films in which a child embodies aspects of the redeemer, the one who saves his people. In this science-fiction film, an exceptional child, Griffin, who has the rare ability to see Good and Evil, and the ability to travel back and forth in time, finds himself in a medieval town threatened by the plague. Identified specifically with Christ crucified as the Messiah when he climbs the bell-tower of the Cathedral to fix a cross on the peak, Griffin has to die in order to save the people. Another and a rather unlikely film to represent an image of Christ in a child is James Cameron's *Terminator 2: The Day of Judgment* (1991). The film is clearly meant to be an action-packed adventure vehicle for Arnold Schwarzenegger, but the critic, Michael Graff identifies as a Christ-figure the boy pursued by the evil "Terminator" because he has extraordinary powers and is destined to become leader of a future human resistance-liberation movement. Graff proposes the boy's name as the definitive clue to his christological identity: John Connors, the initials J.C. for Jesus Christ.[86] Graff does not push the synthesis any further and justly so, for the film with its repeated scenes of exaggerated and gratuitous violence does not warrant it.

7. The Dramatic Role of Jesus as Christ-Figure

One of the rarest and most curious guises for the filmic Christ-figure is that of Jesus in a dramatic presentation. In this modality, the Christ-figure is embodied in the person and actions of an actor playing the role of Jesus in a representation of the passion. One of these films in Dassin's *He Who Must Die*, based on Nikos Kazantzakis' novel, *The Greek Passion*. Dassin represents the Christ-figure in a rather weak man, chosen to play the role of Jesus in the passion play of his village, and who then finds the courage to resist the injustice of the local Orthodox priest and finally to offer himself as sacrificial victim to save a group of poor refugees. Arcand's film, *Jesus of Montreal*, as we saw in chapter one, not only repeats this pattern but creates a much closer identification between the young actor and the role he is playing, and perhaps even with the real Jesus "behind" that role. Then in Pasolini's *La ricotta*, there is a fascinating variation on the theme: Stracci, the film's Christ-figure, in fact dies on the cross ridiculed and abandoned; but, as we have already noted, Stracci is acting the role, not of Christ but of the good thief.

8. The Popular Adventure Hero as Christ-Figure

One of the most common vehicles of the Christ-figure in cinema is the popular adventure film. In these films the protagonists, in dimensions of their personalities and in aspects of their behavior, reflect elements of the story of Jesus Christ, though clearly in a less intense and less authentic manner than in some of the spiritual masterpieces already examined. In George Lucas' science-fiction blockbuster *Star Wars* (1977), for example, the protagonist, a young, innocent but very brave Luke Skywalker becomes a "disciple"[87] of an older figure, Obi-Wan Kenobi, who on a number of levels represents Jesus Christ: he "lives simply, imparting wisdom and giving good example to people like Luke"[88] and he opposes evil in the person of the villain Darth Vader. A man totally dedicated to his "mission,"[89] Obi-Wan even " physically resembles . . . Jesus.[90] He greets Luke with the expression "blessing,"[91] "The Force be with you!" thus calling to mind the words Jesus spoke to greet and reassure his fearful disciples after his death and Resurrection, "Peace be with you." (Jn 20:19). Finally, in his death, Obi-Wan Kenobi "completes the allegorical link to Christ."[92]

A paraphrase of "the Life and Passion of Christ in a southern chain gang,"[93] Stuart Rosenberg's film *Cool Hand Luke* represents in the person and behavior of the protagonist the basic dynamics of the Christ-event. For a minor offence committed while drunk, Luke, played very effectively by Paul Newman, is sent to prison and is working on a chain gang. Because the punishment is much exaggerated for his crime, there is a sense in which Luke is innocent. A sympathetic character with a very "independent spirit,"[94] Luke does not let himself be defeated or broken by the system and for this, he suffers cruel treatment at the hands of the guards, yet wins the respect of the fellow inmates for whom he becomes the object of "hero worship."[95] At one point, Luke has a fistfight with the boss of the chain-gang, and afterwards Rosenberg creates a clear visual reference to Jesus in a shot of Luke with a white towel over his head and his "disciples" around him. "It is Luke's dwelling among sinners, his being prepared to suffer for the other convicts who have become his 'disciples,' and for being the 'man who will not conform,' that makes him a kind of Christ figure."[96]

As with Christ and the religious authorities of his time, the tension builds between Luke and the prison authorities, to the point where it becomes clear that he has to be eliminated, that is, sacrificed for the good of the prison population. Like Jesus, he is betrayed by one of his friends. As he hides in a chapel awaiting death, he makes an impassioned and very personal prayer to God, clearly a reference to Jesus' prayer to God in Gethsemane. After Luke's death, his fellow inmates gather in the prison yard and recall with "nostalgic fondness"[97] and hope his great courageous deeds, suggesting the beginning of an oral tradition. "A kind of resurrection is implied in this scene."[98]

Elia Kazan's film, *On the Waterfront,* is dense with themes from the New Testament, a veritable "biblical concordance."[99] Based on the true story of the Jesuit priest, John Corridan, who worked as chaplain to dock workers in New York in the 1950s, it stars Karl Malden as Father Barry,[100] a priest who is represented as a Christ-figure. Boldly proclaiming the rights of the workers against corrupt union leaders and the mob, at one point Kazan has him preach a dramatic sermon from the hold of a ship where one of his men has been killed by the mob. He is hit by an object thrown by a mob bully, and bleeds from the side of his head, but he does not stop speaking the truth.

Opposite Malden is a young Marlon Brando, playing an ex-boxer Terry Malloy, who has thrown a fight for the mob. He regretfully insists he could have been a "contenduh." Having met Father Barry, Malloy has a conversion-experience, by which Barry's Christ-figure role is given another facet: like the healing Christ, he is a bridge "reconciling a fallen man to a forgiving God."[101] Through Barry, Malloy learns self-respect and integrity, and becomes a "contenduh" morally – and the second Christ-figure of the film – by revealing important information about the mob to the authorities. Clearly Malloy is destined to die, a conclusion consistent with the plot and the development of the character, but the producers opted for a happy ending. In "a ritual sacrifice,"[102] Malloy is badly beaten and in his bruised body and bloody face, Kazan represents a "muted crucifixion . . . a waterfront crucifixion without the nails."[103] At the end of the fight, Kazan includes a shot in which this

Christ-figure, blood flowing down his face, is held up by Father Barry and his girlfriend, a clear visual reference to the "Pietà." The violence Malloy suffers for having chosen to speak the truth becomes the image of the passion of Christ, a "veritable *via crucis*,"[104] and by giving the film a happy ending, showing Malloy rising from the brutal beating, Kazan concludes with an "uplifting resurrection motif."[105]

Another popular film with an incontrovertible and powerful christological subtext, as we have already suggested, is Milos Forman's *One Flew Over the Cuckoo's Nest*. Based on the best-selling homonymous novel by Ken Kesey, it became an international hit and won five Academy Awards.[106] A black comedy set in a hospital for the criminally insane, its protagonist is Randle Patrick McMurphy, played superbly by Jack Nicholson, and in the course of the film, he becomes "an unlikely, even irreverent, messianic figure . . . in whose life, suffering, and death he [Forman] finds an analogue to the Jewish-Christian figure of the Suffering Servant."[107] Forman clearly intends the asylum as a "metaphor for contemporary society itself,"[108] a world in which there is a situation of repression, of total control by violence, overt and covert, which denies the people living in it freedom, hope and a future. There is no doubt that this world needs a savior, a Christ-figure. The savior is given in the person of McMurphy who comes to the hospital, after having feigned insanity to avoid going to work on a prison farm for statutory rape.[109]

As soon as the perfectly-sane McMurphy arrives, he begins to live a series of major confrontations with Nurse Ratched. He realizes the inmates are not in fact crazy but rather totally intimidated by the authorities. He eventually gets them on his side by speaking the truth to them, what he calls "reality therapy," intended to liberate them. When McMurphy and another inmate, a Native American called Chief Bromden, are subjected to shock therapy, he asks ironically but significantly, "Do I get a crown of thorns?" The confrontations between McMurphy and the authorities continue, and finally he realizes that his time is up, that he is about to be lobotomized. His only chance is to escape, but he insists on having one last party with his friends, for which he smuggles whiskey and two women into the ward. An image of the Last Supper, the party becomes a liturgy of freedom and individual integrity and life. As Ratched and the authorities arrive, McMurphy risks all by staying behind to help Ratched's worst victim, Billy Bibbit get back his human integrity. Of course, he is caught, and Bibbit, intimidated once again by Nurse Ratched, betrays him, tells all, and then out of remorse, kills himself. McMurphy attacks Ratched, is subdued and lobotomized, and subsequently Chief Bromden, wanting to release McMurphy from this living death, smothers him in his arms, and then runs to his freedom, cheered on by the inmates.

Clearly the story of McMurphy is full of "disguised parallels to the life of Jesus."[110] Thus the sacrifice and liberation dynamic of McMurphy's mission does not stand merely on its own, but is widened and strengthened by "the spiritual and cultural power of two thousand years of tradition."[111] Some of these christic parallels have already been suggested above: the liberator entering an oppressive world and into conflict with the authorities, the calling of disciples, the teaching and healing ministry, the death plot against him of which he is aware, the last meal, the betrayal, arrest and crucifixion. But there are many other signs of McMurphy's christological identity. When, for example, the director of the hospital asks him who he "really" is, McMurphy, pointing to his dossier, answers, "What does it say there?" clearly echoing Jesus' "Who do the crowds say that I am?" (Lk 9:18).[112] McMurphy is different from the inmates but he enters fully into their world, a suggestion of the Incarnation, and he proceeds, as did Jesus, to "defy the petty legalisms imposed by the authorities."[113] He takes his "disciples" on an outing to a nearby river, so that they can fish, insisting: "You're no longer loonies, but fisherman," a precise reference to Jesus' calling the apostles and making them "fish for people" (Lk 4:19).

At the end, knowing the danger involved, McMurphy freely chooses to stay behind to help Bibbit. Bibbit's betrayal and suicide echoes those of Judas. The lobotomy on McMurphy becomes his crucifixion, after which one of the staff says that McMurphy is "upstairs, meek as a lamb," a reference to the sacrificial lamb, Jesus the Christ, the Lamb of God. When Chief Bromden holds the dead McMurphy in his arms, Forman creates a composition reminiscent of the "Pietà," and when Bromden, having ripped out a water fountain (living water flows), breaks out of the asylum, he is cheered on by enthusiastic shouts of "He is risen." The concluding images are an unequivocal visual metaphor of Paschal victory: "The Chief, the camera, and we are all liberated from the enprisonment [sic] of the ward and returned to that freedom and beauty of the natural wilderness."[114]

7

Christ-Figures in the Films of Bresson and Tarkovsky

Beyond studying the representation of Christ-figures in single films, one can approach the theme by considering how film *auteurs* develop images of Christ in several of their films. This *auteur* approach to the Christ-figure would be fruitful with, for example, the earlier films of Pier Paolo Pasolini, some of which we have already discussed, or with the films of John Ford. There are however two other film-makers, both *auteurs*, both within the Christian tradition, both giants in world of cinema, whose work stands out for its high Christian spiritual significance and impact. The Frenchman, Robert Bresson, and the Russian, Andrei Tarkovsky, of whom we have already spoken repeatedly, create in their films a variety of complex figurative images of Christ. In this concluding chapter, we shall take a brief look at a selection of these films.

The Films of Robert Bresson

Robert Bresson made thirteen films between 1934 and 1983, on a variety of subjects, but all of them shot through and through with Christian and christological themes, in which "analogies to Christ and relationships with the scriptures never cease."[1] Already we have considered in some detail Bresson's *The Trial of Joan of Arc* and his masterpiece *Au hasard Balthazar*. Here we will analyze two other Bresson films. Though most of the French director's protagonists represent "allusions to the life of Christ,"[2] each represents different dimensions of the Christ-event: Bresson "multiplies the images of Christ in his work, refusing, as did the Evangelists themselves, to present a single unique of the Savior."[3] Often however, the Bressonian Christ-figure assumes the guise of the suffering servant: "the figure of the Just One, scoffed at and insulted, which represents Jesus in the profound depths of his Incarnation, overpowered by human misery and suffering."[4]

This dynamic pattern of the passion of Christ, operative in most of Bresson's films, is not always easy to discern, in part because he has a very sophisticated and often extremely subtle style, difficult to follow and appreciate, and in part because, for Bresson, "every human being carries his own cross, different from that of others, but in the end always identifiable with that of the son of God."[5] His characters are complex: some are innocent, others guilty; some die, others live; some are victims till the end, others are victorious. But they are all intelligent and aware, and mysterious: "even in their most extreme confidences, they never fundamentally reveal anything but their mystery – like God himself."[6]

One of Bresson's most common approaches to human suffering is the use of the metaphor of the prison: people in prison, people locked into mental or moral prisons, people going into prison, people escaping. "All of Bresson's films have a common theme: the meaning of confinement and liberty."[7] The Christ-symbolism in the protagonist is perhaps most clear when the experience of confinement, that is the passion suffered, is due to the sinfulness of others, when it is "the alienation caused by the egoism and the hostility of other people."[8]

Elements of Bresson's film-style underline the transcendent or christological reach of his protagonists. In a landmark book, Paul Schrader analyzes in detail what he refers to as Bresson's "transcendental style,"[9] which includes the use of unknown actors, an anti-dramatic acting style and non-expressive recitation. In his compositions and in the photography of his protagonists, Bresson imitates Byzantine iconography: "the long forehead, the lean features, the closed lips, the blank stare, the frontal view, the flat light, the uncluttered background, the stationary camera, these identify Bresson's protagonists as objects suitable for veneration."[10] Finally, in the concluding shot of each of his films, Bresson creates an image of stasis: "Stasis is the quiescent, frozen or hieratic scene which succeeds the decisive action and closes the film."[11] In *The Diary of a Country Priest*, the stasis is in the shadow of a cross; in *A Man Escaped* (1956), it is expressed in "the long shot of the darkened street,"[12] and the music of the Mozart "Kyrie;" in *The Trial of Joan of Arc*, it is the charred stump of the stake"[13] at which Joan has been burned; and in *Au hasard Balthazar*, the stasis is created by the long shot held on the dying donkey. For Bresson, this moment of stasis, supported by the other techniques, points to the Transcendent.

Perhaps Bresson's best known film, *The Diary of a Country Priest*, recounts the story, told in the first person, of the parish priest of Ambricourt, a young man who has had little success in his parish and who is dying of cancer. In the life and death of the priest, Bresson represents more transparently than in any other of his films the passion and death of Christ, thus creating in the priest an eloquent Christ-figure. Bresson suggests the identification of the young man with Christ, first of all because, as we have already said in the preceding chapter, as a priest, he is an *alter Christus*, a figure of Christ, and more specifically especially by creating in him an eloquent example of the suffering servant of Yahweh, that is, of Christ in his passion. The stomach cancer from which the priest suffers and which brings about his death becomes his "stigmata;"[14] the identification with Christ is underlined by the fact that because of the disease, the priest limits himself to eating bread dipped in wine, a distinct allusion to the Eucharist and to the Last Supper.

Though the priest's physical suffering is important, Bresson builds the suffering servant-Christ analogy mostly on the basis of the man's moral, psychological suffering, his experience of isolation, of being in a sense imprisoned. Bresson suggests the first motif of isolation-imprisonment in the man's priesthood. Susan Sontag says that in Bresson, "the imagery of the religious vocation and of crime are used jointly. Both lead 'to the cell.'"[15] In the case of the priest of Ambricourt, the "cell" is multileveled. The Bresson-expert Jean Sémolué speaks of three levels of the priest's imprisonment or aliena-tion.[16] Beyond the first level, that of the priest's sickness, his sense of being prisoner in a body that is slowly, painfully destroying him, there is the second level of the priest's social imprisonment, for the man is almost totally isolated from the people to whom he is to minister. He is full of fears and doubts about his ministry, about his effectiveness as a priest; the people avoid him, they walk away from him, they reject him. "The priest is condemned to suffer in the 'prison' created by the indifference, the mistrust or the hostility of others."[17] Bresson represents this isolation from the people in a "*leitmotiv* created by the shots of fences and grills,"[18] barriers with which repeatedly he separates the priest from other people.

The third level of the priest's isolation is that of the sacred solitude of his struggle with evil and sinfulness: "The priest is unable to cope with the world of sin, either in himself or others. The normal recourse of a Christian, prayer, is not open to him."[19] Bresson represents this terrible struggle of his protagonist by having him describe it in first person, both in the diary we see him writing, and in the voice-over commentary through which he reveals the depths of his soul. It seems as if the priest is, in fact, unable to relate to any of the elements in his environment; "even nature . . . seems hostile to the suffering priest as he collapses under the gray sky and tall dark barren trees."[20] Bresson has the face of the young actor, Claude Laydu, become a mirror which, by reflecting "his trials, his failures, the outrages inflicted on him, his wounds, [reveals] the Way of the Cross, the Passion, which reaches its fulfillment in the final image of the Cross, towards which the entire film has been moving."[21]

Bresson gives his protagonist a high degree of self-awareness in this passion: his diary which acts as a spiritual frame for the film, reveals this. "Little by little, as if moving down the Way of the Cross, the priest comes to realize"[22] that, in his own words, he is a "prisoner of His [Christ's] Sacred Passion," the priest "associates his agony with the sacrificial agony of Christ."[23] Speaking with his spiritual director, the Vicar of Torcy, a superfi-cial man much in contrast to him, the priest of Ambricourt says that he feels he has the divine mission to accomplish and prolong in his own flesh and spirit the holy agony of Christ. Bresson gives biblical allusions to this conver-sation by having it take place on the summit of a hill – "clearly an image of Calvary"[24] – and during the scene, he has us hear the barking of a sheepdog and the bells of a flock of lambs, going to the slaughter: "A holocaust of lambs representing the sacrifice of the Lamb of God, and of all those who carry on his work of love."[25] It is clear from his conversations and from the words in his diary that the priest lives his awful suffering with a conscious redemptive intention: he opens himself up completely "to the strikes against him,"[26] convinced on both the human and the supernatural levels, that letting himself be killed by these blows and accepting with joy this murderous fate, will assure the liberation of these bound souls [his parishioners]."[27]

Bresson supports the content of his film by surrounding the priest with a heavy funereal atmosphere, in low-contrast black and white and somber grey tones, thus creating a world from which the presence of God seems to have withdrawn, clearly an appropriate atmosphere for the passion. Bresson breaks the heaviness in one moment, in the scene when the priest goes for an exhilarating lyrical motorcycle ride with a friend. But even this moment points to Calvary: it is Palm Sunday and the joyful ride is a transparent image of the entry of Jesus into Jerusalem.

Already in *The Diary of Country Priest*, the director reveals some aspects of his transcendental style: the compositions and images in the style of Eastern iconic art, seen in the many close-ups of the priest and in a remarkable shot of him at the top of a barren hill looking skyward, a "composition familiar to Byzantine [mosaic] wall painting."[28] Finally, in the conclusion of the film, the moment of the priest's death and resurrection, Bresson creates a long moment of contemplative stasis: in a shot held for a long ninety seconds, he creates "the shadow of the cross cast on a wall . . . a blatant symbol"[29] of the salvific death of Jesus Christ lived in the death of the country priest.

Bresson's fourth film, *A Man Escaped* (1956), already in its original title suggests the christological motif of Resurrection: *Un condamné à mort s'est échappé* or "A man condemned to death has escaped." Based on the true story of a resistance fighter imprisoned by the Gestapo in Montluc Prison in Lyon who in 1943 escaped from the prison, the action of the film is limited mostly to the prison and to the cell of the protagonist, Fontaine. In this confined space, through the few contacts Fontaine has with his fellow-prisoners, and particularly in his voice-over commentary as he later recounts the story of his escape, Bresson creates in Fontaine an image of profound human nobility, of undying hope.

Christological echoes abound in Fontaine's behavior throughout the film: he becomes a focus of the interest and the hope of the other prisoners, a moral leader. He plays a clearly soteriological role for the old man Blanchet in the cell next to his, who is in despair and to whom Fontaine "gives back a desire to live."[30] On one of his furtive night-time excursions within the prison, he erases from the cell door of one of his neighbors the indication that this man is to be deprived of visits to the yard and of food. Certainly for the young Jost, his cellmate, he is a guide and help: at one point Bresson has him (Fontaine – fountain) give Jost water to drink, a gesture dense with Gospel echos, and in the end he leads Jost to freedom. Curiously, Bresson also gives Fontaine a precursor, a kind of John the Baptist who prepares the way for him, in the person of Orsini. Orsini's ill-fated attempt to escape gives Fontaine the information he needs to escape. As they hear the gunshots of Orsini's execution, the old man Blanchet says to Fontaine: "He had to fail so that you might succeed," echoing the dynamic of John the Baptist and ultimately, of the redemptive salvific mission of Jesus, who died so that we might live.

In addition to these christological allusions, Bresson includes several "explicit, salvific references"[31] in the film. One is the Gospel story of the conversation between Jesus and Nicodemus (Jn 3:1-10), a text given to Fontaine by a priest-prisoner, a text which Bresson has Fontaine read to Blanchet just when Orsini is executed. In the Gospel text, the dynamic is that of Christ revealing himself to Nicodemus as the salvific Son of Man. Bresson has the text, of which the crucial phrase is: "The wind blows where it chooses . . . but you do not know where it comes from or where it goes" (vs. 8), become an announcement of the post-Resurrection Pentecost Spirit, the Spirit of the Risen Christ. Undoubtedly the most crucial christological reference in *A Man Escaped* is that of the music and words of the "Kyrie Eleison" from Mozart's "Mass in C Minor," which Bresson periodically inserts on the otherwise ascetic soundtrack of the film, and each time, the "Kyrie" is connected with the motif of escaping, of resurrection. In the conclusion of the film, as Fontaine and Jost walk down the road into the night and freedom, "the choirs explode again,"[32] with the Mozart "Kyrie," clearly praising the mercy of God who gives Resurrection-victory.

Four Films of Andrei Tarkovsky

The films of the great Russian director Andrei Tarkovsky[33] are dense with Christian and christological themes, and his protagonists embody incontrovertible dimensions of the Christ-figure. Tarkovsky is far too intelligent and complex an artist to create simple and straightforward allegories of the Christ-event in his films: it would be better to speak of multiple allusions to the Christ-event in his characters. In *Andrei Roublev* (1966), a stunningly beautiful film of epic scope, more a "historical fresco"[34] than a narrative, about the Russian monk and icon-painter Roublev, Tarkovsky alludes repeatedly to the Christ-event. He even entitles one chapter of the film "The Passion of Andrei,"[35] and in it, he has his protagonist experience a vision of Christ carrying his cross – a "Breughel-like"[36] *via crucis* through a Russian setting – to Calvary: and the "Christ dragging his cross looks very much like Andrei."[37] During his vision, Tarkovsky has Andrei recite a long monologue in which he reflects on the sense of the death of Christ relative to the situation of the suffering of the peasants in Russia in his day, a monologue which also clearly refers to Andrei's own suffering and passion:

> Evils continue to fall on the back of the peasant. . . . He [Christ-the peasant] carries his cross with courage, without losing hope, enduring all without a complaint. . . . You talk to me about Christ. Perhaps it is for that reason that he was crucified. To reconcile God and humanity.[38]

In Andrei's "own perception of Golgotha,"[39] in the uncontrolled violence and terrifying social chaos that he is witnessing as he travels through Russia, he seems to consider himself as a "willing victim to redeem these ignorant and innocent people, a meek Christ walking barefoot through the snow of a village street."[40]

It is however, especially in the conclusion of *Andrei Roublev* that Tarkovsky allows his film to explode with imagery of the passion and Resurrection of Christ. After the miraculous casting of a great bell for a cathedral, in itself "an image of renewal and hope,"[41] Tarkovsky has Andrei kneel at the foot of an upright wooden beam (the cross), cradling in his arms the young man-creator of the bell in an evident Pietà reference, and it is at this point, to the sound of the ringing bell, that Andrei dies to his vow, made earlier in the film, not to paint. Tarkovsky marks his decision to resume painting – to rise from death to new life as an artist, "to show this life transformed"[42] – by shifting his film from black-and-white to color, and by marking its conclusion with an explosion of images in brilliant colors from Roublev's greatest icons, including such details as: crosses, Christ on the donkey on Palm Sunday, Christ in the Garden of Gethsemane, the dove of the Spirit, the crib of Bethlehem, John the Baptist, the baptism of Christ, and finally, the three angels of the masterpiece, "The Trinity." Tarkovsky himself says of this concluding montage: "We wanted to lead the spectator, by a succession of details, to a total view of the 'Trinity,' the summit of Roublev's art."[43] This brilliant celebration of Resurrection-victory extends beyond Roublev all the way to the film-maker himself: "The images of *The Trinity* become the sign of the fulfillment not only of Roublev but also of Tarkovsky, as if the old monk, painter of icons . . . had succeeded, through the centuries, in transmitting his secret to the young film-maker."[44]

In the protagonist of *Stalker* (1979), "a Dostoevskian blessed one,"[45] a poor man "who is weak in the world's eyes but determined to maintain his integrity, a 'Fool for Christ,'"[46] Tarkovsky incarnates dimensions of Christ the Master, the one who leads and teaches his disciples. In this eerie, semi-science-fiction film[47] – "Neither the country nor the date are made clear"[48] – the Stalker, the only name Tarkovsky gives him, at great risk guides two others, Writer and Scientist, men who search for the truth, into a forbidden and forbidding "Zone." He leads them on the voyage deeper and deeper into its secrets, and in the end persuades them not to violate its ultimate mystery. The journey takes on aspects of a religious pilgrimage, "an interior, spiritual journey in which time and space operate in an oneiric rather than a naturalistic fashion."[49] "There is a sacred region (the Zone) in the heart of which there hides a sanctuary (the House) which has in it a tabernacle (The Room)."[50] It becomes a voyage of spiritual discovery and initiation, "which is to lead . . . from a world without God to the revelation of the Spirit."[51] Telegraph towers in the form of crosses mark the landscape, as a "sign of the spiritual and of hope,"[52] a crown of thorns suggests the christological mysteries of sacrifice and redemption; and mysterious rain showers allude to divine grace. In a dream of Stalker, Tarkovsky has us see, among other things, "a fragment of the [Van Eyck] altar-piece beneath the water . . . [and] around it swimming fish, a symbol for the Christ."[53]

The dynamic of pilgrimage in the entire film, as well as a series of shots of Stalker seated with the other two men touched by "a strange sweetness, a profound peace having descended upon them,"[54] and clearly suggesting the three angels of the Roublev icon of the Trinity allude to the biblical event of the post-Resurrection Jesus who meets and speaks with the two pilgrims on the road to Emmaus (Lk 24:13). This christological allusion is announced earlier when Stalker reads that Gospel passage to his companions, a scene which "could very well be the interpretative key of the film,"[55] and whose importance Tarkovsky marks by shifting the film's color from sepia to full color.

Beyond his actions, Stalker himself has certain definite traits of the Christ-figure. He "seems to be weak, but essentially it is he who is invincible because of his faith and his will to serve others."[56] "Stalker's shaven head suggests suffering"[57] and he has a "Christ-like beard."[58] Marks on his head and face, "his scars and his stigmata[,] give witness to a long procession of sufferings, to a calvary."[59] This christological identity is admitted by Tarkovsky. In answer to the comment, "Stalker has something of the prophet. He is a kind of Christ," the director answered, "Yes, of a prophet who believes that humanity will perish because they have no spiritual life."[60] A couple of critics see Stalker "in a direct line with those famous christic figures which enlighten the world of Doestoevski's novels."[61] In the conclusion of the film, Tarkovsky has Stalker's wife look directly into the camera and speak about him: significantly he describes him in a way that reflects the suffering servant of Yahweh in Isaiah: she says he is a "blessed fool" – the Russian word *"bogenny"* means "man of God" – and she adds that "Everyone laughed at him, he was so pitiful."

In the conclusion of his penultimate film, *Nostalghia* (1983), Tarkovsky creates two Christ-figures, both of whom die sacrificial deaths to save the world from destruction. First there is the Italian, Domenico, representing the prophet, unheeded and rejected, the apocalyptic madman, "the lucid fool who wants to save humanity,"[62] who immolates himself in a final paradoxical gesture of prophecy-sacrifice. A "'voice crying in the wilderness,'"[63] Domenico[64] is a courageous man "who is prepared to take upon himself the burden of the sorrows of the world and their redemption."[65] Tarkovsky announces the ultimate christological victory of his sacrifice: he falls flaming to the ground collapsing face down, "in the parody of the pose of a man crucified,"[66] and as he dies, Tarkovsky inserts on the soundtrack a thunderous rendition of Beethoven's "Ode to Joy."

Opposite Domenico, there is the Russian poet Andrey Gorchakov, "in exile" in Italy and clearly representing Tarkovsky, who about Andrey says: "The protagonist [is] a mirror image of me."[67] Gorchakov recognizes the greatness of Domenico: the film is replete with suggestions, often made with mirrors, of a "shared or common identity of the two men,"[68] and he repeats

Domenico's strange prophetic gesture of carrying a "sacerdotal candle – paradoxical image of hope"[69] across the thermal pool at Bagno Vignoni in Tuscany. Photographed in an awesome, contemplative *plan-séquence* shot of more than eight minutes, the poet's walking across the pool several times, "penetrating into the territory of death,"[70] becomes "Andrey's Road to Calvary."[71] At the end, having achieved his mission of bringing light into the darkness, he collapses and dies: for Andrey as for Domenico, "the bearing of the candle has become a giving of the self,"[72] and by completing "the mission given to him by the 'madman' . . . Gorchakov has preserved a fragile glimmer of life and of hope, by sacrificing *his* life."[73]

The Sacrifice, Tarkovsky's final film – he died of cancer shortly after its editing was completed – is a masterpiece dense with religious, biblical and christological symbolism and allusions, such as the music of the Bach "Passion of Saint Matthew" which opens and closes the film, the Leonardo da Vinci painting of "The Adoration of the Magi," which is repeatedly referred to, and the phrase from the Gospel of John, "In the beginning was the Word." (Jn 1:1) In this film, considered "a parable which reflects an esthetic of the Incarnation,"[74] Tarkovsky, in his own words, wants to represent "the christian concept of self-sacrifice."[75]

But it is especially in Alexander, the film's protagonist, that Tarkovsky represents the sacrificial-salvific death of Jesus, clearly referred to in the film's title. Aware that the imminent threat of a nuclear war "requires a radical, absolute sacrifice,"[76] Alexander makes an impassioned plea-vow to God, beginning with the christological "Our Father," to accept his life in exchange for the salvation of his son and family. Then, "conscious of his link with ultimate reality [and] merely obeying his vocation,"[77] Alexander fulfills the vow by deliberately sacrificing everything in a fiery holocaust, burning his house and everything in it, a scene photographed in a *plan-séquence* shot lasting almost seven minutes.[78] In the epilogue of the film, Alexander's little son, who before was mute, now sits by a tree – "the cross of salvation,"[79] the "ideogram of sacrifice"[80] – planted by his father in the opening of the film, and speaks. He is alive, and "plainly the 'redeeming hope.'"[81] The sacrifice was efficacious. New life, resurrection-life is given. Tarkovsky announces this new life in the final shot of the film:

> Then the camera pans slowly up the length of the dead tree, and through the stumps of the branches we see the sky and the flat sea, depth and distance and height. The effort of resurrection which was the driving force in all of Tarkovky's films, has been achieved in *The Sacrifice*.[82]

Epilogue

This book takes a first systematic step towards proposing as an alternative to the literal representation of Jesus in film, the more adequate metaphorical representation, that is, the Christ-figure. As a first step it is introductory. Much remains to be done in this area, by way of moving forward the discussion. In this very brief conclusion, I would like to suggest a number of directions in which future research might go. One area for further work comes to mind immediately because it was considered (only) briefly in the penultimate chapter of this book, and that is a wider research into some of the typical guises or modalities of the filmic Christ-figure. There is still much material regarding metaphorical images of Christ to be investigated in films about saints and films about priests and nuns. The *genres* of the western, the prison film, the war film, all of which we considered in a limited way in this book, still offer fertile ground for research, as does the work of a number of film-*auteurs.*

The films of Tarkovsky and Bresson, some of which we considered here, certainly deserve further investigation, as do the early films of Pasolini and Bergman and some of Buñuel, and the films of John Ford and Carl Dreyer. Beyond the work of these *auteurs,* a number of individual films only mentioned in the present discussion offer interesting possibilities for discussion of the filmic Christ-figure: Fellini's *La dolce vita* (1960), for example, or Pasolini's *Teorema* (1968) or John Schlesinger's *Midnight Cowboy* (1969).

To recall the first part of the present study, there are still a number of Jesus-films that might be researched fruitfully, for example, a comparative investigation, with a theological-aesthetic hermeneutic, of the Jesus-protagonist of the primitive passion play films would prove fruitful. A more thorough treatment of some of the early and later Jesus epics, some of which we treated briefly in this book, would prove interesting. I am thinking, for example, of Robert Wiene's *I.N.R.I.*, DeMille's *The King of Kings*, Philip Van Loan's *Jesus of Nazareth* (1928), Julien Duvivier's *Golgotha*, William Beaudine and Harold Daniels' seldom seen and curious film about an American "Oberammergau," *The Lawton Story* (1949), Irving Pichel and John T. Coyle's *Day of Triumph* (1954), Peter Sykes and John Kirsh's *Jesus: The Man Who Changed the World* (1979) and Franco Rossi's apocryphal *A Child Called Jesus* (1989).

To move to more theoretical themes, clearly there is still much to be done in the area of the inevitable and fundamental contrast between filmic representations of the Jesus of Nazareth who is recognized (only) as a prophetic figure of history and world culture, and filmic representations of Jesus of Nazareth, historical figure but also focal point and center of the Christian faith, Jesus the Christ, Eternal Word of God. Regarding the metaphorical representations of the Jesus of culture, a serious study should be done of the protagonist-heros of many popular adventure and science-fiction films, characters referred to, perhaps too casually, by many film critics as "popular Christ-figures." An analytical approach operating with a clear theological-christological hermeneutic to the films of the *Superman* or the *Batman* series, for example, would I think, point out the limits of these "popular Christ-figures," demonstrating precisely how they are fundamentally inadequate, and at times invalid, vehicles for imaging the Christ.

Another area of more theoretical research is precisely the concept of the filmic Christ-figure. Just how does it function? What dynamic takes place in the viewing audience as they experience the protagonist of one of these films, a dynamic which allows them to make both identifications and distinctions between the metaphor, the concrete and specific Christ-figure, and the transcendent reality it points to, the Christ figured? Then there is the fascinating question of the fundamental distinctions between the filmic Christ-figure and the Christ-figure in prose fiction, in theater or in pictorial art, an argument only touched upon to in this book. For example, one could do a detailed comparative study of the Babette of Axel's film and the Babette of Blixen's novella, or a study of Shane in Schaefer's novel and Shane in Stevens' film. What are the differences in the degree and the modality of Christ-figuring between one *genre* and the other? This same approach could be fruitfully applied to the Jesus of Kazantzakis' novel in contrast to Scorsese's filmic Jesus.

There is also the rather wide field of the varieties of filmic Christ-figures, of the distinctions between the strict allegorical approach, and the looser, more open analogical or parabolical approaches. There are, for example, essential distinctions between the simple narrative of a biblical parable and the fully fleshed out filmic narrative in sound and images and color that is analogical to the story of Jesus or of the Christ. The filmic fiction narrative with its complex plot and character development is clearly in contrast to the elemental and even abstract quality of the biblical parable. Clearly in this particular investigation, one working tool of the hermeneutic would be the relatively new scholarly field of narrative theology pioneered by Michael Goldberg and John Navone.[1]

In this book, the chapter on *Jesus of Montreal* functioned as a bridge between the investigation of the Jesus-film and that of the Christ-figure-film. A further area very worthy of exploration would be precisely the good number of films of this type, that is, in which a person impersonating Jesus Christ in a play or a film becomes a Christ-figure, with the many levels of meaning generated by this dynamic. There are, for example two filmic versions of Michael Bulgakov's *The Master and Margherite*, a novel which features a *Jesus of Montreal*-type Christ-figure: Aleksander Petrovic's *The Master and Margarita* (1977) and Andrei Wajda's *Pilatus und Andere* (1972). The two films are quite different from each other and both move away from the novel. Then more investigation using this Christ-figure-within-a-Jesus-figure hermeneutic, and focussing in particular on the fascinating theme of the self-consciousness of the Christ-figure protagonist, could fruitfully be done on Pasolini's *La ricotta* and on Dassin's *He Who Must Die*, two films which we discussed briefly in this present work.

And now in conclusion, we ought to consider briefly Carl Theodor Dreyer's *Jesus of Nazareth* script[2] for the much beloved film which the great master never made. Though it is not in fact a Jesus-film, we are including it here because, judging from the quality and the power of the script and from the consummate skill and spiritual power of Dreyer in the films he did make, his Jesus-film might well have been the best of them all. The *Jesus of Nazareth* project absorbed Dreyer's interest and energy for almost thirty years of his life and informed all the films he made during that time, for example *Ordet*. The miracle-working Johannes of that film, as we have already noted, is clearly a Christ-figure. But he is also a preparatory exercise for the radical, uncompromising Jesus of the film Dreyer was hoping to make.

Dreyer's reflection and preparation, which included the study of exegesis, biblical archaeology, the history of Palestine and even the Hebrew language, was aimed not only at creating an authentic image of Jesus, but also at researching the theoretical and practical possibilities of the film medium to represent Jesus of Nazareth "without betraying him."[3] Dreyer wanted to represent Jesus as a human being with his existence profoundly rooted in this world, an exceptional man not a superman, "in whom the creativity inherent in every human being, manifested itself with such power that neither before him nor after him did human history ever witness anything similar."[4] In his script, Dreyer insisted on Jesus' humanity, his Jewishness – the film was subtitled *Jesus the Jew* – and his living and dying in occupied territory. Having spent time in Berlin in the 1930s and in occupied Denmark in the early 1940s, and having witnessed the growth of antisemitism in western Europe and the subsequent holocaust, Dreyer wanted his Jesus-film – in which the responsibility for the death of Jesus is unequivocally that of the Roman occupying power – to be an uncompromising attack on the moral and social evil of antisemitism.

As much as he tried, Dreyer was unable to obtain the financing to make his Jesus-film. Several trips to the United States and even to Hollywood produced some promises, none of which bore fruit. A eleven-year association with the American impresario Blevins Davis resulted a signed contract but for a variety of reasons – mainly Davis' total unreliability – the contract was never honored. Various plans were made but never carried out: to make the film in Israel, for which Dreyer traveled there; to make it in the United States and in English; to film it in panoramic wide-screen like *King of Kings* and *The Greatest Story Ever Told*, a suggestion which Dreyer refused categorically.[5] There was a serious offer made by a Swede living in New York to finance the film but only if it were made by both Dreyer and Ingmar Bergman, an offer immediately turned down by the Danish director. The possibility of help from O.C.I.C. did not work out, nor did the proposal of Gabriel Axel, who later filmed *Babette's Feast*, to promote the financing of the project.

Finally in 1967, RAI, the Italian national television network, undertook negotiations regarding the possibility of financing and producing the film.[6] Dreyer was full of hope and insisted only on two conditions: that the film be made on location in Israel and that its pro-Semitic theme not be tempered. He saw this latter condition as very much in keeping with the "spirit of religious reconciliation promoted by Pope John XXIII and the Vatican Council."[7] Dreyer further indicated that his "film of liberation"[8] would be in color, would have unknown actors, Israelis for Jesus and the apostles, and Italians for Pilate and the Romans and that it would be shot in English and then dubbed into Italian.[9] Tragically, before the negotiations could be finalized and the production could get underway, Dreyer, seventy-nine years of age at the time, became increasingly weak and incapacitated. In March 1968, perhaps after a fall, he was admitted to hospital and a short time later, he died. And with Dreyer died a little known hope for the creation of a Jesus-film that might have gone beyond all the others in accurately and authentically representing the Jesus of the gospels and the Christ of the Gospel.

Endnotes

Part One: The Jesus Film

General Introduction

1. Peter Malone, *Movie Christs and Antichrists* (New York: Crossroad, 1990), 21.

2. The best description and critique of this development I have come across is in a brief article by Joseph Marty, a French priest-film critic: *"Chromo, patro, mélo: le cinéma, côté Saint Sulpice,"* in *Le film religieux – CinémAction No.49* (Paris: Corlet, 1988), 62-70.

Introduction

1. The only exceptions here are the most hypothetical non-Christians who have somehow lived totally isolated from the Christian religious or cultural tradition and who find themselves facing a film about Jesus.

Chapter One: The Early Years

1. André Gaudreault, "La Passion du Christ: une forme, un genre, un discours," in *An Invention of the Devil? Religion and the Early Cinema. Une Invention du Diable? Le Cinéma des Premiers Temps et Religion,* edited by Roland Cosandey, André Gaudreault, Tom Gunning (Sainte Foy, Canada: Les Presses de l'Université Laval, 1992), 95.

2. Frank Kermode, "John," in *The Literary Guide to the Bible,* edited by Robert Alter and Frank Kermode (Cambridge: Belknap Press, 1987), 459.

3. Isabelle Raynauld, "Les scénarios de la Passion selon Pathé (1902-1914), in *An Invention of the Devil?*, 130.

4. Charles Keil, "From the Manger to the Cross: The New Testament Narrative and the Question of Stylistic Retardation," in *An Invention of the Devil?*, 112.

5. Ibid. Keil is referring here to one film, but clearly what he says applies to the *genre.*

6. Ibid.

7. Ibid., 118.

8. Ibid., 106.

9. Ibid., 107.

10. Ronald Holloway, *Beyond the Image: Approaches to the Religious Dimension in the Cinema* (Geneva: Oikoumene, 1977), 48.

11. In the literature, there is considerable confusion about this film. A French listing speaks of an 1897 passion filmed by an operator of Louis Lumière in Austria. [Jean-Luc Douin, "Filmographie," in *Le film religieux,* 42.] Kinnard and Davis seem to refer to it twice. Once it is simply referred to as a film "released by Lumière" [Roy Kinnard and Tim Davis, *Divine Images: A History of Jesus on the Screen* (New York: Citadel Press-Carol Publishing Group, 1992), 27.] but earlier in this book, there is a longer description of a film of the Passion Play performed in Horwitz [*sic*], Bohemia, produced by an American representative of Auguste Lumière. The authors go on to say that it was "crudely shot and disappointed audiences" [Ibid., 19], an opinion clearly contradicted by the detailed evidence amassed by Musser whom I follow in this commentary. [Charles Musser, "Les Passions et les Mystères de la Passion aux États-Unis (1880-1900)," in *An Invention of the Devil?*, 145-186.] Kinnard and Davis seem to imply that these are two films, when the evidence indicates that they are one and the same. The usually reliable publication *Film-Dienst* mentions the film twice: once it says that it was produced by Lumière (using the singular form of the name) [Gerd Albrecht, "Jesus – Eine Filmkarriere," in *Film-Dienst Extra: Jesus in der Hauptrolle* (Köln: Katholisches Institut für Medieninformation [KIM], November 1992): 10.] and later indicates that it was a French production, in (only) thirteen scenes, of the Lumière brothers. [P[eter]. H[asenberg]., "Jesus im Film – Eine Auswahlfilmographie," in Ibid., 74.] Finally Ronald Holloway refers to it as "a fake Parisian reproduction of the Horitz (Bohemia) Passion . . . a rather lengthy 15-minute version, arranged in 13 tableaux-scenes." [Holloway, 48.]

12. Like many of these early films, it was available to buyers or distributers in a variety of editions.

13. Holloway, 48.

14. Not all the critics agree on the dating of these three early films. Kinnard and Davis date the first two as 1897 and the Hollaman production as 1897-98, with its first showing on 30 January 1998. [Kinnard and Davis, 27, 19-20.] Castellani puts the first two films in 1895, and the Hollaman production in 1897. [Leandro Castellani, *Temi e figure del film religioso* (Leumann TO: Editrice Elle Di Ci, 1994), 190.] Hasenberg's dating places them all in the same year, 1897. [H[asenberg]., "Jesus im Film – Eine Auswahlfilmographie," 74.]

15. Holloway, 48.

16. For fear of scandal, the fact that Russell was paid for his six weeks of work was kept a secret.

17. Holloway, 48.

18. Musser, 172.

19. Kinnard and Davis, 21.

20. H[asenberg]., "Jesus im Film – Eine Auswahlfilmographie," 74.

21. Holloway dates it as 1899. [Holloway, 50.]

22. Kinnard and Davis, 29.

23. Herbert Reynolds, "From the Palette to the Screen: The Tissot Bible as Sourcebook for *From the Manger to the Cross,*" in *An Invention of the Devil?*, 276.

24. James Jacques Joseph Tissot, *The Life of Our Saviour Jesus Christ,* 4 Vols., translated by Mrs. Arthur Bell (New York: McClure-Tissot Co., 1899). The book is not a Bible in the traditional sense, but rather a "Life of Christ," with readings from the gospels supplemented by illustrations and commentaries by Tissot. [Reynolds, 276.]

25. Ibid., 281.

26. Ibid.

27. Kinnard and Davis, 22.

28. Holloway, 55.

29. Les and Barbara Keyser, *Hollywood and the Catholic Church: The Image of Roman Catholicism in American Movies* (Chicago: Loyola University Press, 1984), 16.

30. The terms "extradiegetical" and "intradiegetical" will be used repeatedly in this book and are meant to distinguish between elements of form and style in a film, and elements of content. The word "intradiegetical" – meaning literally "within the diegesis" – indicates elements which have to do with the narrative or storyline of a film and includes characters, plot, action, setting and even music, if the source of the music is seen or can be justified within the narrative of the film. The word "extradiegetical" – meaning "outside the diegesis" – refers to specifically filmic elements of the production. It includes, for example, photography, movements and angles of the camera, actors and style of acting, editing, special effects and theme music.

31. Kinnard and Davis, 27.

32. Keyser, *Hollywood and the Catholic Church,* 17.

33. Kinnard and Davis, 27.

34. Ibid., 33.

35. The film premiered on 12 May 1918. The armistice was signed six months later, on 11 November.

36. Castellani, *Temi e figure del film religioso,* 30.

37. Alan Pavelin, *Fifty Religious Films* (Chislehurst, Kent: A. P. Pavelin, 1990), 35.

38. Ibid.
39. DeMille quoted in Keyser, *Hollywood and the Catholic Church,* 22.

40. Ibid.

41. Kinnard and Davis, 43.

42. Pavelin, 31.

43. Both citations are from Kinnard and Davis, 44.

44. Keyser, *Hollywood and the Catholic Church,* 22.

45. Ibid. In Europe there is a tradition of pious devotional images of Jesus, stressing the formal pose and the soft, sentimental features, parallel to that of Hallmark cards in the U.S. It began in Paris in the mid-nineteenth century, developing in religious bookstores around the Church of St. Sulpice, this popular approach to the sacred image, which also influenced the cinema art, was known as the *"style sulpicien."* A fine analysis, which also notes the political

undertones of the "sulpician" style, is the already-mentioned article by Joseph Marty.

46. H[asenberg]., "Jesus im Film – Eine Auswahlfilmographie," 76.

47. Kinnard and Davis, 44.

48. Jean-Luc Douin, "Jésus superstar: Certains préfèrent l'invisible," in *Le film religieux*, 37.

49. H[asenberg]., "Jesus im Film – Eine Auswahlfilmographie," 76. The tendency to avoid closeups of Jesus is common in these early films. Dreyer's film, for example, has many expressive close-ups of Satan and Judas, but very few of Jesus.

50. The word "peplum," originally from the Greek *"peplos,"* refers to the loose outer garment worn by the women in these films. Gerald Forshey does a careful analysis of many of these films, identifying in them social, ethical, political subtexts particularly relevant to the American scene at the time they were made. [Gerald E. Forshey, *American Religious and Biblical Spectaculars* (Westport CT: Praeger, 1992).]

51. Claude Aziza, "Les premiers chrétiens: les lions ne sont jamais loin," in *Le film religieux*, 27.

52. Kinnard and Davis, 53.

53. Forshey, 30.

54. Kinnard and Davis, 73, 74.

55. Kinnard and Davis indicate the film was produced by Centurion Films of Rev. James K. Friedrich, and distributed by Buena Vista, a Disney company. Most other sources refer to it simply as a Disney film. [Kinnard and Davis, 115.]

56. The first version of *Ben-Hur,* a 1907 American production, was directed by Olcott and Oates. The second version, a 1925 MGM production, was directed by Fred Niblo, and many of the critics consider it superior in many ways to the 1961 version.

57. Keyser, *Hollywood and the Catholic Church,* 31.

58. Ibid., 38.

59. Bosley Crowther quoted in Ibid., 37. The original source is named as Bosley Crowther, *Vintage Films* (New York: G.P. Putnam, 1977), without a page reference.

60. Keyser, *Hollywood and the Catholic Church,* 31.

61. It was preceded by an eminently forgettable British production in 1949 and by a memorable Swedish production in 1953. Expertly and sensitively directed by Alf Sjöberg, the Swedish production reaches profound levels of human and spiritual significance going far beyond its later remake.

62. *Pontius Pilate* was made in 1961, but, perhaps because the distributers feared the worse, it was not released in Europe till 1964. Only in 1967, and evidently for the same reasons, was it distributed in the United States. The fears of the distributers were not unfounded: the film was a flop.

63. Kinnard and Davis, 154.

Chapter Two:
The Gospel According to Hollywood:
King of Kings *and the* Greatest Story Ever Told

1. Moira Walsh, "Christ or Credit Card?: A Review of *King of Kings,*" *America,* 21 October 1961, 71.

2. Ibid., 71. Walsh is, of course, referring to more than just these two films.
   3. Robert Benayoun, *"Le Roi des Rois:* A teen-age Jesus," *Positif* n.45 (May 1962): 63.

4. Bruce Petri, *A Theory of American Film: The Films and Techniques of George Stevens* (New York: Garland Publishing Company, 1987), 206.

5. Welles is not credited because, as the director Ray himself explains, "He asked for credit equal to that of Jeffrey Hunter or no credit at all. That made it very easy for the executives of Metro-Goldwyn-Mayer." [Adriano Aprà, Barry Boys, Ian Cameron, José Luis Guarner, Paul Mayersberg, and V.F. Perkins, "Interview with Nicholas Ray," *Movie,* n.9 (May 1963): 24.]

6. For *King of Kings,* the production team was composed of Sam Bronston. the producer, Philip Yordan, the writer of the screenplay and the director, Ray.

7. The American (Catholic) Legion of Decency concurs, saying about the film: "The poetic license taken in the development of the life of Christ renders the film theologically and scripturally inaccurate." [Walsh, 72.]

8. Bruce Babington and Peter William Evans, *Biblical Epics: Sacred Narrative in the Hollywood Cinema* (Manchester: Manchester University Press, 1993), 128.

9. Edward O'Connor, *"King of Kings,"* *Films* v.12, n.9 (November 1961): 548.

10. Land., "Film Reviews: *King of Kings,"* *Variety,* 11 October 1961, 6.

11. Ibid., 73.

12. Babington and Evans, 106.

13. O'Connor, 548.

14. Crowther, *"Kings of Kings,"* *The New York Times Film Reviews 1959-1968 – Volume 5* (New York: The New York Times and Arno Press, 1970) (12 October 1961).

15. Victor Erice and Jos Oliver, *Nicholas Ray y su Tiempo* (Madrid: Filmoteca Espanola, 1986), 154. The story of this "formal approval" is worth describing for it reveals a great deal about the attitudes and working methods of those behind the film. *King of Kings* was being filmed on location in Spain. At some point during the shooting, the producer went to Rome, during which visit, "Bronston, fully aware of the benefits of publicity during production, obtained script approval from Pope John XXIII." [Geoff Andrew, *The Films of Nicholas Ray: The Poet of Nightfall* (London: Charles Letts, 1991), 180.] The news of the papal interest made the front page of *Variety,* the most important film industry daily newspaper in America, and the article read as follows: "Producer Sam Bronston received Papal approval of his biblical film project, "The King of Kings," [*sic*] . . . in private audience with John XXIII at the Vatican last week, after the Phil Yordan-Diego Fabri screenplay was read and accepted by the highest New Testament authorities. The Pope blessed the production and urged Catholic support." ["Pope's Direct OK Simplifies 'Kings' Coin Problems." *Variety* v.218,

n.2 (9 March 1960), 1.] Regardless of what really went on between Bronston and company and the Pope – probably little, because in the Vatican, "private audience" can mean that one sees the Pope along with five thousand other people in the "private" audience hall, and it is highly unlikely that the world's top biblical scholars were convoked to the Vatican to read Ray's screenplay – here we have a perfect example of Vatican contacts being abused by the film producers as a publicity stunt whose final end is economic in nature. The title of the *Variety* article gives it all away.

16. Babington and Evans, 104.

17. Land., 6.

18. O'Connor, 549.

19. Forshey, 89.

20. Elizabeth Quigley, "Cinema: The Dainty Crucifixion," *The Spectator* n.207 (24 November 1961), 763.

21. Andrew, 180.

22. Crowther, *"King of Kings."*

23. "Fitzgerald's Views," *Variety* n.226 (8 November 1961), 5.

24. Ray himself explains, "When I shot it, I thought that it should last from twenty to thirty minutes." [Erice and Oliver, p.205.] Between the shooting of the scene and the final editing of the film, *King of Kings* was sold to MGM. As a result Ray lost all control over the final cut of the film. In the editing done by MGM, the Sermon on the Mount scene was cut down considerably. Ray was not amused: "They cut the sequence of the Sermon very badly, and now it does not have the harmony that I was looking for." [Ibid.]

25. Forshey, 91.

26. Martin Scorsese interviewed in Jean-Luc Sablon, "Martin Scorsese: Dieu est avec moi." *Revue du Cinéma-Image et Son* n.442 (October 1988): 59.

27. Benayoun, 62.

28. Andrew, 183. Ray justifies the bizarre question and answer style because that was how the masters taught in the synagogues. [Erice and Oliver, 204.] Another critic tries very hard to explain, ultimately unconvincingly, what Ray tried to do in this sequence. "The tracking shot of the Sermon on the Mount in the film is Ray's version – based on historical research – of how he supposed Jesus constantly moved around and engaged small groups of ever-different people in Socratic dialogue about Christianity, and thus, that Jesus never stood still on the top of the mount, as icons picture him, talking to the multitude of ten thousand." [John Francis Kreidl, *Nicholas Ray* (Boston: Twayne Publishers, 1977), 194.]

29. Jean Douchet and Jacques Joly, "Nouvel entretien avec Nicholas Ray," *Cahiers du Cinéma* v.22, n.127 (January 1962): 10.

30. What Ray ought to know is that imitating Leonardo's fresco or not, depends not so much on the shape of the table as on the compositions of the shots, the camera angles and movements, and the editing.

31. Apparently it never occurred to Ray that the washing of the feet would necessarily have taken place before the group arrived at the table, as in Rossellini's *The Messiah*.

32. Douchet and Joly, 10. With considerable pride and enthusiasm, and with no sense of the irony involved, Ray describes how he built the table: "I took a cross and broke it in such a way that the horizontal arms did not meet. Then I placed Jesus at the head of the cross." [Ibid.]

33. About this shot, Ray admits "It's an almost successful shot, but not quite," and then he attempts, rather feebly, to explain what he was trying to do: "I wanted to dramatize, in the sense of giving the moment more emotional value, by using the camera in this way and bringing Mary and John into the shot fully and organically." [Aprà, Boys, Cameron, Guarner and others, 24.]

34. Kinnard and Davis, 132.

35. Ibid. Quoted without, indicating source.

36. Keyser, *Hollywood and the Catholic Church,* 38.

37. Douin, "Jésus superstar: Certains préfèrent l'invisible," in *Le film religieux.* 37.

38. Walsh, 73. Obviously, the film reviewer for Vatican Radio was of a different opinion: "It has to be said that the physical appearance of the Divine Master corresponds in a surprising and respectfully faithful manner to the traditional iconography. And this, thanks to the solemn nobility of Jeffrey Hunter, to the sweetness of his look which reveals a dominating power, both human and mystical." [Ibid.] Quoted without indicating source.

39. Erice and Oliver, 154.

40. One frustrated reporter explains how he was refused contact with the actor: "I was told that 'he has requested that his personal life be cloaked and that the Press of the world try to understand why it is impossible for him to grant interviews on the subject of his portrayal of Jesus.'" [Peter Baker, "Making It B-I-G," *Films and Filming* v.7, n.2 (November 1960): 15.]

41. Forshey, 89. Quoted without indicating source.

42. Babington and Evans, 130.

43. Ibid.

44. Andrew, 182.

45. Baker, 15.

46. François Truchaud, *Nicholas Ray* (Paris: Editions Universitaires, 1965), 165.

47. Babington and Evans, 136.

48. Forshey, 90.

49. Walsh, 73.

50. Forshey, 90.

51. Babington and Evans, 138.

52. One critic rather feebly attempts to find some deep spiritual meaning in the shadow of Christ interpreting it as "a revealing light, chasing away the darkness." [Truchaud, 169.]

53. Forshey, 91.

54. Ibid., 89.

55. Babington and Evans, 135.

56. Forshey, 91.

57. Walsh, 73.

58. Ibid., 74, 73.

59. The fact of Stevens' "retaining the tawdry title to the Fulton Oursler book" is interpreted by one critic as a transparent marketing device, a "bow to moneymen." [Petri, 202.] Oursler's book generated more than one spin-off. It was also the source of a popular serial drama on radio. [*Spuren des Religiösen im Film,* edited by Peter Hasenberg, Wolfgang Luley and Charles Martig (Mainz: Matthias-Grünewald-Verlag and Köln: Katholisches Institut für Medieninformation [KIM], 1995), 83.]

60. Ernesto G. Laura, "La vita di Gesù in cinerama," *Rivista del Cinematografo* n.6 (June 1965): 290.

61. Forshey, 95.

62. Holloway, 119.

63. Forshey, 96.

64. Ibid., 102.

65. A number of critics note that this was not Stevens' original intention, that in fact he wanted to avoid the errors of the colossal. The film, however, ended up being just that. [Forshey, 95.]

66. Interestingly, Stevens' work previous to *The Greatest Story Ever Told,* includes the classical Western, *Shane,* made in 1953 (discussed at length in part two, chapter 3), *Giant,* made in 1956 and *The Diary of Anne Frank,* made in 1959, all of them quite successful both at the box-office and among the critics.

67. A.S., "Greatest Story Ever Told, The," *The Monthly Film Bulletin* (BFI) v.32, n.376 (May 1965): 69.

68. Kinnard and Davis, 161.

69. One source lists five versions of the film, of 260 min., 238 min., 197 min., 190 min. and 191 min. [Kinnard and Davis, 161, 158.] Another source adds a 225 min. and a 141 min. version to the puzzle. [Forshey, 95.] A third source adds a 195 min. version ["Microsoft Cinemania 94," Interactive Movie Guide CD, Microsoft Corporation.] and a fourth, a 200 min. version. ["CinEnciclopedia 2: La banca dati del cinema mondiale," CD, Editoria Elettronica Editel and Ente dello Spettacolo, 1994.] Finally, a version of 127 min. is noted, evidently the briefest. [*Spuren des Religiösen im Film,* 84.]

70. Tom Aitkin, "The greatest story – never told," *The Tablet,* 23-30 December 1995, 1657.

71. Ibid.

72. A decision, as we shall see again later, taken also by Pier Paolo Pasolini regarding his Jesus film, *The Gospel According to Saint Matthew.* But his alternative – isolated, primitive, poor villages in Southern Italy and the dusty, desert-like slopes of Mount Etna, especially when rendered in black and white – is very different from, and more appropriate than that of Stevens' film.

73. Aitkin, 1658.

74. Shana Alexander, *"The Greatest Story Ever Told,"* in *Life,* 25 February 1965, 25.

75. Dwight Macdonald, *Dwight Macdonald on Movies* (Englewood Cliffs, NJ: Prentice Hall, 1970), 436.

76. Babington and Evans, 141

77. One critic notes that Stevens' choice of setting for *The Greatest Story Ever Told* was "undoubtedly influenced by the visual power and scope that had give Stevens' Shane its mythic power." [Forshey, 100.] The difference, of course, is that in *Shane,* the spectacular landscape never distracts from the people in them; the characters belong in the landscapes; the Western myth is complete, consistent, coherent.

78. Ibid., 101.

79. Michael Singer, "Cinema Savior," *Film Comment* v.24, n.5 (September-October 1988): 46.

80. Kinnard and Davis, 161.

81. Babington and Evans, 101.

82. This is the term used by Robert Bresson, the great French director, who never used well-known actors in his films.

83. Land., 6.

84. Keyser, *Hollywood and the Catholic Church,* 38.

85. Forshey, 101.

86. Singer, 46

87. Aitkin, 1658. Michael Singer has a bit of fun with this scene. Commenting on the setting amidst the "plateaus and buttes of Utah's Monument Valley, made so popular in John Ford westerns," he adds, "we half expect John Wayne leading the cavalry to save the day at Calvary. And holy mackerel – the Duke is there, dressed as a Roman centurion on a windswept hill and drawling, 'Truly this was the Son of Gawd.' " [Singer, 46.]

88. A.S., 70.

89. Laura, 293.

90. The critic Felix Barber qualifies Winters' infirmity with a touch of irony: "Shelley Winters has a brief attack of leprosy." [Quoted in Babington and Evans, 148.]

91. A.S., 69.

92. Aitkin, 1657.

93. One critic, comments on the effects of the physicality of Heston: "John the Baptist here is sheer muscleman and has about as much religious feeling as Steve Reeves in *The Thief of Baghdad.*" [Raymond Durgnat, *"The Greatest Story Ever Told:* Raymond Durgnat on the Images of Jesus," *Films and Filming* v.11, n.9 (June 1965), 26.]

94. Kinnard and Davis, 161.

95. Aitkin, 1658.

96. Forshey, 96.

97. Ibid., 102.

98. Durgnat, *"The Greatest Story Ever Told:* Raymond Durgnat on the Images of Jesus," 26.

99. Castellani considers this dangerous "Klu Klux Klan rally" scene and the omnipresent "landscape of the Western" as evidence that Stevens' film is "incurable ill of Americanisms." [Castellani, *Temi e figure del film religioso,* 31.]

100. A.S., 96.

101. One critic rather astonishingly, and erroneously, sees a close resemblance between this lackluster Jesus and the energetic and fiery prophet-protagonist of *The Gospel According to Saint Matthew.* "It is astounding how the Jesus of Max Von Sydow . . . resembles the Jesus of the Italian film of Pasolini." [Laura, 292.]

102. Durgnat, *"The Greatest Story Ever Told:* Raymond Durgnat on the Images of Jesus," 26.

103. Aitkin, 1658.

104. Ibid., 1657.

105. Durgnat, *"The Greatest Story Ever Told:* Raymond Durgnat on the Images of Jesus," 25-26.

106. Ibid., 26.

107. Ibid.

108. Forshey, 96.

109. Malone, *Movie Christs and Antichrists,* 30.

110. Forshey, 96.

111. Ibid.

112. Ibid.

113. Ibid., 99.

114. Page Cook, "The Sound Track," *Films in Review* v.16, n.4 (April 1965): 245.

115. James M. Wall, "Biblical Spectaculars and Secular Man," in *Celluloid and Symbols,* edited by John C. Cooper and Carl Skrade (Philadelphia: Fortress Press, 1970), 52.

116. Babington and Evans, 139.

117. Ibid., 100.

118. Douin, "Jésus superstar: Certains préfèrent l'invisible," 37.

119. Forshey, 103.

120. Petri, 203.

121. Castellani, *Temi e figure del film religioso,* 30.

122. Forshey, 98.

123. Ibid.

124. Ibid., 103.

125. Philip, T. Hartung, "The Screen: The Greatest Is Average," *Commonweal* v.81, n.24 (12 March 1965), 765.

126. Aitkin, 1657.

127. This unnecessary and annoying idiosyncracy reaches its extreme point in the crucifixion scene: When Jesus says "My God, my God, why hast thou forsaken me?," I counted six full seconds between his first and second "my God."

128. Durgnat, *"The Greatest Story Ever Told:* Raymond Durgnat on the Images of Jesus," 25.

129. Ibid.

Chapter Three:
The Jesus Musicals: Jesus Christ Superstar *and* Godspell

1. There was a third "Jesus musical," also released in 1973 by Twentieth-Century Fox. *The Gospel Road* was produced by country-western singer Johnny Cash and his wife June Carter Cash, and starring her as Mary Magdalene and featuring him as occasional narrator and guide through the holy sites in Palestine. The film is a strange blend of historical-devotional drama and documentary, including some social-ecological comments, and "enhanced" by songs and music by John Denver, Kris Kristofferson, Johnny Cash and others. It had limited distribution and success in the United States, and almost none elsewhere.

2. Forshey, 104.

3. Renato Filizzola, *I film degli anni '70* (Roma: Edizioni Paoline, 1980), 369.

4. Ibid.

5. Kinnard and Davis, 177.

6. The review in the entertainment weekly *Variety* spoke of a "3,000,000 album bestseller (retail gross $35,000,000)." Quoted in Holloway, 121, without further information about the source.

7. Peter Hasenberg, "Clown und Superstar: Die Jesus-Musicals der 70er Jahre," *Film-Dienst Extra,* 40.

8. Forshey, 105.

9. Malone, *Movie Christs and Antichrists,* 34.

10. Ibid.

11. Castellani, *Temi e figure del film religioso,* 29.

12. Review in *Newsweek* (9 July 1973), 82, quoted in Forshey, 116.

13. Ibid., 106.

14. Bert Reisfeld, "Norman Jewison talks to Bert Reisfeld about *Jesus Christ Superstar,"* *Photoplay* (G.B.) v.24, n.4 (April 1973), 26.

15. "Andrew Lloyd Webber (the composer) and Tim Rice (the lyricist) never intended for their opera to be biblical scholarship, historical realism, or official doctrine." [Forshey, 106.]

16. Ibid.

17. Ibid.

18. Ibid., 109.

19. Tony Rayns, "Review of *Jesus Christ Superstar,*" *The Monthly Film Bulletin* (BFI) v.400, n.476 (September 1973): 192.

20. Peter Hasenberg sees in this caricature of Herod "a satirical representation of the audience (present in the cinema) who have 'tasted' the *Jesus Christ Superstar* show with the same culinary attitude [as Herod] and so, without any interest in the person and message of Jesus." ["Clown und Superstar," 41.]

21. Filizzola, 369.

22. Forshey, 107.

23. Alan R. Howard, "Review of *Jesus Christ Superstar,*" *The Hollywood Reporter* v.226, n.47 (25 June 1973), 10.

24. Forshey, 107.

25. Kinnard and Davis, 177. Michael Singer with tongue in cheek speculates that Ted Neeley-Jesus' "irritating falsetto" is the reason "why Yvonne Ellimann's Mary Magdalene didn't know how to love him." [Singer, 46.]

26. Rayns, 192.

27. Hasenberg, "Clown und Superstar," 39-40.

28. Forshey, 104.

29. Ibid., 110.

30. From the cross, Jesus speaks his last words, mentioning the Father, but he does it so formally that it is as if he is quoting the Gospel rather than speaking the words with passion.

31. For some strange reason, Jewison has Jesus then repeat the traditional formula: "This is my blood you drink. . . . This is my body you eat." The awkward redundance and the offhand way he speaks the words are without explanation.

32. Review of *Jesus Christ Superstar* in *Christianity Today,* quoted in Kinnard and Davis, 177.

33. The only reference to a kingdom is when Jesus says rather lamely to Pilate: "There may be a kingdom for me somewhere." It hardly qualifies as a theological reference.

34. In the film, Jesus is named "Christ," sometimes as if it were his second name, sometimes as a blasphemy. But it is never used in the proper sense of "The Christ," "The Savior" or "The Holy One of God."

35. In its representation of Jesus, Jewison's film seems to anticipate several elements of Martin Scorsese's *The Last Temptation of Christ.* I shall discuss this curious, but I think significant, correspondence, in the chapter on Scorsese's film below.

36. Hasenberg, "Clown und Superstar," 40.

37. I find it very difficult to imagine the reasoning behind Filizzola's comment that Jewison restores to us "a young Christ, strong but gentle, decisive but smiling, with an intensely human power of communication." [Filizzola, 371.]

38. Forshey notes the ambiguity of Jesus' relationship with Mary Magdalen. [Forshey, 107.] But he does not comment on what seems rather obvious to me, the

exaggeratedly intense quality of Jesus' contacts with Judas; in fact, in the composition of a number of shots showing Jesus, Magdalene and Judas, Jewison seems to suggest a rather tense *ménage à trois.*

39. In one such occasion, while Mary Magdalene is for the nth time sensuously anointing Jesus' face, Jesus turns toward Judas, caresses his hand and exchanges intense looks with him. Also significant in this regard is that at different moments in the film, both Mary Magdalene and Judas – who is clearly jealous of Jesus' attention to Magdalene – sing the *Jesus Christ Superstar*'s best known song, "I don't know how to love him, I don't know why he moves me." Significantly, Judas adds the phrase, "Does he love [pregnant pause] does he love me too? Does he care for me?"

40. One critic evidently was not impressed by this concluding number for he comments: "Finally 'Superstar' blares forth with the shallow impact of an inferior imitation of Isaac Hayes." [Murf., "Film Reviews: *Jesus Christ Superstar,"* Variety, 27 June 1973, 20.] Another was even less impressed by the song and music in general, and by the finale: "the songs tend to sound alike, the rock beat being more Las Vegas than Rolling Stones, while the lyrics are less than poetic and the drama collapses in the finale." [Howard, 10.]

41. Rayns, 192.

42. Ibid.

43. Hasenberg, "Clown und Superstar," 40.

44. Ibid.

45. Forshey, 107.

46. Singer, 44.

47. Joy Gould Boyum, "From Porno to Piety: Religious Themes Appearing in Today's Films," *Making Films in New York,* April 1973, 20.

48 Sege., "Film Reviews: *Godspell,"* Variety, 28 March 1973, 18.

49. Hasenberg, "Clown und Superstar," 38.

50. Sege., 18.

51. Hasenberg, "Clown und Superstar," 40, 38. The word Hasenberg uses here is "Actualizierung."

52. "Godspell" (An interview with David Greene and Michael Heimann), *Making Films in New York,* v.7, n.2 (April 1973), 10.

53. Malone, *Movie Christs and Antichrists,* 34.

54. Ibid.

55. Alexander Stuart, "Review of *Godspell,"* Films and Filming v.19, n.11 (August 1973): 52.

56. Malone, *Movie Christs and Antichrists,* 32, 34.

57. Betty Jeffries Demby, "The Making of Godspell: An Interview with Director David Greene," *Filmmakers Newsletter* v.6, n.7 (May 1973), 33.

58. Ibid.

59. *"Godspell"* (An interview with David Greene and Michael Heimann), 13.

60. Ibid., 14.

61. Greene explains that the colors of the costumes were bleached, "to be less vivid, dramatic, bright, violent for a 'watercolor look.'" [Ibid.]

62. Demby, 33.

63. Ibid., 34.

64. "Roger Ebert Review," *Microsoft Cinemania* 94, Interactive Movie Guide, Microsoft Corporation, 1993. I find it difficult to understand the reasoning behind the criticism that sincerity is "what is most lacking in *Godspell.*" [Kinnard and Davis, 177.]

65. None of the characters in the film have names but in the case of the Jesus character and the character of John the Baptist-Judas (same actor), the specific identity is clear. The critic Roger Ebert indicates that Jesus and John the Baptist-Judas have names. [Ibid.] The copy of the film that I analyzed does not confirm this.

66. Paul Madden, "Review of *Godspell,*" *The Monthly Film Bulletin* (BFI) v.40, n.474 (July 1973): 148.

67. A scene corresponding to the account in Matthew 3. Hereafter, all references to the Bible will be made in abbreviated form in the text. All citations of biblical material are from the *New Revised Standard Version* of *The Holy Bible* (Nashville: Thomas Nelson Publishers, 1989).

68. Kinnard and Davis, 177.

69. Malone, *Movie Christs and Antichrists,* 34.

70. Peter's confession is witnessed to in the four gospels: Matthew 16:16-23; Mark 8:27-33; Luke 9:18-22; John 6:68-69 and 20:21-23.

71. This event too is witnessed to in the four gospels: Matthew 21:12-13; Mark 11:15-19; Luke 19:45-48; and John 2:13-17.

72. As we have already noted, the same actor plays both roles, John the Baptist and then Judas.

73. Hasenberg, "Clown und Superstar," 39.

74. Ibid.

75. Ibid.

76. Holloway, 121.

77. Hasenberg, "Clown und Superstar," 39.

78. Stuart, "Review of *Godspell,*" 52.

79. The anthropologist Victor Turner investigates the dimension of liminality in human experience, the psychologist Abraham Maslow speaks of peak experience and the sociologist Peter Berger examines marginal situations and the philosopher Karl Jaspers writes about the *Grenzsituation*. The concept is then appropriated by a number of theologians – who speak of limit experiences, critical points, disclosure situations and the dimension of ultimacy – to describe and explain qualify of human experiences that are opportunities of breakthrough to the transcendent. For the discussion of *Godspell* and liminality in this chapter, I want to acknowledge a debt of gratitude to my friend and Jesuit confrère, Gregorius Budi Subanar. We saw the film together, he offered me his written reflections on it, and after some discussion he convinced me to think about it in

terms of Victor Turner's theories and synthesis. His advice was good, the analysis bore fruit.

80. One critic would disagree with my interpretation here. She is convinced that *Godspell* does not bring even a trace of devotional sentiment or theological interest to its subject matter. [Boyum, 20.]

Chapter Four:
The Scandal Films: Monty Python's Life of Brian
and The Last Temptation of Christ

1. This is in fact the full title of the film. Hereafter I will use the abbreviated form, *Life of Brian.*

2. Dennis Altman, "Film Reviews: *The Life of Brian." Cinema Papers* (Australia), n.24 (December-January 1979-1980): 659.

3. Chris Petit, "Half a Dinari [*sic*] For My Bloody Life Story?," *Time Out* n.499 (5 November 1979), 21.

4. Clyde Jeavons, "Review of *Monty Python's Life of Brian," The Monthly Film Bulletin* (BFI) v.46, n.550 (November 1979): 229.

5. Altman, 659.

6. An Italian critic suggests the film was blocked by the Vatican: "It's interesting to note that in Italy, where 'the man in white [the Pope] reigns,' the film was never distributed . . . though Academy Pictures [Italy] negotiated several times with Handmade Pictures [British producer] for the rights." I suspect the reason for its non-distribution in Italy was much more pragmatic: the fear that the highly specialized Monty Python brand of humor would not be understood and appreciated by the Italian public and that the film would be an economic flop. [Marco Zatterin, *Il Circo Volante: Viaggio nel grottesco pythoniano (o nel grottiano pythonesco)* (Roma: Quaderni dell'AIACE, 1987), 33.]

7. Gavin Millar, "Cinema: Blessed Brian," *The Listener* v.102, n.6237 (15 November 1979), 678.

8. Petit, 21.

9. Cart., "Review of *Life of Brian," Variety's Film Reviews 1978-1980* – v.15 (New York: R.R. Bowker, 1983). (22 August 1979)

10. "Film Guide: *Monty Python's Life of Brian," Sight and Sound* v.49, n.1 (Winter, 1980): 66.

11. Jeavons, 229.

12. Vincent Canby, "Gospel of Lunacy," *The New York Times Film Reviews 1979-1980* (New York: The New York Times & Arno Press, 1981). (17 August 1979)

13. Zatterin, 31.

14. Canby.

15. Petit, 21.

16. Ibid.

17. Ibid.

18. Marjorie Bilb, "The New Films: *Monty Python's Life of Brian,*" *Screen International* n.217 (24 November 1979): 18.

19. Petit, 21.

20. Altman, 659.

21. Ibid.

22. Bilb, 18.

23. Singer, 47.

24. Ibid.

25. Millar, 678.

26. Ibid.

27. The novel was first published in English in 1961. The edition to which I shall refer in this chapter is that published in paperback by Faber and Faber (London) in 1975.

28. Les Keyser, *Martin Scorsese* (New York: Twayne Publishers, 1992), 167.

29. David Ehrenstein, *The Scorsese Picture: The Art and Life of Martin Scorsese* (New York: Birchlane Press-Carol Publishing Group, 1992, 112. This commission of biblical and theological experts was composed of John L. McKenzie, the (then-) Jesuit scripture scholar, John B. Cobb of Claremont College, with a liberal Protestant perspective, Rosemary Radford Reuther of Garrett Evangelical Theological Seminary, a prominent Catholic feminist theologian and John Elliot of San Francisco State University, a Lutheran scholar. [Mary Pat Kelly, *Martin Scorsese: A Journey* (New York: Thunder's Mouth Press, 1991), 176.]

30. Ehrenstein, 112.

31. *Scorsese on Scorsese,* edited by David Thompson and Ian Christie (Boston: Faber and Faber, 1989), 121.

32. The English title is *Hail Mary.* Jean-Luc Godard's film is a strange contemporary updating of the Mary and Joseph story. More shocking for its style – the Marie of the film is repeatedly pictured nude – than its content, it nonetheless incurred the wrath of Church groups and hierarchies in Europe and America.

33. *Scorsese on Scorsese,* 122.

34. Ehrenstein, 112.

35. Kinnard and Davis, 207.

36. Ibid.

37. David Ehrenstein gives a detailed account of the varied positions and statements of those who objected to the film, which included TV evangelists Pat Robertson, Jerry Falwell, Jimmy Swaggart, Jim Bakker, Catholic Archbishops Mahoney (Los Angeles) and O'Connor (New York), the Catholic Mother Angelica of the Eternal Word Television Network, and Christian pop-singer Pat Boone – who played the Resurrection angel in George Stevens' *King of Kings.* Most of them had not seen the film. [Ehrenstein, 112-113.] Les Keyser follows up with further information on the protest. He adds the name of former White House aide Pat Buchanan who attacked the film in his nationally syndicated newspaper column, and the Reverend Donald Wildmon of the American Family Association, "which added 60,000 new members during the campaign" against the film.

He and his people, armed with antisemitic slogans, picketed the Los Angeles home of Lew Wasserman, the Jewish chairman of MCA, the parent corporation of Universal Pictures. [Keyser, *Martin Scorsese,* 184-186.]

38. Ehrenstein, 113.

39. Ibid. Zeffirelli later denied having made the remarks.

40. Olivier Serre, "Le point de vue de Chrétiens-Médias," in *Le film religieux,* 55.

41. Jonathan Rosenbaum, "Raging Messiah: *The Last Temptation of Christ,"* *Sight and Sound* v.57, n.4 (Autumn 1958): 281.

42. Keyser, *Martin Scorsese,* 186.

43. Kinnard and Davis, 207.

44. Kelly, 161.

45. Marie Katheryn Connelly, *Martin Scorsese: An Analysis of His Feature Films with a Filmography of His Whole Career* (Jefferson NC: McFarland & Company, 1993), 125.

46. Michael Henry, "Entretien avec Martin Scorsese sur *La Dernière Tentation du Christ,"* *Positif* n.332 (October 1988): 7.

47. Kelly, 169. Rather significantly, Scorsese adds that at that time "I was thinking of making a movie from a different novel, *King Jesus* by Robert Graves." [Ibid.]

48. *Scorsese on Scorsese,* 138.

49. Ibid. Scorsese says significantly about *The Gospel According to Saint Matthew* that it has "a script better than mine . . . it's my favorite film on Jesus." [Sablon, 54.]

50. Two critics speak of a "subversion of the Catholic iconology of the sacred heart." [Babington and Evans, 153.]

51. The error of Scorsese's overly literal and material reading of the symbolism of the Sacred Heart icon is immediately sensed by most Catholic, and many non-Catholic, viewers of the film, who inevitably react with vociferous incredulity.

52. *Scorsese on Scorsese,* 18, 21.

53. Keyser, *Martin Scorsese,* 170.

54. *Scorsese on Scorsese,* 136.

55. Ehrenstein, 109.

56. *Scorsese on Scorsese,* 131.

57. Ibid., 133.

58. Michael Morris, "Of God and Man: A Theological and Artistic Scrutiny of Martin Scorsese's *The Last Temptation of Christ,"* *American Film* v.14, n.1 (October 1988): 47.

59. Babington and Evans, 165.

60. "The first half of the film was shot in a village near Marrakesh . . . for Nazareth and the early part of Jesus' mission. And then Meknès, which is in the northern part of the country, was . . . Jerusalem." [Kelly, 210.]

61. Babington and Evans, 107.

62. Rosenbaum, 281.

63. Kinnard and Davis, 208.

64. Kenneth Von Gunden, *Postmodern Auteurs: Coppola, Lucas, De Palma, Spielberg and Scorsese* (Jefferson, NC: McFarland & Company, 1991), 160.

65. Janet Maslin, "The Inner Life of the Absolute," *The New York Times Film Reviews 1987-1988.* (New York: Times Books and Garland Publishing Company, 1990) (12 August 1988). On the other hand, a French critic is very happy with the American accents, saying it is "a perfectly justified choice." [Jean-Pierre Coursodon, "Martin Scorsese: La chair et l'esprit," *Positif* n.332 (October 1988): 3.]

66. Kelly, 224.

67. Babington and Evans, 109.

68. Ibid.

69. Ibid. Jonathan Rosenbaum concludes: "The use of females throughout to signify only motherhood and temptation (of the male) suggests that if anyone should be objecting to this film, it is women of all denominations rather than fundamentalists of both sexes." [Rosenbaum, 281.]

70. His most important films before *The Last Temptation of Christ* were: *Mean Streets,* 1973; *Alice Doesn't Live Here Anymore,* 1974; *Taxi Driver,* 1976; *New York, New York,* 1977; *Raging Bull,* 1980; *The King of Comedy,* 1982; and *The Color of Money,* 1986.

71. Leo Lourdeaux, *Irish and Italian Filmmakers in America: Ford, Capra, Coppola, and Scorsese* (Philadelphia: Temple University Press, 1990), 259.

72. Keyser, *Martin Scorsese,* 170.

73. Ibid.

74. Richard Corliss, "Body . . .", *Film Comment* v.24, n.5 (September-October 1988): 43.

75. Maslin.

76. Corliss, "Body . . .," 43.

77. Scorsese made *Mean Streets* in 1973 and *Raging Bull* in 1980.

78. Von Gunden, 160.

79. Rolando Caputo, "Forbidden Christ," *Cinema Papers* (Australia) n.71 (January 1989): 8.

80. Harlan Jacobson, "You talkin' to me?," *Film Comment* v.24, n.5 (September-October, 1988): 32.

81. Lourdeaux, 259.

82. Caputo, 8.

83. Ibid.

84. Henry, 8.

85. Kelly, 242.

86. Ibid., 243.

87. Von Gunden, 162.

88. Kelly, 243.

89. An image of the Sacred Heart appears in his 1995 film, *Casino,* in the form of a plaster statue conspicuously pictured on the kitchen table at which the powerful mafiosi discuss questions of policy. The reference is, I daresay, ironic.

90. Richard Corliss, ". . . and Blood: An Interview with Martin Scorsese," *Film Comment* v.24, n.5 (September-October 1988): 36.

91. Corliss, "Body . . . ," 42.

92. Keyser, *Martin Scorsese,* 183.

93. *Scorsese on Scorsese,* 118.

94. Sablon, 54.

95. Ibid., 55.

96. *Scorsese on Scorsese,* 12. Significantly, this move was frowned upon by his parents. [Keyser, *Martin Scorsese,* 10.]

97. Ibid.

98. Ibid.

99. Sablon, 55.

100. *Scorsese on Scorsese,* 12.

101. Diane Jacobs, "Martin Scorsese Doesn't Live Here Anymore: Hollywood's Successful Young Director Has Walked Some Pretty Mean Streets," *Viva,* March 1976, 89, quoted in Keyser, *Martin Scorsese,* 10.

102. Ibid., 11.

103. This image is not original to *The Last Temptation:* In Scorsese's script for *Jerusalem, Jerusalem,* a film he never made, "J.R. [the protagonist] imagines a contemporary crucifixion in which blood spurts when Roman soldiers nail Jesus' feet to the cross, a graphic detail recaptured in *Temptation* at the political prisoner's death." [Lourdeaux, 259.]

104. For a more extensive description of this strange fascination with blood in Scorsese's experience of Italo-American Catholicism, see Keyser, *Martin Scorsese,* 184, and Martin Scorsese, "In the Streets," in *Once a Catholic: Prominent Catholics and Ex-Catholics Discuss the Influence of the Church on their Lives and Works,* edited by Peter Occhiogrosso (Boston: Houghton Mifflin, 1987), 88-101.

105. Castellani, *Temi e figure del film religioso,* 161.

106. Rosenbaum, 281.

107. Keyser's explanation – "This bizarre literalism can be traced to Scorsese's encounters with the Sisters of Mercy, who emphasized the sanctity of the host and wine as God's real body and blood to impressionable Catholic youths." [Keyser, *Martin Scorsese,* 184.] – is overly simple, reductive, and neglects the role of Schrader in the writing of the script, who being a Calvinist certainly had no contact, at least as a child, with the Sisters of Mercy.

108. Ibid., 183.

109. *Scorsese on Scorsese,* 118.

110. To give but one example: *Raging Bull* is for the most part in black and white, but the title, seen against an image of De Niro-LaMotta "dancing" in the boxing ring in abstract, poetic slow motion, in bold letters, is blood red in color. And splattering blood is a staple of the film.

111. Scorsese, in Corliss, ". . . and Blood: An Interview with Martin Scorsese," 42.

112. Henry, 12

113. Keyser, 184.

114. Castellani, *Temi e figure del film religioso,* 161.

115. Ibid.

116. There is no specific evidence in the literature that Scorsese was aware of the significance of this piece of music and song. It was chosen by Peter Gabriel, the creator of the soundtrack. Neither is there any specific evidence that Gabriel knew of the words of the song nor of their full significance.

117. Kelly, 223.

118. For the information concerning the Moslem hymn and for some of the commentary that follows, I am grateful to three Jesuit confrères: Gregorius Budi Subanar, a graduate student in Missiology at the Gregorian University and Roland Meynet and Arij Roest Crollius, professors at the Gregorian. All three viewed with me the Last Supper scene in the film and generously shared their knowledge of Arabic and Moslem culture and religion.

119. Scorsese, quoted in Von Gunden, 159.

120. Ehrenstein, 114.

121. Kelly, 230.

122. Corliss, ". . . and Blood: An Interview with Martin Scorsese," 42.

123. *Scorsese on Scorsese,* 117.

124. Keyser, *Martin Scorsese,* 182.

125. Morris, 47.

126. Keyser, *Martin Scorsese,* 171.

127. Kelly, 171-172, and *Scorsese on Scorsese,* 126.

128. Cart., "Film Reviews: *The Last Temptation of Christ,"* *Variety,* 10 August 1988, 12.

129. Scorsese counters this objection with an equally tenuous argument. He speaks of first-century Palestine as a cultural and racial melting pot, and makes Jesus Aryan by "assimilation . . . so we thought Jesus could have had blue eyes." Then he adds rather illogically, "Willem looks like the Jesus we have known over the years." [Kelly, 204.]

130. David Thompson, "Review of *The Last Temptation of Christ,"* *Films and Filming* n.409 (October 1988): 38.

131. Babington and Evans, 157.

132. Connelly, 128.

133. Pam Cook, "Feature Films: The Last Temptation of Christ," *The Monthly Film Bulletin* (BFI) v.55, n.657 (October 1988): 288.

134. Keyser, *Martin Scorsese,* 171.

135. The protagonists of *Mean Streets, Taxi Driver* and *Raging Bull,* respectively.

136. Cook, 288.

137. Babington and Evans, 162.

138. Scorsese explains how he translated the meaning and feeling of the painting into the film medium: in the "painting by Bosch . . . the surrounding faces gave no sense of three dimensions. It took all morning to do that scene, at 120 frames per second [for slow motion]. To keep the people around him, some of them laughing or pointing at him, we had to tie them together with ropes, so they could move only one step at a time." [*Scorsese on Scorsese,* 138.]

139. Babington and Evans, 163.

140. Ibid., 130.

141. One critic actually describes the "human condition" of Scorsese's Jesus as "his sexuality." [Jean-François Pigoullie, "Religion: Les années 80 ou le religieux postmoderne," *Positif* n.340 (June 1989): 21.]

142. The violence is even an stylistic on Scorsese's part: "The fierceness of Jesus's rejection of his mother exceeds narrative necessities." [Babington and Evans, 166.]

143. Henry, 11. Scorsese responds to the comment rather evasively: "The idea of the room in the form of a shoebox, with the bed behind a curtain, comes in fact from Taiwan." [Ibid.]

144. Cook, 288.

145. Babington and Evans, 152.

146. Morris, 45.

147. Cook, 288.

148. Lourdeaux, 259.

149. A significant detail that is found neither in the Bible nor in Kazantzakis' *The Last Temptation.*

150. This intermittent, unpredictable violence of Jesus finds one of its sources in the fundamental attitude of Martin Scorsese towards his film, a good example of which is provided by the following anecdote told by the actor Michael Been, who plays John in the film. He describes how, in the scene of the stoning of Mary Magdalene, Scorsese instructed everyone on the set (including the apostles) to pick up some large rocks (made of rubber). "Everyone went to the bucket and got a rock except me. He [Scorsese] said, 'Michael, do you have one?' And I said, 'No. I really can't imagine John, this gentle John, stoning someone.' He said, 'Bullshit, pick up a rock!'" [Kelly, 217.]

151. Lourdeaux, 254.

152. Keyser, *Martin Scorsese,* 176.

153. Connelly, 131.

154. Morris, 44-45.

155. Ibid., 45.

156. *Scorsese on Scorsese,* 124.

157. Morris, 45.

158. Kinnard and Davis, 208. The sequence seems, at least in its final two shots, a reference to the painting of Giuseppe Pellizza da Volpedo entitled, "Il quarto stato," "The Fourth Estate," which pictures a crowd of peasants advancing and emanating socialist power Bernardo Bertolucci used the painting as a principle of composition in his 1976 political-historical-epic film, *Novecento* or *1900*.

159. Connelly, 130. Commenting negatively on the "contemporary quality" of Scorsese's casting, she adds that the disciples are "too much New York provincial types to be convincing as biblical characters." [Ibid.]

160. Rosenbaum, 282. Making reference to two great film-makers, both with profound, spiritual visions of reality, whose Jesus-films, had they made them, would certainly have been different from *The Last Temptation of Christ*, Rosenbaum comments on Scorsese's limitations: "The pity and compassion of a Dreyer or a Bresson are missing." [Ibid.]

161. Babington and Evans, 161.

162. Ibid., 163.

163. Ibid., 160.

164. Rosenbaum, 281.

165. Castellani, *Temi e figure del film religioso*, 161

166. Cart., 12.

167. Lourdeaux, 260.

168. Cart., 12.

169. Castellani, *Temi e figure del film religioso*, 159.

170. This is the average of the lengths of the versions of the film in video that I studied – the Italian and the British versions, both 156 minutes long – and of the length of the cinema version as reported in various encyclopedias – 158, 161, 164.

171. Scorsese justifies this omission saying, "It's the idea that he [Matthew] creates the legend that gave me trouble. . . . In the book, when Jesus complains to Matthew that he is distorting the facts, Matthew answers, 'An angel speaks into my ear and tells me what to write. I can't do anything about it.' That's a little too easy." Scorsese says nothing about the fact that Kazantzakis' version flies in the face of all serious biblical scholarship about the creation-redaction of the Gospels. [Henry, 10.]

172. Castellani, for example, insists that in the prose narration, Kazantzakis is able to clearly distinguish between various levels of the tale – "it makes very clear the line of demarcation between the rigorously evangelical passages and the imaginary 'last temptation'" – while in Scorsese's narration, the images "do not succeed in distinguishing between the two levels." Though Castellani is both a film critic and a film-maker, he evidently did not view the film very closely. [*Temi e figure del film religioso*, 159.]

173. Cook, 288.

174. Morris, 46.

175. Peter Malone, "Martin Scorcese's [*sic*] *The Last Temptation of Christ,*" *Cinema Papers* (Australia) n.71 (January 1989): 7. No one questions the logic or the psycho-logic of the dying Jesus' temptation to domestic bliss. It seems to me that in the case of a just man dying the shameful and excruciatingly painful death by crucifixion, the temptation to despair is more logical and more credible. I wonder if it ever occured to Scorsese that the earliest Gospel might, in this matter, be recording precisely what happened on Calvary that day: – "'Eloi, Eloi lame sabachthani?' which means, 'My God, my God, why have you forsaken me?' " (Mk 15:34) – that is Jesus tempted to despair.

176. Morris, 46.

177. Charles Krauthammer, "The *Temptation* of Martin Scorsese," *Washington Post,* 19 September 1988, 23, sec.A. Perhaps Scorsese involuntarily reveals one of these "demons," when, with rather strange logic, he attempts to justify the "last temptation" sequence: "You know, the one sexual thing the priest told Catholic boys they could not be held responsible for was nocturnal emission. It was like an involuntary fantasy. And with Jesus it's the same thing. How can you hold him responsible for this fantasy?" [Corliss. ". . . and Blood: An Interview with Martin Scorsese," 38.]

178. Cook, 288.

179. Rosenbaum, 281.

180. The critic Jonathan Rosenbaum uses this title ironically as part of the title of his review of the film: "Raging Messiah: *The Last Temptation of Christ.*"

181. Kinnard and Davis, 207.

182. Scorsese, in typical enigmatic style, explains his solution: "There was no more film. It was an accident. To end . . . on a fade-to-black, too sad, while the death of Christ is a moment of happiness." [Sablon. 59.]

183. A Jewish scholar criticizes Scorsese's solution: "the film's exultation at this moment, clumsily signaled with a burst of joyous music and a dizzying display of psychedelic imagery, does not suffice." [Phillip Lopate, "Fourteen Koans by a Levite on Scorsese's *The Last Temptation of Christ,*" *Tikkum,* November-December 1988: 76, paraphrased in Keyser, *Martin Scorsese,* 175.]

184. Babington and Evans, 128.

185. *Casino* is exceptional in Scorsese in that it has two distinct first-person narrators, which makes for a very dense "subjective" structure.

186. Ehrenstein, 114. In this regard, Les Keyser's analysls is way off the mark: "Where Kazantzakis relied on interior monologues to define Christ's struggle, Schrader and Scorsese turned to dialogue." [Keyser, *Martin Scorsese,* 171.] There is far more first-person interior monologue in Scorsese that in Kazantzakis.

187. Maslin. She points out that this first-person voice-over description of his struggles, his nightmarish visions is "reminiscent of Harvey Keitel's opening inner monologue in *Mean Streets.*" [Ibid.]

188. Ibid.

189. Babington and Evans, 151.

190. Ibid.

191. Ibid., 152.

192. Ibid., 151.

193. Both quotations are from Ibid., 152.

194. This disclaimer, and the quotation from Kazantzakis that precedes it, were, it seems, added at the last minute, after some test audiences voiced serious objections about the film.

195. Castellani, *Temi e figure del film religioso,* 160.

Chapter Five:
Two Recent Classics: Jesus of Nazareth *and* The Messiah

1. Its television premiere in the United States, on NBC, was on 3 and 10 April 1977, in two segments for a total of six hours and thirty-seven minutes; and two years later, an expanded edition was transmitted, again on NBC, in four segments of two hours each, on 1, 2, 3, and 8 April. [Kinnard and Davis, 185, and Richard H. Campbell and Michael R. Pitts, *The Bible on Film: A Checklist 1897-1980* (Metuchen, NJ: The Scarecrow Press, 1981), 179.]

2. ITC (Britain) and RAI (Italy).

3. Kinnard and Davis, 189.

4. Ibid., 187.

5. For example, when it premiered on Italian television, it attracted 28,000,000 viewers, clearly a record for 1977. [Castellani, *Temi e figure del film religioso,* 32.]

6. Kinnard and Davis, 187, 189.

7. Ibid., 187.

8. For the Italian two-cassette version of the film, divided into fourteen episodes, a carefully planned and executed 182 page study guide is available, prepared by Bartolino Bartolini of the Catechetical Center run by the Salesians in Torino, and published by Editrice Elle Di Ci and Sampaolo Audiovisivi. Costing LIT10.000 ($7.50). Presupposing the viewing by small groups of the special "catechetical" video version of the film in brief segments, each chapter in divided into four parts: a reflection on the theme of the episode-scenes to be considered, a detailed summary of the plot with the dialogue, series of suggested questions and suggestions for teachers, and finally a brief liturgical celebration to close the experience.

9. Campbell and Pitts, 180. This development boggles the mind. It clearly means that many people prefer to read the "novelized" version of the facts, finding the fictional form and content more satisfying than the biblical. Worse, it suggests that some people might even not be aware of the biblical "original version." Further, it raises the point that perhaps Zeffirelli's film version of the biblical "facts" is closer to fiction that to facts. One can almost imagine someone in the not-too-distant future wondering, about the *Jesus of Nazareth* phenomenon – which came first, the Barclay novel or the Zeffirelli film? – while remaining in the dark about the ur-source of both these mass-culture media-products.

10. Franco Zeffirelli, *Il mio Gesù,* raccontato a Luigi Gianoli (Milano: Sperling & Kupfer Editori, 1992).

11. Ibid., 19.

12. Ibid., 18.

13. Ibid., 19.

14. William Aldridge, "Franco Zeffirelli on Telling the Story of Christ from Its Real Roots," *Screen International* n.48 (7 August 1976): 9.

15. I can't imagine what David Ehrenstein is thinking of when he speaks of Zeffirelli's film as "Pasolini-inspired." [Ehrenstein, 111.] All the evidence indicates unequivocally that Zeffirelli's film is the polar opposite of Pasolini's, both in content and in form. Recently, in response to the inclusion of Pasolini's *Gospel* in a Vatican-prepared list of exceptional religious films, Zeffirelli said: "*The Gospel* of Pasolini, best religious film? Who are they trying to kid? It's well known that Pasolini, in my opinion a mediocre director, was an atheist. His vision of Christianity was totally distorted." [Giuseppina Manin, "Sul cinema Chiesa in malafede," *Corriere della Sera,* 25 February 1996, 13.]

16. Zeffirelli, 73-74.

17. Filizzola, 373.

18. Ibid., 372. Filizzola continues: "All that went on [in the Catholic world] during and after the Second Vatican Council – the discussions, the crises, the innovations – seems not to interest him in the least." [Ibid., 373.]
19. Andrew Rissik, "A Pallid Pageant," *Films and Filming* v.23, n.10 (July 1977): 5.

20. Zeffirelli, 151.

21. Ibid., 152.

22. Kinnard and Davis erroneously refer to this passage as the "Immaculate Conception." [Kinnard and Davis, 189.] The error is rather common in commentaries on Jesus-films. The "Immaculate Conception" is a recently-declared [1956] dogma of the Catholic Church having to do with the conception of Mary, the mother of Jesus and has nothing to do directly with the Annunciation or the birth of Jesus.

23. Rissik, 5.

24. Zeffirelli, 122.

25. Ibid., 159.

26. In fact, Zerah is a creation of Anthony Burgess. But when Zeffirelli rewrote the script he retained Zerah, and so ultimately the responsibility for this strange character is his.

27. Rissik, 5.

28. Campbell and Pitts, 179.

29. Zeffirelli spends a whole Chapter of his book, entitled "Did Judas betray?," justifying his position on Judas. [Zeffirelli, 186-198.]

30. Campbell and Pitts, 179.

31. The review of *Jesus of Nazareth* in *Newsweek* praises the great "ecumenical deference" of the film. [Kinnard and Davis, 189.] I wonder, though, if one should praise ecumenical deference – or perhaps political correctness, in view of the investments in the film – when it achieved by Zeffirelli's brand of highly fictional and sentimental revisionism. One might wonder further if Zeffirelli's ecumenical deference is motivated more by his desire to combat antisemitism, clearly a just cause, or by his not wishing to alienate a large part of the viewing public.

32. Rissik, 5.

33. Castellani, *Temi e figure del film religioso,* 31.

34. Philippe Hodara, "*Jésus de Nazareth* de Franco Zeffirelli," *Lumière du Cinéma* n.11 (January-February 1978): 23.

35. Rather like the famous Botticelli painting of "Venus Rising from the Conch Shell."

36. Castellani, *Temi e figure del film religioso,* 31.

37. Hodara, 23.

38. It is not as if Zeffirelli had been compelled by the producers of the film to use these "stars," as was Ray because his film was in trouble. Zeffirelli's own comments in *Il mio Gesù* regarding the well-known actors he was working with seem to indicate just the opposite. Zeffirelli says: "I felt it was essential for the health and the success of the film that it be solidly anchored to artists of talent, professionals whose presence is a guarantee of success" (52). I don't think it is exaggerated to hear the word "economic" whispering softly behind the repeated words "success." For the role of Jesus, Zeffirelli quite incredibly considered Dustin Hoffmann and Al Pacino (91). Concerning Mary Magdalene, he says, "The ideal Magdalene would be Anne Bancroft; I always remember her as a terrific actress, from *The Miracle Worker* to *The Graduate;* but then I thought that I was wishing for the impossible" (50). Then, he indicates his satisfaction that Laurence Olivier has accepted his invitation to play Nicodemus "especially because of his Christian faith and our strong and long-lasting friendship" (47), and notes that "the Joseph of Arimathea of James Mason [was] an example of style and wonderful balance" (55), The clincher, I think, is when Zeffirelli defends this "very rich gallery" of actors (Would the word "stable" perhaps have been more appropriate?) by insisting that "not one of these actors had been chosen because of his famous name or his actual popularity" (46). Gertrude's line in *Hamlet* comes to mind: "The lady doth protest too much, methinks" (act 3, scene 2).

39. Kinnard and Davis, 189.

40. Ibid.

41. Hodara, 23.

42. Evidently Kinnard and Davis would not agree with me, for they insist: "The ingredient that sets this Jesus film apart from the others is its naturalness, its simplicity." [Kinnard and Davis, 189.]

43. Rissik, 4.

44. Ibid., 5.

45. Ibid. Rissik's comparison is to a "Gorden Fraser" Easter card, the British equivalent of Hallmark devotional cards, appropriate for every sacred occasion.

46. Ferdinando Camon, in *Corriere della Sera* (25 April 1977), quoted in Filizzola, 373.

47. Ibid.

48. Castellani, *Temi e figure del film religioso,* 32.

49. Ibid.

50. Gianni Baget Bozzo, *Stampa Sera,* 25 April 1977, quoted in Filizzola, 374.

51. Virgilio Fantuzzi, "Vangeli cinematografici a confronto," *La Civiltà Cattolica* an.128, n.2 qd.3048 (18 June 1977): 582.

52. Ibid.

53. Ibid.

54. This fact probably accounts for the number of people who, having seen *Jesus of Nazareth,* are firmly convinced that the entirely-fictional Zerah is in fact a Gospel figure.

55. Fantuzzi, "Vangeli cinematografici a confronto," 582.

56. Ibid., 583.

57. This is precisely what Jesus in his life, and in his preaching and particularly in his parables, *does not do.* Jesus issues challenges, he offers invitations, allowing for the movement of the grace of the Spirit in the listeners to move them in freedom to respond.

58. Fantuzzi, "Vangeli cinematografici a confronto," 583.

59. As we will see in the following section and in the next chapter, both Rossellini and Pasolini must have sensed the peril of this pseudo-naturalistic approach to the *vita Christi,* because each "in his own way, attempted to follow the approach of an anti-realism far from the results sought by Zeffirelli." [Ibid.]

60. Zeffirelli, 18.

61. Ibid., 15.

62. Ibid., 54.

63. Ibid., 119-120.

64. Ibid., 55.

65. Ibid., 115.

66. Ibid.

67. Ibid., 116.

68. Ibid., 96.

69. Ibid., 79.

70. Ibid., 83.

71. Ibid., 78.

72. Ibid., 79. One critic is convinced that Zeffirelli succeeds in this enterprise: he speaks of "certain 'portraits' of Christ in which his face has a transparence and a luminosity that is almost divine." [Hodara, 23.]

73. Even a critic otherwise well-disposed to Zeffirelli's film has reservations about the music score, saying: "the music of Mr. Maurice Jarre seemed to us rather insipid, affected and syrupy." [Ibid., 24.] Zeffirelli, however, was happy with the music: when he saw the film for the first time with the music score edited in, he says, "I became again a virgin of all these experiences and I viewed the film as if I was seeing it for the first time." [Zeffirelli, 204.]

74. Singer, 47.

75. Fantuzzi, "Vangeli cinematografici a confronto," 586.

76. Ibid., 583.

77. Ibid.

78. An Italian critic, himself obviously ideologized, imputes an almost reactionary ideological motivation to Zeffirelli. In the film, he sees an insistence that "the sovereignty of Christ, coming from God, is transmitted directly to the apostles and to Peter and so, for Roman Catholics, to the Bishops and the Pope." According to him, this makes of *Jesus of Nazareth* a "symbolic seal of legitimacy of the hierarchy and the Pope, the only legitimate heirs of the movement that had that same God as exceptional protagonist." [Liborio Termine, "Conformismo intellettuale per il *Gesù* di Zeffirelli," *Cinema Nuovo* v.26, n.248 (July-August 1977): 256.]

79. For Italy, Orizzonte 2000, and for France, Procinex-France 3-Téléfilm (Paris).

80. Singer, 46. Ehrenstein, speaking of Scorsese's Jesus-film says in passing that *The Messiah* was "little seen in the United States." [Ehrenstein, 111.]

81. For example, the authoritative checklist of films on the Bible by Campbell and Pitts, published in 1981, and referred to several times in this book, does not mention *The Messiah,* a rather conspicuous and inexplicable omission. Nor does it mention Rossellini's other biblical film, *Acts of the Apostles* (1968).

82. *The Flowers of St. Francis* (1950), *Joan of Arc at the Stake* (1954), *Acts of the Apostles* (1968), and *Augustine of Hippo* (1972).

83. To name four: *The Man with the Cross* (1943), *Open City, Paisan* and *Stromboli: Land of God* (1949).

84. In addition to several early didactic works, between 1968 and 1975 when he made *The Messiah,* Rossellini made six didactic films for television: *Acts of the Apostles, Socrates* (1970), *Blaise Pascal* (1971), *Augustine of Hippo, The Age of the Medici* (1972), and *Descartes* (1974).

85. Mireille Latil Le Dantec, "Les Films: *Le Messie,*" *Cinématographe* n.18 (April-May 1976): 37.

86. Peter Bondanella, *The Films of Roberto Rossellini* (Cambridge: Cambridge University Press, 1993), 25.

87. Fantuzzi, "Vangeli cinematografici a confronto," 580.

88. Ibid.

89. Ibid.

90. Bondanella, *The Films of Roberto Rossellini,* 25.

91. Fantuzzi, "Vangeli cinematografici a confronto," 580.

92. Gianni Rondolino, *Roberto Rossellini* (Firenze: La Nuova Italia, 1977), 118.

93. Virgilio Fantuzzi, *"Il Messia* di Roberto Rossellini," *La Civiltà Cattolica* an.126, n.4, qd.3010 (15 November 1975): 341.

94. Fantuzzi, "Vangeli cinematografici a confronto," 581.

95. Castellani, *Temi e figure del film religioso,* 33.

96. Rondolino, 118.

97. "Conversazione con Roberto Rossellini," edited by Edoardo Bruno, Alessandro Cappabianca, Enrico Magrelli, Michele Mancini, *Filmcritica* v.27, nn.264-265 (May-June 1976): 134.

98. At least this is so in the Italian original of the film, in which version the formal "distancing" tone is augmented bv the dubbing of the dialogue.

99. Luigi Bini, *"Il Messia* di Roberto Rossellini," *Letture* v.31, qd.326 (April 1976): 312.

100. Ibid., 313.

101. The biblical and theological advisors to the film were, first, the Jesuit Carlo Maria Martini, then professor at the Pontifical Biblical Institute in Rome and now Cardinal-Archbishop of Milan, and later, Father E. Segneri.

102. The austere style of the film, however, is more like that of Mark's Gospel than the "literary and theological elaboration of John." [Fantuzzi, *"Il Messia* di Roberto Rossellini," 342.]

103. Guy Bedouelle, *Du spirituel dans le cinéma* (Paris: Editions du Cerf, 1985), 66.

104. Rondolino, 119.

105. Hollywood, with its casts of thousands and its Grand Opera productions of the raising of Lazarus, has conditioned us to presume that there were hundreds of first-hand witnesses to every miracle of Jesus. According to the text of the gospels, and to biblical scholarship, this is highly improbable. As it is highly improbable that Jesus was followed continually by crowds of enthralled listeners. Rossellini, Scorsese and Pasolini try to dismantle this filmically-created expectation.

106. Fantuzzi, *"Il Messia* di Roberto Rossellini," 343.

107. Bini, *"Il Messia* di Roberto Rossellini," 312.

108. Bedouelle, 66.

109. Rossellini interviewed by Father C. Sorgi, *Avvenire,* 26 October 1975, quoted in Fantuzzi, *"Il Messia* di Roberto Rossellini," 343.

110. There apparently was no objection to this unambiguous position from the film's major source of funding in the United States, explained perhaps by the fact that Father Peyton and the Family Theatre group tended to be on the conservative end of the Catholic religious-ideological spectrum. The lack of public objection from Jewish organizations was probably because the film was not distributed (or at least not widely) in the States.

111. Fantuzzi, *"Il Messia* di Roberto Rossellini," 345.

112. Bedouelle, 66.

113. Bini, *"Il Messia* di Roberto Rossellini," 312.

114. Latil Le Dantec, 38.

115. Johannes Horstmann, *"Der Messias," Film-Dienst* v.41, n.19 (19 September 1989), reprinted in *Film-Dienst Extra,* 67.

116. Latil Le Dantec, 38.

117. Horstmann. The word he uses is *"Urbild,"* literally "first image."

118. Rondolino, 119.

119. Alessandro Cappabianca, Enrico Magrelli, Michele Mancini, "Appunti su Rossellini," *Filmcritica* v.27, nn.264-265 (May-June 1976): 155.

120. Ibid, 155.

121. Fantuzzi, "Vangeli cinematografici a confronto," 580-581.

122. Ibid., 580

123. Ibid., 584.

124. Fantuzzi, *"Il Messia* di Roberto Rossellini," 343.

125. Latil Le Dantec, 38.

126. Bini, *"Il Messia* di Roberto Rossellini," 312.

127. Ibid.

128. Fantuzzi, *"Il Messia* di Roberto Rossellini," 340.

129. Bini, *"Il Messia* di Roberto Rossellini," 312.

130. Rondolino, 119.

131. "Conversazione con Roberto Rossellini," 136.

132. Ibid., 137.

133. Ibid., 135.

134. Bini, *"Il Messia* di Roberto Rossellini," 312.

135. Rossellini explains his use of the *plan-séquence* shot, also known as a sequence shot: "If you want to arrive at the concrete, you have to offer a large number of elements, which each viewer will then synthesize according to his personality, his nature. The *plan-séquence* shot allows me to offer all these data, without falling into the 'privileged' point of view of the fixed frame." ["Conversazione con Roberto Rossellini," 135.]

136. The zoom lens can, of course, be used for strong dramatic effects. Scorsese operates it with this intention, obtaining strong emotional and psychological results. Avoiding the psychological effect, Rossellini gives the zoom lens a much cooler, didactic-analytical role.

137. Bini, *"Il Messia* di Roberto Rossellini," 313.

138. Fantuzzi, "Vangeli cinematografici a confronto," 584.

139. Ibid.

140. Ibid.

141. Fantuzzi speaks of the difficulty (if not the impossibility) of cinematographically illustrating the Gospel, because of the "basic incompatibility between the essentiality of the sacred and the pseudo-naturalistic approach promoted by the pervasive audio-visual communications mass-media." He argues that Rossellini succeeds exceptionally and admirably because he develops a counter cultural style, the "way of anti-naturalism." [Ibid, 583.]

142. "Conversazione con Roberto Rossellini," 137.

143. The exception, in my opinion, is Pasolini's *The Gospel According to Saint Matthew,* made eleven years before *The Messiah,* and subject of the next chapter of this book.

144. Fantuzzi, *"Il Messia* di Roberto Rossellini," 347.

145. Ibid.

146. St. Paul says that after his Resurrection, Jesus appeared to many, "most of whom are still alive." (1 Cor 15:6) This question of eyewitness reports of the resurrected Lord, and not of the Resurrection itself to which there could not be eyewitnesses, is crucial in the understanding of the primitive community, for its proclamation of Jesus as the Christ.

147. Bini, *"Il Messia* di Roberto Rossellini," 313.

148. Rondolino, 119.

149. Stefano Masi and Enrico Lancia, *I film di Roberto Rossellini* (Roma: Gremese Editore, 1987), 133.

150. Bedouelle, 66.

151. Masi and Lancia, 133.

152. Bini, *"Il Messia* di Roberto Rossellini," 313.

153. Ibid.

154. Ibid.

155. Fantuzzi, *"Il Messia* di Roberto Rossellini," 344.

156. Ibid., 337.

157. Bini, *"Il Messia* di Roberto Rossellini," 314.

158. Fantuzzi, "Vangeli cinematografici a confronto," 581.

159. Fantuzzi, *"Il Messia* di Roberto Rossellini," 349.

160. Fantuzzi, "Vangeli cinematografici a confronto," 585.

161. Rossellini interviewed in *Avvenire,* 26 October 1975, quoted in Bini, *"Il Messia* di Roberto Rossellini," 311-312.

162. Fantuzzi, *"Il Messia* di Roberto Rossellini," 346.

Chapter Six:
The Masterpiece: The Gospel According to Saint Matthew

1. The original title is *Il Vangelo secondo Matteo, "The Gospel According to Matthew."* The title was changed – "Saint" added – by the distributors of the English-language version against Pasolini's wishes and protests. As were also changed the titles of the Spanish and French versions of the film. Pasolini considered the change an "outrage." [*Pasolini su Pasolini: Conversazioni con Jon Halliday* (Parma: Ugo Guanda Editore, 1992), 76.]

2. Maurizio Viano, *A Certain Realism: Making Use of Pasolini's Film Theory and Practice* (Berkeley: University of California Press, 1993) 134.

3. In Italy, Arco Film (Rome) and in France, Lux Compagnie Cinématographique (Paris).

4. Campbell and Pitts, 153.

5. The *Pro Civitate Christiana* was founded in Assisi after the Second World War by the Catholic priest, Don Giovanni Rossi. Made up mostly of lay people, it promotes religious-cultural activities by giving moral, organizational and at times financial support to worthy projects.

6. Pier Paolo Pasolini, in a letter of February 1963 to Lucio S. Caruso of the *Pro Civitate Christiana,* published in Pier Paolo Pasolini, *Il Vangelo secondo Matteo* (Milan: Garzanti, 1964), 16-17, and quoted in Enzo Siciliano, *Pasolini,* translated by John Shepley (New York: Random House, 1982), 269.

7. Pasolini, in his book of *Il Vangelo second Matteo,* 14, quoted in Siciliano, 270.

8. *Accattone,* in 1961; *Mamma Roma* in 1962; *La ricotta* (one episode of four in *Rogopag*) and *La rabbia* (first part) in 1963; and *Comizi d'amore* and *Sopralluoghi in Palestina,* in 1964. Pasolini's published works are listed in Siciliano, 421-422. His complete film credits are listed in Stefano Murri, *Pier Paolo Pasolini* (Milan: Editrice Il Castoro, July-August 1994), 159-172.

9. The crusading public prosecutor, Giuseppe De Gennaro, did not enjoy unanimous support of the Italian public. Pasolini's biographer notes, for example, that "not all Catholics" shared his opinion, and he continues: "The priests who taught at the Pontifical Gregorian University in Rome did not find the film insulting." [Siciliano, 254.] As a professor at the Gregorian thirty-two years later, I can confirm what Siciliano says. My confrère Paolo Valori, Professor Emeritus at the Gregorian, has several times spoken to me about the occasion in 1964 in which a special private showing of *The Gospel According to Saint Matthew* was arranged for the Jesuit fathers of the Gregorian. He was present at the screening as was Pasolini himself, and he reports that after the film, Pasolini spoke informally with the fathers. Valori recalls very clearly that his confrères reacted positively to the film and that the conversation with Pasolini afterwards was warm and friendly.

10. Murri, *Pier Paolo Pasolini,* 53.

11. Pasolini in Marisa Rusconi, "4 Registi al magnetofono," *Sipario* (October 1964): 16, quoted in Naomi Greene, *Pier Paolo Pasolini: Cinema as Heresy* (Princeton: Princeton University Press, 1990), 72.

12. *Pasolini su Pasolini,* 89.

13. Ibid.

14. Viano, 133.

15. *Pasolini su Pasolini,* 78.

16. Pasolini in "Una visione del mondo epico-religiosa," a conversation with Pier Paolo Pasolini, in *Bianco e nero,* v.25, n.6 (June 1964), quoted in Virgilio Fantuzzi, "La 'visione religiosa' di Pier Paolo Pasolini," in *Cinema sacro e profano* (Roma: Edizioni "La Civilta Cattolica," 1983), 316, note 84.

17. *Pasolini su Pasolini,* 82.

18. Pasolini in letter to Lucio Caruso, quoted in Siciliano, 270.

19. Ibid.

20. Viano, 140. Then, in a long note on pages 331-333 of his book, Viano traces very precisely the correspondences between the text of Pasolini's film and that of Matthew's Gospel.

21. *Pasolini su Pasolini,* 90.

22. Luciano De Giusti, *I film di Pier Paolo Pasolini* (Roma: Gremese Editore, 1983), 68. Clearly both Zeffirelli's and Rossellini's films were made after Pasolini's.

23. Pasolini, responding to criticism of the film in Paris, quoted in De Giusti, 69.

24. Stefano M. Paci, "Prudence Counsels Daring," *Thirty Days* v.7, n.1 (1995), 65. The words are in a letter from Siri to Father Giovanni Rossi, dated 22 February 1963, and quoted in its entirety in Paci's article.

25. Siciliano, 272.

26. Ibid., 273.

27. Sam Rohdie, *The Passion of Pier Paolo Pasolini* (Bloomington: Indiana University Press, 1995), 162. André Ruszkowsky, film scholar and President of the O.C.I.C. Jury at the Venice festival responded to the strong criticism of the Catholic prize given to the film of a Communist by insisting that "Any jury, and especially a jury that is just and impartial as must be that of O.C.I.C., must make its judgment based on the film in question and not on the person and the positions of its director." [*Rivista del cinematografo* nn.6-10 (1964): 439.]

28. Paci, "A Blessed Clapperboard," *Thirty Days* v.7, n.1 (1995), 68.

29. The Italian word, *"laico,"* has stronger connotations that the English word. If "layperson" means simply one who is not a member of the clergy, *"laico"* carries suggestions of religious non-belief, and non-practice, perhaps of atheism with political-ideological overtones.

30. Paci, "A Blessed Clapperboard," 68.

31. Ibid., 67-68.

32. The *Osservatore Romano* reviewer said: "There is no doubt that the author [Pasolini] does not consider the Gospel a historical document. It is equally evident that he shows no interest in underlining its more profound truth, namely the divinity of Christ." [Giacinto Ciaccio, "Fedele al racconto, non all'ispirazione del Vangelo il film di Pasolini," *L'Osservatore Romano* n.206 (31.679), 6 September 1964, 6.]

33. The list of great films was prepared on the occasion of the centenary of cinema, by a special committee of the Vatican's Pontifical Commission for Social Communications whose president is the American Archbishop John Foley and of which this author was a member. It was first circulated as part of a document entitled "I cinema al servizio della religione, dei valori e dell'arte," ("Cinema in the Service of the Faith, of Moral Values and of Art") and then was picked up and published by the *Corriere della Sera* on 25 February 1996, 13, as part of an article by Giuseppina Manin entitled "Sul cinema Chiesa in malafede," to which I have already made reference in the previous chapter.

34. Siciliano, 275.

35. The title itself is a composite of the first letters of the surnames of the directors of its four episodes: RO-ssellini, GO-dard, PA-solini, and G-regoretti.

36. Maurizio Ponzi, "La Ricotta," in "Quatre films inédits de Pier Paolo Pasolini," *Cahiers du cinéma* n.169 (August 1965): 28.

37. The two painters imitated in the still tableaux are Rosso Fiorentino and Pontormo. [Mario Verdone, "I film: *Rogopag,*" *Bianco e Nero* v.24, n.3 (March 1963): 58-61.]

38. Ponzi, 28.

39. Mario Verdone, "Da Bergman ad Antonioni," *Bianco e Nero* v.24, nn.8-9 (August-September 1964): 18. For "epics," Verdone uses the word *"polpettoni." "Polpettone"* means literally "big meatball," that is, cheap meat ground together and served, well-disguised, in a spicy sauce. But a meatball – even in *la bella Italia* – is still a meatball. The word is used to describe elaborate, overinflated, pretentious films, whose epic size and reach, elaborate music scores, major stars and casts of thousands, and costs of millions, do not succeed in effectively disguising the moral, spiritual and esthetic void within.

40. Ibid.

41. There is some evidence that Pasolini had in fact made this choice before the trip to Palestine, and that the places seen and the conversations with Father Andrea Carraro, recorded in *Sopralluoghi in Palestina* were Pasolini's way of confirming and elaborating a decision already taken.

42. De Giusti, 69.

43. Pasolini in *Vie nuove,* 19 November 1964, quoted in De Giusti, 69.

44. Siciliano, 274.

45. Literally "the stones," they are ancient dwellings built around hillside caves.

46. *Pasolini su Pasolini,* 81.

47. Murri, *Pier Paolo Pasolini,* 57.

48. Mosk., "Venice Film Fest Reviews: *Il Vangelo secondo Matteo,*" *Variety,* 16 September 1964, 17.

49. Verdone, 17.

50. Ermanno Olmi's 1983 film, *Camminacammina,* literally "Keep walking, Keep walking," is made in the style of the popular sacred drama. Like Pasolini's film, *Camminacammina* is based on the Gospel of Matthew, but since it limits itself to a consideration of the significance of the journey of the Magi to Bethlehem, it can hardly be considered a Jesus-film.

51. Leandro Castellani, "Venezia XXV Edizione: *Il Vangelo secondo Matteo,*" *Rivista del Cinematografo* nn.9-10 (September-October 1964): 430.

52. Castellani, *Temi e figure del film religioso,* 150.

53. Ibid.

54. Franz Everschor, "Die Darstellung religiöser Inhalte im Film," *Stimmen der Zeit* v.193, n.6 (June 1975): 393.

55. Verdone, 18.

56. Fantuzzi, "Vangeli cinematografici a confronto," 581.

57. Pasolini, in letter to Lucio Caruso, quoted in Siciliano, 270.

58. Greene, 71.

59. Ibid.

60. Pasolini, "Cristo e il Marxismo: Dialogo Pasolini-Sartre," *L'Unità*, 22 December 1964, 26, quoted in Greene, 71.

61. Douin, "Jésus superstar: Certains préfèrent l'invisible," 38.

62. Ibid.

63. Viano, 134.

64. John R. May, "Visual Story and the Religious Interpretation of Film," in *Religion in Film,* edited by John R. May and Michael Bird (Knoxville: University of Tennessee Press, 1982), 27.

65. Eckhard Bieger, "Revolte und Religion: Gedanken zu Pasolini's Jesus Gestalten im Abstand von 30 Jahren," in *Film-Dienst Extra,* 35.

66. *Pasolini su Pasolini,* 78.

67. Ibid., 77.

68. Ibid.

69. To name only a few, the writer (and Pasolini's biographer) Enzo Siciliano as Simon, the writer Natalia Ginzburg, as Mary of Bethany, Mario Socrate as John the Baptist, the writer Francesco Leonetti as King Herod II.

70. Maurizio Viano says that Susanna Pasolini is "too old to be a credible Madonna" and more importantly, that she "ruthlessly exposes the film's autobiographical dimension and indirectly suggests that Christ's story is like an open matrix for the most personal and diverse appropriations." [Viano, 145.]

71. Sandro Petraglia, *Pier Paolo Pasolini* (Firenze: La Nuova Italia-Il Castoro Cinema, July-August 1974), 58.

72. Viano, 143. Much of the brief comment in this paragraph is based on Viano's more detailed and rather convincing argumentation which he refers to as a feminist reading. [Ibid., 142-145.]

73. Ibid., 143. We recall how Cecil B. DeMille used this conventional representation of the Magdalene in the opening of his film and how Scorsese pushed it to its outer limits, suggesting Jesus' sexual desire for her.

74. Ibid.

75. Ibid.

76. Ibid., 144.

77. Petraglia, 62.

78. Viano, 145.

79. Davoli was only when fifteen years old when Pasolini met and "fell in love with him." [Siciliano, 285.]

80. Here I am translating literally from the original soundtrack of the film.

81. Ehrenstein, in his book on Martin Scorsese, speaks of Pasolini's film as representing a Jesus "whose behavior could easily be interpreted as paranoid schizophrenic." [Ehrenstein, 111.] The overwhelming evidence of the film goes against this opinion.

82. J. Lajeunesse, *"L'Evangile selon Saint Matthieu," Image et Son* n.184 (May 1965): 100.

83. Viano, 141.

84. Malone, *Movie Christs and Antichrists,* 30.

85. Ibid., 17.

86. Peter Bondanella, *Italian Cinema from Neorealism to the Present* (New York: Continuum-Frederick Ungar. 1990), 183.

87. Jean-Louis Bory, *Des Yeux pour Voir: Cinéma I* (1961-1966) (Paris: Union Génerale d'Edition, 1971), 75.

88. Castellani, "Venezia XXV Edizione: *Il Vangelo secondo Matteo,* " 432.

89. A.C.L., *"Vangelo secondo Matteo, Il (The Gospel According to Saint Matthew),"* The Monthly Film Bulletin (BFI) v.34, n.402 (July 1965): 104.

90. Malone, *Movie Christs and Antichrists,* 30.

91. A.C.L., 104.

92. Fantuzzi, "Vangeli cinematografici a confronto," 583.

93. Luigi Bini, *"Il Vangelo secondo Matteo,"* Letture v.19, n.l0 (October 1964): 707.

94. Ehrenstein, 111.

95. Castellani. "Venezia XXV Edizione: *Il Vangelo secondo Matteo,* " 431.

96. Holloway, 22.

97. Franz Everschor, *"Das 1. Evangelium-Matthäus,"* in *Film-Dienst Extra,* 63.

98. Castellani, *Temi e figure del film religioso,* 154.

99. A.C.L., 105.

100. Ibid.

101. Wall, 53.

102. Viano. 142.

103. Not, however, to the extent suggested by Bini when he says that Pasolini "wanted to remove from the film every explicit reference to the divinity of Jesus." [Bini, *"Il Vangelo secondo Matteo,"* 706.]

104. Thomas M. Martin, *Images and the Imageless: A Study in Religious Consciousness and Film* (Lewisburg: Bucknell University Press – London: Associated University Presses, 1981), 124.

105. Greene, 79.

106. Castellani, *Temi e figure delfilm religioso,* 156.

107. Fulvio Lungobardi, *"Il Vangelo* di Pasolini," Filmcritica v.16, n.154 (February 1965): 119.

108. Greene, 79. An Italian critic perhaps exaggerates a little when he says: "There is not a single scene in which a character in the crowd succeeds in resisting the exclusivist pride of the messiah, not a single frame which raises one of them out of a perspective which crushes everything and flattens the variety [of the people] into a sub-human homogeneity." [Petraglia, 61.]

109. Geneviève Szabō, *"L'évangile selon Saint-Matthieu,"* Jeune Cinéma n.6 (March-April 1965): 15.

110. One of the first attempts to inculturate the Eucharistic liturgy, the "Missa Luba" is a Mass which was created within the Congolese culture. It is sung in Latin but with the voices, the musical instruments and rhythms of that African nation.

111. Bondanella, *Italian Cinema from Neorealism to the Present,* 184.

Part Two: The Christ-Figure

Introduction

1. Holloway, 187.

2. I considered this question of the analogical approach to the biblical event, as opposed to the direct approach, in some articles published in the last couple of years. ["Il film biblico: Meglio il modello analogico che gli effetti speciali," *Letture* an.49, qd.512 (December 1994): 40-42; "Cinema, cultura, spiritualità: Sintonia possibile," *Consacrazione & Servizio* an.44, n.5 (May 1995): 33-40; "Un approccio teologico-spirituale al cinema," *Consacrazione & Servizio* an.44, n.10 (October 1995): 26-36.] In a much longer article, I did a detailed analysis of the whole question of the religious and biblical film: its nature and form, its theological significance, its various modalities, and approaches to its analysis. ["Cine profano, cine religioso," *Teologia y Catequesis* (Madrid) n.56 (October-December 1995): 11-44.]

3. 2 Corinthians 4:4; Colossians 1:15.

4. Michael Goldberg notes that "much of what the Bible has to say is cast in story form." [*Theology and Narrative: A Critical Introduction* (Nashville, TN: Abington, 1982), 147.]

5. May, "Visual Story and the Religious Interpretation of Film," 30.

6. Holloway, 187. Here and in the subsequent three points, Holloway is referring to an article by Robert Detweiler, "Christ and the Christ Figure in American Fiction," of which he does not give the coordinates. " I was able to trace it to: *New Theology* n.2. Edited by Martin Marty and Dean G. Peerman. New York: MacMillan, 1965.

7. Holloway, 187. Holloway uses as an example of the mythical approach, Pasolini's *The Gospel According to Saint Matthew.* As I argued in the chapter on Pasolini's film, I think Holloway is rather off the mark in this opinion.

8. Ibid.

9. Malone, *Movie Christs and Antichrists,* 158.

10. Neil P. Hurley, "Cinematic Transfigurations of Jesus," in *Religion in Film,* 64.

11. Ibid., 66.

12. Ibid.

13. Ibid., 64.

14. Ibid.

15. Malone, *Movie Christs and Antichrists,* 158.

Chapter One:
Jesus of Montreal: *A Transitional Film*

1. Since the script of the film has been published and is very close to the text of the film, I shall rely on it for citations of dialogue. The translation from the French is mine. [Denys Arcand, *Jésus de Montréal* (Montreal: Boréal, 1989), 119.] Further citations will be identified by page number in brackets in the text or in the notes.

2. Marc Gervais, "A Canadian Film Event," *Compass* (Canada) (September 1989): 38.

3. Ibid., 41.

4. Luigi Bini, "*Il declino dell'impero americano di Denys Arcand,*" *Letture* an.42, qd.437 (May 1987): 458.

5. Allan Hunter, "Passion Play," *Films and Filming* v.423 (January 1990): 13.

6. Peter Malone uses the term "Christ-figure" to describe Daniel. ["Review of *Jesus of Montreal*," *Cinema Papers* (Australia) n.80 (August 1990): 57.] Tom O'Brien uses it too. ["Review of *Jesus of Montreal*," *Film Quarterly* v.44, n.1 (Autumn 1990): 49.] Many other critics say the same thing but without using the phrase.

7. Janis Pallister offers some interesting interpretations of the biblical significance of the names and surnames of the major characters of the film. [*The Cinema of Québec: Masters in Their Own House* (Madison, WI/Teaneck, NJ: Fairleigh Dickinson University Press, 1995), 383-384.]

8. Ibid., 386.

9. I have screened *Jesus of Montreal* many times, and with a variety of age groups and inevitably, during this scene of the tradition passion play, the viewers inevitably laugh: a reaction clearly expected and intended by Arcand. The audience too, rejects this image of Jesus.

10. François Ramasse, "Denys Arcand: Etre tendre malgré tout," *Positif* v.340 (June 1989): 14. A number of critics mistakenly identify the Gospel as that of Matthew, saying, for example, "Daniel plays Jesus and . . . acts out parts of His life as they appear in the Gospel according to St. Matthew." [Maria Garcia, "Review of *Jesus of Montreal*," *Films in Review* v.41, n.10 (October 1990): 491.] It is true however, that the scene of the temptations of Daniel "in the desert" of the modern metropolis reflects more Matthew's Gospel than Mark's.

11. Apparently not noticing the woman's later appearance with the New-Age guru, one critic misunderstands her identity, and interprets "Arcand's library scene as an encounter with an angelic 'messenger.'" [O'Brien, 49.]

12. Nor, interestingly enough, do many members of the film audience. In my experience with the film, this line brings very few laughs.

13. The closest Arcand comes to a title is when he has the radio show hostess speaks of "the Passion on the mountain" (117), not intending it, however, as a specific title.

14. Gilles Marsolais, "Dossier Denys Arcand: Du spirituel dans l'art – Critique de *Jésus de Montréal*," *24 Images: La revue québécoise du cinéma* nn.44-45 (Fall 1989): 41.

15. Malone, "Review of *Jesus of Montreal*," 58.

16. Gervais, 40.

17. One critic does not seem to appreciate this subtle technique of Arcand. She describes rather accurately the way he presents the passion play but misses his reason for doing it this way, and I think her basic premise is wrong. "We assume Arcand intended that portion of Christ's life to be a central theme. Yet we never see *The Passion Play* in its entirety, and what we do see are often not even identifiable Stations or portions of the story." [Garcia, 492.]

18. Gervais, 40.

19. Strat., "Competing at Cannes: *Jésus of Montréal* [*sic*] (*Jesus of Montreal*)," *Variety's Film Reviews 1989-1990 – Vol. 21* (New York: R.R. Bowker, 1991) (17 May 1989).

20. Gervais, 40.

21. Ibid., 39.

22. Ibid., 40.

23. Regarding the seriousness of Daniel's-Arcand's research for the historical Jesus, Reinhold Zwick in a major study does an excellent, detailed analysis of the passion play, noting several factual errors and weaknesses, several points at which Daniel-Arcand's version differs widely from the Gospel. [Reinhold Zwick, "Entmythologisierung versus Imitatio Jesu: Thematisierungen des Evangeliums in Denys Arcand's Film *Jesus von Montreal*," *Communicatio Socialis: Zeitschrift für Publizistik in Kirche und Welt*, v.23, n.2 (Paderborn: Ferdinand Schöning Verlag, 1990): 17-47.] Daniel-Arcand presents as fact based on "recent new discoveries" and "computer-assisted textual analysis," (Arcand, 35) that Jesus was the illegitimate son of a Roman soldier, for which the actual evidence is extremely tenuous. He places the beginning of the written tradition about Jesus at one hundred years after his death (60) when biblical scholarship agrees overwhelmingly that Mark's Gospel was written thirty to thirty-five years after Jesus died. His offhand comment that disciples writing about their leader after his death "lie, embellish," (60) flies in the face of overwhelming evidence to the contrary, evidence available to anyone who reads the Bible even superficially. Zwick does not suggest that these errors and weaknesses are conscious on Arcand's part, but I would like to suggest precisely that as a possibility, that is as one more element subverting the passion play. In that case, it would become a question of the limited biblical research of Daniel, not of Arcand. Gervais, for instance, insists that "Arcand makes it clear that Daniel is not posing as an expert," so why should his research be faultless? [Gervais, 39.]

24. The media people are based on entertainment personalities active on the Montreal scene, but they are, in Arcand's own words, reinterpreted by the actors "to create characters who are kind of archetypes." [Marcel Jean, "Dossier Denys Arcand: Entretien avec Denys Arcand," *24 Images: La revue québécoise du cinéma* nn.44-45 (Fall 1989): 53.]

25. Louis Goyette, "Dossier Denys Arcand: Quand le cinéma devient un spectacle," *24 Images: La revue québécoise du cinéma* nn.44-45 (Fall 1989): 59.

26. Maria Garcia would disagree with me here. She maintains mistakenly that the disciples of Daniel do not change at all: "The actors have no apparent motiva-

tion and we never see their transformation." The profound conversion experience represented in Mireille, for example, is obvious. [Garcia, 492.]

27. Hunter, 11.

28. In fact on two crosses, the one in the *via crucis*, under which his head is crushed, and the cruciform operating table on which his body is stretched for the removal of his organs.

29. Janis Pallister gets the analogy right but the detail wrong. She says: "that Daniel has started a theater is equated to Christ starting a church, for his theater is of the purest, the most essential nature." [Pallister, 384.] Clearly Daniel is not the one to start a theater. The idea comes from the lawyer and only after Daniel's death. The analogy works well, for in a sense Christ's Church is formed by the action of the Spirit of the Risen Lord in his disciples after his death. The traditional occasion for the event is the feast of Pentecost.

30. Zwick, 30.

31. Ibid.

32. Arcand creates a quite remarkable shot in the subway station, after Daniel has collapsed (died), of Mireille cradling his head in her lap, forming the unequivocal visual analogue of a "Pietà."

33. Janis Pallister identifies these young women as Constance and Mireille, who sing the "Stabat Mater" in the subway station as "they collect money in a cigar box for their newly founded theater-church." [Pallister, 383.] Here she is in error on two points: quite obviously the singers are not Constance and Mireille, and they have nothing to do with the lawyer's project to found a theater as a memorial to Daniel.

34. Several critics evidently did not notice this rather obvious fact. One comments that Daniel "has an affair" with Mireille. [Strat., "Competing at Cannes: *Jésus of Montréal* [*sic*] (*Jesus of Montreal*)."] Another says Mireille is Daniel's "friend and his lover." [Kevin McMahon, "*Jésus de Montréal* and the Culture of Nihilism," *Take One*, Summer 1995, 43.]

35. O'Brien, 48.

36. André Roy, "Dossier Denys Arcand: Jésus des médias – Critique de *Jésus de Montréal*," *24 Images: La revue québécoise du cinéma* n.44-45 (Fall 1989): 45.

37. Hunter, 13.

38. O'Brien, 50. Speaking of his choice of the actor Lothaire Bluteau for the role of Daniel, Arcand reveals how he wanted to avoid the usual "handsome young man image that Jesus too often is given." He goes on to indicate his intention of opposing, in his film, Martin Scorsese's portrayal of a heavy sexual atmosphere between Jesus and Mary Magdalene and he concludes: "I purposely avoided this possibility by my choice of actors. I wanted no sexual suggestions." [Christine Haas, "*Jésus de Montréal* – Denys Arcand: La Passion revisitée par l'auteur du *Déclin de l'empire américain*," *Première* n.146 (May 1989), 145.]

39. The lawyer's name, Richard Cardinal, is a play on "rich Cardinal," a not-so-subtle dig at the Roman Catholic hierarchy, all the tougher when the "true identity" of the lawyer is revealed.

40. O'Brien, 50.

41. Ibid.

42. Zwick, 34.

43. Mark 13:1-27. Zwick also sees an Gospel reference in the two hospitals Daniel is rushed to: the first, *"Hôpital Saint Marc,"* overcrowded, with no room for Daniel, is likened to the situation at Bethlehem when Jesus is born: no room in the inn; the second, a Jewish hospital, he sees as a reference to the parable of the Good Samaritan. I only note the irony that it is the Jewish hospital, with its transplant surgery, that makes possible Daniel's "resurrection." [Zwick, 34.]

44. Ramasse, "Denys Arcand: Etre tendre malgré tout," 15.

45. Pallister, 388. Daniel's surname "Coulombe" means dove, and so the reference to the Holy Spirit.

46. There is even here the suggestion that some of Daniel's words are not in the original script, but that he improvises them, inspired (so to speak) by the occasion. That, of course, raises the level of the identification between the Christ-figure and the Christ figured.

47. Pallister, 392.

48. Zwick, 36. Some of the material that follows is adapted from Zwick's article.

49. Ramasse, "Denys Arcand: Etre tendre malgré tout," 14.

50. Zwick, 36.

51. Ibid., 31-33.

52. Literally "chaste prostitute," a term first used by St. Ambrose to describe the Church, in his commentary on the Gospel of Luke. [Sant'Ambrogio, *Opera Omnia: Opere esegetiche IX/I: Esposizione del Vangelo secondo Luca*, edited by Giovanni Coppa (Milano: Biblioteca Ambrosiana, 1978), 263.] The concept is ancient, with its roots in the Old Testament's and then the New Testament's reflections on the sinful people of God. The theologian Hans Urs von Balthasar traces in great detail the development of the concept of "casta meretrix" from the Old Testament, through the New Testament and in the early and later Church Fathers. [Hans Urs von Balthasar, "Casta Meretrix," in *Sponsa Verbi: Skizzen zur Theologie II* (Einsiedeln: Johannes Verlag, 1961), 203-305.]

53. Bini, *"Jesus of Montreal*, di Denis [sic] Arcand," *Letture* an.45, qd.463 (January 1990): 69.

54. There are several dissolves in the *plan-séquence*, but they are so subtle as to be practically invisible.

55. Goyette, 57. He notes how the rhythm of the "Stabat Mater" sung in the opening of the film is fast, in contrast to the slower rhythm when it is sung by the same young women in the conclusion.

56. *Quando corpus morietur, / Fac, ut animae donetur, / Paradisi gloria. / Amen.*

57. Zwick, 33.

58. Neither Zwick nor Ramasse – who notes single movement of the camera "all the way to the mountain" [Ramasse, "Denys Arcand: Etre tendre malgré tout," 17.] – notice this remarkable *double* vertical movement.

59. Zwick, 33.

Chapter Two:
The Woman as Christ-Figure

1. It is not by chance that they are played by the same actress, Giulietta Masina, who is also Fellini's wife.

2. Pierre Leprohon, *The Italian Cinema*, translated by Roger Greaves and Oliver Stallybrass (London: Secker & Warburg, 1972), 147.

3. In the Italian original, he is called "il matto," literally "the crazy one," "the fool."

4. Gilbert Salachas, "Le bonheur," *L'Avant-Scène Cinéma* n.381 (May 1989): 7.

5. Two of the critics do not think very highly of the nun's advice. Gordon Gow, speaking first of "the special Italian hang-up about religion," says that the nun's "words of comfort turn out to be short-lived relief." [Gordon Gow, *"La Strada,"* *Films and Filming* v.16, n.1 (October 1969): 58.] Frank Burke says, much in the same vein, that the nun's words are "commonplace Christian 'wisdom,' yet . . . they are life-denying and escapist. Paradoxically, they are also antispiritual, anti-religious." [Frank Burke, *Federico Fellini: Variety Lights to La Dolce Vita* (Boston: Twayne Publishers, 1984), 48.] Obviously, I do not agree. In answer to Gow, it is important to say that the point of the Christian challenge is not so much to provide relief as to reveal the truth and show the way. Concerning Burke's comments, the true Christian wisdom of spiritual freedom is profoundly life-affirming. It promotes commitment, not escapism.

6. Toby Goldberg, *Federico Fellini: A Poet of Reality – Film Studies #6* (Boston: Boston University Broadcasting and Film Division), 42.

7. Frank Burke, doing a feminist analysis of Gelsomina's servitude, concludes: "By adopting 'service' as the principal condition of their relationship, Gel-somina accepts the most traditional, the most unliberated, of female roles. (This, along with the fact that *Il matto*'s philosophy is mere Christian doctrine, reveals how fully the characters have succumbed to the traditional modes of experience by now.)" [Burke, 47.]

8. J.W., *"Strada, La (The Way),"* *The Monthly Film Bulletin* (BFI) v.23, n.264 (January 1956): 5.

9. Gow, 58.

10. Donald Costello, *Fellini's Road* (Notre Dame: University of Notre Dame Press, 1983), 6.

11. Frank Burke clearly denies this conversion of Zampanò, saying that "Zampanò is reduced to brutish futility, then to inertia as *La Strada* comes to a close. He notes that in the conclusion, Zampanò looks "tragically simian," and finally that "he slumps forward, face down, turned away from the last bit of illumination offered by the night sky. The fall back to the beast and beyond even that – to mere inanimate existence – is complete." [Burke, 51, 52, 53.] Burke is vastly outnumbered by the critics who recognize a conversion in Zampanò.

12. André Bazin, *"La Strada,"* *Cross Currents* 6 n.3 (1956): 203.

13. Henri Agel, "Néo-réalisme franciscain?" *Radio-Cinéma-Télévision* n.271 (27 March 1955): 3.

14. Geneviève Agel, *Les Chemins de Fellini* (Paris: Editions du Cerf, 1956), excerpted in Gilbert Salachas, *Federico Fellini* (New York: Crown Publishers, 1963), 173-174, and quoted in Costello, 6. I checked this reference of Costello to Agel in Salachas, against the text of Agel's original piece on *La strada* (see note 15) in *Les Chemins de Fellini* but was unable to locate the match.

15. Ibid., 30. Geneviève Agel is even more specific, connecting Gelsomina's salvific act with a Christian initiation for Zampano: "he plunges into the water in a sort of baptism . . . Gelsomina has accomplished her redemptive action." [Geneviève Agel, 66.]

16. Federico Fellini, "Letter to a Jesuit Priest," in *Fellini on Fellini*, edited by Anna Keel and Christian Strich (London: Eyre Methuen, 1976), 66.

17. Harvey G. Cox Jr., "The Purpose of the Grotesque in Fellini's Films," in *Celluloid and Symbols,* edited by John C. Cooper and Carl Skrade (Philadelphia: Fortress Press, 1970), 105.

18. Peter Bondanella and Manuela Gieri, "Fellini's *La Strada* and the Cinema of Poetry," in *La Strada – Federico Fellini, director*, edited by Peter Bondanella and Manuela Gieri (New Brunswick NJ: Rutgers University Press, 1987), 15.

19. Some of the critics identify "The Clown" as the Christ-figure. Donald Costello makes some interesting suggestions in this regard. But then Costello speaks of "angel imagery," and, along with others, goes on to present a better case for Gelsomina as the Christ-figure [Costello, 18-19, 22-23], a position clearly taken by Edward Murray who says "Unlike Christ, the Fool does not willingly sacrifice his life for Zampanò; Gelsomina performs that function." [Edward Murray, *Ten Film Classics: A Re-Viewing* (New York: Frederick Ungar, 1978), 75.]

20. Costello speaks of Gelsomina's resolve as being "tested, three times:" the temptation to leave the circus, the temptation to escape with "The Clown," "a harder one to resist," and finally the nun's invitation to Gelsomina to stay in the convent. [Costello, 21-22.]

21. Costello very convincingly traces this gradual opening up and change in Zampanò. [Ibid., 27-29.]

22. Gerald Mast, *A Short History of the Movies* (New York: MacMillan Publishing Company, 1986), 323.

23. Charles B. Ketcham, *Federico Fellini: The Search for a New Mythology* (New York: Paulist Press, 1976), 45.

24. Burke, 43.

25. Geneviève Agel, 64.

26. Both quotations from ibid.

27. Edouard de Laurot, "*La Strada*: A Poem on Saintly Folly," *Film Culture* v.2, n.1 (1956): 14.

28. Ketcham, *Federico Fellini: The Search for a New Mythology*, 47.

29. Costello, 29.

30. Neil P. Hurley, *Towards a Film Humanism* (New York: Dell Publishing Co., 1975), 150.

31. Federico Fellini, "The Continuity Script," in *La Strada – Federico Fellini, director*, 164.

32. Edward Murray, *Fellini the Artist* (New York: Frederick Ungar, 1985), 83.

33. Murray, *Ten Film Classics: A Re-Viewing*, 84.

34. "Notes on the Continuity Script," in *La Strada – Federico Fellini, director*, 175, note 23.

35. Burke, 70.

36. Peter Baker, "*Le Notti di Cabiria*," *Films and Filming* (March 1958): 23.

37. Stuart Rosenthal, *The Cinema of Federico Fellini* (New York: A.S. Barnes and Company, 1976), 41.

38. Andrew Sarris, "*Cabiria: Le Notti di Cabiria*," *Film Culture* v.4, n.6 (January 1958): 20.

39. Mast, 323.

40. Goldberg, 52.

41. Fellini repeats this exercise in the longer, more exaggerated and terrifying episode of the apparition of the Madonna in *La dolce vita* (1960).

42. Michael Graff, "Christus Inkognito: Eine theologische Spurensicherung im Film," *Film Dienst Extra: Jesus in der Hauptrolle* (November, 1992): 51.

43. Goldberg, 52.

44. Graff, 51.

45. Burke, 79.

46. Mast, 323.

47. The image of Cabiria surrounded by the young people has echoes of the victory-of-life-Resurrection scenes in two other films: the conclusion of Bresson's *Au hasard Balthazar* (1966), in which the dying Balthazar is surrounded by sheep in a pastoral setting; and that of Ermanno Olmi's *The Legend of the Holy Drinker* (1988), in which the dying Andreas, having completed his mission, is seated on the Bishop's throne surrounded by priests.

48. André Bazin, "*Cabiria*: The Voyage to the End of Neorealism," in *What is Cinema? – Vol. II*, edited by Hugh Grey (Berkeley: University of California Press, 1971), 91.

49. Ibid.

50. Murray, *Fellini the Artist*, 109.

51. John R. May, "Federico Fellini," in *Religion in Film*, 175.

52. Graff, 50.

53. Burke, 77.

54. Ibid., 75.

55. Ibid., 81.

56. Ibid.

57. Fellini, "Letter to a Jesuit Priest," 66.

58. Claudia Gorbman, "Music as Salvation: Notes on Fellini and Rota," *Film Quarterly* v.28, n.2 (Winter 1974-1975): 24.

59. Burke, 81.

60. Ibid., 83.

61. The novella sets the action in Norway. Axel makes several changes, most of which streamline the film, make it smoother. I shall refer to the English edition: Karen Blixen (Isak Dinesen), "Babette's Feast" in *Anecdotes of Destiny* (London: Penguin Books, 1986). Citations will be identified by page number in brackets in the text or in the notes.

62. Richard Combs, "Films on TV: *Babette's Feast*," *The Listener* v.122, n.3145 (21 December 1989), 49.

63. Named, of course, after Philipp Melanchthon and Martin Luther.

64. Geoffrey Hill, *Illuminating Shadows: The Mythic Power of Film* (Boston: Shambhala, 1992), 139.

65. QSF, "Review of *Babette's Feast*," *Screen International* n.642 (5 March 1988): 24.

66. Citations without reference notes are of narration or dialogue from the soundtrack of the film, in this case from the English-subtitled, original version.

67. Some might wish to consider Babette's festive meal as the heavenly banquet, the eschatological feast, promised by Jesus to the Roman centurion (Mt 8:11), to the disciples (Mt 26:29 and Mk 14:25), and to others (Lk 22:18 and 23:30). This meal in the Kingdom of Heaven is a future promise, a reward to be shared with Jesus in glory. The text of the film does not give much support to this interpretation but rather points to the eucharistic banquet that is inaugurated in the Last Supper: twelve people at table; Babette present eucharistically in the meal, if not at the table; a sacrificial-sacramental celebration which brings about the salvation of the participants.

68. QSF, 24.

69. Margaret Walters, "Cinema: *Babette's Feast*," *The Listener* v.119, n.3052 (3 March 1988), 37.

70. Frédéric Strauss speaks of a neat two-part structure: forty-five minutes before the feast and forty-five during the feast. ["La dernière cène," *Cahiers du Cinéma* n.405 (March 1988): 43-44.] The simplicity of this analysis does not allow for the rich complexity of the film, better served by a more subtle analysis.

71. Anna Manzato, "*Il pranzo di Babette* di Gabriel Axel," *Letture* an.43, qd.450 (October 1988): 760.

72. *Kenosis* is a Greek word meaning "emptying out," and refers to the mystery of God's choosing to "put aside" the power, the majesty, the greatness, of the Divinity in order to enter fully into the limits of human experience. In the New Testament, it is best expressed in the Letter to the Philippians: "Jesus Christ, / who, though he was in the form of God, / did not regard equality with God / as something to be exploited, / but emptied himself, / taking the form of a slave, / being born in human likeness. / And being found in human form, / he humbled

himself / and became obedient to the point of death – / even death on a cross."
(Phil 2:6-8)

73. In the novella, Blixen indicates that Babette, "the refugee never learned to speak the language of her new country." (36) Axel's film suggests just the opposite.

74. Jean Claude Guiguet, "Choix de films: *Le Festin de Babette* de Gabriel Axel," *Etudes* v.368, n.5 (May 1988): 663.

75. Walters, 37.

76. Combs, "Review of *Babette's Feast*," *The Monthly Film Bulletin* (BFI) v.55, n.65 (March 1988): 75.

77. Ibid., 74.

78. Everything that comes into contact with Babette is redeemed. Around her, nothing material is void of spiritual value, not even lottery winnings. Axel's choice here is not unlike the audacious choice of Ermanno Olmi in *The Legend of the Holy Drinker*, to make the repeated gifts of money to the protagonist a symbol of divine grace.

79. Regarding the meal, "the sequence took a fortnight to shoot and employed one of Copenhagen's top chefs Jan Pederson of La Cocotte, as its second unit director." [Combs, "Review of *Babette's Feast*," 74.]

80. Hill, 158.

81. Kell., "Review of *Babette's gästebud* (*Babette's Feast*)," *Variety* (6 May 1987), 564.

82. Françoise Audé, "*Le Festin de Babette*: La générosité et la sorcellerie," *Positif* n.326 (April 1988): 70.

83. Strauss, 44.

84. Combs, "Review of *Babette's Feast*," 74.

85. Pavelin, 15.

86. Strauss, 44.

87. In Blixen's text, they remain in the kitchen.

88. Hill, 150.

89. Guiguet, 664.

90. Kell., 564.

91. The English subtitles err twice when they use the word "mercy" here for the Danish "*gnoden*," clearly audible on the soundtrack. Elsewhere in the speech, they correctly translate as "mercy" the Danish "*barmherzichkeit*."

92. Audé, 69.

93. Jill Forbes, "Axel's Feast," *Sight and Sound* v.57, n.2 (Spring 1988): 106.

94. Audé, 70.

95. Walters, 37.

96. Only once in the film does a prayer mention Jesus Christ, that of Philippa, who, speaking with a penitent, says, "Christ loved us and cleansed us of our sins with His blood," apparently a this-worldly prayer. But the christological reference is immediately shifted to the other-worldly by Martina, who continues, "You who

seek Christ turn your eyes to heaven." Axel seems to suggest that for them, Christ is not to be found in this world.

97. In the English subtitle, it is weakened to "Dear God."

98. Hill, 150.

99. In the novella, the snow is seen on the ground earlier in this scene, when the guests leave. Shifting the snowfall to the end and subtly associating it with Babette is far more effective.

100. Walters, 37.

101. Hill, 157.

102. The film is generally known by its original German title, *Bagdad Cafe.*

103. Philippe Niel, *"Bagdad Cafe*: De l'image mirage à l'image magique," *Positif* n.328 (June 1988): 75.

104. Giuliana Mercorio, "A Bavarian in Bagdad," *Films and Filming* n.409 (October 1988): 13.

105. In Italian, the name Jasmine becomes Gelsomina. I suspect it is not by chance that Adlon gives his protagonist the same name as Fellini's greatest Christ-figure.

106. The film is totally neglected in a number of recent book-length studies of religious themes in cinema. Where it is discussed, no reference is made to the christological identity and function of its protagonist.

107. Virginie Danglades, "Percy Adlon: L'image est primordiale," *Cinema 88* (22 June 1988): 6.

108. Adriano Piccardi, "Scheda: *Bagdad Café*," *Cineforum*, an.28, n.9 (September 1988): 79.

109. Ibid., 80.

110. One critic speaks of the inhabitants of the Cafe as the "authentic America of Percy Adlon, that of the black population (Brenda, the owner of Bagdad Cafe), the minorities (the local sheriff, an Indian), the emarginated (Cox, the painter, the tattoo artist, the backpacker)" [N.S., "Notes sur d'autres films: *Bagdad Café*," *Cahiers du Cinéma* nn.407-408 (May 1988): 144.]

111. Edna., "Rio Festival Reviews: *Out of Rosenheim,*" *Variety* v.6, n.329 (2 December 1987), 33.

112. Percy Adlon says of Palance, archetypal bad guy of the western movie, "that *walking* in cowboy boots, his western attitude . . . and then instead of a gun, I give him a paint brush! I needed Jack Palance, he *smells* of Hollywood!" [Mercorio, 15.]

113. Tom Milne, "Review of *Out of Rosenheim (Bagdad Café),*" *The Monthly Film Bulletin* (BFI) v.55, n.657 (October 1988): 309.

114. Niel, *"Bagdad Cafe*: De l'image mirage à l'image magique," 75.

115. N.S., 143.

116. Virginie Danglades, "Bagdad Café en plein désert Mojave," *Cinema 88* (20 April 1988): 6.

117. Peter Green, "Germans Abroad: Herzog, Wenders, Adlon," *Sight and Sound* v.57, n.2 (Spring 1988): 129.

118. Marcel Martin, "La voleuse de Bagdad," *L'Avant-Scène Cinéma* nn.375-376 (November-December, 1988): 9.

119. Milne, 308.

120. Matthew 17:1-8; Mark 9:2-8; Luke 9:28-36.

121. Milne, 308.

122. In fact, the canvases are seen to be numbered on their reverse side from I to VIII. Apparently two of them were suppressed during the editing of the film.

123. Milne, 309.

124. Green, 131.

125. Frédéric Strauss, "Critiques: *La Dernière Marche* (*Dead Man Walking*)," *Cahiers du Cinéma* n.501 (April 1996): 80.

126. One has only to imagine how Martin Scorsese, Jean-Luc Godard or David Lynch would have made this film.

127. At the prestigious Berlin Festival, the Silver Bear is the second highest award. The Oscar was given to Susan Sarandon for her performance as the protagonist in the film.

128. Alain Charbonneau, "La peine du mort: *Dead Man Walking* de Tim Robbins," *24 Images: La revue québécoise du cinéma* n.82 (Summer 1996): 49.

129. Philip Kemp, "*Dead Man Walking*," *Sight and Sound* v.6, n.6 (April 1996): 44.

130. Ibid., 43. These qualities also stand out in Robbins' previous film, *Bob Roberts* (1992), in which he keeps careful control of his protagonist, a right-wing western-singer-become-politician. By making him an intelligent, personable and even likeable person, Robbins avoids caricature, thus creating a more complex and convincing, and ultimately more frightening representation of evil.

131. Ibid.

132. Jean-Paul Jeancolas, "La Dernière Marche: S'en fout pas, la mort," *Positif* n.442 (April 1996): 45.
133. Kemp, 44.

134. Ibid.

135. In a beautiful moment of total authenticity, the two nuns share a bit of black humor. When it is decided that Poncelet's body will be buried in the nuns' lot in the local cemetery, they laugh about the irony that an old nun, who always aggressively defended celibacy as the only valid choice, will thus end up lying next to a ferocious man "for all eternity."

136. Kemp, 44.

137. Ibid.

138. Bob Dufford, "Be Not Afraid," *Glory and Praise* (Phoenix, AZ: North American Liturgy Resources – G.I.A. Publications, 1987), 32.

139. Charbonneau, 49.

140. Virgilio Fantuzzi, "Film: *Dead Man Walking – Condannato a morte*," *La Civiltà Cattolica* an.147, qd.3500 (20 April 1996): 220.

141. Charbonneau, 49.

142. Strauss says that Poncelet "ends christically . . . on the cross." [Strauss, "Critiques: La Dernière Marche (Dead Man Walking)," 80.] I am convinced that the Christ-analogy is built around Sister Prejean, and that in this scene, Poncelet is analogous to the good thief. Of course, it is true that, in a very wide sense, the good thief died christically, that is, saved or "christified" by his contact with Jesus.

143. Ibid.

144. Kemp, 44.

145. Strauss, "Critiques: *La Dernière Marche* (*Dead Man Walking*)," 80.

Chapter Three:
The Hero of the Western as Christ-Figure: Shane

1. Produced by Paramount Pictures and released in 1953, the film is based on the novella "Shane," written by Jack Schaefer and first published in *The American Indian* by Curtis Publishing Company in 1956. The film differs considerably from the novella. In general more streamlined, faster moving, it is also different in a number of ways that are significant for the film's development of the protagonist, Shane, as a Christ-figure, a development not nearly as clear in the novella. In this chapter, from time to time and in footnotes, I shall indicate how the film shifts the meaning of the novella. I shall refer by page number in brackets to the text of "Shane" published in Jack Schaefer, *Shane and Other Stories* (London: Penguin-Puffin, 1994).

2. For citations of dialogue, I rely on the soundtrack of the film, which I have analyzed in the video version.

3. *The BFI Companion to the Western*, edited by Edward Buscombe (London: André Deutsch – BFI Publishing, 1993), 297.

4. Bruce Petri, *A Theory of American Film: The Films and Techniques of George Stevens* (New York: Garland Publishing, 1987), 166.

5. Penelope Houston, "*Shane* and George Stevens," *Sight and Sound* v.23, n.2 (October-December 1953): 72.

6. In the novella, the social reality is more advanced. The town is larger: it has houses, stores and even a schoolhouse. (48) In his film, Stevens creates a more primitive social reality which, by not permitting townspeople and social structures to act as buffers, renders more clearly the clash between the forces of good and evil and makes this conflict more critical.

7. Houston, 72.

8. Hill, 118.

9. Alan Stanbrook, "The Return of *Shane*," *Films and Filming* v.12, n.8 (May 1966): 40.

10. "The enemy is usually without a family, indicating faithfulness to none other than himself, by whom any peace or prosperity comes through force or avarice." [Hill, 121.]

11. Stanbrook, 40.

12. In his text, Schaefer reveals much more about Shane's past, through a series of complicated, and at times awkward flashbacks, through anguished reactions of Shane when the subject of gunfighters is raised, and through Shane's own direct admissions. Stevens is more subtle and ultimately more successful. He suggests Shane's past in a series of light touches: his own glances, looks, expressions, reactions and the voiced suspicions of others. These low-key effects create and preserve around Shane an aura of mystery.

13. In three moments, the actual fighting lasts almost five minutes on-screen, exceptionally long for such a scene.

14. In the book, it is Joe Starrett who gives this warning to his son. Stevens makes Marian more perceptive than her husband, more sensitive to reality in general and to Shane in particular.

15. Hill, 122.

16. The entire episode of the burial of Torrey is Stevens' creation; it is only mentioned after the fact in Schaefer's text. (91-92) The film thus makes much more explicit Shane's conscious commitment to the future of the community, and it does so using Christian religious imagery.
17. Petri, 167.

18. At this point, the novella continues the story. The boy, called "Bob," goes home. There is a discussion of Shane's actions, then a moment of desperate indecision on the part of Joe Starrett, and finally a triumphant happy ending. Schaefer also frames his entire story in a flashback memory account of Bob Starrett as an adult. Stevens removes this fictional frame and has his "story" begin and end with Shane, thus placing the main dynamic there.

19. Hill, 121.

20. This element is much stronger in the film than in the book. Schaefer takes longer to reveal the powerful threat represented by the Ryker clan. In the book, they are called "Fletcher;" the name Stevens gives them more effectively suggests their evil, as do the actions he gives them from the beginning of the film.

21. Houston, 71.

22 Geoffrey Hill sees in Wilson a reference to the "evil one . . . the beast" of the Book of the Apocalypse. [Hill, 122.]

23. Roger Horrocks does not notice this rather evident detail, repeated in a several ways, of Shane working for Starrett and helping Starrett and the other homesteaders in variety of ways. He insists that "Ladd [Shane] himself is useless except for carrying out the primitive task of justice that is required. But such men then become outcasts, scapegoats . . . and must be cast out from the community." [Roger Horrocks, *Male Myths and Icons: Masculinity in Popular Culture* (London: MacMillan Press, 1995), 69.] Horrocks' outcast-scapegoat comment is also questionable. Shane is not cast out of the community, in fact he chooses to leave it.

24. Schaefer spends more time developing explicitly the experience of bonding between the two men. The film keeps it subtle, delicate, thus maintaining another aspect of the mystery of Shane.

25. Michael Graff, in his comprehensive survey-essay on Christ-figures in film, admits Shane's role as "a stranger" who comes into town "restoring order and

setting free" but he seems to prefer another, darker, side to Shane, considering him the "venging angel" who brings "death and destruction . . . not mercy but judgement, not benevolence but power." [Graff, 53.] In Schaefer's text, Shane is several times described as being ambivalent, as being both safe and dangerous at the same time. Stevens largely suppresses this ambivalence.

26. In Schaefer's text, Shane is described quite differently: he is a "dark figure" with a "lean and hard" face; his eyes are "hooded in the shadow," (8) and he has "dark hair." (9) He wears "dark trousers," a "coat of the same dark material," a brown shirt, a kerchief of "black silk," and a black hat. (7) Clearly Stevens wants a more "solar" appearance for his protagonist.

27. Petri, 167.

28. Except in the brief moment when two homesteaders misunderstand his passivity regarding the insults of Ryker's men the first time he meets them.

29. David Desser, "Kurosawa's Eastern 'Western': *Sanjuro* and the Influence of *Shane*," *Film Criticism* v.8, n.1 (Autumn 1983): 56. This article of Desser is a fascinating study of significant parallels and divergences in content and style between the classical western, and Kurosawa's film. [Ibid., 54-65.]
30. Ibid., 56.

31. Jon Tuska, *The Filming of the West* (Garden City NY: Doubleday and Company, 1976), 530.

32. Stanbrook, 40.

33. Stevens suggests a similar freedom and trust in Joe Starrett on this occasion. It is, in fact, he who makes it possible for his wife to dance with Shane. As the music begins, she is coming towards him to dance, but he quickly moves outside the gate of the corral, leaving her with Shane. Feigning helplessness and laughing, he says, "Marian, they've fenced me out here." As his wife and Shane dance, he watches smiling, evidently happy for both of them. At one point, and only for a moment, his expression becomes rather serious: the logic of the whole sequence seems to deny this being a sign of his jealousy, a point confirmed towards the end of the film when Joe confesses his total trust in Marian. I suggest that Starrett's reaction is quite the opposite of jealousy, that, at that moment, he has a premonition of the day that Shane, for one reason or another, will "be moving on," will no longer be part of their lives.

34. Roger Horrocks does not seem to appreciate either Shane's celibacy or his spiritual freedom. He says, "Shane is a male pin-up, a kind of vamp, seducing everyone in sight with his buckskin fringes and his fluttering eye-lashes. There is something both beguiling and irritating about this portrayal." Horrocks is simply wrong on several counts. In my repeated screenings of the film, I neither saw nor sensed anything of the vamp in Shane. Throughout most of the film he does not wear his buckskin clothes, he does not flutter his eyelashes and to suggest that Shane seduces "everyone in sight" is erroneous and deliberately misleading. Horrocks continues his highly ideological and quite outrageous interpretation, when, speaking of how the Starretts react to Shane, he writes: "The farmer's wife seems to long for him in a veiled sexual manner; the boy longs for him as a superfather; and possibly the farmer himself longs for him as a male lover." Particularly the suggestion of a possible homoerotic longing in Starrett for Shane is a deliberate perversion of the noble and open relationship

of care and trust that exists between the two men. [Both quotations from Horrocks, 69.]

35. Hill, 118. It is strange that Hill connects the film with all kind of myths – "While *Shane* plays out a common western movie motif, it also carries more ancient mythical elements of a drama far older and more numinous than the inspiration of the film narrative" [Ibid., 121]. – including the Old Testament myth-story of Cain and Abel, the story of Joseph and Mary and their journey into Egypt, and he barely notes the many and significant correspondences between Shane and the person and activity of Jesus.

36. K.R., "Review of *Shane*," *The Monthly Film Bulletin* (BFI), v.20, n.236 (September 1953): 132.

37. Both Wilson's mysterious evil and his complexity are much clearer in the film than in the book.

38. The Starretts' names are echoes of those of Joseph and Mary, the New Testament ur-couple.

39. The moral complexity of the relationship of Starrett and his wife, and of their relationship with Shane, is more subtly suggested in the film than in the book, and is more interesting and more credible because of that.

40. Stevens does not offer easy answers to this question. In fact, in Joey's uncontrolled "shooting spree" towards the end of the film, probably its most terrifying moment, he creates an emblem of the terrible moral ambiguity of the whole question. Significantly, this episode is original to the film. Geoffrey Hill's comments on violence and war, in relation to *Shane*, provide some interesting and helpful insights.

41. Tuska, 530.

42. Stevens keeps Joey away from the brutal killing of Torrey. As a result, what we see and hear is much less dramatic than the other violence.

43. Nina W. Stern, "Review of *Shane*," *Films in Review* v.4, n.4 (April 1953): 196.

44. Here too, Stevens reinvents what Schaefer writes in his novella. Schaefer has the whole story narrated by Bob as an adult, years after the events, giving his own well thought out, definitive interpretation of every aspect of the events recalled. Stevens' choice of showing only several crucial scenes from the boy's point of view, and of letting the spectator of the film interpret the events, is a more interesting and challenging approach.

45. Shane's arrival and humble mingling with the other homesteaders in the store is in radical contrast to the later arrival of Wilson as gunfighter. He comes into the bar alone, and in his looks and slow, deliberate movements, not unlike a venomous snake, he exudes the power of evil so much that the dog in the bar gets out of his way. There is little of the kenotic incarnation there.

46. In the old West, marriage, family, stability are obvious virtues; celibacy for the sake of the kingdom is a rather ambiguous choice; its significance is less obvious.

47. Stevens tones down the almost neurotic self-awareness of Shane in Schaefer's text.

48. Tuska, 530.

49. One critic speaks literally of Shane's "ascension" at the end of the film. [Pierre Berthomieu, "L'homme des vallées perdues," *Positif* n.397 (March 1994): 91.]

50. John 14; John 16:16-24.

51. All this is original with Stevens' film. In Schaefer's text, Shane neither comes down from, nor goes back up into the mountains. Nor does he cross a river.

52. This element of gratuitousness is missing from Schaefer's text.

53. Hill, 124.

54. Malone, *Movie Christs and Antichrists*, 105. The biblical reference is to Luke 2:34.

55. Hill speaks of Shane's sacrifice: "He tried to break the mold of his gunfighter nature by attempting domesticity, but duty bound him to further violence for a righteous cause." [Hill, 123-124.]

56. Ibid., 135. In the film, Shane's choice to stay and work with Starrett, to incarnate himself and ultimately to sacrifice himself, is entirely his own initiative. In Schaefer's text, it is a choice inspired by the impassioned plea of Marian, desperately concerned for her husband and herself. (65-67) The film, in giving the initiative to Shane, is more effective.

57. Again all of these elements are original to the film. In Schaefer's text, Shane does not ride through the cemetery and there are no references to crosses. After the gunfight, Shane rides out onto the plain, not into the mountains, and by moonlight.

Chapter Four:
A Christ-Figure in Two Films of Kieślowski

1. The question of the titles of films-in-translation is generally a complicated one: Stevens' *Shane,* for example, becomes in Italian *Il cavaliere della valle solitaria,* literally, "The Horseman of the Lonely Valley"; Pasolini's *Il Vangelo secondo Matteo,* "The Gospel according to Matthew," becomes in English version, *The Gospel According to Saint Matthew.* In the case of the two films of Kieślowski discussed in this chapter, the situation becomes more complicated. The longer version of the film, whose Polish title, *Krotki Film o Miłosci,* means "A Short Film about Love," has precisely that title in the English version. Not so in the Italian version, *Non desiderare la donna d'altri*: literally "Do not desire the wife of another." Evidently the Italian translator did not know the Commandments very well and confused the sixth with the ninth. Doubly ironical this translation because the shorter version of the film (in Polish simply *Dekalog, sześć* "Decalogue Six," which is also the English title) in Italian is titled: *Decalogo sei: Non commettere atti impuri,* "Decalogue Six: Do not commit impure acts." Whoever did *that* translation evidently looked up the Commandments.

2. The idea of *The Decalogue* began with Krzysztof Piesiewicz, Kieślowski's lawyer-friend and scriptwriter, and was concretized as a project of ten one-hour films for Polish television. Originally they were to be filmed by ten different young directors, as their first films, but when Piesiewicz and Kieślowski completed the screenplays, Kieślowski decided to direct them himself. Some

money for the project came from Polish television, but not enough, and so Kieślowski went to the Ministry of Culture and offered to make two of the films for cinema: he chose the fifth commandment, they the sixth. He got the money, wrote (with Piesiewicz) longer versions of the screenplays, and while shooting the films, made two versions of each one. The longer versions, *A Short Film about Killing*, and *A Short Film about Love*, were completed and released in 1988 before the entire work, *The Decalogue* was premiéred at the Venice Film Festival in 1989. [Information from: *Kieślowski on Kieślowski*, edited by Danusia Stok (London: Faber and Faber, 1993), 143-159 and *Krzysztof Kieślowski*, edited by Mario Sesti (Roma: Dino Audino Editore, 1993), 23.] Some critics confuse the chronology of the two longer films and *The Decalogue*. Charles Eidsvik, for example, says: "These two films [the longer ones] were produced as theatrical by-products of a Decalog on contemporary issues." [Charles Eidsvik, "Kieślowski's 'Short Films': *A Short Film about Killing*; *A Short Film about Love*," *Film Quarterly* v.44, n.1 (Autumn 1990): 51.]

3. Gina Lagorio, *Il Decalogo di Kieślowski: Ricreazione narrativa* (Casale Monferrato AL: Edizioni Piemme, 1992), 130.

4. Yung., "San Sebastian Reviews: *Krotki Film o Miłosci* (*A Short Film about Love*)," *Variety*, 5 October 1988, 15.

5. Roberto Escobar, in a review in *Il Sole 24 Ore*, quoted in *Krzysztof Kieślowski*, edited by Sesti, 42.

6. Emanuela Imparato, *Krzysztof Kieślowski: Il Decalogo: Per una lettura critica* (Roma: A.I.A.C.E., 1990), 24.

7. Krzysztof Kieślowski, "Introduction," in Krzysztof Kieślowski and Krzysztof Piesiewicz, *Decalogue: The Ten Commandments,* translated by Phil Cavendish and Susanna Bluh (London: Faber and Faber, 1991), xiv.

8. Lagorio, 129.

9. Ibid., 30.

10. Charles Eidsvik misses this important point when he says that the characters of *The Decalogue* films "live in drab concrete silos, virtually caged, cut off from normal contact." Kieślowski in fact creates a complex web of contacts among them. [Eidsvik, 51.]

11. Though the critics universally recognize the interconnectedness of the films, Kieślowski waffles considerably on the question. On the one hand, he seems almost to deny the fact: "You have to pay great attention and concentrate very hard to . . . notice that the films are interconnected." [*Kieślowski on Kieślowski*, edited by Danusia Stok, 155.] On the other hand, he affirms it, imagining the interconnectedness as an advantage: "Television viewers following the series from the beginning would be able to recognize in the individual films people from other parts of the series." [Kieślowski, "Introduction," xiii.]

12. Sauro Borelli, in *L'Unità*, quoted in *Krzysztof Kieślowski*, edited by Mario Sesti, 44.

13. *Kieślowski on Kieślowski,* edited by Danusia Stok, 156. In fact, in two episodes, he uses the same "lighting cameraman."

14. Claudio Carabba, in *L'Europeo*, quoted in *Krzysztof Kieślowski*, edited by Mario Sesti, 43.

15. All three quotations are from Lagorio, 136.

16. Philippe Rouyer, "Voir et être vue (*Décalogue, six*)" in "Krzysztof Kieslowski – *Decalogue*: la preuve par dix," *Positif*, n.351 (May 1990): 37.

17. Jonathan Keates, "Heartburn: *A Short Film about Love*," *Sight and Sound* v.59, n.2 (Spring 1990): 132.

18. His interpretation limited by a tightly-closed psychoanalytic hermeneutic, one commentator insists that the boy uses the telescope to "better observe the sex life" of the woman. The analysis is reductionistic and the results are simply wrong. [Francis J. Rigney, M.D., "*The Decalogue*: A Psychoanalytic Deadlock," *Film Criticism* v.14, n.3 (Spring 1990): 62.]

19. Again here Rigney misses the point. He speaks of Tomek's "phony milkman act." [Ibid., 63.] Whether Tomak's delivering of milk is considered literally or as a metaphor of something more profound, it is anything but "phony."

20. The quotations of dialogue from A *Short Film about Love* are based on the English-subtitled version of the film, not on the published script: Kieślowski and Piesiewicz, *Decalogue: The Ten Commandments. The* question of published film scripts is a complicated one. In some cases, for example, Arcand's *Jesus of Montreal,* the published script is very close to the released film. Other times, the published script does not reflect accurately the film. In the case of the scripts in English of Kieślowski's *The Decalogue* this is very much the case. Both the opening and especially the conclusion of *Decalogue One, Decalogue Five and Decalogue Eight* in the published text are very different from those of the films, quite clearly giving a different meaning, in each case, to the entire film. Regarding *Decalogue Six,* the book indicates it is the "feature-length script" of A *Short Film about Love,* and so, one might presume, not of the shorter *Decalogue Six.* But, in fact, it is *not* at all the script of the longer version, and, in fact, differs considerably in the beginning, in the end, and in many others details, from *both* released versions of the film. For this reason, for both citations of dialogue and for my interpretation of the films, I will rely on the films, in the English-subtitled versions. One further comment on the English published scripts of *The Decalogue.* The editors saw fit to list the text of the Ten Commandments at the end of the "Introduction." Not a bad idea. Except that those who handled the text (There are no references, not even to the edition of the Bible from which the text is taken.) were rather confused, a confusion not even resolved by their viewing of Kieślowski's films: as listed there, the Fourth Commandment has to do with the keeping holy the Sabbath; the Fifth, with honoring one's parents; the Sixth, with not killing, etc.]

21. Virgilio Fantuzzi, "*Non desiderare la donna d'altri*," *La Civiltà Cattolica* an.140, v.14, qd.3347 (2 December 1989): 520.

22. Eidsvik, 53.

23. Rigney, 63.

24. Eidsvik, 53.

25. Gian Carlo Bertolina, "*Non desiderare la donna d'altri* di Krzysztof Kieślowski," *Letture* an.45, qd.463 (January 1990): 71. Bertolina does not go much beyond this interpretation in his review. With this and with a number of specific details of his reading, I do not agree.

26. I speak here from personal experience. More than once, in public film-forums using *A Short Film About Love*, I have seen members of the audience walk out of the hall before the discussion even began. Sometimes, members of the public have criticized me for including such a "perverted" film in a cycle of religious cinema. For some, even the erroneous Italian title, *Do Not Desire the Wife of Another*, is already too much.

27. Lagorio, 86.

28. Imparato, 63.

29. Serafino Murri, *Krzysztof Kieslowski* (Milano: Editrice Il Castoro, January-February 1996), 113.

30. Kieślowski has Tomek make this proclamation of love at the very center point of the film, both chronologically and psychologically.

31. B.U., "*A Short Film about Love (Krotki Film o Miłosci)*," *Screen International* n.688 (21 January 1989): 22.

32. The critic Imparato supports my argument when, using an ironically appropriate word, she says: "It is the hemorrhage of feelings provoked by the woman in the boy, that brings healing to the woman." [Imparato, 67.]

33. It is not because he is reticent to show such a violent gesture that Kieślowski uses an ellipse here, something underlined by the unusually graphic violence of *A Short Film about Killing* and *Decalogue 5*, which includes perhaps the longest killing scene every filmed.

34. Lagorio, 81.

35. Bertolina, 72.

36. Fantuzzi, "*Non desiderare la donna d'altri*," 520.

37. Lagorio, 84.

38. Ibid., 87.

39. Tomek says to her "I love you" several times. Given the context of his declaration, his adamant refusal to enter her apartment, it is clearly more than a mere sentiment.

40. Lagorio, 84.

41. Fantuzzi, "*Non desiderare la donna d'altri*," 520.

42. To attribute Tomek's shyness, awkwardness and sexual inhibition to his having been raised in an orphanage is too easy. It also betrays considerable ignorance about life in that environment.

43. The published script includes only the man's voice saying "Magda?" and her answering "Yes." (182) The English subtitles of the film do not shows these words, but they are clearly audible on the soundtrack.

44. Some critics note the biblical reference in the name of the woman, and even insists that it is "not by chance" that she has this name, but, inexplicably, they do not take the logical further step of asking what that name might mean for the identity of Tomek. [Imparato, 68, and Fantuzzi, "Non desiderare la donna d'altri," 519.]

45. I disagree with Fantuzzi who speaks of Tomek's love as "a kind of armor that separates him from all the rest of reality." [Fantuzzi, "*Non desiderare la donna*

d'altri," 520.] Clearly, his love for Magda opens him up to her, makes him vulnerable to suffering, and ultimately, at least symbolically, to death. Kieślowski himself says about the love of his two protagonists: "We are always looking at this love from the point of view of the person who is suffering because of this love . . . love is always tied up with some sort of suffering." [*Kieślowski on Kieślowski,* edited by Danusia Stok, 169.]

46. Murri, *Krzysztof Kieslowski,* 114.

47. The Samaritan woman: John 4:4-24; the appearance to Mary: John 20:11-18; on the road to Emmaus: Luke 24:13-35.

48. Emanuela Carozzi, "Lenti, vetri e porte: un cinema tra partecipazione e distacco," in *Krzysztof Kieślowski,* Special Issue of *Garage: Cinema, Autori, Visioni.* (Torino: Edizioni Scriptorium, February 1995), 64.

49. Philippe Niel, "Dix blasons de la morale (*Le Décalogue*)," *Positif* 346 (December 1989): 31.

50. It is mysterious because Kieślowski shows neither the window nor the breaking, but only the violent noise of the shattering glass and the shards raining to the floor, a sound and an action repeated twice.

51. In *A Short Film about Love,* the fact that Tomek, as Christ-figure, is not strong, macho and sure of himself, like Magda's men friends, but rather shy, awkward, chubby, his dress clothes outmoded, his being without a home and alone in the world, all are metaphorical expressions of the kenosis of Jesus Christ, of which the highest point in Tomek is his sacrificial "death" for love of Magda.

52. At least three critics seem to misunderstand this sequence. One says simply that in the woman's final emotional reaction "there is no redemption." [Murri, *Krzysztof Kieślowski,* 114.] Another interprets Magda's spiritually insightful "seeing" as unreal: "Magda sees herself, upsetting the bottle of milk, then crying, before being comforted by Tomek in a fantasy that has no more reality than do Tomek's hopes for his relationship with her." [Pascal Pernod, "L'amour des personnages: *Brève Histoire d'amour,*" *Positif* 346 (December 1989): 27.] A third critic is way off the mark on several counts: "Given the distinctively East European sinisterness which pervades Kieślowski's way of viewing things, it is unsurprising that this concluding transference should less akin to a dream than to a nightmare." [Tim Pulleine, *Krotki Film o Miłosci (A Short Film about Love), The Monthly Film Bulletin* (BFI) v.57, n.676 (May 1990): 132.]

53. A diminutive and affectionate form of "Magda" or "Magdalena."

54. Lagorio, 85.

55. Kieślowski, in *Kieślowski on Kieślowski,* edited by Danusia Stok, 170. In contrast to this, he says about the cinema version, that is, about *A Short Film about Love,* "the possibilities are open . . . it's a far more optimistic ending [though] not necessarily a happy ending." Kieślowski also indicates that the actress who plays Magda, Grazyna Szapołowska, expressed her dissatisfaction with the ending of the television version, as a result of which Kieślowski and Piesiewicz wrote the other, "more optimistic" ending for her. [Ibid.] Perhaps Szapołowska, living the experience of Magda, had the better spiritual insight.

56. Gianfranco Ravasi, "Le grandi 'Dieci Parole' del Sinai," in Lagorio, 203.

Chapter Five:
An Exceptional Christ-Figure: Au Hasard Balthazar

1. Jean Collet, "Le drôle del chemin de Bresson à Balthazar," *Études* v.325 (July-August 1966): 81.

2. Jean Sémolué, *Bresson ou l'acte pur des métamorphoses* (Paris: Flammarion, 1993), 126.

3. P. Adams Sitney, "The Rhetoric of Robert Bresson," in *The Essential Cinema: Essays on Films in The Collection of Anthology Film Archives*, edited by P. Adams Sitney (New York: Anthology Film Archives and New York University Press, 1975), 199.

4. Collet, 81.

5. Ibid., 80.

6. Bresson interviewed in *Les Nouvelles littéraires*, 26 May 1966, quoted in Michel Estève, *Robert Bresson: La passion du cinématographe* (Paris: Editions Albatros, 1983), 52, note 1.

7. Xavier Tilliette, "Des ânes et des hommes," *Etudes* v.324 (June 1966): 831.

8. Collet, 80.

9. Ibid., 88.

10. An outstanding study of Bresson's style, perhaps not definitive but only because it is limited to his first six films, is Paul Schrader's *Transcendental Style in Cinema: Ozu, Bresson, Dreyer* (Berkeley: University of California Press, 1966).

11. Eric Rhode, *Tower of Babel: Speculations on the Cinema* (London: Weidenfeld and Nicolson, 1965), 44.

12. Bresson, quoted in Schrader, 61.

13. From *Les anges du péché* (1943) to *L'argent* (1983); in addition, there is a short film, *Affaires publiques* (1934), not usually noted in Bresson filmographies.

14. Sémolué, *Bresson ou l'acte pur des métamorphoses*, 150.

15. René Maurice, "De Lucifer à Balthazar, en suivant Robert Bresson," *Lumière et Vie* n.78 (1966): 31.
16. Estève, *Robert Bresson: La passion du cinématographe,* 52-53.
17. Holloway, 189.

18. Matthew 2:1-12.

19. Estève, *Robert Bresson: La passion du cinématographe,* 52. The rhythm-rhyme of the title is "very regular, in three syllables repeated twice, it hammers, after the first syllable, the same vowel five times, very open. These sounds and rhythms characterize the gait of the donkey and the regular open movement of the film." [Sémolué, *Bresson ou l'acte pur des métamorphoses*, 135.]

20. Maurice, 46.

21. Maurice, 47.

22. Matthew 21:1-11; Mark 11:1-11; Luke 19:28-39; John 12:12-19.

23. Maurice, 47.

24. Bresson, in P. Gilles, "Robert Bresson une patience d'âne," *Arts*, 9 December 1965, n.3, quoted in Giorgio Tinazzi, *Il cinema di Robert Bresson* (Venezia: Marsilio Editori, 1979), 100, note 1.

25. Collet, 88.

26. Estève, *Robert Bresson: La passion du cinématographe*, 53.

27. Both quotations are from ibid.

28. Michel Delahaye, François Weyergans, Jean-Louis Comolli, Jean Narboni, André S. Labarthe, "Balthazar au hasard: Table ronde," *Cahiers du Cinéma* n.180 (July 1966): 78.

29. Estève, *Robert Bresson: La passion du cinématographe*, 53.

30. Sitney, 201.

31. The citations of dialogue from the film are my own translations from the soundtrack of the Italian (dubbed) version of the film, compared to, and at times corrected by, two published (but incomplete and different) summaries of the script in French: in Philippe Arnaud, *Robert Bresson* (Paris: Cahiers du Cinéma, 1986) and in Sémolué, *Bresson ou l'acte pur des Métamorphoses*.

32. The only extradiegetical music heard in the film is brief excerpts from Schubert's "Sonata for Piano Number 20," which Bresson inserts in certain crucial moments. In this summary of the plot of the film, I will simply indicate in the text the presence of music with the notation: "[music]."

33. Luigi Bini, "*Au hasard Balthazar*," *Letture* v.21, n.10 (October 1966): 712.

34. Delahaye, Weyergans, Comolli and others, 78.

35. J.[ean] S.[émolué], "L'éminente dignité des humbles (*Au Hasard Balthazar*, de Robert Bresson)," *Esprit* v.34, n.350 (June 1966): 1250.

36. Holloway, 189.

37. Tilliette, 833.

38. Ibid., 832.

39. Jean-Luc Godard in *Les Nouvelles littéraires*, 26 May 1966, quoted in Sémolué, *Bresson ou l'acte pur des métamorphoses*, 134.

40. René Prédal, "*Au Hasard Balthazar*," in *Robert Bresson: L'aventure intérieure – L'Avant-Scène Cinéma*, edited by René Prédal, nn.408-409 (January-February 1992): 81.

41. Estève, *Robert Bresson: La passion du cinématographe*, 54.

42. Arnaud, 60.

43. Ibid., 72.

44. Durgnat, "*Balthazar*," *Films and Filming* v.13, n.3 (December 1966): 52.

45. Estève, *Robert Bresson: La passion du cinématographe*, 55-56.

46. Adelio Ferrero, *Robert Bresson* (Firenze: La Nuova Italia-Il Castoro Cinema, May 1979), 71.

47. Maurice, 40.

48. Ferrero, 69.

49. Neil Hurley suggests that this makes Arnold a Jesus-figure. ["Cinematic Trans-figurations of Jesus," 188.] Charles Barr admits that Arnold "receives a 'Judas kiss' before dying, from Gérard; he rides on a ass; he even . . . has 'a little the look of Christ.' . . . The association is there, but delicate." And then he insists that "Arnold is not a Christ figure." [Charles Barr, "*Au hasard, Balthazar*," in Amédée Ayfre and others, *The Films of Robert Bresson* (London: Studio Vista Ltd., 1979), 110.] I think Bresson's point is to focus attention on Gérard as a Judas-figure, the incarnation of evil, betraying innocence. If anything Arnold's fate here prefigures that of Balthazar, who later is betrayed by Gérard in vaguely similar circumstances.

50. Sémolué, *Bresson ou l'acte pur des métamorphoses*, 145.

51. Ibid, 137.

52. Collet, 87.

53. Ibid.

54. Bresson interviewed in by Yves Kovacs in *Cahiers du Cinéma* n.140, quoted in Collet, 82, note 2. Regarding this particularly sensitivity of animals, we can recall the dogs in *Shane*: the one in the bar who twice leaves the room when the evil gunman enters, and the other who seems to mourn the death of his master, Torrey.

55. Delahaye, Weyergans, Comolli and others, 79.

56. Bresson's respectful treatment of the donkey who on screen is "Balthazar" extends beyond the latter's on-screen presence and behavior. While defending the intelligence of donkeys in general, Bresson "did not want to make of his Balthazar a wise animal," [Sémolué, *Bresson ou L'acte pur des métamorphoses*, 142-143.] at least in the typical sense. Preferring a maximum of opacity, he searched for a donkey who has no training: "So I took a donkey that knew how to do absolutely nothing. Not even how to pull a cart." [Jean-Luc Godard and Michael Delahaye, "The Question: Interview with Robert Bresson," *Cahiers du Cinéma in English* n.8 (February 1967): 25. (original: *Cahiers du Cinéma*, n.178, May 1966)] Regarding the circus scene, where Balthazar has to be trained, Bresson explains: "I did not want him to be professional, and I filmed the circus scene, the scene where the donkey does mathematical calculations, long after the rest, to give time to the trainer to train the donkey, to teach him to do calculations. I wanted to keep the donkey absolutely free of all training, free of all falsification." [Sémolué, *Bresson ou l'acte pur des métamorphoses*, 143.] In order to disturb the donkey's routine as little as possible, Bresson had Balthazar accompanied home to his stable each evening, to a village some kilometres from where the filming was taking place.

57. Very strangely, most of the critics refer to it as a lion: there is absolutely no doubt that it is a tiger.

58. Sémolué, *Bresson ou l'acte pur des métamorphoses*, 143-144.

59. Collet, 87.

60. Sémolué, *Bresson ou l'acte pur des métamorphoses*, 144.

61. Maurice, 38.

62. Ibid.

63. Bini, *"Au hasard Balthazar,"* 711.

64. T.M., *"Au hasard, Balthazar (Balthazar),"* *The Monthly Film Bulletin* (BFI) v.34, n.396 (January 1967): 2.

65. Maurice, 37.

66. Bini, *"Au hasard Balthazar,"* 711. The Italian phrase he uses is "connubio di vita," which clearly has the sense of marriage union.

67. Ibid.

68. Tinazzi, 102.

69. Maurice, 38.

70. Ibid., 20.

71. Jean-Louis Bory, *Des Yeux pour voir: Cinéma I (1961-1966)* (Paris: Union Générale des Editions, 1971), 86.

72. Prédal, *"Robert Bresson: L'aventure intérieure – L'Avant-Scène Cinéma,"* 12.

73. There are, in fact, a several instances in which Balthazar seems to take the initiative. He tries to resists the cruel treatment of his first master after Marie, he runs wild with the hay cart and when it overturns he runs off from crowd chasing him and comes home to Marie's. He walks away from Arnold outside the courthouse, and, in the end, he climbs to the summit of the mountain from where he is abandoned by Gérard.

74. Delahaye, Weyergans, Comolli and others, 78. They continue, noting that "several times in the film he reacts." [Ibid.]

75. Bedouelle, 71.

76. Tilliette, 832.

77. Maurice, 45.

78. Prédal, *"Au Hasard Balthazar,"* *"Robert Bresson: L'aventure intérieure – L'Avant-Scène Cinéma,"* 84. The analogy has its limits because Jesus was also very much a human being.

80. Graff, 51.

80. Tilliette, 833.

81. Arnaud, 57.

82. Maurice, 43.

83. This ought not to surprise. Bresson's style, as we have noted, is often referred to as self-consciously spiritual or theological. Bedouelle speaks of Bresson's "theological esthetic: exercises of photography and sound, but at the same time, spiritual exercises." [Bedouelle, 29.] More to the point here, Paul Schrader, in his detailed discussion of Bresson's "transcendental style," quotes Bresson on his use of music, saying that music "can transport us into a region that is no longer simply terrestrial, but rather cosmic, I would even say divine." [Schrader, 82.] His carefully selective and disciplined use of brief passages from the Schubert piano sonata have precisely this effect. Then, the photography, the iconic images of Balthazar. Of Bresson's pictorial style, Schrader says: "Bresson uses methods of representation very similar to those represented by Byzantine painters and mosaicists . . . non-expressive faces, hieratic positions,

symmetric compositions, and two-dimensionality [emphasizing the] long fore-head, the lean features, the closed lips, the blank stare, the frontal view, the flat light, the uncluttered background." [Ibid., 99.]

84. Maurice, 43.

85. Bini, "*Au hasard Balthazar*," 712.

86. Ibid.

87. Maurice, 44.

88. Angelo L. Lucano, "La grazia secondo Bresson," in *Tutto Bresson: Gli 80 anni di un maestro: Dossier* (Roma: ANCCI, 1987), 21-31. Excerpted from *Cultura e religione nel cinema* (Torino: ERI Edizioni, 1975), 28-29.

89. Collet, 89.

90. Maurice, 44-45.

91. Tilliette, 832; Graff, 51.

92. Maurice, 44-45.

93. René Gilson, "My God, Wilt Thou Forsake Me?," *Cahiers du Cinéma in English* n.11 (September 1967): 54. (original: *Cahiers du Cinéma*, n.182, September 1966) The phrase in the original article is "*poème-parabole*," rendered awkwardly into "parabola-and-parable poem" in the English translation. The literal translation is more accurate.

94. Ibid., 55.

95. Lindley Page Hanlon, *Narrative Structure in the Later Films of Robert Bresson*, a doctoral dissertation submitted to New York University, June 1977. University Microfilms International, Ann Arbor, MI, 125.

96. Ibid.

97. Gilson, 55.

98. Michel Estève, "Il settimo film di Robert Bresson," *Cineforum* v.6, n.56 (June 1966): 433.

99. Maurice, 42.

100. Ibid.

101. St. Paul speaks of God's "plan for the fullness of time to gather up all things in him [Christ] things in heaven and things on earth" (Eph 1:10), a plan worked out in Christ's redeeming blood. He repeats the same idea in his Letter to the Colossians: "Through him God was pleased to reconcile to himself all things, whether on earth or in heaven, by making peace through the blood of his cross." (Col 1:20)

102. Maurice, 41.

103. Roger Greenspun, "Bresson Feature Opens at the New Yorker," *The New York Times Film Reviews 1969-1970* (New York: The New York Times & Arno Press, 1971). (20 February 1970)

104. Sémolué, *Bresson ou l'acte pur des métamorphoses*, 149.

105. Ibid., 150.

106. Durgnat, "*Balthazar*," 52.

107. Sémolué, *Bresson ou l'acte pur des métamorphoses*, 150.

108. Ibid., 138.

109. Ibid., 149.

110. Bini, "*Au hasard Balthazar*," 712.

111. Lucano, 28.

112. Bory, 85-86.

113. Sémolué, *Bresson ou l'acte pur des métamorphoses*, 150.

Chapter Six:
Dimension and Guises of the Christ-Figure

1. Three of the principal references for the material presented and discussed in this chapter are: Peter Malone's book, *Movie Christs and Antichrists*, Neil P. Hurley's article, "Cinematic Transfigurations of Jesus," and Michael Graff's article, "Christus Inkognito: Eine theologische Spurensicherung im Film."

2. Graff, 52.

3. Ibid., 53.

4. Ibid., 51.

5. Ibid., 55.

6. The original title of Dassin's film is *Celui qui doit mourir*. Evidently it is not a well-known film for it is not mentioned in a number of critical biographical pieces on Dassin. Also there seems to be little agreement regarding the year of its release. I found a variety of dates purporting to be its year of production: 1956, 1957, 1958. I chose 1957 because it was the date indicated by three sources.

7. Viano, 103.

8. Understandably, a number of these dates are disputed by scholars. Here I am following the dates given by Henri Agel, in the "Filmographie" following his article "Jeanne La Pucelle en dix-huit films. Sainte et conquérante," in *Le film religieux*, 88.

9. There is some disagreement concerning the number of Joan of Arc films. Castellani, for example, counts fifteen. [Castellani, *Temi e figure del film religioso*, 191-192.] Agel, on the other hand, speaks of eighteen. [Henri Agel, "Jeanne La Pucelle en dix-huit films. Sainte et conquérante," in *Le film religieux*, 88.]

10. Keyser, "*Hollywood and the Catholic Church: The Image of Roman Catholicism in American Movies*," 29.

11. Pierre Leprohon, "L'hagiographie à l'écran: Par-delà des apparences," in Etudes cinématographiques: Jeanne d'Arc à l'ecran, n.18-19 (Fall 1962): 128. Lephron continues: "Perhaps never has hagiographical cinema gone so far into the ridiculous and bad taste. A 'grand spectacle' film, with battles, tourneys, banquets, it makes the admirable 'poor one' into a figure which is absolutely foreign, not only to his message but even to his legend." [Ibid.]

12. For her first Francis, Cavani chose Lou Castel, *enfant terrible* of Italian cinema in the 1960s. Her choice of Rourke, *enfant terrible* of American cinema and fresh from the soft-porn *Nine and a Half Weeks*, was perhaps even more daring,

given his reputation and his large size and boxer's physique: Francis was small and slight of build. But in both cases, she succeeded well in capturing crucial dimensions of Francis' person and experience.

13. Hiroshi Komatsu, "Dreyer e la coscienza estetica come continuum," in *Il cinema di Dreyer: L'eccentrico e il classico,* edited by Andrea Martini (Venezia: Marsilio Editori, 1987), 60.

14. David Bordwell, *The Films of Carl-Theodor Dreyer* (Berkeley: University of California Press, 1981), 90.

15. Castellani, *Temi e figure del film religioso*, 122.

16. Sémolué, "Passion et Procès: (De Dreyer à Bresson)," in *Etudes cinématographiques: Jeanne d'Arc à l'écran*, 104.

17. The twenty-nine sessions of Joan's trial are concentrated symbolically into one day.

18. Castellani, *Temi e figure del film religioso*, 121.

19. Bedouelle, 74.

20. Ibid.

21. Bordwell, 90.

22. Sémolué, *"La Passion de Jeanne d'Arc*: Prise de conscience de Carl Dreyer," in *Etudes cinématographique: Jeanne d'Arc à l'ecran*, 46.

23. Roger Manvell, "Revaluations – 6: *La Passion de Jeanne d'Arc*, 1928," *Sight and Sound* v.19, n.8 (December 1950): 338.

24. Deborah Linderman, "Uncoded Images in the Heterogenous Text," *Wide-Angle* v.3, n.3 (1979): 38.

25. It reads "Heretique relapse, Apostate Ydolatre." [Bordwell, 92.]

26. The inscription I.N.R.I., represents "Iesus Nazarenus, rex Iudaeorum," or "Jesus of Nazareth, the King of the Jews." Ordered by Pontius Pilate, the inscription is spoken of in John 19:19-21.

27. Michele Canosa, "La passione del volto," *Cinema & Cinema* v.12, n.44 (September-December 1985): 64.

28. Amédée Ayfre, *Cinéma et mystère* (Paris: Editions du Cerf, 1969), 48.

29. In French, the words for daughter and son are very close: "fille de Dieu," and "fils de Dieu."

30. Schrader, 123.

31. Ibid.

32. Ayfre, "Les voix du silence," *Cahiers du Cinéma* n.17 (November 1952): 59. Dreyer also counts on painting for other elements in the film. The instruments of torture, for example, are clearly related to Flemish paintings such as the "Tower of Babel" and "The Census of Bethlehem" of Breughel. [Andrea Martini, "La scelta scandalosa di Dreyer," in *Il cinema di Dreyer: L'eccentrico e il classico,* 151.]

33. Maurice Bardèche and Robert Brassillach, *Histoire du Cinéma*, edited by André Martel, quoted in *"La Passion de Jeanne d'Arc*: Dossier-film no.3," *L'Avant-Scène Cinéma* n.100 (February 1970): 53.

34. Bordwell, 91.

35. Castellani, *Temi e figure del film religioso*, 122.

36. Hurley, *Towards a Film Humanism*, 186.

37. Leo Murray, "*Le procès de Jeanne d'Arc*," in *The Films of Robert Bresson*, edited by Amédée Ayfre (London: Studio Vista Ltd., 1969), 96.

38. "Entretien avec Robert Bresson et Jean Guitton," in *Etudes cinématographiques: Jeanne d'Arc à l'ecran*, 87.

39. Leo Murray, 94.

40. Susan Sontag, "Spiritual Style in the Films of Robert Bresson," in *Against Interpretation and Other Essays* (New York: Farrar, Straus and Giroux, 1966), 194.

41. Ibid., 183.

42. Ibid., 184. Sontag says that with Carrez, "Bresson has experimented with the limit of the unexpressive [*sic*]." [Ibid.]

43. Ibid.

44. "Entretien avec Robert Bresson et Jean Guitton," 91.

45. Schrader, 77.

46. Sémolué, "*Procès de Jeanne d'Arc* dans l'oeuvre de Robert Bresson," *Esprit* v.31, n.318 (June 1963): 1192. Another French critic is not at all convinced by Bresson's portrait of Joan as an intelligent woman: "One has the impression of hearing a doctor of theology in discussion with other doctors of theology, rather than a country girl in front of her judges." [M.M., "*Procès de Jeanne d'Arc*," *Cinéma 62* n.67 (June 1962): 95.]

47. Murray speaks of these words as "Christic." [Leo Murray, 97.]

48. Jean Guitton maintains that "this cry of Joan evokes the tears of Jesus over Jerusalem." ["Entretien avec Robert Bresson et Jean Guitton," 89.] He adds that "the fact that Joan was condemned by very literate men of the Church puts her very close to Jesus who was condemned by a religious tribunal." [Ibid.]

49. Estève, "Une tragédie au présent de narration," in *Etudes cinématographiques: Jeanne d'Arc à l'ecran*, 112.

50. Ibid., 109.

51. Claude Beylie, "Corps memorable," *Cahiers du Cinéma* v.24, n.143 (May 1963): 41.

52. Ian Cameron, "Interview with Robert Bresson," *Movie* n.7 (February-March 1963): 29.

53. Pavelin, 91.

54. Estève, "Une tragédie au présent de narration," 111.

55. Leo Murray, 105.

56. Ibid., 101.

57. Ibid., 103.

58. Schrader, 82.

59. "Entretien avec Robert Bresson et Jean Guitton," 88.

60. Malone, *Movie Christs and Antichrists*, 102.

61. Ibid., 101.

62. Hurley, "Cinematic Transfigurations of Jesus," 62.

63. Holloway, 188.

64. Ibid.

65. Malone, *Movie Christs and Antichrists*, 161.

66. The "luxury-loving" bishop, complete with cellular telephone is a heartless manager; the pastor is leading a double life, sleeping with his young and attractive housekeeper. One older and violently unbalanced priest in the opening of the film breaks into the bishop's residence using a huge crucifix as a battering ram and another older, "ugly, misanthropic priest," pastor of a remote country parish, speaks only Latin and is cruel and sadistic. The young priest-protagonist, a "handsome, starched, blond, south-of-England conservative," all rubrics and orthodoxy, suddenly discovers he is a homosexual, and deals with the issue by going to a gay bar and going home with the first man he meets. Citations from Donald Lyons, "Priests," [*Film Comment* v.31, n.3 (May-June 1995): 83, 85, 82.]

67. Hurley, "Cinematic Transfigurations of Jesus," 64.

68. Neil Hurley errs in twice identifying the film's setting as Montréal. Clearly it is Québec City. [Ibid., 64, 66.]

69. Lyons, 81.

70. Pavelin, 69.

71. Malone, *Movie Christs and Antichrists*, 78.

72. Ibid., 79.

73. In this brief synthesis, I use material from: Malone, *Movie Christs and Antichrists*, 79.

74. Ibid., 65.

75. Ibid.

76. Hurley, "Cinematic Transfigurations of Jesus," 72.

77. Ibid.

78. Castellani, *Temi e figure del film religioso*, 125.

79. Bedouelle, 88.

80. Holloway, 121. Holloway dates the Fair as 1966. In fact it was held in 1964-65.

81. Malone, *Movie Christs and Antichrists*, 66.

82. Viano, 100. He continues: "*La ricotta* reveals the extent to which appearances (Stracci deserves contempt and ridicule) conceal a quite opposite truth (Stracci is sublime), dramatizing at once the existence of the mask and the discovery of what lies beneath it." [Ibid.] Another Italian critic clearly appreciates the way the religious and political themes move parallel to one another other in *La ricotta*. With some irony, he summarizes the plot in a credo, in which little Stracci is the Christ-figure. "Behold once again, the divine descends to earth, is made human, incarnates itself in the new Christ, the subproletariat, suffers under neocapitalism, is crucified through the shots of a biblical film made by the

new Pharisees, the bourgeois class, and in death, redeems himself." [U.F., *"Rogopag,"* *Cinema Nuovo* v.16, n.162 (March-April 1963): 137.]

83. Graff, 55.

84. Ibid.

85. Hurley, "Cinematic Transfigurations of Jesus," 67.

86. Graff, 49.

87. Hurley, "Cinematic Transfigurations of Jesus," 76.

88. Ibid.

89. Ibid.

90. Ibid.

91. Ibid.

92. Ibid.

93. Holloway, 121.

94. Hurley, "Cinematic Transfigurations of Jesus," 70.

95. Ibid.

96. Pavelin, 21.

97. Hurley, "Cinematic Transfigurations of Jesus," 71.

98. Ibid.

99. Hurley, *"On the Waterfront*: Rebirth of a 'Contenduh,'"* in *Image and Likeness: Religious Visions in American Film Classics*, edited by John R. May (New York: Paulist Press, 1992), 103.

100. Malden was awarded an Academy Award in 1954 for his classic performance. Two other Oscars went to the film, for Best Picture and Best Director.

101. Hurley, *"On the Waterfront*: Rebirth of a 'Contenduh,'"* 103.

102. Ibid.

103. Ibid., 102, 101.

104. Ibid., 103.

105. Ibid.

106. At the 1975 Academy Awards, the film won the Oscars for Best Picture, Best Actor, Best Actress, Best Director and Best Screenplay.

107. Mara E. Donaldson, "Love and Duty in *Casablanca*," in *Image and Likeness: Religious Visions in American Film Classics*, 146.

108. Ibid.

109. He explains to the doctor: "She was fifteen, goin' on thirty-five, Doc."

110. Charles B. Ketcham, *"One Flew Over the Cuckoo's Nest*: A Salvific Drama of Liberation," in *Image and Likeness: Religious Visions in American Film Classics*, 151.

111. Ibid.

112. Ibid., 152.

113. Ibid.

114. Ibid.

Chapter Seven:
Christ-Figures in Bresson and Tarkovsky

1. Gilson, "'My God, Wilt Thou Forsake Me?," 55.

2. Prédal, *Robert Bresson: L'aventure intérieure – L'Avant-Scène Cinéma,* 12.

3. Bedouelle, 70.

4. Ibid., 71.

5. Prédal, *Robert Bresson: L'aventure intérieure – L'Avant-Scène Cinéma,* 12.

6. Amédée Ayfre, "The Universe of Robert Bresson," in Amédée Ayfre and others, *The Films of Robert Bresson,* 14.

7. Sontag, 186.

8. Estève, *Robert Bresson: La passion du cinématographe,* 108.

9. Schrader, 59.

10. Ibid., 100.

11. Ibid., 82.

12. Ibid.

13. Ibid.

14. Henri Agel and Amédée Ayfre, *Le cinéma et le sacré* (Paris: Cerf, 1961), 36.

15. Sontag, 59-60.

16. Jean Sémolué, *Bresson* (Paris: Editions Universitaires, 1960), 69.

17. Estève, *Robert Bresson: La passion du cinématographe,* 108.

18. Ibid.

19. Schrader, 75.

20. Ibid., 73.

21. Agel and Ayfre, 36.

22. Schrader, 72.

23. Ibid., 73.

24. Agel and Ayfre, 35.

25. Ibid.

26. Ibid., 36.

27. Ibid., 35.

28. Schrader, 100-101.

29. Ibid., 79.

30. Sémolué, *Bresson ou l'acte pur des métamorphoses,* 84.

31. Arnaud, *Robert Bresson,* 20.

32. Sémolué, *Bresson ou l'acte pur des métamorphoses,* 86.

33. Though in the published criticism, Andrei Tarkovsky's name is spelled in a wide variety of ways, I shall spell it this way. In citations, I shall respect the spelling used by the authors whom I am quoting.

34. Mark Le Fanu, *The Cinema of Andrei Tarkovsky* (London: BFI Publishing, 1987), 42.

35. In fact, at one point – at the end of 1966, when the first cut of the film was ready – this was intended as the title for the entire film. [Vida T. Johnson and Graham Petrie, *The Films of Andrei Tarkovsky: A Visual Fugue* (Bloomington: University of Indiana Press, 1994), 80.]

36. Ibid., 252.

37. Le Fanu, 38.

38. Guy Gauthier, *Andrei Tarkovski* (Paris: Edilig, 1988), 56.

39. Maya Turovskaya, *Tarkovsky: Cinema as Poetry* (London: Faber and Faber, 1989), 40.

40. Ibid.

41. Le Fanu, 47.

42. Johnson and Petrie, 97.

43. Gauthier, 82.

44. Jacques Demeure, *"Andrei Roublev*: Nous sommes tous des peintres mediévaux," in *Andrei Tarkovski*, edited by Gilles Ciment (Paris: Dossier Positif-Rivages, 1988), 81.

45. Estève, "Andrei Tarkovski: Un art de l'icône," in *Le film religieux*, 138.

46. Pavelin, 81.

47. In a bizarre image of death and resurrection, the film itself "was shot twice over, a very rare occurrence in commercial cinema . . . owing to a processing fault at the laboratories which ruined the negative." [Le Fanu, 94.]

48. Emmanuel Carrère, *"Stalker*: Troisième plongée dans l'océan, troisième retour à la maison," in *Andrei Tarkovski*, edited by Gilles Ciment, 115.

49. Johnson and Petrie, 152.

50. Carrère, 117.

51. Jacques Gerstenkorn and Sylvie Strudel, *"Stalker*: La quête de la foi ou le dernier souffle de l'esprit," in *Etudes cinématographiques 135-138: Andreï Tarkovsky*, edited by Michel Estève (Paris: Lettres Modernes-Minard, 1986), 85.

52. Estève, "Andrei Tarkovski: Un art de l'icône," 139.

53. Turovskaya, 113.

54. Bedouelle, 87.

55. Ibid., 88.

56. Andrei Tarkovsky, *Sculpting in Time: Reflections on the Cinema* (London: The Bodley Head, 1988), 181.

57. Le Fanu, 98.

58. Carrère, 119.

59. Gerstenkorn and Strudel, 82.

60. Aldo Tassone, "Entretien avec Andrei Tarkovski," in *Andrei Tarkovski*, edited by Gilles Ciment, 127.

61. Gerstenkorn and Strudel, 82.

62. Estève, "Andrei Tarkovski: Un art de l'icône," 138.

63. Turovskaya, 125.

64. Domenico is played by the Swedish actor Erland Josephson, who in Tarkovsky's next and final film, *The Sacrifice*, plays the role of Alexander, the protagonist and a Christ-figure.

65. Turovskaya, 127.

66. Ibid., 133.

67. Tarkovsky in Tony Mitchell, "Andrei Tarkovsky and *Nostalghia*," *Film Criticism 8*, n.3 (1984): 5, quoted in Johnson and Petrie, 159. The director goes on to say: "I have never made a film which mirrors my own states of mind with so much violence, and liberates my inner world in such depth." [Ibid.]

68. Ibid., 164.

69. Le Fanu, 119.

70. Gauthier, 123.

71. Turovskaya, 133.

72. Ibid., 134.

73. Ramasse, "*Nostalghia*: 'Souviens-toi de Sisyphe,'" in *Etudes cinématographiques 135-138: Andreï Tarkovsky*, 140.

74. Estève, "Andrei Tarkovski: Un art de l'icône," 139.

75. Andrei Tarkovski, "Le Sacrifice, Offret, Sacrificatio: A propos du *Sacrifice*," in *Andrei Tarkovski*, edited by Gilles Ciment, 144.

76. Estève, "Une esthétique de l'incarnation: *Le Sacrifice*," in *Etudes cinématographiques, 135-138: Andreï Tarkovsky*, 182.

77. Andrei Tarkovsky, *Sculpting in Time: Reflections on the Cinema*, 209.

78. Johnson and Petrie, 179. After the earlier disaster with the print of *Stalker*, in another twist of fate, the camera blocked at the beginning of this crucial shot. The house had to be rebuilt, and the scene shot again.

79. Estève, "Andrei Tarkovski: Un art de l'icône," 139.

80. Estève, "Une esthétique de l'incarnation: *Le Sacrifice*," 184.

81. Le Fanu, 137.

82. Turovskaya, 149.

Epilogue

1. Michael Goldberg, *Theology and Narrative: A Critical Introduction* (Nashville, TN: Abington, 1982); John Navone, *Gospel Love: A Narrative Theology* (Wilmington, DE: Glazier, 1984); and John Navone, *Seeking God in Story* (Collegeville, MN: Liturgical Press, 1990).

2. The script was written by Dreyer in English and published in 1972 by the Dial Press in New York. A more complete version of the script – the Dial Press edited some material out of Dreyer's manuscript – has been published in French, accompanied by an excellent introductory essay by Maurice Drouzy, in which he explains the development of Dreyer's ill-fated project: Carl Theodor Dreyer, *Jésus de Nazareth, Médée*, edited by Maurice Drouzy (Paris: Editions du Cerf, 1986).

3. Dreyer in ibid, 14.

4. Dreyer in ibid.

5. Dreyer knew Ray's film and had no intention of imitating it. He did not know Pasolini's *The Gospel According to Saint Matthew*. [Giacomo Gambetti, "Testimonianza a proposito di *Jesusfilm*," in *Il cinema di Dreyer: L'eccentrico e il classico*, 179.]

6. In his introductory essay Drouzy suggests that the RAI made a serious and concrete proposal to finance the film. [Dreyer, *Jésus de Nazareth, Médée*, 31.] The Italian Giacomo Gambetti, who participated in the RAI-Dreyer negotiations, insists that Drouzy is wrong and that the discussions were quite preliminary. [Gambetti, "Testimonianza a proposito di *Jesusfilm*," 173-174.]

7. Ibid., 179.

8. Dreyer in ibid.

9. Ibid., 180.

Bibliography

The following bibliography is a listing of the works from which I cited material in the book and of a few other significant works which I consulted but from which I quoted no material. Clearly it does not pretend to be exhaustive. It consists of two parts. In the first part are listed books and articles of a more general nature or works which refer to more than one film discussed in this book or from which I quote material in more than one chapter of the book. The second part, subdivided according to the chapters of the book, and in some cases further subdivided according to sections of a chapter, lists works from which I quote material in that chapter or section of a chapter.

When the material quoted is from a source which is itself quoting an earlier source, only the source to which I had access is included in the bibiliography. Clearly the two and sometimes three sources are included in the notes. Finally, when the material quoted is from one essay in a collection of essays, in this bibliography I note as the principal reference the title and bibliographical details of the collection. Then I list the essays in that collection from which I have quoted material. In the case of works published in languages other than English, the original form of the title and of the place of publication and publisher are respected.

Regarding the abbreviations used in the entries, "v" is for volume, "n" for number and "nn" for numbers. In the entries for some Italian journals, "an" is for "*anno*" or year, meaning (roughly) volume; "qd" is for "*quaderno*" or "copy-book," meaning (roughly) "issue." All the numbers are rendered in Arabic, even if in the original sources, they are in Roman numerals.

Part One: General Bibliography

Agel, Henri and Amedée Ayfre. *Le cinéma et le sacré*. Paris: Editions du Cerf, 1961.

Arnaud, Philippe. *Robert Bresson*. Paris: Cahiers du Cinéma, 1986.

Ayfre, Amédée. *Cinéma et mystère*. Paris: Editions du Cerf, 1969.

_____. *Le cinéma et la foi chrétienne*. Paris: Librairie Arthème Fayard, 1960.

_____. *Le cinéma et sa vérité*. Paris: Editions du Cerf, 1969.

_____. *Contributi a una teologia dell'immagine*. Roma: Edizioni Paoline, 1966.

_____. *Conversion aux images? I. Les images et Dieu; II. Les images et l'homme*. Paris: Editions du Cerf, 1964.

_____. *Dieu au cinéma: Les problèmes esthétiques du film religieux*. Paris: Presses Universitaires de France-Privat, 1953.

Babington, Bruce, and Peter William Evans. *Biblical Epics: Sacred Narrative in the Hollywood Cinema*. Manchester: Manchester University Press, 1993.

Baugh, Lloyd. "Un approccio teologico-spirituale al cinema." *Consacrazione & Servizio* an.44, n.10 (October 1995): 26-36.

_____. "Cinema, cultura, spiritualità: Sintonia possibile." *Consacrazione & Servizio* an.44, n.5 (May 1995): 33-40.

_____. "Cine profano, cine religioso." *Teologia y Catequesis* (Madrid) n.56 (October-December 1995): 11-44.

_____. "Il film biblico: Meglio il modello analogico che gli effetti speciali." *Letture* an.49, qd.512 (December 1994): 40-42.

Bedouelle, Guy. *Du spirituel dans le cinéma*. Paris: Editions du Cerf, 1985.

Bondanella, Peter. *Italian Cinema from Neorealism to the Present*. New York: Continuum-Frederick Ungar, 1990.

Butler, Ivan. *Religion in the Cinema*. New York: A. S. Barnes, 1969.

Campbell, Richard H. and Michael R. Pitts. *The Bible on Film: A Checklist 1897-1980*. Metuchen, NJ: The Scarecrow Press, 1981.

Castellani, Leandro. *Temi e figure del film religioso*. Leumann, TO: Editrice Elle Di Ci, 1994.

Il cinema di Dreyer: L'eccentrico e il classico, Il. Edited by Andrea Martini. Venezia: Marsilio Editori, 1987.

In this collection:

    Gambetti, Giacomo. "Testimonianza a proposito di *Jesusfilm*," 173-183.

    Komatsu, Hiroshi. "Dreyer e la coscienza estetica come continuum," 55-62.

    Martini, Andrea. "La scelta scandalosa di Dreyer," 149-158.

Cinéma et Spiritualité. In the series "Collection Alternatives." Bruxelles: Editions O.C.I.C., 1988.

"CinEnciclopedia 2: La banca dati del cinema mondiale," CD, Editoria Elettronica Editel and Ente dello Spettacolo, 1994.

Cox, Harvey. *The Feast of Fools: A Theological Essay on Festivity and Fantasy*. New York: Harper and Row, 1969.

Detweiler, Robert. "Christ and the Christ Figure in American Fiction." In *New Theology n.2*. Edited by Martin Marty and Dean G. Peerman. New York: MacMillan, 1965.

Estève, Michel. *Robert Bresson: La passion du cinématographe*. Paris: Editions Albatros, 1983.

Everschor, Franz. "Die Darstellung religiöser Inhalte im Film." *Stimmen der Zeit* v.193, n.6 (June 1975): 388-396.

Fantuzzi, Virgilio. "Vangeli cinematografici a confronto." *La Civiltà Cattolica* an.128, n.2 qd.3048 (18 June 1977): 579-586.

Ferlita, Ernest, and John R. May. *Film as a Search for Meaning*. Dublin: Veritas, 1977.

Ferrero, Adelio. *Robert Bresson.* Firenze: La Nuova Italia-Il Castoro Cinema, May 1979.

Filizzola, Renato. *I film degli anni '70.* Roma: Edizioni Paoline, 1980.

Film-Dienst Extra: Jesus in der Hauptrolle (Köln: Katholisches Institut für Medieninformation [KIM], November 1992).
In this collection:

    Albrecht, Gerd. "Jesus – Eine Filmkarriere," 9-14.

    Bieger, Eckhard. "Revolte und Religion: Gedanken zu Pasolini's Jesus Gestalten im Abstand von 30 Jahren," 32-35.

    Eichenberger, Ambros. *"Der Messias,"* in *Zoom-Filmberater* v.30, n.8 (19 April 1978), Reprinted in *Film-Dienst Extra,* 67-68.

    Everschor, Franz. *"Das 1. Evangelium-Matthäus,"* 62-64.

    Gasper, Hans. "Blasphemie oder Fremdprophetie? Jesus-Filme als Skandal," 41-43.

    Graff, Michael. "Christus Inkognito: Eine theologische Spurensicherung im Film," 48-56.

    Hasenberg, Peter. "Clown und Superstar: Die Jesus Musicals der 70er Jahre," 36-41.

    _____. "Jesus im Film – Eine Auswahlfilmographie," 74-84.

    _____. "Zehn ausgewählte Jesus-Filme – Kritiken und Materialen," 58-73.

    Horstmann, Johannes. *"Der Messias," Film-Dienst* v.41, n.19 (19 September 1989). Reprinted in *Film-Dienst Extra,* 66-67.

Le film religeux - CinémAction n.49. Paris: Corlet, 1988.
In this collection:

    Agel, Henri. "Jeanne La Pucelle en dix-huit films. Sainte et conquérante," 84-88.

    Aziza, Claude. "Les premiers chrétiens: les lions ne sont jamais loin," 26-32.

    Boitel, Philippe. "Editorial: Rendre visible l'invisible?," 5-7.

    Di Falco, Jean Michel. In "Deux films contestés," 41.

    Douin, Jean-Luc. "Filmographie," 42.

    _____. In "Deux films contestés," 41.

    _____. "Jésus superstar: Certains préfèrent l'invisible," 33-38.

    Estève, Michel. "Andrei Tarkovski: 'Un art de l'icône,' 138-139.

    _____. "Robert Bresson: le janséniste," 140-141.

    Marty, Joseph. "Chromo, patro, mélo: le cinéma, côté Saint-Sulpice," 62-70.

    Oms, Marcel. "Quatre Bernanos au cinéma: La grâce sous la braise," 89-93.

    Serre, Olivier. "Le point de vue de Chrétiens-Médias," 54-55.

The Films of Robert Bresson. Edited by Amédée Ayfre and others. London: Studio Vista Ltd., 1979.
In this collection:

    Ayfre, Amédée. "The Universe of Robert Bresson," 6-24.

    Barr, Charles. *"Au hasard, Balthazar,"* 106-114.

    Murray, Leo. *"Le procès de Jeanne d'Arc,"* 90-105.

Ford, Charles. *Le cinéma au service de la foi*. Paris: Présence Plon, 1953.

Forshey, Gerald E. *American Religious and Biblical Spectaculars*. Westport, CT: Praeger, 1992.

Gilson, René. "My God, Wilt Thou Forsake Me?" *Cahiers du Cinéma in English* n.11 (September 1967): 54. [Original: *Cahiers du Cinéma*, n.182, September 1966)].

Goldberg, Michael. *Theology and Narrative: A Critical Introduction*. Nashville, TN: Abington, 1982.

Heumann, E. "Zwischen Blasphemie und Erbauung: Die vielen Gesichtes Jesus im Film." *Religio* v.1 (1989): 30-32

Hill, Geoffrey. *Illuminating Shadows: The Mythic Power of Film*. Boston: Shambhala, 1992.

Holloway, Ronald. *Beyond the Image: Approaches to the Religious Dimension in the Cinema*. Geneva: Oikoumene, 1977.

Huizinga, Johan. *Homo Ludens: A Study of the Play Element in Culture*. Boston: Beacon Press, 1955.

Hurley, Neil P. *Towards a Film Humanism*. New York: Dell Publishing Co., 1975.

Image and Likeness: Religious Visions in American Film Classics. Edited by John R. May. New York: Paulist Press, 1992.

In this collection:

Donaldson, Mara E. "Love and Duty in *Casablanca*," 119-125.

Hurley, Neil P. "*On the Waterfront*: Rebirth of a 'Contenduh,'" 96-103.

Ketcham, Charles B. "*One Flew Over the Cuckoo's Nest*: A Salvific Drama of Liberation," 145-152.

Keyser, Les and Barbara. *Hollywood and the Catholic Church: The Image of Roman Catholicism in American Movies*. Chicago: Loyola University Press, 1984.

Kinnard, Roy and Tim Davis. *Divine Images: A History of Jesus on the Screen*. New York: Citadel Press-Carol Publishing Group, 1992.

Lynch, William. *Christ and Apollo: The Dimensions of the Literary Imagination*. New York: Sheed and Ward, 1960.

_____. *Images of Faith: An Exploration of the Ironical Imagination*. Notre Dame, IN: University of Notre Dame, 1973.

Leon-Dufour, Xavier. "Jésus-Christ sur l'écran." *Etudes* (March 1965): 390-395.

Macdonald, Dwight. *Dwight Macdonald on Movies*. Englewood Cliffs, NJ: Prentice Hall, 1970.

Malone, Peter. *Movie Christs and Antichrists*. New York: Crossroad, 1990.

Maritain, Jacques. *Approaches to God*. Translated by Peter O'Reilly. New York: MacMillan, 1964.

_____. "Preface" in William Congdon, *Nel mio disco d'oro: Itinerario a Cristo*. Assisi: 1961.

Martin, Thomas M. *Images and the Imageless: A Study in Religious Consciousness and Film*. Lewisburg: Bucknell University Press – London: Associated University Presses, 1981.

Mast, Gerald. *A Short History of the Movies.* New York: MacMillan Publishing Company, 1986.

"Microsoft Cinemania '94," Interactive Movie Guide CD, Microsoft Corporation.

Navone, John. *Gospel Love: A Narrative Theology.* Wilmington, DE: Glazier, 1984.

_____. *Seeking God in Story.* Collegeville, MN: Liturgical Press, 1990.

New Revised Standard Version of *The Holy Bible.* Nashville, TN: Thomas Nelson Publishers, 1989.

Niebuhr, H. Richard. *Christ and Culture.* New York: Harper Torchbook, 1956.

Ong, Walter. *The Presence of the Word.* New Haven: Yale University Press, 1967.

Passion du Christ comme thème cinématographique. Edited by Michel Estève. *Etudes cinématographiques* nn.10-11 (1971).

Pavelin, Alan. *Fifty Religious Films.* Chislehurst, Kent: A. P. Pavelin, 1990.

Pigoullie, Jean-François. "Religion: Les années 80 ou le religieux postmoderne." *Positif* n.340 (June 1989): 18-21.

Rahner, Hugo. *Man at Play.* New York: Herder and Herder, 1967.

Religion im Film: Lexicon mit Kurzkritiken und Stichworten zu 1200 Kinofilmen. Edited by Peter Hasenberg, Johannes Horstmann and others. Köln: Katholisches Institut für Medieninformation (KIM), 1993.

Religion in Film. Edited by John R. May and Michael Bird. Knoxville: University of Tennessee Press, 1982.

In this collection:

Bird, Michael. "Film as Hierophany," 3-22.

_____. "Ingmar Bergman," 142-150.

May, John R. "Federico Fellini," 170-176.

_____. "Visual Story and the Religious Interpretation of Film," 23-43.

Hurley, Neil P. "Cinematic Transfigurations of Jesus," 61-78.

Robert Bresson: L'aventure intérieure – L'Avant-Scène Cinéma. Edited by René Prédal. nn.408-409 (January-February 1992).

In this collection:

Prédal, René. "*Au Hasard Balthazar*," 81-84.

Santayana, George. *Poetry and Religion.* New York: Harper Torchbook, 1957.

Schrader, Paul. *Transcendental Style in Cinema: Ozu, Bresson, Dreyer.* Berkeley: University of California Press, 1966.

Schillaci, Anthony. *Movies and Morals.* Notre Dame, IN: Fides, 1968.

Scott, Nathan A. *The Broker Center: Studies in the Theological Horizon of Modern Literature.* New Haven, CT: Yale University Press, 1968.

Screening the Sacred: Religion, Myth and Ideology in Popular American Film. Edited by Joel W. Martin and Conrad E. Ostwalt Jr. Boulder, CO: Westview Press, 1995.

Singer, Michael. "Cinema Savior." *Film Comment* v.24, n.5 (September-October 1988): 44-47.

Sontag, Susan. "Spiritual Style in the Films of Robert Bresson." In *Against Interpretation and Other Essays*. New York: Farrar, Straus and Giroux, 1966, 177-195.

Spuren des Religiösen im Film. Edited by Peter Hasenberg, Wolfgang Luley and Charles Martig. Mainz: Matthias-Grünewald-Verlag and Köln: Katholisches Institut für Medieninformation [KIM], 1995.

Turner, Victor. *Dramas, Fields and Metaphors: Symbolic Action in Human Society*. Ithaca, NY: Cornell University Press, 1974.

_____, and Edith Turner. *Image and Pilgrimage in Christian Culture: Anthropological Perspectives*. New York: Columbia University Press, 1978.

Verdone, Mario. "Da Bergman ad Antonioni." *Bianco e Nero* v.24, nn.8-9 (August-September 1964): 7-29.

Wall, James M. "Biblical Spectaculars and Secular Man." In *Celluloid and Symbols*. Edited by John C. Cooper and Carl Skrade. Philadelphia: Fortress Press, 1970: 51-60.

_____. *Church and Cinema: A Way of Viewing Film*. Grand Rapids, MI: William B. Eerdsmans, 1971.

Wollen, Peter. *Signs and Meaning in the Cinema*. London: Secker and Warburg, 1974.

Ziolkowski, Theodore. *Fictional Transfigurations of Jesus*. Princeton, NJ: Princeton Univeristy Press, 1972.

Zwick, Reinhold. "Die Ressourcen sind nicht erschöpft." *Herder Korrespondenz* v.11 (November 1995): 616-620.

Part Two: Bibliography According to Chapters

Part One, Chapter One: The Early Years

An Invention of the Devil? Religion and the Early Cinema. Une Invention du Diable? Cinéma des Premiers Temps et Religion. Edited by Roland Cosandey, André Gaudreault, Tom Gunning. Sainte Foy, Canada: Les Presses de l'Université Laval, 1992.

In this collection:

Gaudreault, André. "La Passion du Christ: une forme, un genre, un discours," 91-101.

Keil, Charles. "*From the Manger to the Cross*: The New Testament Narrative and the Question of Stylistic Retardation," 112-120.

Musser, Charles. "Les Passions et les Mystères de la Passion aux États-Unis (1880-1900)," 145-186.

Raynauld, Isabelle. "Les scénarios de la Passion selon Pathé (1902-1914)," 131-141.

Reynolds, Herbert. "From the Palette to the Screen: The Tissot Bible as Sourcebook for *From the Manger to the Cross*," 275-310.

The Literary Guide to the Bible. Edited by Robert Alter and Frank Kermode. Cambridge: Belknap Press, 1987.

Part One, Chapter Two:
King of Kings, The Gospel According to Hollywood

Baker, Peter. "Making It B-I-G." *Films and Filming* v.7, n.2 (November 1960): 14-15, 42.

Benayoun, Robert. "*Le Roi des Rois*: A teen-age Jesus." *Positif,* n.45 (May 1962): 62-63.

Crowther, Bosley. "*Kings of Kings.*" In *The New York Times Film Reviews 1959-1968, v.5.* New York: The New York Times and Arno Press, 1970 (12 October 1961).

Cutts, John. "*King of Kings.*" *Films and Filming* v.8, n.4 (January 1962): 32-33.

Fieschi, Jean-André. "Le regard et le don: *King of Kings.*" *Cahiers du Cinéma* v.22, n.129 (March 1962): 56-58.

"Fitzgerald's Views." *Variety* n.226, 8 November 1961, 5.

H.H. "*King of Kings.*" *Films* v.12, n.9 (November 1961): 545-546.

Land. "Film Reviews: *King of Kings.*" *Variety,* 11 October 1961, 6.

"Nick Ray Comments." *Variety* n.224, 18 October 1961, 5.

O'Connor, Edward. "*King of Kings.*" *Films in Review* v.12, n.9 (November 1961): 546-549.

Petri, Bruce. *A Theory of American Film: The Films and Techniques of George Stevens.* New York: Garland Publishing Company, 1987.

P.H. "*King of Kings.*" *The Monthly Film Bulletin* (BFI) v.29, n.336 (January 1962): 7.

"Pope's Direct OK Simplifies 'Kings' Coin Problems." *Variety* v.218, 9 March 1960, 1.

Quigly, Elizabeth. "Cinema: The Dainty Crucifixion." *The Spectator* n.207, 24 November 1961, 763.

Walsh, Moira. "Christ or Credit Card?: A Review of *King of Kings.*" *America,* 21 October 1961, 71.

The Greatest Story Ever Told

Aitkin, Tom. "The greatest story – never told." *The Tablet,* 23-30 December 1995, 1657.

Alexander, Shana. "*The Greatest Story Ever Told.*" *Life,* 25 February 1965, 25.

Andrew, Geoff. *The Films of Nicholas Ray: The Poet of Nightfall.* London: Charles Letts, 1991.

A.S. "The Greatest Story Ever Told." *The Monthly Film Bulletin* (BFI) v.32, n.376 (May 1965): 69-70.

Aprà, Adriano, Barry Boys, Ian Cameron, José Luis Guarner, Paul Mayersberg and V.F. Perkins. Interview with Nicholas Ray. *Movie* n.9 (May 1963): 14-25.

Cook, Page. "The Sound Track." *Films in Review* v.16, n.4 (April 1965): 244-246.

Douchet, Jean and Jacques Joly. "Nouvel entretien avec Nicholas Ray." *Cahiers du Cinéma* v.22, n.127 (January 1962): 10.

Durgnat, Raymond. *"The Greatest Story Ever Told*: Raymond Durgnat on the Images of Jesus." *Films and Filming* v.11, n.9 (June 1965): 25-26.

Erice, Victor and Jos Oliver. *Nicholas Ray y su Tiempo.* Madrid: Filmoteca Española, 1986.

Hartung, Philip T. "The Screen: The Greatest Is Average." *Commonweal* v.81, n.24, 12 March 1965, 765.

Kreidl, John Francis. *Nicholas Ray.* Boston: Twayne Publishers, 1977.

Land. "Film Reviews: *The Greatest Story Ever Told.*" *Variety*, 16 February 1965, 6.

Laura, Ernesto G. "La vita di Gesù in cinerama." *Rivista del Cinematografo* n.6 (June 1965): 290-293.

Macdonald, Dwight. *Dwight Macdonald on Movies.* Englewood Cliffs, NJ: Prentice Hall, 1970.

Patterson, Frances Taylor. "Film Reviews: *The Greatest Story Ever Told.*" *Films in Review* v.16, n.3 (March 1965): 173-176.

Ray, Nicholas. *I Was Interrupted: Nicholas Ray on Making Movies.* Edited by Susan Ray. Berkeley: University of California Press, 1993.

Richie, Donald. *George Stevens: An American Romantic.* New York: The Museum of Modern Art, 1970.

Truchaud, François. *Nicholas Ray.* Paris: Editions Universitaires, 1965.

Part One, Chapter Three: The Jesus Musicals

Jesus Christ Superstar

Howard, Alan R. "Review of *Jesus Christ Superstar.*" *The Hollywood Reporter* v.226, n.47, 25 June 1973, 3, 10.

Murf. "Film Reviews: *Jesus Christ Superstar.*" *Variety,* 27 June 1973, 20.

Rayns, Tony. "Review of *Jesus Christ Superstar.*" *The Monthly Film Bulletin* (BFI) v.400, n.476 (September 1973): 192.

Reisfeld, Bert. "Norman Jewison talks to Bert Reisfeld about *Jesus Christ Superstar.*" *Photoplay* (G.B.) v.24, n.4, April 1973, 26-27.

Godspell

Boyum, Joy Gould. "From Porno to Piety: Religious Themes Appearing in Today's Films." *Making Films in New York,* April 1973, 20, 31, 45.

Demby, Betty Jeffries. "The Making of *Godspell*: An Interview with Director David Greene." *Filmmakers Newsletter* v.6, n.7, May 1973, 32-35.

"Godspell" (An interview with David Greene and Michael Heimann). *Making Films in New York* v.7, n.2, April 1973, 10, 13, 14, 18.

Madden, Paul. "Review of *Godspell.*" *The Monthly Film Bulletin* (BFI) v.40, n.474 (July 1973): 148.

Sege. "Film Reviews: *Godspell.*" *Variety*, 28 March 1973, 18.

Stuart, Alexander Stuart. "Review of *Godspell.*" *Films and Filming* v.19, n.11 (August 1973): 52.

Part One, Chapter Four: The Scandal Films

Monty Python's Life of Brian.

Altman, Dennis. "Film Reviews: *The Life of Brian.*" *Cinema Papers* (Australia) n.24 (December-January 1979-1980): 659-660.

Bilb, Marjorie. "The New Films: *Monty Python's Life of Brian.*" *Screen International* n.217 (24 November 1979): 18.

Canby, Vincent. "Gospel of Lunacy." *The New York Times Film Reviews 1979-1980.* New York: The New York Times and Arno Press, 1981 (17 August 1979).

Cart. "Review of *Life of Brian.*" *Variety's Film Reviews 1978-1980,* v.15. New York: R.R. Bowker, 1983 (22 August 1979).

"Film Guide: *Monty Python's Life of Brian.*" *Sight and Sound* v.49, n.1 (Winter 1980): 66.

Jeavons, Clyde. "Review of *Monthy Python's Life of Brian.*" *The Monthly Film Bulletin* (BFI) v.46, n.550 (November 1979): 229.

Millar, Gavin. "Cinema: Blessed Brian." *The Listener* v.102, n.6237, 15 November 1979, 78-79.

Petit, Chris. "Half a Dinari [*sic*] For My Bloody Life Story?" *Time Out* n.499, 5 November 1979, 21.

Rogers, Tom. "Review of *Life of Brian.*" *Films in Review* v.31, n.2 (January 1980): 56.

Zatterin, Marco. *Il Circo Volante: Viaggio nel grottesco pythoniano (o nel grottiano pythonesco).* Roma: Quaderni dell'AIACE, 1987.

The Last Temptation of Christ

Caputo, Rolando. "Forbidden Christ." *Cinema Papers* (Australia) n.71 (January 1989): 7-8.

Cart. "Film Reviews: *The Last Temptation of Christ.*" *Variety*, 10 August 1988, 12.

Connelly, Marie Katheryn. *Martin Scorsese: An Analysis of His Feature Films with a Filmography of His Whole Career.* Jefferson, NC: McFarland & Company, 1993.

Cook, Pam. "Feature Films: *The Last Temptation of Christ.*" *The Monthly Film Bulletin* (BFI) v.55, n.657 (October 1988): 287-288.

Corliss, Richard. ". . . and Blood: An Interview with Martin Scorsese." *Film Comment* v.24, n.5 (September-October 1988): 36-39, 42.

_____. "Body . . ." *Film Comment* v.24, n.5 (September-October 1988): 34, 42-43.

Coursodon, Jean-Pierre. "Martin Scorsese: La chair et l'esprit." *Positif* n.332 (October 1988): 2-5.

Di Caprio, Lisa. "*The Last Temptation of Christ*: Spirit and Flesh." *Jump Cut* n.35 (April 1990): 108-109.

Ehrenstein, David. *The Scorsese Picture: The Art and Life of Martin Scorsese.* New York: Birchlane Press-Carol Publishing Group, 1992.

Henry, Michael. "Entretien avec Martin Scorsese sur *La Dernière Tentation du Christ.*" *Positif* n.332 (October 1988): 6-12.

Jacobson, Harlan. "You talkin' to me?" *Film Comment* v.24, n.5 (September-October 1988): 32-33.

Jenkins, Steve. "From the Pit of Hell." *The Monthly Film Bulletin* (BFI) v.55, n.659 (December 1988): 352-353.

Keyser, Les. *Martin Scorsese.* New York: Twayne Publishers, 1992.

Krauthammer, Charles. "The *Temptation* of Martin Scorsese." *Washington Post*, 19 September 1988, 23, sec.A.

Lopate, Phillip. "Fourteen Koans by a Levite on Scorsese's *The Last Temptation of Christ.*" *Tikkum*, November-December 1988, 74-78.

Lourdeaux, Leo. *Irish and Italian Filmmakers in America: Ford, Capra, Coppola, and Scorsese.* Philadelphia: Temple University Press, 1990.

Malone, Peter. "Martin Scorcese's [*sic*] *The Last Temptation of Christ*," *Cinema Papers* (Australia) n.71 (January 1989): 4-8.

Maslin, Janet. "The Inner Life of the Absolute." *The New York Times Film Reviews 1987-1988.* New York: Times Books and Garland Publishing Company (12 August 1988).

_____. "Two Directors Put Their Stamps on Their Dream" [on Coppola and Scorsese]. *The New York Times Film Reviews 1987-1988.* New York: Times Books and Garland Publishing Company (21 August 1988).

Morris, Michael. "Of God and Man: A Theological and Artistic Scrutiny of Martin Scorsese's *The Last Temptation of Christ.*" *American Film* v.14, n.1 (October 1988): 44-49.

Newman, Kim. "Short Films: *The Big Shave.*" *Sight and Sound* v.2, n.2 (June 1992): 56.

Rosenbaum, Jonathan. "Raging Messiah: *The Last Temptation of Christ.*" *Sight and Sound* v.57, n.4 (Autumn 1958): 281-282.

Sablon, Jean-Luc. "Martin Scorsese: Dieu est avec moi." *Revue du Cinéma-Image et Son* n.442 (October 1988): 52-59.

Schrader on Schrader. Edited by Kevin Jackson. London: Faber and Faber, 1990.

Scorsese, Martin. "In the Streets." In *Once a Catholic: Prominent Catholics and Ex-Catholics Discuss the Influence of the Church on Their Lives and Works.* Edited by Peter Occhiogrosso. Boston: Houghton Mifflin, 1987, 88-101.

Scorsese on Scorsese. Edited by David Thompson and Ian Christie. Boston: Faber and Faber, 1989.

Thompson, David. "Review of *The Last Temptation of Christ.*" *Films and Filming* n.409 (October 1988): 37-38.

Von Gunden, Kenneth. *Postmodern Auteurs: Coppola, Lucas, De Palma, Spielberg and Scorsese.* Jefferson NC: McFarland & Company, 1991.

Part One, Chapter Four: Two Modern Classics

Jesus of Nazareth

Aldridge, William. "Franco Zeffirelli on Telling the Story of Christ from Its Real Roots." *Screen International* n.48 (7 August 1976): 8-9
Hodara, Philippe. "*Jésus de Nazareth* de Franco Zeffirelli." *Lumière du Cinéma* n.11 (January-February 1978): 20-25.
Manin, Giuseppina. "Sul cinema Chiesa in malafede." *Corriere della Sera*, 25 February 1996, 13.
Rissik, Andrew. "A Pallid Pageant." *Films and Filming* v.23, n.10 (July 1977): 4, 6.
Termine, Liborio. "Conformismo intellettuale per il *Gesù* di Zeffirelli." *Cinema Nuovo* v.26, n.248 (July-August 1977): 253-256.
Zeffirelli, Franco. *Il mio Gesù*. Raccontato a Luigi Gianoli. Milano: Sperling & Kupfer Editori, 1992.

The Messiah

Bondanella, Peter. *The Films of Roberto Rossellini*. Cambridge: Cambridge University Press, 1993.
Bini, Luigi. "*Il Messia* di Roberto Rossellini." *Letture* v.31, qd.326 (April 1976): 311-314.
Cappabianca, Alessandro, Enrico Magrelli, Michele Mancini. "Appunti su Rossellini." *Filmcritica* v. 27, nn.264-265 (May-June 1976): 150-157.
"Conversazione con Roberto Rossellini." Edited by Edoardo Bruno, Alessandro Cappabianca, Enrico Magrelli, Michele Mancini. *Filmcritica* v. 27, nn.264-265 (May-June 1976): 134-137.
Fantuzzi, Virgilio. "*Il Messia* di Roberto Rossellini." *La Civiltà Cattolica* an.126, n.4, qd.3010 (15 November 1975): 337-349.
Le Dantec, Mireille Latil. "Les Films: *Le Messie*." *Cinématographe* n.18 (April-May 1976): 37-38.
Masi, Stefano and Enrico Lancia. *I film di Roberto Rossellini.* Roma Gremese Editore, 1987.
Miccichè, Lino. *Cinema italiano degli anni '70.* Venezia: Marsilio Editori, 1980.
Moscati, Italo. "Occhio critico: *Il Messia* di Roberto Rossellini." *Cinemasessanta* v.113 (January-February 1977): 52-53.
Rondolino, Gianni. *Roberto Rossellini.* Firenze: La Nuova Italia, 1977.
Tomasino, Renato. "*Il Messia*: Il film come equilibrio instabile." *Filmcritica* v.27, nn.264-265 (May-June 1976): 147-149.

Part One, Chapter Six: The Masterpiece –
The Gospel According to Saint Matthew

A.C.L. "*Vangelo secondo Matteo, Il. (The Gospel According to St. Matthew)*." *The Monthly Film Bulletin* (BFI) v.34, n.402 (July 1965): 104-105.

Bini, Luigi. "*Il Vangelo secondo Matteo.*" *Letture* v.19, n.10 (October 1964): 703-708.

Bory, Jean-Louis. *Des Yeux pour Voir: Cinéma I (1961-1966)*. Paris: Union Générale d'Edition, 1971.

Castellani, Leandro. "Venezia XXV Edizione: *Il Vangelo secondo Matteo*." *Rivista del Cinematografo* nn.9-10 (September-October 1964): 430-434.

Ciaccio, Giacinto. "Fedele al racconto, non all'ispirazione del Vangelo il film di Pasolini." *L'Osservatore Romano* n.206 (31.679), 6 September 1964, 3, 6.

C[omolli]., J[ean.]-L[ouis]. "*Il Vangelo secondo Matteo,*" *Cahiers du Cinéma* v.27, n.159 (October 1964): 24-27.

De Giusti, Luciano. *I film di Pier Paolo Pasolini*. Roma: Gremese Editore, 1983.

Delahaye, Michel, "Tout Droit: *Il Vangelo secondo Matteo (L'Evangile selon Saint Matthieu)*." *Cahiers du Cinéma* [v.28] nn.166-167 (May-June 1965): 125-126.

Fantuzzi, Virgilio. "La 'visione religiosa' di Pier Paolo Pasolini." In *Cinema sacro e profano*. Roma: Edizioni "La Civiltà Cattolica," 1983, 275-351. First published in *Bianco e Nero*, v.37, nn.1-4 (January-April 1976): 53-112.

Greene, Naomi. *Pier Paolo Pasolini: Cinema as Heresy*. Princeton: Princeton University Press, 1990.

Lajeunesse, J. "*L'Evangile selon Saint Matthieu.*" *Image et Son* n.184 (May 1965): 100-101.

Lungobardi, Fulvio. "Il *Vangelo* di Pasolini." *Filmcritica* v.16, n.154 (February 1965): 117-119.

Mosk. "Venice Film Fest Reviews: *Il Vangelo secondo Matteo.*" *Variety*, 16 September 1964, 17.

Murri, Stefano. *Pasolini*. Milano: Editrice Il Castoro, July-August 1994.

Paci, Stefano M. "A Blessed Clapperboard." *Thirty Days* v.7, n.1 (1995), 66-68.

_____. "Prudence Counsels Daring." *Thirty Days* v.7, n.1 (1995), 64-65.

Pasolini su Pasolini: Conversazioni con Jon Halliday. Parma: Ugo Guanda Editore, 1992.

Petraglia, Sandro. *Pier Paolo Pasolini*. Firenze: La Nuova Italia-Il Castoro Cinema, July-August 1974.

Ponzi, Maurizio. "La Ricotta," in "Quatre films inédits de Pier Paolo Pasolini." *Cahiers du Cinéma* n.169 (August 1965): 28.

Rohdie, Sam. *The Passion of Pier Paolo Pasolini*. Bloomington: Indiana University Press, 1995.

Ruszkowsky, André. In *Rivista del Cinematografo* nn.9-10 (September-October 1964): 439.

Siciliano, Enzo. *Pasolini*. Translated by John Shepley. New York: Random House, 1982.

Szabō, Geneviève. "*L'évangile selon Saint-Matthieu.*" *Jeune Cinéma* n.6 (March-April 1965): 14-15.

Verdone, Mario. "I film: *Rogopag.*" *Bianco e Nero* v.24, n.3 (March 1963): 58-61.

Viano, Maurizio. *A Certain Realism: Making Use of Pasolini's Film Theory and Practice.* Berkeley: University of California Press, 1993.

Part Two, Chapter One: A Film of Transition – *Jesus of Montreal*

Ambrogio, Sant.' *Opera Omnia: Opere esegetiche IX/I: Esposizione del Vangelo secondo Luca.* Edited by Giovanni Coppa. Milano: Biblioteca Ambrosiana, 1978.

Arcand, Denys. *Jésus de Montréal.* Montreal: Boréal, 1989.

Barker, Adam. "Review of *Jésus de Montréal.*" *The Monthly Film Bulletin* (BFI) v.57, n.672 (January 1990): 3-4.

Bini, Luigi. "*Il declino dell'impero americano* di Denys Arcand." *Letture* an.42, qd.437 (May 1987): 458-459.

_____. "*Jesus of Montreal,* di Denis [*sic*] Arcand." *Letture* an.45, qd.463 (January 1990): 67-70.

Garcia, Maria. "Review of *Jesus of Montreal.*" *Films in Review* v.41, n.10 (October 1990): 491-492.

Gervais, Marc. "A Canadian Film Event." *Compass* (Canada) (September 1989): 38-41.

Goyette, Louis. "Dossier Denys Arcand: Quand le cinéma devient un spectacle." *24 Images: La revue québécoise du cinéma* nn.44-45 (Fall 1989): 56-59.

Haas, Christine. "*Jésus de Montréal* – Denys Arcand: La Passion revisitée par l'auteur du *Déclin de l'empire américain.*" *Première* n.146 (May 1989), 142-145.

Hunter, Allan. "Passion Play." *Films and Filming* v.423 (January 1990): 10-13.

Jean, Marcel. "Dossier Denys Arcand: Entretien avec Denys Arcand." *24 Images: La revue québécoise du cinéma* nn.44-45 (Fall 1989): 46-53.

Malone, Peter. "Review of *Jesus of Montreal.*" *Cinema Papers* (Australia) n.80 (August 1990): 57-58.

Marsolais, Gilles. "Dossier Denys Arcand: Du spirituel dans l'art – Critique de *Jésus de Montréal.*" *24 Images: La revue québécoise du cinéma* nn.44-45 (Fall 1989): 40-43.

Marsolais, Gilles and Claude Racine. "Entretien avec Denys Arcand à propos de *Jésus de Montréal.*" *24 Images: La revue québécoise* n.43 (Summer 1989): 4-9.

McMahon, Kevin. "*Jésus de Montréal* and the Culture of Nihilism." *Take One,* Summer 1995, 43-44.

O'Brien, Tom. "Review of *Jesus of Montreal.*" *Film Quarterly* v.44, n.1 (Autumn 1990): 47-50.

Pallister, Janis. *The Cinema of Québec: Masters in Their Own House.* Madison, WI/ Teaneck, NJ: Fairleigh Dickinson University Press, 1995.

Ramasse, François. "Denys Arcand: Etre tendre malgré tout." *Positif* v.340 (June 1989): 12-17.

Roy, André. "Dossier Denys Arcand: Jésus des médias – Critique de *Jésus de Montréal*." *24 Images: La revue québécoise du cinéma* n.44-45 (Fall 1989): 44-45.

Strat. "Competing at Cannes: *Jésus of Montréal* [sic] (*Jesus of Montreal*)." *Variety's Film Reviews 1989-1990,* v.21. New York: R.R. Bowker, 1991 (17 May 1989).

Tadros, Jean-Pierre. "The Second Coming of Denys Arcand?" *Cinema Canada* n.164 (June-July 1989): 16-17.

von Balthasar, Hans Urs. "Casta Meretrix." In *Sponsa Verbi: Skizzen zur Theologie II*. Einsiedeln: Johannes Verlag, 1961. 203-305.

Weinmann, Heinz. *Cinéma de l'imaginaire québécois: De* La petite Aurore *à* Jésus de Montréal. Saint-Laurent (Québec, Canada): l'Heragone, 1990.

Zwick, Reinhold. "Entmythologisierung versus Imitatio Jesu: Thematisierungen des Evangeliums in Denys Arcands Film *Jesus von Montreal*." *Communicatio Socialis: Zeitschrift für Publizistik in Kirche und Welt* v.23, n.2. Paderborn: Verlag Ferdinand Schöning, 1990, 17-47.

Part Two, Chapter Two: The Woman as Christ-Figure

La strada and *Nights of Cabiria*

Agel, Geneviève. *Les Chemins de Fellini*. Paris: Editions du Cerf, 1956.

_____. "Giulietta Masina or God's Little Clown." *Radio-Cinéma-Télévision* n.271, 27 March 1955, 38.

Agel, Henri. "Néo-réalisme franciscain?" *Radio-Cinéma-Télévision* n.271, 27 March 1955, 3.

Alpert, Hollis. *Fellini*. New York: Atheneum, 1986.

Aristarco, Guido. "Il mestiere del critico: *Le notti di Cabiria*." *Cinema Nuovo* v.6, n.118 (15 November 1957): 263-265.

Aubier, Dominique. "Mythologie de *La Strada*." *Cahiers du Cinéma* v.9, n.49 (July 1955): 3-9.

Baker, Peter. "*Le Notti di Cabiria*." *Films and Filming* (March 1958): 23.

Baxter, John. *Fellini*. London: Fourth Estate, 1993.

Bazin, André. "*Cabiria*: The Voyage to the End of Neorealism." In *What is Cinema? – Vol. II*. Edited by Hugh Grey. Berkeley: University of California Press, 1971. 83-92.

_____. "*La Strada*." *Cross Currents* 6 n.3 (1956): 203.

_____. "*La Strada*: Une preuve de l'existence de l'âme." *Radio-Cinéma-Télévision* n.271 (27 March 1955), 4.

Benayoun, Robert. "*La strada* ou quand Fellini s'ouvre aux chimères." *Positif* v.2, n.13 (March-April 1955): 26-28.

Burke, Frank. *Federico Fellini: Variety Lights to La Dolce Vita*. Boston: Twayne Publishers, 1984.

Costello, Donald P. *Fellini's Road*. Notre Dame: University of Notre Dame Press, 1983.

Cox, Harvey, Jr. "The Purpose of the Grotesque in Fellini's Films." In *Celluloid and Symbols*. Edited by John C. Cooper and Carl Skrade. Philadelphia: Fortress Press, 1970, 89-106.

de Laurot, Edouard. *La Strada*: A Poem on Saintly Folly." *Film Culture* v.2, n.1 (1956): 11-14.

Fellini on Fellini. Edited by Anna Keel and Christian Strich. London: Eyre Methuen, 1976.

In this collection:

Fellini, Federico. "Letter to a Jesuit Priest," 65-66.

Goldberg, Toby. *Federico Fellini: A Poet of Reality – Film Studies #6*. Boston: Boston University Broadcasting and Film Division.

Gorbman, Claudia. "Music as Salvation: Notes on Fellini and Rota." *Film Quarterly* v.28, n.2 (Winter 1974-1975): 17-25.

Gow, Gordon. *"La Strada."* *Films and Filming* v.16, n.1 (October 1969): 58.

Hawk. "Film Reviews: *La Strada* (*The Road*)." *Variety*, 22 September 1954, 6.

J.W. *"Strada, La* (*The Way*)." *The Monthly Film Bulletin* (BFI) v.23, n.264 (January 1956): 5.

Ketcham, Charles B. *Federico Fellini: The Search for a New Mythology*. New York: Paulist Press, 1976.

Kezich, Tullio, and Federico Fellini. "The Long Interview." In *Federico Fellini's Juliet of the Spirits*. Edited by Tullio Kezich. New York: Orion Press, 1965, 9-65.

Leprohon, Pierre. *The Italian Cinema*. Translated by Roger Greaves and Oliver Stallybrass. London: Secker & Warburg, 1972.

Murray, Edward. *Fellini the Artist*. New York: Frederick Ungar, 1985.

_____. *Ten Film Classics: A Re-Viewing*. New York: Frederick Ungar, 1978.

P.J.D. *"Notti di Cabiria* (*Cabiria*)." *The Monthly Film Bulletin* (BFI) v.25, n.292 (May 1958): 57-58.

Rosenthal, Stuart. *The Cinema of Federico Fellini*. New York: A.S. Barnes and Company, 1976.

Salachas, Gilbert. "Le bonheur." *L'Avant-Scène Cinéma* n.381 (May 1989): 4-7.

Sarris, Andrew. "Cabiria: *Le Notti di Cabiria*." *Film Culture* v.4, n.6 (January 1958): 18-21.

La Strada – Federico Fellini, director. Edited by Peter Bondanella and Manuela Gieri. New Brunswick, NJ: Rutgers University Press, 1987.

In this collection:

Bazin, André. "The Crisis of Neo-Realism: *La Strada*," 199-203.

Bondanella, Peter, and Manuela Gieri. "Fellini's *La Strada* and the Cinema of Poetry," 3-22.

Fellini, Federico. "The Continuity Script," 35-164.

"Notes on the Continuity Script," 165-175.

Babette's Feast

Audé, Françoise. "*Le Festin de Babette*: La générosité et la sorcellerie." *Positif* n.326 (April 1988): 69-70.

Blixen, Karen (Isak Dinesen). "Babette's Feast." In *Anecdotes of Destiny*. London: Penguin Books, 1986.

Brisse, Stéphane. "Deux films qui étonnent le cinéma." *Cinema Quatre-Vingt Huit* (22 June 1988): 3-5.

Combs, Richard. "Films on TV: *Babette's Feast*." *The Listener* v.122, n.3145, (21 December 1989), 49.

_____. "Review of *Babette's Feast*." *The Monthly Film Bulletin* (BFI) v.55, n.65 (March 1988): 74-75.

Forbes, Jill. "Axel's Feast." *Sight and Sound* v.57, n.2 (Spring 1988): 106-107.

Guiguet, Jean Claude. "Choix de films: *Le Festin de Babette* de Gabriel Axel." *Etudes* v.368, n.5 (May 1988): 662-664.

Kell. "Review of *Babette's gästebud* (*Babette's Feast*)." *Variety*, 6 May 1987, 564.

Manzato, Anna. "*Il pranzo di Babette* di Gabriel Axel." *Letture* an.43, qd.450 (October 1988): 759-761.

QSF. "Review of *Babette's Feast*." *Screen International* n.642 (5 March 1988): 24.

Strauss, Frédéric. "La dernière cène." *Cahiers du Cinéma* n.405 (March 1988): 43-44.

Walters, Margaret. "Cinema: *Babette's Feast*." *The Listener* v.119, n.3052, 3 March 1988, 37.

Out of Rosenheim (Bagdad Cafe)

Alster, Laurence. "Review of *Bagdad Café*." *Films and Filming* n.409 (October 1988): 30.

Boujut, Michel. "Citizen Adlon." *L'Avant-Scène Cinéma* nn.375-376 (November-December 1988): 3-5.

Danglades, Virginie. "Percy Adlon: L'image est primordiale." *Cinema 88* (22 June 1988): 6.

_____. "Bagdad Café en plein désert Mojave." *Cinema 88* (20 April 1988): 6.

Edna. "Rio Festival Reviews: *Out of Rosenheim*." *Variety* v.6, n.329, 2 December 1987, 33.

Green, Peter. "Germans Abroad: Herzog, Wenders, Adlon." *Sight and Sound* v.57, n.2 (Spring 1988): 126-130.

Martin, Marcel. "La voleuse de Bagdad." *L'Avant-Scène Cinéma* nn.375-376 (November-December 1988): 7-9.

Mercorio, Giuliana. "A Bavarian in Bagdad." *Films and Filming* n.409 (October 1988): 12-14.

Milne, Tom. "Review of *Out of Rosenheim* (*Bagdad Café*)." *The Monthly Film Bulletin* (BFI) v.55, n.657 (October 1988): 307-309.

Niel, Philippe. "*Bagdad Cafe*: De l'image mirage à l'image magique." *Positif* n.328 (June 1988): 74-75.

N.S. "Notes sur d'autres films: *Bagdad Café*." *Cahiers du Cinéma* nn.407-408 (May 1988): 143-144.

Piccardi, Adriano. "Scheda: *Bagdad Café*." *Cineforum*, an.28, n.9 (September 1988): 79.

Dead Man Walking

Charbonneau, Alain. "La peine du mort: *Dead Man Walking* de Tim Robbins." *24 Images: La revue québécoise du cinéma* n.82 (Summer 1996): 48-49.

Dufford, Bob. "Be Not Afraid." In *Glory and Praise*. Phoenix AZ: North American Liturgy Resources – G.I.A. Publications, 1987. Number 32.

Fantuzzi, Virgilio. "Film: *Dead Man Walking – Condannato a morte*." *La Civiltà Cattolica* an.147, qd.3500 (20 aprile 1996): 219-220.

Jeancolas, Jean-Paul. "La Dernière Marche: S'en fout pas, la mort." *Positif* n.442 (April 1996): 45.

Kemp, Philip. "*Dead Man Walking*." *Sight and Sound* v.6, n.6 (April 1996): 43-44.

Strauss, Frédéric. "Critiques: *La Dernière Marche (Dead Man Walking)*." *Cahiers du Cinéma* n.501 (April 1996): 80.

Part Two, Chapter Three:
The Hero of the Western as a Christ-Figure – *Shane*

Archer, Eugene. "George Stevens and the American Dream." *Film Culture* v.3, n.1 (11) (1957): 25-32.

Berthomieu, Pierre. "L'homme des vallées perdues." *Positif* n.397 (March 1994): 90-91.

The BFI Companion to the Western. Edited by Edward Buscombe. London: Andre Deutsch-BFI Publishing, 1993.

Desser, David. "Kurosawa's Eastern 'Western': *Sanjuro* and the Influence of *Shane*." *Film Criticism* v.8, n.1 (Autumn 1983): 54-65.

Horrocks, Roger. *Male Myths and Icons: Masculinity in Popular Culture*. London: MacMillan Press, 1995.

Houston, Penelope. "*Shane* and George Stevens." *Sight and Sound* v.23, n.2 (October-December 1953): 71-76.

K.R. "Review of *Shane*." *The Monthly Film Bulletin* (BFI), v.20, n.236 (September 1953): 132-133.

Miller, Gabriel. "*Shane* Redux: *The Shootist* and the Western Dilemma." *Journal of Popular Film & Television* v.11, n.2 (Summer 1983): 66-77.

Petri, Bruce. *A Theory of American Film: The Films and Techniques of George Stevens*. New York: Garland Publishing, 1987.

Schaefer, Jack. *Shane and Other Stories*. London: Penguin-Puffin, 1994.

Stanbrook, Alan. "The Return of *Shane*." *Films and Filming* v.12, n.8 (May 1966): 36-41.

Stern, Nina W. "Review of *Shane*." *Films in Review* v.4, n.4 (April 1953): 194-197.

Tuska, Jon. *The Filming of the West*. Garden City, NY: Doubleday and Company, 1976.

Part Two, Chapter 4:
A Christ-Figure in Two Films of Kieślowski

Bertolina, Gian Carlo. "*Non desiderare la donna d'altri* di Krzysztof Kieślowski." *Letture* an.45, qd. 463 (January 1990): 70-72

B.U. "*A Short Film about Love* (*Krotki Film o Miłosci*). *Screen International* n.688 (21 January 1989): 22.

Carozzi, Emanuela. "Lenti, vetri e porte: un cinema tra partecipazione e distacco." In *Krzysztof Kieślowski*, Issue of *Garage: Cinema, Autori, Visioni*. Torino: Edizioni Scriptorium, February 1995, 58-73.

Cavendish, Phil. "Kieslowski's *Decalogue*." *Sight and Sound* v.159, n.33 (Summer 1990): 162-165.

Ciment, Michel, and Hubert Niogret. "*Le Décalogue*: entretien avec Krzysztof Kieślowski." *Positif* 346 (December 1989): 36-43.

Eidsvik, Charles. "Kieślowski's 'Short Films': *A Short Film about Killing*; *A Short Film about Love*." *Film Quarterly* v.44, n.1 (Autumn 1990): 50-55.

Fantuzzi, Virgilio. "*Non desiderare la donna d'altri*," *La Civiltà Cattolica* an.140, v 14, qd.3347 (2 December 1989): 519-520.

Fisher, William. "*The Ten Commandments (Dekalog)*." *Screen International* n.748 (17 March 1990): 22-23.

Imparato, Emanuela. *Krzysztof Kieślowski: Il Decalogo: Per una lettura critica*. Roma: A.I.A.C.E., 1990.

Keates, Jonathan. "Heartburn: *A Short Film about Love*." *Sight and Sound* v.59, n.2 (Spring 1990): 132.

Kieślowski, Krzysztof, and Krzysztof Piesiewicz. *Decalogue: The Ten Commandments*. Translated by Phil Cavendish and Susanna Bluh. London: Faber and Faber, 1991.

Kieślowski on Kieślowski. Edited by Danusia Stok. London: Faber and Faber, 1993.

Krzysztof Kieślowski. Edited by Mario Sesti. Roma: Dino Audino Editore, 1993.

Lagorio, Gina. *Il Decalogo di Kieślowski: Ricreazione narrativa*. Casale Monferrato, AL: Edizioni Piemme, 1992.

Lubaszenko, Olaf. "Travailler avec Kieślowski." *Positif* 346 (December 1989): 32.

Murri, Serafino. *Krzysztof Kieślowski*. Milano: Editrice Il Castoro, January-February 1996.

Niel, Philippe. "Dix blasons de la morale (*Le Décalogue*)." *Positif* 346 (December 1989): 28-31.

Pernod, Pascal. "L'amour des personnages: *Brève Histoire d'amour*." *Positif* 346 (December 1989): 26-27.

Pulleine, Tim. *"Krotki Film o Miłosci (A Short Film about Love)." The Monthly Film Bulletin* (BFI) v.57, n.676 (May 1990): 132-133.

Rigney, M.D., Francis J. *"The Decalogue:* A Psychoanalytic Deadlock." *Film Criticism* v.14, n.3 (Spring 1990): 55-71.

Rouyer, Philippe. "Voir et être vue *(Décalogue, six)"* in "Krzysztof Kieślowski – *Décalogue:* la preuve par dix." *Positif,* n.351 (May 1990): 37.

Yung. "San Sebastian Reviews: *Krotki Film o Miłosci (A Short Film about Love)." Variety,* 5 October 1988, 15.

Chapter Five:
An Exceptional Christ-Figure – *Au hasard Balthazar*

Bini, Luigi. *"Au hasard Balthazar." Letture* v.21, n.10 (October 1966): 710-714.

Bory, Jean-Louis. *Des Yeux pour voir: Cinéma I (1961-1966).* Paris: Union Générale des Editions, 1971.

Briot, René. *Robert Bresson.* Paris: Editions du Cerf, 1957.

Collet, Jean. "Le drôle de chemin de Bresson à Balthazar." *Etudes* v.325 (July-August 1966): 80-91.

Delahaye, Michel, François Weyergans, Jean-Louis Comolli, Jean Narboni, André S. Labarthe. "Balthazar au hasard: Table ronde." *Cahiers du Cinéma* n.180 (July 1966): 76-79.

Droguet, Robert. *Robert Bresson. Premier Plan* (Serdoc, Lyon) n. 42 (November 1966).

Durgnat, Raymond. *"Balthazar." Films and Filming* v.13, n.3 (December 1966): 18, 51-52.

Estève, Michel. "Il settimo film di Robert Bresson." *Cineforum* v.6, n.56 (June 1966): 429-442.

Gilson, René. "'My God, Wilt Thou Forsake Me?'" *Cahiers du Cinéma in English* n.11 (September 1967): 54-57 (original: *Cahiers du Cinéma* n.182, September 1966).

Godard, Jean-Luc and Michel Delahaye. "The Question: Interview with Robert Bresson." *Cahiers du Cinéma in English* n.8 (February 1967): 5-27. (original: *Cahiers du Cinéma* n.178, May 1966)

Graham, Peter. *"Balthazar." Films and Filming* v.12, n.4 (January 1966): 56-57.

Greenspun, Roger. "Bresson Feature Opens at the New Yorker." *The New York Times Film Reviews 1969-1970.* New York: The New York Times & Arno Press, 1971.

Hanlon, Lindley Page. *Narrative Structure in the Later Films of Robert Bresson,* a doctoral dissertation submitted to New York University, June 1977. University Microfilms International, Ann Arbor, Michigan.

Johnson, William. "Film Reviews: *Balthazar." Film Quarterly* v.20, n.3 (April 1966): 24-28.

Lucano, Angelo L. "La grazia secondo Bresson." In *Tutto Bresson: Gli 80 anni di un maestro: Dossier.* Roma: ANCCI, 1987, 21-31. Excerpted from *Cultura e religione nel cinema.* Torino: ERI Edizioni, 1975, 28-29.

Maurice, René. "De Lucifer à Balthazar, en suivant Robert Bresson." *Lumière et Vie* n.78 (1966): 31-53.

Rhode, Eric. *Tower of Babel: Speculations on the Cinema.* London: Weidenfeld and Nicolson, 1965.

Robert Bresson. Camera-Stylo. Ramsey Poche Cinéma, 1989.

Sémolué, Jean. *Bresson ou l'acte pur des métamorphoses.* Paris: Flammarion, 1993.

S[émolué]., J[ean]. "L'éminente dignité des humbles (*Au Hasard Balthazar*, de Robert Bresson)." *Esprit* v.34, n.350 (June 1966): 1249-1251.

Sitney, P. Adams. "The Rhetoric of Robert Bresson." In *Essential Cinema: Essays on Films in The Collection of Anthology Film Archives, The.* Edited by P. Adams Sitney. New York: Anthology Film Archives and New York University Press, 1975. 182-207.

"Testimonianze su Balthazar." *Cineforum* v.6, n.56 (June 1966): 516-519.

Tilliette, Xavier. "Des ânes et des hommes." *Etudes* v.324 (June 1966): 831-833.

Tinazzi, Giorgio. *Il cinema di Robert Bresson.* Venezia: Marsilio Editori, 1979.

T.M. "*Au hasard, Balthazar (Balthazar).*" *The Monthly Film Bulletin* (BFI) v.34, n.396 (January 1967): 2.

Tournès, Andrée. "*Au hasard Balthazar.*" *Jeune Cinéma* n.17 (September-October 1966): 22-23.

Chapter Six:
Essential Dimensions and Typical Guises of the Christ-Figure

Ayfre, Amédée. "Les voix du silence." *Cahiers du Cinéma* n.17 (November 1952): 58-60.

Beylie, Claude. "Corps memorable." *Cahiers du Cinéma* v.24, n.143 (May 1963): 40-41.

Bordwell, David. *The Films of Carl-Theodor Dreyer.* Berkeley: University of California Press, 1981.

Bresson, Robert. *Notes on the Cinematographer.* London: Quartet Books, 1986.

Cameron, Ian. "Interview with Robert Bresson." *Movie* n.7 (February-March 1963): 28-29.

Canosa, Michele. "La passione del volto." *Cinema & Cinema* v.12, n.44 (September-December 1985): 63-69.

Etudes cinématographiques: Jeanne d'Arc à l'ecran, n. 18-19 (Fall 1962).
In this collection:
Entretien avec Robert Bresson et Jean Guitton," 85-97.
Estève, Michel. "Une tragédie au présent de narration," 108-119.
Leprohon, Pierre. "L'hagiographie à l'écran: Par-delà des apparences," 125-130.
Mambrino, Jean. "*Procès de Jeanne d'Arc* de Robert Bresson: les voix et la parole," 83-84.
Pinel, Vincent. "*Joan of Arc* de Victor Fleming, ou l'hagiographie spectaculaire," 59-64.

Sémolué, Jean. "*La Passion de Jeanne d'Arc*: Prise de conscience de Carl Dreyer," 38-52.

_____. "Passion et Procès: (De Dreyer à Bresson)," 98-107.

Kermabon, Jacques. "L'espace aboli." *L'Avant-Scène Cinéma* n.367-368 (January-February 1988): 34-35.

"*Jeanne d'Arc* e l'antiteatro: Colloquio con Robert Bresson." *Bianco e Nero* v.24, n.3 (March 1963): 9-20.

Kovacs, Yves. "Entretien avec Robert Bresson." *Cahiers du Cinéma* v.24, n.140 (February 1963): 4-10.

Landy, Marcia. "Woman, Iconography, and Transcendence in Dreyer's *The Passion of Joan of Arc.*" *Field of Vision* nn.9-10 (Winter-Spring 1980): 12-18.

Linderman, Deborah. "Uncoded Images in the Heterogenous Text." *Wide-Angle* v.3, n.3 (1979): 34-41.

Manvell, Roger. "Revaluations – 6: *La Passion de Jeanne d'Arc*, 1928." *Sight and Sound* v.19, n.8 (December 1950): 337-339.

Mayersberg, Paul. "*The Trial of Joan of Arc.*" *Movie* n.7 (February/March 1963): 30-33.

M.M. "*Procès de Jeanne d'Arc.*" *Cinéma 62* n.67 (June 1962): 94-95.

Mosk. "Procès de Jeanne d'Arc." *Variety,* 30 May 1962, 6.

Passion de Jeanne d'Arc: Dossier-film no.3, *La. L'Avant-Scène Cinéma* n.100 (February 1970).

Sémolué, Jean. "*Procès de Jeanne d'Arc* dans l'oeuvre de Robert Bresson." *Esprit* v.31, n.318 (June 1963): 1190-1194.

Stranbrook, Alan. "Great Films of the Century – no.12: *The Passion of Joan of Arc.*" *Films and Filming* v.7, n.9 (June 1961): 11-13, 40-41.

Tone, Pier Giorgio. *Carl Theodor Dreyer.* Firenze: La Nuova Italia, May 1978.

U.F. "*Rogopag.*" *Cinema Nuovo* v.16, n.162 (March-April 1963): 136-138.

Vas, Robert. "The Trial of Joan of Arc." *Sight and Sound* v.32, n.1 (Winter 1962-1963): 37-38.

Vecchiali, Paul. "*Procès de Jeanne d'Arc*: Fausses apparences." *Cahiers du Cinéma* v.24, n.143 (May 1963): 35-37.

Part Two, Chapter Seven:
Christ-Figures in the Films of Bresson and Tarkovsky

Andrei Tarkovski. Edited by Gilles Ciment. Paris: Dossier Positif-Rivages, 1988. In this collection:

Carrère, Emmanuel. "*Stalker*: Troisième plongée dans l'océan, troisième retour à la maison," 114-124.

Demeure, Jacques. "*Andrei Roublev*: Nous sommes tous des peintres mediévaux," 80-81.

Tarkovski, Andrei. "Le Sacrifice, Offret, Sacrificatio: A propos du *Sacrifice*," 144-146.

Tassone, Aldo. "Entretien avec Andrei Tarkovski," 125-129.

Antermite, Costanzo, Giovanni Attolini, Vincenzo Camerino, Massimo Garritano, Romano Sambati and Andrej Tarkovskij. *Andrej Tarkovskij: Le ragioni della poesia.* Cavallino di Lecce: Capone Editore, 1990.

Etudes cinématographiques 135-138: Andreï Tarkovsky. Edited by Michel Estève. Paris: Lettres Modernes-Minard, 1986.

In this collection:

Estève, Michel. "Une esthetique de l'incarnation: *Le Sacrifice*," 179-186.

Gerstenkorn, Jacques and Sylvie Strudel, "*Stalker*: La quête de la foi ou Le dernier souffle de l'esprit," 75-112.

Ramasse, François. "*Nostalghia*: 'Souviens-toi de Sisyphe,'" 113-145.

Frezzato, Achille. *Andrej Tarkovskij.* Firenze: Il Castoro Cinema-La Nuova Italia, December 1977.

Gauthier, Guy. *Andrei Tarkovski.* Paris: Edilig, 1988.

Jacobsen, Wolfgang, Klaus Kreimeier, Hans-Joachim Schlegel, Eva M. J. Schmid and Alexander Sokurow. *Andrej Tarkowskij.* (Reihe Film 39) München: Karl Hanser Verlag, 1987.

Johnson, Vida T., and Graham Petrie. *The Films of Andrei Tarkovsky: A Visual Fugue.* Bloomington: University of Indiana Press, 1994.

Le Fanu, Mark. *The Cinema of Andrei Tarkovsky.* London: BFI Publishing, 1987.

Mitchell, Tony. "Andrei Tarkovsky and *Nostalghia*." *Film Criticism 8*, n.3 (1984): 2-11.

Tarkovsky, Andrei. *Sculpting in Time: Reflections on the Cinema.* London: The Bodley Head, 1988.

Turovskaya, Maya. *Tarkovsky: Cinema as Poetry.* London: Faber and Faber, 1989.

Epilogue

Dreyer, Carl Theodor. *Jésus de Nazareth, Médée.* Edited by Maurice Drouzy. Paris: Editions du Cerf, 1986.

Index

Names of Film-Makers

This index of names includes all the film-makers named both in the text and in the endnotes.

Index

Titles of Films

This index of titles includes all films mentioned both in the text and in the endnotes.